A Twenty-First-Century Bible

Part 2

ESTABLISHING THE KINGDOM

(Second Edition)

Books by Brian A Curtis

A Twenty-First-Century Bible (5 volumes)	*The Promised Land* *Establishing the Kingdom* *Prophets and Kings* *Exile and Restoration* *The New Covenant*
Other Biblical Books	*Keys to a Godly Life: An A to Z of the Laws of Moses and the Proverbs of Solomon*
Bible Study Books	*Radical Thinking: 16 Studies on the Laws of Moses*
Children's Stories	*A Day in the Life of a Pair of Trousers & Other Stories*

A Twenty-First-Century Bible

Part 2

ESTABLISHING THE KINGDOM

(Second Edition)

Brian A Curtis

Copyright © 2016, 2022 by Brian A Curtis

First Edition 2016
Second Edition 2022

All rights reserved. No part of this book may be reproduced or transmitted in any form or by any means, electronic or mechanical, including photocopying, recording, or by any information storage and retrieval system, without permission in writing from the copyright owner.

Hardback ISBN: 978-0-6451240-5-7
Paperback ISBN: 978-0-6451240-6-4

CONTENTS

Preface to . . . A Twenty-First Century Bible		vii
Introduction to . . . Part 2. Establishing the Kingdom		ix

C. NARRATIVE

C1	A People without a Leader	13
C2	A Levite	18
C3	Jonathan	26
C4	Othniel	30
C5	Ehud	31
C6	Shamgar	33
C7	Deborah	34
C8	Gideon/Jerub-baal	39
C9	Ruth	47
C10	Abimelech	54
C11	Tola	59
C12	Jair	60
C13	Jepthath	61
C14	Ibzan	66
C15	Elon	67
C16	Abdon	68
C17	Samson	69
C18	Eli	78
C19	Samuel	87
C20	Saul	
	a). King Saul	96
	b). Saul and David	109
C21	Ishbaal/Ishbosheth	155
C22	David	
	a). King of Israel and Judah	163
	b). A Problem of Succession	197
	c). King Solomon and the Temple	224
C23	Solomon/Jedidiah	
	a). Establishing the Throne	247
	b). Building the Temple	258
	c). Love Songs	271
	d). The Highs and Lows of Solomon	283
	e). Reflections on Life	290

D. SONGS, SAYINGS AND YHWH'S TEMPLE

D1	David's Song Book	
	a). Introduction and Songs of Praise	307
	b). The Life of Faith	320
	c). Sin	333
	d). Enemies	354
D2	Solomon's Song Book	393
D3	Other Songs	396
D4	The Sayings of Solomon	
	a). Introduction and Priority of Wisdom	414
	b). The Nature of Wisdom	422
	c). The Use and Abuse of Wisdom	431
	d). The Celebration of Wisdom	435
	e). Family Responsibilities	436
	f). The Sanctity of Life	441
	g). The Sanctity of Marriage	453
	h). Respect for Other People's Property	456
	i). Justice	458
	j). Right Thinking	471
D5	Other Sayings of the Wise	481
D6	YHWH's Temple	490
	Select Biography	499
	Index to Establishing the Kingdom	505

PREFACE TO...
A TWENTY-FIRST CENTURY BIBLE

A Twenty-First-Century Bible is an attempt to present the biblical story of God's people in a new and perhaps more readable way. It was inspired by many people telling me of attempts to read the Bible cover to cover, and in most cases, the person had given up two-thirds of the way through the book of Exodus.

To achieve my aims, I have needed to consider a number of things:

	Matters Considered
1	The need to merge two or more versions of the same story (i.e., the giving of the Ten Commandments, the four gospels, etc.);
2	The need to recognise that the modern reader does not always know or understand the culture and thinking behind biblical events;
3	The need to iron out some of the anomalies in the original text. For example: a. The name 'YHWH' for God is used in the book of Genesis, and yet the book of Exodus makes it quite clear that God was not known as YHWH before the time of Moses; b. Places, particularly in the book of Genesis, are often referred to by the names they were given in the future, not the names they were known as at the time (e.g., Jerusalem would have been known as Jebus in its early history); and c. The inconsistent use of names, particularly where there had been a name change (e.g., Jacob is often referred to as Jacob even after he had been renamed Israel);
4	The need to reinstate cultural aspects of biblical thinking, which have often been changed in modern translations. For example: a. The cultural idea of God being referred to as male; b. The use of the Tetragrammaton 'YHWH' in the English text, in line with the Hebrew practice (Kethibh and Qere) of writing God's name 'YHWH' but reading it aloud as 'Adonai' (or in English 'LORD'); and c. The restoration of idioms and expressions, which help in the understanding of the culture.
5	To retain, as much as possible, the full text of the Bible.
6	The need to use shorter sentences so that the narrative can be more easily read.

As a consequence, the text is presented in two types: a translation of the original languages in normal print; and embellishments, enlightening the twenty-first century reader to some of the cultural background and meaning *in italics*.

Like all translations of the Bible, this version is not perfect. In many ways it can be seen as a work in progress—a precursor of what, I hope, will be many more attempts to come. But my hope is that these books will give the reader a better understanding of the Bible so that they can return, with greater insight, to the original (in all its various translations).

As with any translation, some interpretation of the original text and biblical culture has been required. I do not expect that everyone will agree with every translation or interpretation that I have made. But I am grateful for the myriad contributions that have been made over the centuries, which have aided our understanding of the Bible and without which this attempt would not have been possible.

Finally, in common with all translations before it, it must be remembered that the Bible is not a continuous flowing story but a series of events, feelings, and expressions in the lives of God's people. As a consequence, the narrative remains unavoidably disjointed at times.

Brian A Curtis

PREFACE TO . . . THE SECOND EDITIONS

I am a great believer that no matter what one does, or how much effort is put into a project, there is always room for improvement.

But then, learning never stops. Indeed, when the fifth and final volume—*The New Covenant*—was published in 2020, it incorporated fifteen years of work, learning, and experience.

So although the complete *A Twenty-First-Century Bible* has been published, I am now revisiting each volume, in turn, to make the necessary improvements. Despite that, the thrust of the project remains the same.

Brian A Curtis

INTRODUCTION TO...PART 2: ESTABLISHING THE KINGDOM

Part 2 continues the feature, introduced in Part 1, of dividing the text into two parts. This time:

    C. Narrative; and
    D. Songs, Sayings, and YHWH's Temple

This allows the historical narrative to flow more freely, while maintaining the importance of the other material.

Section C: Narrative

As one of the aims was to present the narrative in chronological order, some shuffling of the biblical material has been required. This, of course, has met with many complications.

In the book of Judges, the total numbers of years stated would indicate a much longer time frame than the period of the judges would allow. As a consequence, recognition that many of the judges were local judges, and that there was some overlap between them, has needed to be made.

In addition, the compilers of 1 and 2 Samuel and 1 Chronicles were not overtly concerned about putting David's life into chronological order either. So, for example, in the book of 1 Samuel, David is introduced into Saul's service, but in the very next story (David and Goliath) Saul is unaware of David's ancestry—which is culturally very odd unless the stories are in the wrong order. But then even when the writers of 1 and 2 Samuel and 1 Chronicles use the same material, the stories are often placed in different orders.

Furthermore, the books of Judges and 2 Samuel both include appendices, which has required further shuffling of the material.

As a consequence, while dates have been provided at the beginning of each chapter, *in italics*, to give some idea of chronology, they should not be taken too literally.

The Narrative section also includes all psalms which relate to those events which can be identified in the period. The Song of Songs and Ecclesiastes have also been included, as they form a very important part of Solomon's story.

Section D: Songs, Sayings and YHWH's Temple

While some psalms are included in the Narrative section of the book, section D includes all the psalms of the period for which no specific event can be identified. They are presented in thematic order.

As with the treatment of YHWH's laws (in Book 1), attempts have been made to deal with aspects of the psalms for which the meaning has been lost over time—particularly the musical and other directions. Unfortunately, some things remain unexplained (e.g, the 'lost' term 'Selah', which may be an instruction to sing louder, or an instruction for the congregation to prostrate themselves before YHWH.)

This section also includes the entire book of Proverbs.

Each proverb identified as belonging to Solomon has been arranged in thematic order, in a loose arrangement based on the model of the Ten Words (The Ten Commandments). This then provides a link with YHWH's Laws (in Book 1–*The Promised Land*).

Similarly the details of Solomon's Temple are included in this section, to mirror the details of the Tabernacle in Book 1.

Section C

NARRATIVE

C1. A PEOPLE WITHOUT A LEADER
(1375-c. 1365 BC)

Leadership Woes[1]

After Joshua (*'YHWH saves'*), son of Nun, had dismissed the people, every Israelite had gone to his own inheritance, to take possession of the land. *But when* Joshua, YHWH's servant, was 110 years of age, he had died. The people had then buried him in the land he had inherited, at Timnath Heres, in the hill country of Ephraim, to the north of Mount Gaash.

But the death of Joshua then threw Israel into a period of uncertainty. They had enjoyed stable leadership since the Exodus from Egypt, but Joshua had died without a successor being identified.

The people had served YHWH all the days of Joshua, and they *continued to serve him* all the days of the elders who outlived Joshua, who had seen all the great deeds that YHWH had done for Israel. *But what they really wanted was another strong leader, particularly someone who would lead them on their military campaigns.*

The Call of Judah[2]

So following Joshua's death, the Israelites enquired of YHWH. They asked, 'Who will go up before us, as a leader, *to fight* against the Canaanites?' *They asked this because they had been unsuccessful in driving out all the inhabitants of Canaan. Indeed, the sons of Benjamin had not been able to dispossess the Jebusites living in Jebus, who were still living with the sons of Benjamin when this story was written down.*

YHWH answered, '*The tribe of* Judah is to go! Look, I have given the land into their hands.'

Now it was customary for a tribe to be referred to by their tribal ancestor. So Judah said to his brother, Simeon, 'Come with me to my inheritance; we will fight against the Canaanites. Then I will go with you to your inheritance.' So Simeon went with Judah. They marched against the Canaanites and the Perizzites, and YHWH gave them into their hands; they defeated the Canaanites and the Perizzites.

Conquest of the South[3]

They then marched to Bezek and killed ten thousand men.

While there they found Adoni-Bezek, *king of Jebus (a successor to Adoni-Zedek*

---

[1] Judges 2:6-9
[2] Judges 1:1-4a, 5b, 21
[3] Judges 1:4b-5a, 6-11, 16-20

who was executed by Joshua and the Israelites at Makkedah). *So* they fought against him. But Adoni-Bezek fled.

So they chased after him and, when they caught him, they cut off his thumbs and big toes. Adoni-Bezek said 'There are seventy kings whose thumbs and big toes *I have* cut off, who have been picking up the scraps under my table. Now God has done to me what I have done to them.' They *then* took him to Jebus (*later to be renamed Jerusalem*), where he was to die.

The sons of Judah fought against Jebus, seized it, put it to the edge of the sword, and set the city on fire.

Then the sons of Judah went down to fight against the Canaanites who were living in the hill country, the Negev, and the foothills.

Judah marched against the Canaanites *who were still* living in Hebron (Hebron was formerly known as Kiriath Arba), and they defeated *the descendants of* Sheshai, Ahiman, and Talmai. (But as Moses had promised, Hebron remained the property of Caleb, who had driven out the three sons of Anak.)

From there they marched against the inhabitants of Debir (which was formerly known as Kiriath Sepher).

The descendants of Moses's father-in-law, the Kenite, went with the sons of Judah, from the City of Palms. They went to the wilderness of Judah that is in the Negev, near Arad, and settled among the people.

Then Judah went with Simeon, his brother, and fought the Canaanites living in Zephath and devoted it *to YHWH for destruction*. They named the city Hormah (*'destruction'*).

Judah captured Gaza, Ashkelon, and Ekron, and their *surrounding* territories. YHWH was with Judah and they took possession of the hill country. But they were unable to drive out the inhabitants of the plains because the inhabitants had iron chariots.

Conquest of the North[4]

In the same way, the house of Joseph marched on Bethel, and YHWH was with them.

The house of Joseph sent spies to Bethel (which was previously called Luz). They saw a man coming out of the city and said to him, 'Show us the entrance to the city and we will deal kindly with you.' So he showed them the entrance to the city.

They put the city to the edge of the sword, but they let the man and his whole family go. Then the man went to the land of the Hittites and built a city. He called it Luz, which was the name it still had *when this story was written down.*

---

[4] Judges 1:22-36

However, Manasseh was unable to drive out *the inhabitants* of Beth Shan, Taanach, Dor, Ibleam, and Megiddo and their surrounding settlements, for the Canaanites were determined to live there.

As Israel grew stronger, they subjected the Canaanites to forced labour, even though they were still unable to dispossess them.

Ephraim was unable to drive out the Canaanites living in Gezer; the Canaanites remained living among them.

Zebulun was unable to dispossess those living in Kitron and Naholol; the Canaanites remained with them, but they were subjected to forced labour.

Asher was unable to drive out the inhabitants of Acco, Sidon, Ahlab, Aczib, Helbah, Aphek, and Rehob. So the Asherites lived among the Canaanites who inhabited the land, for they were unable to drive them out.

Naphtali was unable to dispossess those living in Beth Shemesh and Beth Anath. So they lived among the Canaanites who inhabited the land, but subjected the inhabitants of Beth Shemesh and Beth Anath to forced labour.

The Amorites restricted the sons of Dan to the hill country; they did not allow them to come into the valley. The Amorites, whose boundary ran from Scorpions Pass to Sela and beyond, were determined to remain in Mount Heres, Aijalon, and Shaalbim. *However*, when the house of Joseph increased in power, they *too* were subjected to forced labour.

The Angel of YHWH at Bokim[5]

An angel of YHWH went up from Gilgal to Bokim (*possibly Bethel*). He said, 'I brought you up out of Egypt and led you into the land that I swore to your fathers *I would give you*. I said I would never break my covenant with you. *In turn*, you were not to make a covenant with those living in this land, *and* you were to break down their altars. Yet you have not observed my covenant. Why have you acted this way?

'Now I tell you, I will not drive them out before you. They will be *thorns* in your sides, and their gods will be a snare to you.'

When the angel of YHWH had finished speaking these words to all the Israelites, the people lifted up their voices and wept. They called the name of that place Bokim (*'weeping'*), and they made sacrifices to YHWH there.

The Following Generations[6]

In due course *that* whole generation was gathered to their fathers, and another generation grew up after them who did not know YHWH or the deeds he had done for Israel. The Israelites did evil in the eyes of YHWH; they served

---

[5] Judges 2:1-5
[6] Judges 2:10-3:6

the Baals. They abandoned YHWH, the God of their fathers, who brought them from the land of Egypt. They followed after other gods, the gods of the people around them. They worshipped them and angered YHWH. They abandoned YHWH and served Baal and the Ashteroths. So YHWH burned with anger against Israel.

He gave them into the hands of raiders, who plundered them, and sold them into the hands of their surrounding enemies. They were no longer able to stand against their enemies. Whenever they went out, the hand of YHWH was against them to defeat *them*, just as YHWH said and just as YHWH had sworn to them. He distressed them greatly.

Then YHWH raised up judges who saved them from the raiders. Yet they wouldn't listen to those who judged them; they prostituted themselves to other gods. They worshipped them; they turned quickly from the way their fathers had walked. They did not obey YHWH's commands.

When YHWH raised up judges for them, YHWH was with *each* judge. While the judge lived, he saved them from the hands of their enemies, for YHWH had compassion on them as they groaned under the affliction of their oppressors. But when the judge died, the *people* turned back. They acted more corruptly than their fathers. They followed after other gods; they served them and worshipped them. They did not give up their practices or their stubborn ways.

So YHWH's anger burned against Israel. He said, 'This nation has broken my covenant—the one I commanded their fathers *to keep*. They refuse to hear my voice. Because *of that*, they can be sure that I will no longer drive out the nations that were still in the land when Joshua died; *I will no longer drive them out* before them. Instead, I will test Israel with them; *I will see* whether they will observe the ways of YHWH, as their fathers did, or not.

So YHWH allowed the nations which he had not driven out, and which he had not been quick to give into the hand of Joshua, to remain.

These are the nations that YHWH left, to test those in Israel who had not known any of the wars in Canaan. He did this to teach warfare to the generations of Israelites who had not experienced it.

The Nations Left to Test Israel

The Five Rulers of the Philistines
The Canaanites
The Sidonians
The Hivites living in the mountains of Lebanon (from Mount Baal Hermon to Lebo Hamath)

These nations *were allowed to* remain to test the Israelites, to see whether they would obey the commands that YHWH gave their fathers by the hand of Moses.

So the Israelites lived among the Canaanites, Hittites, Amorites, Perizzites, Hivites, and Jebusites. They took their daughters for themselves as wives *and, in turn*, they gave their daughters to their sons as wives. They *also* served their gods.

C2. A LEVITE
(c. 1373 BC)

The Journey to Bethlehem[7]

In the days before there was a king in Israel, a certain Levite was living in a remote part of the hill country of Ephraim. He took for himself a concubine from Bethlehem in Judah, but she was unfaithful to him; she returned to her father's house in Bethlehem in Judah, and remained there.

Four months *later the Levite*, her husband, got up and went after her. *He intended* to speak tenderly to her so that she would return. He took with him his servant and two donkeys.
So when he arrived, she took him into her father's house. The girl's father was glad when he saw him. He welcomed him and prevailed upon him, so he stayed with him for three days; they ate and drank and slept there.

On the fourth day they got up early, and he prepared to leave. But the girl's father said to his son-in-law, 'Satisfy yourself with some food, then you can go.' So they both sat and ate and drank together.
Then the girl's father said to the man, 'Please stay *the night*. Make your heart merry.' The man got up to go, but his father-in-law was very persuasive. So he stayed; he spent *another* night there.

On the fifth day he *again* rose early and got ready to go. But the girl's father *tried to delay him further*. He said, 'Satisfy your needs. Wait until later in the day.' So the two of them ate. *But later in the day* the man, his concubine, and his servant got up to go.
His father-in-law, the girl's father, said to him, 'Look, the day is *almost* gone; it is *nearly* evening; the day is over. Spend the night here. Stay and let your heart be merry. Get up *early* tomorrow *and go* on your way. Then you can go to your home.' But the man was not willing to stay *another night*, so he got up and left. He took with him his two saddled donkeys, his concubine, *and his servant and he went in the* direction of Jebus (*later to be renamed* Jerusalem), *eight kilometres from Bethlehem*.

The Return Home[8]

The day was almost gone when they approached Jebus.

---

[7] Judges 19:1-10
[8] Judges 19:11-30

The servant said to his master, 'Come, let us turn aside into the city of the Jebusites. Let us spend the night there.'

But his master said to him, 'We will not turn aside into an alien city. They are not Israelites. We will keep going to Gibeah.'

Now Gibeah was another four kilometres, and Ramah a further five kilometres still. So as they travelled further on, the Levite continued to his servant, 'Come, let us reach one of these places. Let us spend the night in *either* Gibeah or Ramah.' So they continued on.

As they walked, and as they approached Gibeah in Benjamin, the sun set. So they turned aside to spend the night in Gibeah.

They entered the town and sat down in the town square, *but they were not welcomed as they should have been.* Indeed, no one took them into *their* home for the night. (The inhabitants of the town were Benjaminites.)

Later, *they saw* an old man coming in from his work in the fields. He was from the hill country of Ephraim but *now* lived in Gibeah. The old man looked up and saw the traveller in the city square. He said, 'Where have you come from? Where are you going?'

The Levite answered him, 'We are journeying from Bethlehem in Judah to a remote area in the hill country of Ephraim. I live there. I went to Bethlehem in Judah, but now I am going back to my home.' *Then the Levite continued, 'We are self-sufficient.* There is enough straw and fodder for our donkeys. We have *enough* bread and wine for *ourselves: for* me, your servant; *my wife,* your maidservant; and the young man who is with *us, who is standing with* your servants. We have no need of anything. Yet no one *here* has taken me into his house.'

The old man said, 'Peace be with you. Let me *take care of* all your needs. But just don't spend the night in the square.' So the old man took him to his house and fed the donkeys. They then washed their feet, and they ate and drank.

As their hearts were getting merry, some wicked men—men of the city—surrounded the house and *began* pounding on the door. They said to the old man who owned the house, 'Bring out the man who has come to your house. We want to have sex with him.'

The man, who owned the house, went out to them and said, 'No, my brothers, do not be *so* wicked. This man has come into my house *and is entitled to my hospitality and protection.* Do not do so such a disgraceful thing.' *Then, as the men could not be deterred,* he added, 'Look, here is my virgin daughter and his concubine. I will bring them out now. Use them. Do to them whatever is good in your eyes. *But* do not do this disgraceful thing to this man.'

The men refused to listen to him, *so the Levite was forced to take matters into his own hands. He could either hand himself over to the men to be abused, or he could send out his concubine for a similar fate.* So the Levite took his concubine and sent her outside

Establishing the Kingdom

to them. They then raped her and abused her the whole night. Then in the morning, at dawn, they let her go.

So, at the break of day, the woman returned to the house belonging to the old man, where her master was staying. But she collapsed at the door and remained there.

Her master got up in the morning, but it was *full* daylight before he opened the door of the house and went out to continue his journey. He saw the woman, his concubine, who had collapsed at the doorway of the house, with her hands on the threshold.

He said to her, 'Get up. Let's go.' But she didn't answer. So he *picked her up and* placed her on the donkey. The man then set out and continued his journey home.

Then, after he had entered his house, he took a knife and, holding onto his concubine, he cut her up, limb by limb, into twelve parts—*one for each of the tribes of Israel*. He then sent her *parts* throughout Israel.

Everyone who saw it said, 'Nothing *like this* has *ever been done before*. Nothing like this has *ever* been seen, from the day the sons of Israel came up from the land of Egypt until this day.' *Then addressing their leaders, they continued,* 'Put your mind to the problem. Consider and tell *us what needs to be done.*'

Civil War[9]

Then all the Israelites gathered together. They came *from the north—from an area that would later be known as* Dan; *from the south—from* Beersheba; and *from the east—from* the land of Gilead. They assembled as one man before YHWH, at Mizpah, *north of Jebus*. There were four hundred thousand foot soldiers armed with the sword. *Furthermore*, the Benjaminites heard that the Israelites had assembled at Mizpah.

The leaders of all the people, of all the tribes of Israel, stood up in the assembly of the people of God. The Israelites said, 'How did this evil deed come about?'

So the Levite, the husband of the murdered woman, *who had gone to explain his actions*, said, 'I came to Gibeah in Benjamin, with my concubine, to spend the night. But the men of Gibeah rose up against me. They surrounded the house at night because of me; they intended to kill me. But they raped my concubine and she died. So I grasped my concubine and cut her up. I then sent pieces to every region of Israel's inheritance.

'They have committed a wicked and shameful act in Israel. Now all you Israelites speak. Give your verdict in this matter.'

Then all the people stood up as one man. They said, 'None of us will return

---

[9] Judges 20:1-48

Establishing the Kingdom

to his tent and none of us will return to his home *until this matter is resolved*. This is what we will do: we will go against Gibeah by lot. We will take men from all the tribes of Israel: ten from every hundred, a hundred from every thousand, and a thousand from every ten thousand. They will supply food for the army. When the people reach Gibeah in Benjamin, *we will treat them* in accordance with *this* disgraceful deed that they have done in Israel.'

So all the men of Israel were gathered together, as one man, against the town.

Then the tribes of Israel sent men throughout the tribe of Benjamin. They said, 'What is this evil that has been committed in your midst? Hand over the wicked men of Gibeah, so that we may put them to death and purge the evil from Israel.' But the Benjaminites refused to listen to their brother Israelites. *Instead*, the Benjaminites *left* their towns and gathered together at Gibeah, *intending* to go out and fight against the Israelites.

That day, from the towns, the Benjaminites mustered *about* twenty-six thousand men carrying the sword, in addition to the seven hundred mustered men who lived in Gibeah. Of all these men, seven hundred left-handed men were chosen, all of whom could sling a stone at a *strand of* hair and not miss. *These numbers, however, were in stark contrast to* the four hundred thousand men mustered from the Israelites (excluding Benjamin), all of whom were fighting men, who carried the sword.

Then the Israelites arose *from Mizpah* and went up to Bethel—*a journey of about five kilometres. Now normally the Tabernacle, the Ark of the Covenant, and the High Priest would have been in Shiloh, but the Ark had been moved because of this disaster; it had been moved closer to Benjamin, because of the need to consult with YHWH.* So at that time the Ark of the Covenant of God was in Bethel, and Phineas, son of Eleazar, the priest was ministering before it.

So the Israelites enquired of God there. They said, 'Out of all of us, which *tribe* is to be the first to go and fight against the Benjaminites?'

Then YHWH said, *perhaps because the concubine was from the tribe of Judah*, 'Judah is to be first.'

So the *next* morning, the Israelites arose, *marched to Benjamin*, and set up camp near Gibeah. The men of Israel then went out to fight against Benjamin. The men of Israel, *with Judah taking the lead*, took up *their* battle positions at Gibeah, and the Benjaminites came out of Gibeah *and fought the Israelites*.

On that day the Benjaminites cut down twenty-two thousand Israelite men on the battlefield.

The Israelites then returned *to Bethel* and wept before YHWH until evening. They enquired of YHWH. They said, 'Shall we go in battle again, against our brothers, the Benjaminites?'

YHWH said, 'Go against them.'

So the people—the Israelites—were encouraged. They took up the same battle positions they had used on the first day.

So on the second day, the Israelites drew near to the Benjaminites. The Benjaminites then came out from Gibeah to oppose them.

On the second day the Benjaminites cut down, on the battlefield, another eighteen thousand Israelite men. All had drawn the sword. Then all the Israelites, all the people, went back to Bethel.

When they arrived they wept and sat there before YHWH. That day they fasted until evening. Then they presented Burnt Offerings and Fellowship Offerings in YHWH's presence, before enquiring of YHWH. They said, 'Should we go out to battle again against our brothers, the Benjaminites? Or should we not go?'

YHWH said, 'Go! I will give them into your hands tomorrow.'

So on the third day Israel *went and* set up men in ambush around Gibeah, *while others* took up positions against Gibeah, as they had previously. They then went up against the Benjaminites.

The Benjaminites came out to attack the people and began to inflict casualties on the people as they had done before. Indeed, they killed about thirty Israelite men along the road leading from Bethel to Gibeah, and in the open field.

But the men of Israel had given way before Benjamin. They were relying on the men in ambush they had placed near Gibeah. *As a consequence*, the Benjaminites said, 'They are being defeated in our presence, as previously. We have surely defeated them as *we did* at the first battle.'

However, they did not realise that they were being drawn away from the town. *Indeed*, the Israelites had said, 'Let us retreat. Let us draw them away from the town onto the roads.' *As a consequence*, every Israelite *who had been involved in the main charge* retreated to Baal Tamar, where they took up their stand.

Then the Israelites, who had been set up in ambush, west of Gibeah, charged out from their place. They moved suddenly and dashed into Gibeah. Ten thousand chosen men, from all of Israel, made a frontal attack on Gibeah. They then spread out and put the whole city to the edge of the sword. *Despite that*, the fighting was still very heavy, and *even the Israelites* didn't know how close they had come to disaster.

Now the men of Israel had arranged for the ambushers to send up a great cloud of smoke from the city. *That* was *the signal for* the men of Israel to turn in battle. So when the cloud, the column of smoke, began to rise from the city, *they began to attack*. The Benjaminites then looked behind them and saw the whole city *with smoke* going up to the heavens.

The men of Benjamin were terrified; they realised that disaster was near. So they turned away from the Israelites *and ran* in the direction of the wilderness. But the battle followed them. Those *who had been involved in the destruction of the town* then *came* among them, and *helped* destroy them.

The Israelites surrounded the Benjaminites. They chased *those who had escaped the cordon*, and easily overtook them near Geba, *five kilometres north*-east *of Gibeah*. So the Benjaminites saw they had been defeated.

In this way, YHWH defeated Benjamin in Israel's presence. The Israelites struck down *about* twenty-five thousand one hundred men from Benjamin that day. All had borne the sword.

Benjaminite Casualties (approximate)
(All men bearing the sword, all men of valour)

The Israelites' initial attack	18,000 men
When the Benjaminites turned and fled into the wilderness, in the direction of the rock of Rimmon	5,000 men on the roads
At the end of the pursuit, as far away as Gidom	2,000 men
TOTAL	25,000 men

However, six hundred men *escaped*. They turned and fled into the wilderness *in the direction of* the rock of Rimmon. *At the time, the Israelites chose not to pursue them, and those who had escaped* stayed at the rock of Rimmon for four months.

The men of Israel then went *throughout* Benjaminite *territory* and put to the edge of the sword everything in their towns, including animals and whatever else they found, *including women and children*. They then set the towns they found on fire.

Rebuilding Benjamin[10]

With one of the tribes virtually extinguished, the people returned to Bethel and

---

[10] Judges 21:1-25

sat there, in God's presence, until evening. They raised their voices and wept bitterly. They said, 'Why, YHWH, God of Israel, has this happened to Israel? Why is one tribe missing in Israel today?'

Then, in the morning, the people got up, and *presumably because the existing altar could not accommodate the number of offerings*, they built *another* altar there. They then offered *their* Burnt Offerings and Fellowship Offerings.

Now the men of Israel had sworn *certain* oaths at Mizpah. They had made a solemn oath that anyone who failed to join the assembly before YHWH at Mizpah, 'Shall surely be put to death.' They had also said, 'None of us will give his daughter to a Benjaminite as a wife.'

So the Israelites said, 'Which of all the tribes of Israel did not join the assembly before YHWH at Mizpah?' The Israelites then grieved for their brother, Benjamin. They said, 'Today, one tribe has been cut off from Israel.'

Then, looking for a way to restore Benjamin, they continued, 'How can we provide wives for those who remain? We have sworn an oath by YHWH not to give them our daughters as wives?' They then repeated, 'Which of the tribes of Israel did not assemble before YHWH at Mizpah?'

They then realised that no one had come to the camp—to the assembly—from Jabesh Gilead *in Manasseh, on the eastern side of the Jordan River*. Indeed, when they counted the people, there was no one from Jabesh Gilead there. So the assembly sent twelve thousand valiant men to Jabesh Gilead.

They ordered them, 'Go! Put to the edge of the sword all of the inhabitants, including women and children. *More specifically*, kill all the men and every woman who has lain with a man.'

So when the valiant men arrived, they did as they had been instructed, and they found four hundred young women who had not lain with a man, among the inhabitants of Jabesh Gilead.

While the raid was in progress, the Israelites moved their base to Shiloh. Shiloh was north of Bethel, east of the highway that runs from Bethel to Shechem and south of Lebonah. *Bethel had been the base for the attacks on Benjamin, but with the war over, the High Priest (with the Ark) had probably returned to Shiloh.*

So the men brought the young women to the camp at Shiloh, in the land of Canaan. The entire assembly then sent *a delegation* to the *six hundred* Benjaminites at the rock of Rimmon. They spoke to them and offered them peace.

The Benjaminites then returned *to their homes* and were given the women who had been spared from Jabesh Gilead. But there were not enough *women* for them *all*.

But the people were sorry about Benjamin, because of the breach YHWH had made within the tribes of Israel. So the elders of the assembly said, 'How can we provide wives for the remaining *Benjaminites*? Women have been eliminated from Benjamin.'

They said, 'The survivors of Benjamin must have an inheritance. No tribe is to be wiped out from Israel. But we cannot give them our daughters as wives, because we took a solemn oath. We said, "Cursed is anyone who gives a wife to a Benjaminite."'

They *then* realised, 'Look, there is an annual festival of YHWH *coming up* in Shiloh.'

So they told the Benjaminites: 'Go, lie in wait in the vineyards and watch. When you see the daughters of Shiloh come out to participate in the dances, rush out from the vineyards and seize a wife for yourself. Each *man is to take* a daughter of Shiloh. Then return to the land of Benjamin. When their fathers or brothers come to us to complain, we will say to them, "Be gracious to us for their sake. We were unable to get *every* man a wife in the war *with Jabesh Gilead. Besides*, you are not guilty *of breaking your vow*, because you didn't *actually* give them *your daughters*."'

So *when the time came*, that is what the Benjaminites did. They caught the number of women *they needed* from those who were dancing. Then they left and returned to their inheritance. They then rebuilt the towns and lived in them.

At that time, the Israelites also left Shiloh. They all returned to their *own* tribes, to their *own* clans, and to their own inheritances.

In those days there was no king in Israel; everyone did what was fit in his *own* eyes.

C3. JONATHAN
(c. 1368 BC)

Micah's Idols[11]

There was a man named Micah, who lived in the hill country of Ephraim. He said to his mother, 'I heard you utter a curse. *It was* about the eleven hundred *shekels* of silver that were taken from you. Look, I have the silver; I took them.'

His mother said, 'May YHWH bless you my son.'

He *then* returned the eleven hundred *shekels* (*12.54 kilogrammes*) of silver to his mother.

His mother said, 'I solemnly consecrate the silver in my hand to YHWH. I will give it back to you, my son. Then you can make a carved image and a cast idol.'

So *after* he returned the silver to his mother, his mother took two hundred *shekels* (*2.28 kilogrammes*) of silver and gave it to a silversmith, who made it into an image—an idol. It was then placed in Micah's house.

In those days there was no king in Israel; everyone did what was right in their *own* eyes. The man, Micah, made a shrine to *many* gods. He made an ephod *for a priest* and *some* household gods *to bring luck and prosperity*. He then installed one of his sons, to be his own priest.

A Levite from Bethlehem[12]

There was a young man from Bethlehem in Judah, from the clan of Judah. *His name was Jonathan, a descendant of Gershom, son of Moses.* He was a Levite who lived in Bethlehem, *who one day* left the town of Bethlehem in Judah to find somewhere else to live.

As he journeyed along, he came to the hill country of Ephraim, to the house of Micah.

Micah asked him, 'Where have you come from?'

He said to him, 'I am a Levite from Bethlehem in Judah. I am travelling *around*, looking for *the right* place to stay.'

Now Jonathan was not a descendant of Aaron, and was therefore not eligible to be a priest. But despite that, Micah said to him, 'Remain *here* with me. Be my *spiritual* father and my priest. I will give you ten *shekels* (*114 grams*) of silver a year, plus a set of clothes, and your food.' So the Levite went in and agreed to live with the man.

---

[11] Judges 17:1-6
[12] Judges 17:7-13

Micah then consecrated the Levite, and the young man became his priest. He lived in the house of Micah. Indeed, the man treated the young man like one of his *own* sons.

Micah then said, 'I now know that YHWH will bless me, because the Levite has become my priest.'

The Danites Conquer Laish[13]

In those days, there was no king in Israel and the tribe of Dan was looking for a place where they might settle. *They had been granted an inheritance* among the tribes of Israel, but had been unable to take possession of it. So the Danites sent five men from all the men of their clan—men of war from Zorah and Eshtaol—to search and spy out the land.

They told them, 'Go, and explore the land.'

In this way, the men came to the hill country of Ephraim, to the house of Micah. But as they neared Micah's house *they heard* the voice of the young man *and* recognised the Levite's *accent*.

They approached him and asked, 'Who brought you here? What are you doing in this *place*? Why are you here?'

He then told them everything that Micah had done for him. *He said*, 'He has hired me; I am his priest.'

They then said to him, 'Please enquire of God *for us*, so that we may learn whether the journey we are on will be successful.'

They then stayed the night.

In the morning, the priest said to them, 'Go in peace. The journey you are going on has YHWH's approval.' So the five men went on *their way*.

They came to Laish (*48 kilometres north-west of the Sea of Galilee*) and noticed its people living in safety. Like the Sidonians, the people *felt* secure and undisturbed; they lacked nothing, because their land was very prosperous. *They had strong cultural ties with* the Sidonians, but were *some* distance from them. But the people had no *formal* relationships with anyone.

When they returned to their brothers—Zorah and Eshtaol—their brothers said to them, 'What did you *find*?'

They answered, 'Come, let us go up against them. We have seen the land, and it is very good.' *But the Danites apparently needed more convincing. So the five continued*, 'Don't *just sit there* doing nothing. Don't delay in going, entering, and taking possession of the land. When you get there, you will find a people *who*

---

[13] Judges 18:1-31

believe they are secure. God has put into our hands a broad spacious land; a place where nothing is lacking in the land.'

So six hundred armed men, from Zorah and Eshtaol from the tribe of Dan, set out from there, ready for battle.

As they went, they set up camp near Kiriath Jearim in Judah. For this reason they called that place Mahaneh Dan (*'camp of Dan'*), *and it was still known by this name when this story was written down.* It was west of Kiriath Jearim.

From there they passed on to the hill country of Ephraim and came to the house of Micah.

The five men, who had spied out the land *around* Laish, then said to their brothers, 'Do you know that in *one of* these houses there is an ephod, household gods, a carved image, and a cast idol? Now you know what you must do.' So the five men went over and approached the house of the young man—the Levite—the house of Micah.

The priest was standing at the entrance to the gate, so they asked about his welfare. *Then* the six hundred men from the tribe of Dan, armed ready for battle, *came to the* entrance to the gate and stood there with the priest.

The five men who had spied out the land *then* entered *the house and* took the carved image, the ephod, the household gods, and the cast idol.

The priest, *who had followed them in*, said to them, 'What are you doing?'

They said to him, 'Keep quiet! Put your hand over your mouth! Come with us. Be a father and a priest for us. Wouldn't it be better for you to be a priest for a *whole* Israelite tribe or clan than to be a priest for the household of one man?'

The priest was pleased *with the offer, so* he took the ephod, the household gods, and the carved image. He then took his place in the centre of the *six hundred* men, *so they could provide an escort and shield around him. Then, expecting some sort of attack from the rear by Micah,* they placed their children, livestock, and possessions in front of them. They then turned away and resumed their journey.

After the Danites had gone some distance from the house, Micah called together the men who lived in the houses nearby. They *chased after* the Danites *and* caught up *with them. Indeed,* they shouted out to the Danites, who then turned *to face them.*

They said to Micah, 'What do you want? Why did you call out?'

He replied, 'You have taken my gods, the ones I made; *you have taken* my priest and gone away. What else do I have? So how can you ask me, "What do you want?"'

The Danites said to him, 'Do not speak in our hearing. *If you do*, angry men will attack you. Then you and your family will lose your lives.'

Establishing the Kingdom

So when Micah saw that the Danites were too strong for him, he turned away and returned home. The Danites also went on their way.

The Danites took *the items that* Micah had made, and his priest, and continued to Laish. They attacked the people—*who had felt* secure and undisturbed—with the edge of the sword and they burned the city with fire. No one came to their rescue, because Laish was a long way from Sidon and the people had no *formal* relationships with anyone. *Indeed,* Laish *may have been* in a valley near Beth Rehob, *but they did not provide any support either.*

The Danites rebuilt the city and dwelt there. Although the city was named Laish, they called it Dan. They named it after their ancestor Dan, *one of the twelve sons* born to Israel.

The Danites set up the idols for themselves, and *they consecrated* Jonathan, a descendant of Gershom, son of Moses, *to be their priest.*

The idol they set up, made by Micah, remained in Dan all the time that the house of God was in Shiloh. *Jonathon* and his sons acted as priests for the tribe of Dan until the time of the captivity of the land.

C4. OTHNIEL
(c. 1415-1325 BC)

Othniel[14]

The Israelites did what was evil in the eyes of YHWH. They forgot YHWH their God and served the Baals and the Ashteroths.

YHWH's anger burned against Israel. He sold them into the hand of Cushan Rishathaim, king of Aram Naharaim, and the Israelites served Cushan Rishathaim for eight years.

But the Israelites cried out to YHWH, and YHWH raised up a deliverer for the Israelites—Othniel, son of Kenaz, younger brother of Caleb—and he saved them.

The spirit of YHWH was upon Othniel; he judged Israel. He went to war, and YHWH gave Cushan Rishathaim, king of Aram, into his hand. He triumphed over Cushan Rishathaim.

The land then had peace for forty years, until Othniel, son of Kenaz, died.

---

[14] Judges 3:7-11

Establishing the Kingdom

C5. EHUD
(c. 1320 BC)

Ehud[15]

The Israelites, once again, did what was evil in YHWH's eyes. So because of the evil, YHWH gave Eglon, king of Moab, power over Israel. Eglon made an alliance with the Ammonites and the Amalekites, and they attacked Israel and took possession of the City of Palms *(Jericho)*. The Israelites *then* served Eglon, king of Moab, for eighteen years.

But the Israelites cried out to YHWH. So he raised up a deliverer for them—Ehud, the son of Gera, the Benjamite—a man who was left handed. The Israelites then sent him to take tribute to Eglon, king of Moab.

Now Ehud had made for himself a double-edged sword, a cubit in length *(45.7 centimetres)* and had it strapped to his right thigh, under his clothes. He presented the tribute to Eglon king of Moab, *and then left. But when he reached* the place of idols near Gilgal, he sent the people away who had carried the tribute and returned *to the king*.

He said, 'I have a secret message for you, O king.' *So the* king quietened those attending him, who then left.

Ehud then approached him while he was sitting alone in the cool of his upstairs chamber and said, 'I have a message from God for you.' Then, as the king rose from the seat, Ehud reached with his left hand, drew his sword from his right thigh, and plunged it into the king's belly.

Now the king was a very fat man, and both the blade and hilt sank in. The fat closed over the sword, with the blade protruding out of his back. Ehud did not withdraw the sword from his belly. Then Ehud went out to the porch, shut and locked the doors to the upstairs chamber, and left.

After he had left, the servants returned. They saw that the doors of the upper room were locked. *They may even have smelt the excrement released in the stabbing.* So they said *to one other*, 'Surely he is relieving himself in the inner room of his chamber.' So they waited until they became embarrassed.

When he still did not open the doors to the upstairs chamber, they took the key and unlocked them. Then they saw their lord lying on the floor, dead.

While they had waited, Ehud managed to escape. He passed by the idols

---

[15] Judges 3:12-30

and escaped to Seirah. When he arrived in the hill country of Ephraim he blew a trumpet, and the Israelites *gathered around*.

He ordered them, 'Follow me. YHWH has given Moab, your enemy, into your hands.' So, with Ehud leading them, they went down with him from the hill *country*.

As they followed Ehud, *they came across the Moabites, who were already trying to flee Israelite territory. So* they *cut them off* by taking possession of the fords of the Jordan opposite Moab. They refused to let anyone cross.

At that time they struck down about ten thousand Moabites, all strong and able-bodied men. No one escaped. So Moab was subdued under the hand of Israel that day. Then there was peace in the land for eighty years.

C6. SHAMGAR
(c. 1300 BC)

Shamgar[16]

In the days of Ehud, YHWH raised up Shamgar, son of Anath. He struck down six hundred Philistine men with a cattle prod. He also saved Israel.

---

[16] Judges 3:31

C7. DEBORAH
(c. 1290-1230 BC)

Deborah[17]

After Ehud died, the Israelites, again, did evil in YHWH's eyes. So YHWH sold them into the hand of Jabin, King of Canaan. He reigned in Hazor, *a fortified city in Naphtali, fifteen kilometres north of the Sea of Galilee.* The commander of his army was Sisera, who lived in Harosheth Haggoyim, *probably a staging post in a valley.* He had nine hundred iron chariots and violently oppressed the Israelites for twenty years.

So the Israelites cried out to YHWH.

Now Deborah, a prophetess, and the wife of Lappidoth, was judging Israel at the time. She used to sit under the Palm of Deborah, which was between Ramah and Bethel in the hill country of Ephraim. The Israelites came to her *there* for judgements.

She sent *a messenger to* summon Barak, son of Abinoam from Kedesh in Naphtali. She said to him, 'YHWH, the God of Israel, has commanded, "Go! March to Mount Tabor. Take ten thousand men with you from the sons of Naphtali and Zebulun. I will lure Sisera, commander of Jabin's army, with his chariots and his troops to meet you at the Kishon River. I will give him into your hand."'

Barak said to her, 'If you go with me, then I will go. But if you will not go with me, I will not go.'

She said, 'I will indeed go with you. But because you have responded in such a way, the honour *of killing Sisera* will not be yours. YHWH will give Sisera into the hand of a woman instead.'

Deborah then got up and went with Barak to Kedesh; she went with him and with the ten thousand men who marched with him. There Barak summoned Zebulun and Naphtali.

When Sisera was told that Barak, son of Abinoam, had gone up to Mount Tabor, he summoned his entire *base*—all of his nine hundred iron chariots and all of the men who were with him at Harosheth Haggoyim—*and he led them* to the Kishon River.

Then Deborah said to Barak, 'Go! YHWH has given Sisera into your hand today. YHWH has gone ahead of you.'

So Barak descended Mount Tabor with *his* ten thousand men, and YHWH

---

[17] Judges 4:1-24

threw Sisera, all his chariots, and his whole army into confusion. Barak pursued the chariots and the army all the way to Harosheth Haggoyim. He put them to the edge of the sword. *Indeed*, Sisera's entire troop fell by the edge of the sword. Not one was left; not even one.

Sisera, *however*, dismounted his chariot and escaped on foot. He fled on foot to the tent of Jael, wife of Heber the Kenite.

Now the Kenites were all descendants of Hobab, Moses's father-in-law. But Heber, the Kenite, had moved away from the *other* Kenites. He had pitched his tent near Kedesh, by the oak tree of Zaanannim. He was also on friendly terms with Jabin, king of Hazor.

So Jael went out to meet Sisera. She said to him, 'Come, my lord! Come with me. Do not be afraid.' So he entered her tent and she covered him with a rug.

He said to her, 'Please give me some water. I am thirsty.'

Jael, however, was far more generous. She opened a skin of milk, gave him a drink, and covered him up *again*.

He then said to her, 'Stand at the entrance to the tent! If anyone comes by and asks you, "Is anyone here with you?" say, "No".'

However, Jael did not follow the family line; she had sympathy for the Israelite cause. So after Sisera had fallen asleep from exhaustion, Jael, wife of Heber, took a tent peg, grabbed a hammer in her hand, and crept quietly over to him. She then drove the peg into his temple so that it went right through him into the ground. As a consequence, Sisera died.

When Barak came past pursuing Sisera, Jael went out to meet him. She said to him, 'Come, I will show you the man you are looking for.' So he followed her *into her tent*, and there he saw Sisera lying dead with a tent peg through his temple.

So on that day God subdued Jabin, king of Canaan, before the Israelites. *Then, as time passed*, the hand of the Israelites grew stronger and stronger against him, until they finally destroyed him.

The Song of Deborah[18]

On that day Deborah, and Barak son of Abinoam, sang, these words:

> 'When the leaders of Israel take the lead—
>> when the people gladly offer themselves—
>> praise YHWH.

---

[18] Judges 5:1-31

'Hear, O king!
>Listen, O rulers!
I will surely sing to YHWH;
>I will make melody to YHWH, the God of Israel.

'O YHWH, when you went out from Seir,
>when you marched from the land of Edom,
the earth trembled, the heavens poured,
>the clouds poured down rain.
The mountains quaked in the presence of YHWH, the One of Sinai;
>in the presence of YHWH, the God of Israel.
In the days of Shamgar, son of Anath,
>in the days of Jael,
the *main* roads were deserted,
>and travellers took to winding paths.
In Israel, village life was no more.
>It ceased until I, Deborah, a mother in Israel, stood up.
When new gods were chosen,
>war came to the city gates.
Neither shield nor spear were seen
>among forty thousand in Israel.
My heart is with the leaders of Israel—
>with those who gladly offer themselves—
>praise YHWH.

'You who ride white donkeys,
>who sit on saddle blankets,
>and who walk along the road,
>consider the voices of the singers at the watering places.
There they recite the righteous acts of YHWH;
>the righteous acts of his warriors in Israel.

'YHWH's people
>went down to the city gates.
They said, "Wake up! Arouse yourself, Deborah!
>Wake up! Arouse yourself! Sing a song!
Stand up, Barak!
>Take captive your enemies, son of Abinoam."
The survivors came down to *face* the nobles;
>the people of YHWH came to me to fight the mighty.
They came from Ephraim, whose roots are in Amalek.
>Benjamin followed after, with the people.

Commanders from Makir *(from the tribe of Manasseh)* came down,
    and from Zebulun came those carrying a bearer's staff.
The leaders of Issachar were with Deborah;
    Issachar was *also* with Barak, as he ran into the valley.
However, Reuben was very divided;
    there was much indecision.
"Why did you remain with the campfires
    to hear the *shepherds* whistling for the flocks?"
Yes, Reuben was very divided;
    there was much indecision.
Gilead *(from the tribe of Gad) remained* beyond the Jordan;
    and Dan *preferred trade* by staying with the ships.
Asher *also* remained on the coast,
    staying around its harbours.
Despite that, the people of Zebulun put their lives on the line;
    as did Naphtali on the battlefield.

'Kings came, they fought;
    the kings of Canaan fought at Taanach,
    by the waters of Megiddo.
But they were unable to carry off any silver,
    any plunder.
The stars fought from the heavens;
    from their courses they fought against Sisera.
The Kishon River swept them away;
    the ancient River of Kishon.
        March on my soul, with courage.
Then was the thundering of horses' hoofs;
    there was the galloping of Sisera's mighty steeds.
The angel of YHWH said, "Curse Meroz!" *(a town, location unknown)*;
    it's people will be surely cursed.
For they would not help YHWH;
    they refused to help YHWH against the mighty.

'*In contrast*, you are the most blessed of women,
    Jael, wife of Heber the Kenite.
    You are the most blessed of those who live in tents.
He asked for water, *but* she gave him milk;
    she brought curds in a bowl fit for nobles.
She reached out her hand for a tent peg;
    her right hand for the workman's hammer.
She struck Sisera, crushing his head;
    she shattered and pierced his temple.

Between her feet he lay sunken and fallen;
>   between her feet he was sunken and fallen;
>   and where he had sunken and fallen, he was dead.
Meanwhile, Sisera's mother peered through the window;
>   she cried out through the lattice,
"Why is his chariot taking so long to return?
>   Why has the clatter of his chariot been delayed?"
To which the wisest of her ladies answered her,
>   and indeed she repeated the words to herself,
"Are they not finding the spoils, and dividing them:
>   one or two girls for each man;
>   the plunder of colourful garments for Sisera;
>   dyed embroidered garments;
>   and the plunder of embroidered garments for me."
So may all your enemies perish, YHWH!
>   but may those who love you be like the sun when it rises—
>   at full strength.'

Then the land had peace for forty years.

C8. GIDEON/JERUB-BAAL
(c. 1150-1190 BC)

The Wickedness of the Israelites[19]
Once again the Israelites did evil in YHWH's sight. So he gave them into the hand of Midian for seven years.

The hand of Midian was very strong against Israel. They descended as a swarm of locusts *on the land*, with their livestock and tents; there were so many men and camels that they couldn't be counted. They invaded the land *with the deliberate intention of* ruining it.

Whenever the Israelites planted their seed, the Midianites, Amalekites, and others from the east would attack them. They set up camp in the land and ruined the produce of the land *from east to west* as far away as Gaza. They did not leave anything for Israel to eat, including sheep, cattle, and donkeys.

So the Israelites sought shelter against the Midianites in the mountains, caves, and strongholds. Israel was brought to its knees because of Midian.

So the Israelites cried out to YHWH, and YHWH heard the Israelites cry about Midian.

He sent a man (a prophet) to the Israelites. The prophet said to them, 'This is what YHWH, the God of Israel, says. "I was the one who brought you up from Egypt, from the house of slavery. I delivered you from the hand of Egypt, and from the hand of all who oppressed you. I drove them out in your presence and gave their land to you. I said to you, 'I am YHWH your God. You are not to worship the gods of the Amorites, in whose land you dwell.' But you have not listened to my voice."'

YHWH Commissions Gideon[20]
There was an oak tree at Ophrah *(probably in Manasseh)* that belonged to Joash, the Abiezrite. *There was also a stone trough nearby used as a winepress.*

Now Joash had a son named Gideon, *and in order to keep things from the Midianites, he had learned to do things in secret, and in unconventional ways.* So Gideon was using the winepress to thresh wheat, in order to hide the wheat from Midian. *Then what appeared to be* an angel of YHWH came and sat under *the tree.*

The angel of YHWH who appeared said to him, 'YHWH is with you, mighty warrior.'

---

[19] Judges 6:1-10
[20] Judges 6:11-24

Gideon said to him, 'Sir, if YHWH is with us, why is all this happening to us? Where are all his wonders that our fathers have described to us? Did they not say, "YHWH brought us out of Egypt"? But now YHWH has abandoned us. He has given us into the hand of Midian.'

YHWH turned to him and said, 'Take this strength that you have, and *use it to* deliver Israel from the hand of Midian. You are the one I am sending.'

But Gideon, *not realizing who he was addressing*, replied, 'Sir, how can I save Israel? Look, my clan is the poorest in Manasseh, and I am the youngest in my father's house.'

YHWH said to him, 'I will surely be with you. You will strike down Midian, as if they were one man.'

Then Gideon, *suspecting who it was who was talking* to him, said, 'If I have found favour in your eyes, give me a sign that it is you, *YHWH*, who is speaking with me. *Please stay*. I want to get my offering and place it before you. Don't leave here until after I have returned.'

YHWH said, 'I will stay until you return.'

So Gideon went *to his house* and prepared a young goat, and bread without yeast from an ephah (*22 litres*) of flour. He put the meat in the basket; and the water, in which the meat had been boiled, he put in a pot. He then brought them out to YHWH, under the oak, where he offered them.

The angel of YHWH said to him, 'Take the meat and the bread made without yeast. Put them on this rock, and pour the broth over them.' So he did. The angel of YHWH then reached out, and struck the meat and the bread made without yeast, with the tip of his staff. Fire burst from the rock, consuming the meat and bread made without yeast, after which the angel of YHWH vanished from his sight.

Then Gideon *came to fully* realize who the angel of YHWH *really was*. So he cried out, 'Alas Lord YHWH! I have seen the angel of YHWH face-to-face.'

But YHWH said to him, 'Peace be to you. Do not be afraid. You will not die.'

So Gideon built an altar to YHWH there. He called it, 'YHWH is Peace'. It was still there at Ophrah, *in the land of the* Abiezrites, *when this story was written down*.

The Altar of Baal[21]

Later, that night, YHWH said to him, 'Take *two bulls* from the herd—your father's bull (*that he uses for heavy work*) and a second bull (*ideal for breeding*), seven years old. *With the first bull*, pull down your father's altar to Baal and cut down the Asherah pole standing beside it. Then build an altar to YHWH your God,

---

[21] Judges 6:25-32

in a prominent position, on top of this stronghold. Lay the stones with care. Then offer the second bull as a Burnt Offering, using the wood from the Asherah pole that you cut down.'

So Gideon took ten of his male servants and did exactly what YHWH had said. But because he was afraid of his father's house and the men of the town, he did it at night, not during the day.

The next morning, when the men of the town got up, they saw that the altar of Baal had been pulled down and that the Asherah pole beside it had been cut down. *They also saw* that an altar had been built, and that the second bull had been sacrificed on it.

They said to one other, 'Who has done this?' So they asked and searched around.

They concluded, 'Gideon, son of Joash, did it.'

So the men of the town *went to* Joash. They said, 'Bring out your son! He must be put to death for pulling down the altar of Baal and cutting down the Asherah pole beside it.'

But Joash, *having to decide between Baal and YHWH (with the life of his son at risk)*, replied to all who opposed him, 'Are you going to argue on Baal's behalf? Are you going to save him? Whoever fights for him *and kills Gideon*, will *themselves need to be* put to death by morning *for killing a man*. If Baal is a god, let him defend himself now that his altar has been pulled down.'

That day Gideon was named 'Jerub-Baal' (*'let Baal contend'*), because they said, 'Let Baal strive against him, because he pulled down his altar.'

Gideon's Fleece[22]

All the Midianites, Amalekites, and the peoples of the east, gathered together *for another raid*. They crossed *the Jordan River* and camped in the Valley of Jezreel.

The spirit of YHWH came upon Gideon. He blew a trumpet calling *his own clan*, the Abiezrites, to follow him. He sent messengers throughout all Manasseh and called them to follow him too. He *also* sent messengers to *three other Israelite tribes in the vicinity of the valley*—Asher, Zebulun, and Naphtali. So they gathered together too.

Gideon said to God, '*Give me a sign* that you will do as you have said and save Israel by my hand. Look, I am putting a woollen fleece on the threshing floor. If *in the morning there is* dew only on the fleece, while the rest of the ground

---

[22] Judges 6:33-40

is dry, then I will know that you will do as you have said, and save Israel by my hand.'

The next morning it was so. When Gideon got up, he *was able to* squeeze the fleece, and wring out the dew—*enough for* a full bowl of water.

Then Gideon said to God, 'Don't let your anger burn against me. Let me ask just one more thing; please allow one final test with the fleece. *This time*, let only the fleece remain dry, while all the ground is *covered with* dew.'

That night God did *as Gideon had asked.* All the ground was covered with dew, while only the fleece remained dry.

Gideon's Army[23]

Early the following morning, Jerub-Baal (that is, Gideon), and all who had gathered to him, got up, *left Ophrah, and went to a place overlooking the Valley of Jezreel.* They camped beside the spring of Harod, *giving them a good view of* the Midian camp in the valley further to the north, near the hill of Moreh.

YHWH said to Gideon, 'There are too many people with you for me to deliver Midian into your hand. Some might become boastful against me, saying, "My *own* hand has delivered me." To avoid that, make the *following* announcement. Tell the Israelites, "Whoever is afraid, or trembling, may turn back; he may leave Mount Gilboa."' So twenty-two thousand people returned *to their homes* while ten thousand remained.

Then YHWH said to Gideon, 'There are still too many people. Take them down to the water. I will reduce their numbers *further* for you there. Whoever I tell you, "This man will go with you", he will go with you. But to everyone I tell you, "He will not go with you", he will not go.'

So Gideon took the people down to the water. Then YHWH told Gideon, 'Separate the *people into two groups*: everyone who laps the water with their tongue, as a dog laps, and those who kneel on their knees to drink.' (Those who lapped with their hands to their mouths numbered three hundred men; the rest of the people got down on their knees to drink.)

Then YHWH said to Gideon, 'I will deliver you with the three hundred men who lapped; I will give Midian into your hand. Let all the others go, each to his *own* home.'

So Gideon kept the three hundred men and sent the rest of the Israelites *home* to their tents. *Then the three hundred* took over the provisions and the trumpets that had been in the hands *of those who had left.*

The Defeat of the Midianites[24]

The Midian camp was close by in the valley below. So that night YHWH

---

[23] Judges 7:1-8a
[24] Judges 7:8b-25

Establishing the Kingdom

said to Gideon, 'Get up! Go down against the camp, for I am giving it into your hand. But if you are afraid to go down *to fight*, take your servant, Purah, and go down to the camp. Listen to what they are saying. Then your hand will be strengthened, and you will attack the camp.' So taking Purah, his servant, he went down to *the perimeter of* the camp, *and listened to* those posted around *it*.

Now Midian, Amalek, and all the people of the east, were spread out in the valley. They were like locusts and their camels were too numerous to count; their number was like the sand on the sea-shore. Despite that, Gideon arrived and witnessed a man telling his friend a dream.

He said, 'This is the dream that I dreamt. A cake of barley bread came rolling *down the hill* into the camp of Midian. It came to the tent and struck it so that the tent collapsed, was turned upside down, and flattened.'

His friend replied, 'This can only be the sword of Gideon, son of Joash, the Israelite. God has given Midian and the entire camp into his hand.'

Once Gideon heard the account—the dream and its interpretation—he bowed down *in worship*. He returned to the Israelite camp and ordered, 'Get up! YHWH has given the Midian camp into your hands.' He then divided the three hundred men into three companies, and placed in each of their hands, a trumpet, and a torch inside an empty jar.

He said to them, 'Watch what I do, and do the same. When I get to the outskirts of the camp, whatever I do, do the same. When I, and those who are with me, blow on *our* trumpets, *wherever you are* around the camp, blow on your trumpets too. Then shout out, "For YHWH and for Gideon."' Gideon and the hundred men who were with him *then left*.

They reached the perimeter of the camp at the beginning of the middle watch, *at the beginning of the midnight shift*, after the guard had been changed. They blew on the trumpets and broke the jars that were in their hands; *all* three companies blew on their trumpets and smashed their jars. They then took the torches in their left hands, and the trumpets they were to blow in their right, and they shouted, 'A sword for YHWH and for Gideon.'

As every man held his position around the camp, the whole *Midian* camp cried out and fled. When the three hundred trumpets were blown, YHWH caused *confusion in the camp.* Throughout the entire camp, *the Midianites fought with one another*, one sword against the other. The *Midian* camp *then* fled *in a south-easterly direction, heading towards the Jordan River*, to Beth Shittah, in the direction of Zererah, as far as the border of Abel Meholah, near Tabbath.

Armed Israelites from Naphtali, Asher, and all of Manasseh were then summoned *to help*. They pursued Midian.

Gideon *also* sent messengers throughout all the hill country of Ephraim, saying, 'Come down against Midian! Seize the fords for which they are headed, as far as Beth Barah, and the Jordan *River*.'

Establishing the Kingdom

Now Ephraim was south of Manasseh, located along the expected escape route of the Midianites. But why the Ephraimites had not been included in the initial summons is not known. It could have been for strategic purposes, because of the rivalry between the two tribes of Joseph, or they may simply have been overlooked. But now, all the men of Ephraim were summoned. So they took the fords, as far as Beth Barah and the Jordan River.

They captured Oreb and Zeeb, two Midian leaders. They killed Oreb at the rock of Oreb, and they killed Zeeb at the winepress of Zeeb. They pursued Midian, and brought the heads of Oreb and Zeeb to Gideon, *who by then had moved to* the eastern side of the Jordan *River*.

The Pursuit of Zebah and Zalmunna[25]
But the Ephraimites believed that they had been deliberately snubbed by Gideon. So the men of Ephraim said to Gideon, 'What is this thing you have done to us? Why didn't you call us when you *originally* went to fight against the Midianites?' They then rebuked him sharply.

But he said to them, 'What have I achieved in comparison with you? Aren't the gleanings of Ephraim better than the vintage of Abiezer? God gave the leaders of Midian, Oreb, and Zeeb, into your hands. What have I done compared to you?'

Then, as a consequence of what he had said, their resentment against him subsided.

When Gideon, and the three hundred men who were with him, arrived at the Jordan *River*, they *all* crossed it. They were exhausted, but kept up the pursuit.

He said to the men of Succoth *(in Gad)*, 'Please give some cakes of bread for those at my feet. They are fatigued, and I *still need to* pursue Zebah and Zalmunna, kings of Midian.'

But the officials of Succoth, *perhaps fearing reprisals should Gideon fail*, said, 'Why should we give your army bread, when Zebah and Zalmunna are not yet in your hand?'

So Gideon, *offering reprisals of his own*, said, 'For that, once YHWH has given Zebah and Zalmunna into my hand, *I will return*. I will then flail your flesh with thorns from the wilderness and with briers.'

From Succoth, Gideon went up to Penuel. He made the same request of the men of Penuel. But they replied to him as the men of Succoth *had done*.

So he said to the men of Penuel, 'When I return victorious, I will demolish *your stronghold*—this tower.'

---

[25] Judges 8:1-21

Now Zebah and Zalmunna were in Karkor (*about 100 kilometres east of the Salt Sea, deep in Midian territory*) with the remains of their army. From all the peoples of the east, one hundred and twenty thousand of their men had fallen by the sword, and only fifteen thousand were left.

So Gideon *took* the caravan route to the east of Nobah and Jogbehah (*about 130 kilometres*), *so he could take* the army by surprise. He attacked the camp, but Zebah and Zalmunna escaped. He then pursued them, captured Zebah and Zalmunna, two kings of Midian, and routed the whole army. Gideon, son of Joash, then returned from the battle via the Pass of Heres.

He seized a young boy from Succoth, and questioned him. So the boy provided him with *a list* of all seventy-seven elders, the officials of Succoth.

Then Gideon returned to the men of Succoth. He said, 'Here are Zebah and Zalmunna. You taunted me, saying, "Why should we give your exhausted men bread, when Zebah and Zalmunna are not yet in your hand?"' He then took the elders of the town, and thorns from the wilderness and briers, and he flailed the men of Succoth with them. He *then returned to* Penuel, pulled down the tower, and killed the men of the town. *Then he resumed the journey back to Ophrah.*

Gideon *asked* Zebah and Zalmunna *about their exploits in the Valley of Jezreel. In particular*, he asked them about the men they had killed at Tabor.

They answered, 'They were like you. They bore themselves like sons of a king.'

Gideon said, 'They were my brothers, *not just the sons of my father*, but the sons of my mother *too*. As YHWH lives, if you had spared them, I would not be executing you *now*.'

He said to Jether, his first born, 'Stand up! Kill them!' But the boy could not draw his sword. He was afraid, for he was still a boy.

Zebah and Zalmunna *then taunted Gideon. They* said, 'Come! You strike us. As the man is, so is his strength.'

So Gideon stood up and killed Zebah and Zalmunna. He *then* removed the ornaments that were on their camels' necks *and took them as plunder.*

Gideon's Ephod[26]

Now it is not clear how popular Gideon was among the Israelites. The eastern tribes had not received him well, and Ephraim may still have harboured some resentment against him. However, he had proved himself a leader, and like his brothers had borne himself in the manner of a king.

---

[26] Judges 8:22-29

As a consequence, at least some of the Israelites *came to* Gideon, and said to him, 'Rule over us *as a king*—you, your sons, and your son's sons—because you delivered us from the hand of Midian.'

But Gideon *refused.* He said to them, 'I will not rule over you. My son will not rule over you either. YHWH will rule over you.' Gideon continued, 'What I would ask for, though, is that each of you give me an earring from your plunder' (*the invaders, also known as* Ishmaelites, had worn gold earrings).

They said, 'We will gladly give *them.*' So they spread out a garment and every man threw an earring onto it out of their plunder. (The weight of the gold *earrings* he requested amounted to one thousand seven hundred *shekels of* gold [*19.5 kilogrammes*]). In addition, *Gideon threw in his own personal share*—the crescent-shaped ornaments, pendants, and purple garments that the kings of Midian had worn, as well as the pendants that had been around the camels' necks.

Gideon then made them into an ephod, *as a means to focus the people's attention on YHWH's rule,* and he placed it in Ophrah, his *own* town, *where he had built the altar.* Then Jerub-Baal, son of Joash, returned to his house, where he remained.

In this way the Midianites were subdued before the Israelites. They did not raise their head again, and the land had peace for forty years. *However,* the ephod became a snare to Gideon and his family. *It became an object of worship, and* all of Israel prostituted themselves to it there.

Gideon's Death[27]

Gideon had seventy sons, for he had many wives. His concubine in Shechem also bore him a son. He named him Abimelech (*'my father is king'*), *perhaps reflecting a personal desire for the honour he'd refused.*

Gideon, son of Joash, died at a good old age. He was buried in the tomb of his father, Joash, the Abiezrite, in Ophrah.

But as soon as Gideon was dead, the Israelites returned to prostituting themselves to the Baals; they set up Baal-berith as a god. The Israelites did not remember YHWH their God, who had rescued them from all their surrounding enemies. *In addition,* they did not show any kindness to the family of Jerub-Baal (*that is* Gideon) for all the good that he had done for Israel.

---

[27] Judges 8:30-35

C9. RUTH
(c. 1210 BC)

Naomi's Return to Bethlehem[28]

In the days when the judges ruled, *in a time of peace with Moab*, there was a famine in the land *of Israel*. *So* a man named Elimelech (*'my God is king'*), travelled from Bethlehem in Judah to live in the region of Moab. He *took with him* his wife, Naomi, and his two sons, Mahlon and Kilion. They were Ephrathites from Bethlehem in Judah. They went to the region of Moab to settle there. But Elimelech, Naomi's husband, died, leaving Naomi and her two sons.

Now Naomi's sons had *both* married Moabite women: Kilion had married Orpah, and Mahlon had married Ruth (*which may mean 'female companion'*). But *after she had* lived in Moab about ten years, Mahlon and Kilion also died. This left her without her husband and her two sons.

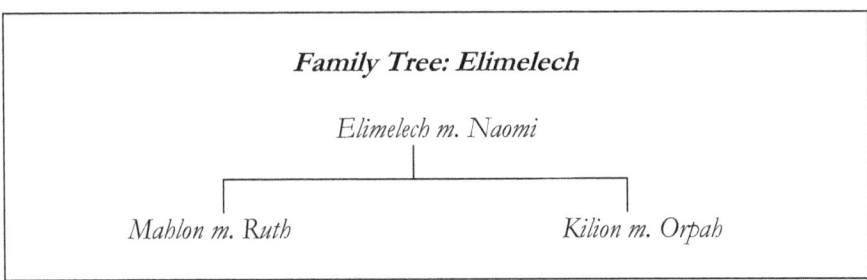

Then *news came to* the region of Moab that YHWH had visited his people *in Israel* and had provided them with food. So when Naomi heard *this*, she got up and, with her daughters-in-law, *began the journey* back from the region of Moab. She left the place where she had been living and, with her two daughters-in-law, set out to return to the land of Judah.

On the way, Naomi said to her two daughters-in-law, 'Go back! Return, both of you, to your mothers' homes. May YHWH deal kindly with you, as you have dealt to the dead and to me. May YHWH grant you both security—a home with a husband.' Then she kissed them *goodbye*, and they raised their voices and wept.

They said to her, 'No! We will go with you to your people instead.'

But Naomi said, 'Turn back my daughters! Why come with me? Will I have any more sons in my womb who could become you husbands? Return my daughters! Go! For I am too old to have *another* husband. *Even* if I thought there

---
[28] Ruth 1:1-22

was hope for me, *even* if I had a husband tonight and I then bore sons, would you wait for them until they were fully grown? Would you keep yourselves for them and not marry another man? No, my daughters, it is more bitter for me than for you, for the hand of YHWH has turned against me.' They *then* raised their voices and wept again. Orpah *then* kissed her mother-in-law *goodbye and left*, but Ruth kept close to her.

Naomi said *to Ruth*, 'Look! Your sister-in-law is returning to her people and to her gods. Return with her.'

But Ruth said, 'Don't urge me to leave you, *or discourage me* from following you. I will go where you go. I will stay where you stay. My people will be your people. My God will be your God. I will die and be buried in the same place that you die. May YHWH deal with me, and may he be ever so severe, should anything but death separates us.'

When Naomi saw that Ruth was determined to go with her, she stopped encouraging her *to return with Orpah*. So the two of them continued their journey, until they arrived in Bethlehem.

When they arrived in Bethlehem, the whole town was stirred *with excitement* at their presence. The women, *who had not expected to see Naomi ever again, were amazed. They* said, '*Can* this *really be* Naomi?'

Naomi said to them, 'Don't call me Naomi (*'pleasant'*). Call me Mara (*'bitter'*). The Almighty has dealt very bitterly with me. I went away full, but YHWH has brought me back empty. YHWH has dealt harshly with me; the Almighty has afflicted me. Why would you *still* call me Naomi?'

In this way, Naomi returned from the region of Moab, with Ruth the Moabitess—her daughter-in-law—and they arrived in Bethlehem at the beginning of the barley harvest.

Ruth Gleans in Boaz's Field[29]

Immediately on their arrival, and with the need to provide food for both herself and her mother-in-law, Ruth, the Moabitess, said to Naomi, 'Let me go to the fields. Let me pick up the ears of grain *dropped on the ground by the reapers. Let me find work following* behind someone in whose eyes I find favour.'

Naomi said to her, 'Go, my daughter.' So she left. She went and gleaned in a field behind the reapers.

This is how it happened.

There was a man of great wealth *in Bethlehem. He was* a kinsman of Naomi's husband, from Elimelech's clan. His name was Boaz and, as it happened, Ruth had gone to the section of the field belonging to Boaz from Elimelech's clan, *to*

---

[29] Ruth 2:1-23

seek permission to glean. Furthermore, she was still seeking favour when Boaz arrived from Bethlehem *to check on the progress of his servants.*

He greeted the reapers, 'May YHWH be with you.'

They said to him, 'May YHWH bless you *too.*'

Boaz, *then noticing Ruth standing there*, said to his servant in charge of the reapers, 'To whom does this young woman belong?'

The servant in charge of the reapers said, 'This young woman is a Moabitess. She is the one who came back with Naomi from the region of Moab. She asked, "Please let me glean. Please let me gather among the sheaves behind the reapers." She came and has been standing here since then *seeking permission.* Except for a short rest in the shelter, *she has been here* from *early* morning until now.'

Now Boaz was probably much older than Ruth; indeed he may well have been Naomi's age. So Boaz *turned* to Ruth *and* said, 'Listen to me, my daughter. Stay here with my servant girls. Do not move on from here. Do not go and glean in another field. Keep your eyes on *this* field which is being harvested; follow after the reapers. I have ordered the men not to touch you. When you are thirsty, go and get a drink from the water jars that the young men have filled.'

Ruth *then* fell to her face; she bowed to the ground. She said to him, 'Why have I found favour in your eyes? Why do you pay me any regard, since I am a foreigner?'

Boaz replied. He said to her, 'All that you have done for your mother-in-law, since the death of your husband, has been reported to me in great detail. *I know* that you have left your father, your mother, and *even* your birthplace, and you have come to a people who before yesterday were *completely* unknown to you. May YHWH reward you for what you have done; may YHWH, God of Israel, under whose wings you have come for refuge, reward you richly.'

Then she said, 'May I *continue to* find favour in your eyes, my lord, for you have comforted me. You have spoken kindly to your servant, even though I am not like one of your servant girls.'

Later, at lunchtime, Boaz said to her, 'Come here. Eat some bread. Dip your piece in the wine vinegar.' So she sat down with the reapers. He then offered her some roasted grain. So she ate until she was satisfied, and even had some left over.

Now there were rules about where people could glean. But Boaz considered that Ruth would be ignorant of such Hebrew customs. In any event, he did not want any such restrictions to be placed on Ruth. So Boaz ordered his servants, 'You are not to embarrass her, even if she gleans between the sheaves. Moreover, *I want you to* deliberately pull out *stalks* from the bundles for her. Leave *them on the ground* so that she can pick *them* up. But do not rebuke her.'

Then once lunch was over, Ruth got up to glean.

In this way, Ruth gleaned in the field until evening. She then beat out what she had gleaned—about an ephah of barley *(22 litres), the equivalent of about three week's wages*. She then picked it up, *probably in her head shawl which she then slung over her shoulder*, and returned to the town.

Her mother-in-law could see how much she had gleaned, so Ruth took it out and gave it to Naomi. *She* also *gave her* what she had had left over from her meal.

Her mother-in-law then said to her, 'Where did you glean today? Where have you been working? May the man who noticed you be blessed.'

Ruth then told her mother-in-law with whom she had worked. She said, 'The name of the man I worked with today was Boaz.'

Naomi said to her daughter-in-law, 'May he be blessed by YHWH. He has not withheld his kindness *either* to the living or the dead.' Then Naomi continued, 'That man is very close to us. He is one of our redeemers *under the levirate marriage law. He is someone who could fulfil his duty in carrying on the family name of Elimelech.*'

Then Ruth, the Moabitess, said, 'He also said to me, "Stay with my servants, until they have completed bringing in my harvest."'

So Naomi said to Ruth, her daughter-in-law, 'It is good, my daughter, that you should go out with his girls. They will not harm you, *and you may not be so safe in* another *man's* field.'

So from the time of the barley harvest to the completion of the wheat harvest, Ruth stayed close to Boaz's servant girls. *She* gleaned in his field, and she stayed with her mother-in-law.

Ruth's Proposal of Marriage[30]

Some time later, Naomi, her mother-in-law, said to her, 'My daughter, should I not seek security for you? *Some*where that would be good for you? Now isn't Boaz, whose girls you have been with, our kinsman?

'Look, he will be winnowing barley at the threshing floor tonight. So wash and perfume *yourself*. Put on your *best* clothes. Then go down to the threshing floor. *But* do not make your presence known to the man until he has finished eating and drinking. Take special note of where he lies down. Then, *at the appropriate time*, go over, uncover his feet, and lie down. He will tell you what you are to do *next*.'

Now in Naomi's plan, there was no suggestion that Ruth should do anything improper. To wash, put on perfume, and to dress up were symptomatic of a good reputation. So too was

---

[30] Ruth 3:1-18

allowing Boaz to initiate any discussion. But with other men present at the threshing floor, Naomi wanted to avoid misunderstanding. The principle issue was to find a way, under levirate marriage law, to maintain Elimelech's family line and, as Boaz was a very busy man, she was seeking an opportunity for Ruth to propose marriage. Her plan may well have included aspects of Moabite custom.

But regardless of the dangers, Ruth said to Naomi, 'I will do everything that you have asked me to do.'

So Ruth went down to the threshing floor and did everything that her mother-in-law had said.

At the end of the working day, Boaz ate *his meal* and *had a* drink. He was in good spirits. Then, *after dinner, to protect his grain from robbers,* he went over to the far end of the pile of grain and lay down. *Ruth then waited for Boaz to drift off to sleep, before* she quietly went over, uncovered his feet, and lay down.

About midnight Boaz *woke up,* startled. He turned over, and saw a woman lying at his feet.

He asked, 'Who are you?'

She said, 'I am Ruth, your maidservant.' *Then instead of letting Boaz speak further, Ruth took the initiative. Assuming that he would do his duty in marrying her, she asked him to indicate his agreement by responding with a custom with which Ruth was familiar.* 'You are a redeemer. Spread the corner of your cloak over your maidservant.'

But Boaz was not the only possible redeemer. Despite that, he was not offended by Ruth's proposal. On the contrary, he said, 'You are blessed by YHWH, my daughter.' *He then compared what Ruth had just done, with her earlier willingness to leave her homeland and family behind.* 'You have shown greater kindness this time than you did before. You have not gone after young men, rich or poor.

'Now, don't be fearful, my daughter. I will do for you everything you have asked. All my people in the city know that you are a woman of great worth. However, although it is true that I am a *possible* redeemer, there is another redeemer closer than me.' *Then, because Boaz was concerned that Ruth shouldn't be seen walking home in the middle of the night, he continued,* 'Stay here tonight. *We will sort out who will be the redeemer* in the morning. If the other man redeems you, good, let him redeem. But if he is unwilling to redeem you, then as YHWH lives, I will redeem you. Lie down *at my feet* until the morning.' So she lay at his feet until morning.

In the morning, before dawn, at a time when people would have been unable to see each other, she got up.

Boaz said, 'It mustn't be known that a woman came to the threshing floor.'

He *then* continued, 'Let me have the shawl you are wearing. Now grasp it firmly.'

So she held it out, and he poured into it six *seahs* (*44 litres*) *of* barley. He then placed the shawl on her, and went off into the city, while Ruth returned to her mother-in-law.

Naomi said, 'How did things go, my daughter?' So Ruth told her everything that the man had done for her.

Ruth said, 'He *also* gave me these six *seahs* of barley. He told me that I was not to return to my mother-in-law empty-handed.'

Naomi said, '*It is now time to* wait, my daughter, until you find out how the matter is resolved. The man will not rest until he settles the matter today.'

The Kinsman-Redeemer[31]

When Boaz arrived at the *city* gate he sat down. He saw the redeemer he had mentioned passing by, *so he called him over.* He said, 'Come over! Sit down here, my friend.' So he came over and sat down. Boaz then assembled ten men from the elders of the city and asked them to sit down too.

Once they were sat down, he said to the redeemer, 'There's a piece of land that belonged to our brother, Elimelech. Naomi, who has returned from the region of Moab, is selling it. I thought I should tell you personally *and* suggest that you buy it in the presence of those sitting *here*, in the presence of the elders of my people. If you will redeem, redeem. But if you will not redeem, tell me so that I will know. No one but you can redeem *the property. But if you refuse*, I am next in line.'

He said, 'I will redeem *it*.'

Then Boaz said, 'The land you acquire is from the hand of Naomi and *from the hand* of Ruth, the Moabitess, the dead man's widow. The day you buy it, you will take on the responsibility of maintaining the dead man's name and his property.'

But the redeemer was either unable or unwilling to support Ruth. He was also unwilling to sacrifice some or all of the inheritance of his own family, to provide for any offspring from his relationship with Ruth.

So the redeemer said, 'Then I cannot redeem it for myself. I cannot risk my own inheritance. Redeem *it* for yourself. Redeem it for me, because I cannot redeem.'

(Now in earlier times in Israel, *the custom* of finalising any matter involving the redemption and transfer *of property* required a man to take off his sandal and give it to the other. This was the way agreements were finalised in Israel.) So the redeemer said to Boaz, 'Acquire it for yourself.' So *Boaz* removed his sandal.

Boaz said to the elders and all the people, 'You are witness today that I have bought everything belonging to Elimelech, Kilion, and Mahlon from the

---

[31] Ruth 4:1-12

hand of Naomi. I have also acquired Ruth the Moabitess, Mahlon's widow, as a wife. *I will* maintain the name of the dead with his property. This way the dead *man's* name will not disappear from his brothers or from his town gate. You are witnesses today.'

All the people who were at the gate, along with the elders, said, 'We are witnesses.' *They then continued by blessing Boaz, referring to their common ancestors, as well as to Boaz's own family line.* 'May YHWH make the woman, who is coming into your home, like Rachel and Leah, who *between* the two of them built up the house of Israel. May you prosper in Ephrathah, and be well-known in Bethlehem. May your house be like the house of Perez, whom Tamar bore to Judah, through the children that YHWH will give you through this young woman.'

Ruth and Boaz[32]

So Boaz took Ruth, and she became his wife. He went into her, and YHWH made her with child. She *later* bore a son.

The women *around* Naomi, said to her, 'Blessed is YHWH. He has not left you without a redeemer today. May the child's name be well-known throughout Israel. He will be a restorer of life for you; he will sustain you in your old age. Your daughter-in-law, who loves you, has given birth to him. She is better to you than seven sons.'

Then Naomi took the child and laid him in her lap; *she took on* the role of his carer.

The women living *nearby* named him. They said, 'A son has been born to Naomi.' They called his name Obed (*'one who serves'*).

---

[32] Ruth 4:13-17a

C10. ABIMELECH
(c. 1220-1180 BC)

The Sons of Jerub-Baal[33]

Jerub-Baal (Gideon) had publicly rejected the idea of his sons becoming rulers over Israel. Despite that, Abimelech, son of Jerub-Baal, went to Shechem to his mother's brothers. He spoke to them, to all the clans of his mother's father.

He said, 'Speak in the hearing of all the leaders of Shechem. *Ask,* "Which is better for you, for all seventy sons of Jerub-Baal to rule over you, *or* for one man? Remember, I am your bone and your flesh."' So his mother's brothers spoke all these words in the hearing of all the leaders of Shechem on his behalf, and their hearts were inclined towards Abimelech.

They said, 'He is our brother.' They *then* gave him seventy *shekels (0.8 kilogrammes) of* silver *(possibly one for each of his brothers)* from the temple of Baal-berith, which Abimelech used to hire worthless and reckless men, who agreed to follow him.

After this, he went to his father's house in Ophrah and murdered his brothers, the seventy sons of Jerub-Baal. *He ritually slaughtered each of them* on the one stone. *However,* Jotham, the youngest son of Jerub-Baal, had hidden and managed to escape. *Abimelech then returned to Shechem.*

Then all the leaders of Shechem and Beth Millo (*a fortress outside and overlooking the city*) gathered *together.* They went up to the *ceremonial* oak tree that had been placed in Shechem and they crowned Abimelech as *their* king.

Jotham[34]

When Jotham was told *all that had happened,* he went up Mount Gerizim *to confront* the leaders of Shechem. He stood at the top, raised his voice, and shouted, 'Listen to me, so that God may listen to you.

'The trees went out to anoint a king to rule over them. They said to the olive tree, "Be king; *rule* over us."

'But the olive tree replied, "Why should I give up my oil, which is used to honour gods and men, to go and wave over the trees?"

'Then the trees said to the fig tree, "You come! Be king over us."

'But the fig tree replied, "Why should I give up my fruit, good and sweet, to go and wave over the trees?"

'Then the trees said to the vine, "You come! Be king over us."

---

[33] Judges 9:1-6
[34] Judges 9:7-21

'But the vine replied, "Why should I give up my wine, which cheers gods and men, to go and wave over the trees."'

Now the buckthorn was a relatively small plant and could provide only limited shelter. It was also prone to burst into flame. As a consequence, it was an ideal plant for Jotham to use to illustrate Shechem's relationship with Abimelech.

'Then all the trees said to the buckthorn, "You come! Be king over us."'

'The bramble replied, "Be sure that you want to anoint me king over you. *If you are, then* come, take refuge in my shade. But if not, let fire come out of the buckthorn; let it consume the cedars of Lebanon."

'Now, did you act in good faith and with integrity when you made Abimelech king? Did you consider the welfare of Jerub-Baal and his family?

'My father fought for you. He put his life on the line to deliver you from the hand of Midian. But have you treated him as he deserves? *No! Instead, this very* day, you have risen up against my father's house. You have *ritually* slaughtered his seventy sons on the one stone, and you have made Abimelech, the son of his maidservant, king over the leaders of Shechem, because he is your brother.

'So, if you *feel today that you have* acted in good faith and integrity towards Jerub-Baal and his house, rejoice in Abimelech. May he rejoice in you too. But if not, let fire come out of Abimelech and consume the leaders of Shechem and Beth Millo; and let fire come out of the leaders of Shechem and Beth Millo and consume Abimelech.'

Jotham then fled. He escaped and went to Beer, *a place some distance from Shechem on the edge of the wilderness*, and remained there for *fear* of his brother Abimelech.

Gaal, Son of Ebed[35]

Abimelech ruled over Israel three years. Then God sent an evil spirit to put a wedge between Abimelech and the leaders of Shechem. *He did this*, so that the violent deaths of the seventy sons of Jerub-Baal would be avenged—on Abimelech their brother who murdered them, and on the leaders of Shechem who helped him to slaughter his brothers.

Indeed, the leaders of Shechem acted treacherously against Abimelech. The leaders set *themselves up* in opposition to him. They set up ambushes on the tops of the hills and robbed everyone who passed by along the road. *But what they were doing* was reported to Abimelech.

Gaal, son of Ebed, then came to Shechem. He moved there with his brothers, and the leaders of Shechem *began to* put their trust in him.

At the time of the grape harvest, the people went out to the fields and gathered

---

[35] Judges 9:22-41

their grapes. They *then* trod *their grapes* and held a festival. They entered the temple of their god and ate, and drank, and cursed Abimelech.

Then Gaal, son of Ebed, said, 'Who is Abimelech? Who is *this* Shechemite that we should serve him? He may be the son of Jerub-Baal, *but he is also the son of a concubine.* Isn't Zebul, *the governor of this city, only* here because he is his deputy? Why should we serve him? We should be serving the men of Hamor, father of Shechem, *instead*.'

Now Hamor had been the clan leader who had founded the city. As a consequence, Gaal's appeal was aimed for a more full-blooded Shechemite to lead the people—and Gaal and his brothers were direct descendants of Hamor. So he deliberately undermined Abimelech, with the intention of putting himself forward as an alternative leader.

Gaal continued, 'Now if these people were under my authority, I would dispose of Abimelech. I would tell Abimelech, "Gather your army. Come out and face me."'

When Zebul, the governor of the city, heard what Gaal, son of Ebed, had said, his anger burned. He secretly sent messengers to Abimelech, telling *him,* 'Look, Gaal son of Ebed, came to Shechem with his brothers. They are inciting the city against you. You, and the people with you, should come at night and lie in wait in the fields. Then in the morning, as the sun rises, you can get up and attack the city. When Gaal, and those who are with him, come out against you, you can do to them as you think fit.'

So Abimelech, and all those with him (four companies), set out at night, and lay in wait near Shechem.

Now Gaal, son of Ebed, *was probably expecting the city to be attacked.* So he went out and stood at the entrance to the city gate. *However, he was not expecting the attack yo be so soon. So when* Abimelech, and those who were with him, *arose* from their hiding place, *it took a while for him to realise what was happening.*

When Gaal saw the people, he told Zebul, 'Look, there are people coming down from the tops of the mountains.'

But Zebul said to him, '*You are mistaking* the shadows on the mountains for men.'

Gaal spoke again. He said, 'No! There are people coming down from the highest peaks. One company is coming via the Diviners' Oak.'

Then Zebul said to him, 'Now where is your boasting? Where are your words, "Who is Abimelech that we should serve him?" Aren't these the people you ridiculed? So go against him; fight against him now.'

So Gaal led out the leaders of Shechem. He fought against Abimelech and many fell wounded at the entrance *to the city* gate. Gaal, however, fled from Abimelech, so Abimelech chased *after* him.

In this way, Zebul drove out Gaal and his brothers; *they were unable to* live in Shechem. *Meanwhile*, Abimelech, *with issues remaining between himself and the people of Shechem*, settled in Arumah, *five kilometres to the south-east.*

Shechem[36]

The next day the people *of Shechem resumed their normal way of life and* went out into their fields. So when this was reported to Abimelech, he took his men, divided them into three companies, and lay in wait *for them* in the fields. Then, when he saw the people coming out from the city, he rose up and attacked them.

Abimelech, and the company with him, rushed forward. They took up a position at the entrance to the gate of the city, *blocking any retreat*. The *other* two companies then charged those in the field and slaughtered them.

Abimelech *then turned to the city itself. Indeed*, all that day he attacked the city. He captured the city and the people in it. Then he killed *the people*, levelled the city, and *cursed it by* scattering salt all over it.

When the leaders of the tower of Shechem heard *what had happened*, they all gathered for refuge in the underground chamber in the temple of El Berith, *(part of the tower's complex)*. *So when* Abimelech was told that all the leaders of the tower of Shechem had assembled *there*, he, and all the men who were with him, went up Mount Zalmon.

Abimelech took an axe in his hand and cut off a branch of a tree. He then picked it up, and placed it on his shoulder.

He ordered the men who were with him, 'You have seen what I have done. Quickly do the same.' So every man cut a branch for himself. Then they followed Abimelech *back to the tower*.

They piled *all the branches* against the tower and, with people still inside, set it on fire. *That day*, everyone who was in the tower of Shechem, about a thousand men and women, died.

Death of Abimelech[37]

Abimelech then marched to Thebez, and he besieged the town and captured it.

In the middle of the city, however, was a strong tower. All the people of the city—men and women—had fled there. They had locked themselves in, and climbed onto the roof of the tower *so that they could watch* Abimelech as he came to the tower and attacked it.

Abimelech approached the entrance to the tower *with the intention of* burning

---

[36] Judges 9:42-49
[37] Judges 9:50-57

it with fire. But a woman threw an upper millstone down on Abimelech's head and crushed his skull.

Immediately he called to his servant, an armour bearer. He ordered, 'Draw your sword; kill me. Then no one will be able to say about me, "A woman killed him".'

So his servant ran him through, and he died.

As soon as the Israelites saw that Abimelech was dead, they each returned to their *own* home.

In this way, God repaid Abimelech's wickedness—what he done to his father by slaughtering his seventy brothers. God also repaid the men of Shechem for their wickedness. *Indeed*, the curse of Jotham, son of Jerub-Baal, was fulfilled on them.

C11. TOLA
(c. 1210-1152 BC)

Tola[38]
Abimelech's strengths had included military might, but he had been very weak on administration, and promoting and defending the worship of YHWH. As a consequence, there was a vacuum that needed to be filled.

So after Abimelech *had died,* Tola son of Puah, son of Dodo, from the tribe of Issachar, arose to deliver Israel. He lived in Shamir, in the hill country of Ephraim. He judged Israel for twenty three years, *in the same way that Othniel and Deborah had judged before him.* He then died, and was buried in Shamir.

---

[38] Judges 10:1-2

C12. JAIR
(c. 1187-1134 BC)

Jair[39]
After Tola *had dealt with the crisis in Israel, peace came to the land. That peace then continued throughout the time of* Jair, the Gileadite, who arose *to judge Israel. It was also a time of great prosperity.*

Jair had thirty sons, who rode on thirty donkeys. They had thirty towns in the land of Gilead, *on the eastern side of the Jordan River. At the time this story was written down* the towns were known as Jair Havvoth (*'the towns of Jair'*).
Jair judged Israel for twenty-two years. He then died and was buried in Kamon.

---

[39] Judges 10:3-5

C13. JEPHTHAH
(c. 1164-1110 BC)

A Plea for Help[40]

The Israelites, again, did what was evil in YHWH's eyes. They served the Baals, the Ashteroths, and the gods of Aram, Sidon, Moab, Ammon, and the Philistines. They abandoned YHWH and no longer served him. *So* YHWH's anger burned against Israel. He sold them into the hands of the Philistines and the Ammonites.

For eighteen years the Ammonites crushed and oppressed every Israelite who was living on the eastern side of the Jordan *River—those who lived* in Gilead, in the *former* land of the Amorites. Then the Ammonites crossed the Jordan *River* to fight against Judah, Benjamin, and Ephraim.

It was a very distressing *time* for Israel. So the Israelites cried out to YHWH. They said, 'We have sinned against you. Indeed, we have abandoned our God, and served the Baals.'

But YHWH said to the Israelites, 'Did you not *also* cry out each time the Egyptians, Amorites, Ammonites, Philistines, Sidonians, Amalekites, and the Maonites oppressed you? *Did* I *not* then save you from their hands? Yet you have abandoned me *again*, and have served other gods. I will no longer deliver you. Go! Cry out to the gods you have chosen. Let them deliver you in your time of distress.'

But the Israelites said to YHWH, 'We have sinned. Do to us whatever seems good in your eyes. But please deliver us today.' They then turned away from the foreign gods that were in their midst, and served YHWH, who had become frustrated with the *continual cycle of* misery in Israel.

Jephthah[41]

Now *there* was a mighty warrior *named* Jephthah, a Gileadite. His father was Gilead. *Although* Gilead's wife had borne him sons, Jephthah was the son of a prostitute. *So* when his wife's sons grew up, they drove him away.

They said to him, 'You are the son of another woman. You will not *receive an* inheritance in our father's house.'

So Jephthah fled from his brothers. He settled in the land of Tob (*95 kilometres south of Damascus*). There, *a group of* worthless men gathered around and went *on raiding parties* with him.

---

[40] Judges 10:6-16
[41] Judges 10:17-11:11

Some time later, the Ammonites made war on Israel. The Ammonites were called to arms, and they set up camp in Gilead. *In response,* the Israelites gathered together and set up camp *nearby* in Mizpah *of Gilead.*

The leaders of the people of Gilead said to one other, 'Whoever begins the fight against the Ammonites will become the leader of all who live in Gilead.'

Then the elders of Gilead went to fetch Jephthah from the land of Tob. They said to Jephthah, 'Come, be our leader! Then we can fight against the Ammonites.'

But Jephthah said to the elders, 'Don't you hate me? *Didn't you* drive me from my father's house? Why have you come to me now that you are in trouble?'

Now the elders of Gilead *could hardly deny the charges. But rather than focus on the mistakes of the past, they countered* Jephthah*'s questions with a proposal. They* said to him, 'Despite what has happened, we have now turned to you. Come with us. Fight against the Ammonites. Be the leader of all who live in Gilead.'

But Jephthah did not believe that the elders would uphold their agreement; he needed to be convinced that their offer was genuine. So Jephthah said to the elders of Gilead, 'If you take me back to fight against the Ammonites, and YHWH gives them over to me, will I be your leader?'

The elders of Gilead said to Jephthah, 'YHWH will be witness against us if we do not do as you have said.'

So Jephthah went with the elders of Gilead, and the people made him leader and ruler over them. Jephthah then repeated all his words in the presence of YHWH in Mizpah.

The Ammonite Territorial Claim[42]

Jephthah then sent messengers to the king of the Ammonites. *They* said, 'What *is there between* you and me? Why have you come to me to do battle against my country?'

The king of the Ammonites said to Jephthah's messengers, '*I have come* because Israel took away my land when they came from Egypt. *They seized the land* from the Arnon *River in the south,* to Jabbok *in the north, and* to the Jordan *River in the west.* Now return the land in peace.'

When the king's reply was reported to Jephthah, he again sent messengers to the king of the Ammonites.

They said to him, 'This is what Jephthah said. "Israel did not take the land of Moab, or the land of the Ammonites. When Israel came out of Egypt, they journeyed through the wilderness to the Sea of Reeds, and arrived at Kadesh-

---

[42] Judges 11:12-28

barnea. Israel then sent messengers to the king of Edom, saying, 'Please let us pass through your country.' But the king of Edom wouldn't listen. They also sent *a similar message* to the king of Moab, but he refused *too*. So Israel remained in Kadesh.

"'They then travelled through the wilderness, going around the lands of Edom and Moab. They journeyed to the east of *Edom and* Moab, and camped on the other (*northern*) side of the Arnon *River*. But they did not cross the boundary of Moab, for the Arnon *River* is the *northern* border of Moab.

"'Israel then sent messengers to Sihon king of the Amorites, king of Heshbon. They said to him, 'Please let us pass through your country to our *own* place.' But Sihon did not trust Israel to pass through his territory. Instead, he gathered all his people together. They set up camp at Jahaz and he fought with Israel. Then YHWH, God of Israel, gave Sihon and all his people into the hand of Israel. Israel defeated them and captured all the land of the Amorites, who were the inhabitants of that country. So they took possession of all the territory of the Amorites, from the Arnon *River in the south* to Jabbok *in the north*, and from the wilderness *in the east* to the Jordan *River in the west*.

"'Now *it was* YHWH, the God of Israel, *who* drove out the Amorites in the presence of his people Israel. So are you *now determined to* take over the land *from us*?'"

For the previous three hundred years, Ammon had been located to the east of the Israelite territories on the eastern side of the Jordan River, and Moab had been to the south. However, in more recent days, Ammon had taken occupation of Moab, and was trying to do the same with the Israelite territories.

Then the messengers continued Jephthah's message, 'Do you not possess what Chemosh, *the god of the Moabites*, your *adopted* god, has given you? In the same way, we will *keep* possession of what YHWH, our God, has given us. Are you better than Balak son of Zippor, king of Moab? Did he ever quarrel against Israel? Did he ever go to war against them? Israel has occupied Heshbon, Aroer, and their settlements, and all the towns along the *northern* bank of the Arnon *River* for three hundred years. In all that time, why haven't you taken them?

'It is not I who has wronged you, but you have wronged me by making war against me. So may YHWH, the judge, decide today between the Israelites and the Ammonites.'

But the king of the Ammonites took no notice of the message that Jephthah sent him.

Jephthah's Vow[43]

The Spirit of YHWH then came upon Jephthah. So Jephthah passed through Gilead and Manasseh, through Mizpah of Gilead, and from there he

---

[43] Judges 11:29-40

went on to the Ammonites. *But being unsure of himself and fearing being rejected again,* Jephthah made a solemn vow to YHWH. *However, his vow was impulsive; it gave little thought to the safety of his family.*

He said, 'If you will indeed give the Ammonites into my hand, then whatever comes out of the door of my house to meet me, when I return victorious from the Ammonites, will be yours. I will sacrifice it as a Burnt Offering.' Jephthah then engaged the Ammonites in battle, and YHWH gave them into his hand.

Jephthah inflicted devastation on twenty towns, from Aroer, to the area surrounding Minnith, and as far away as Abel Keramim. In this way, the Ammonites were subdued in the presence of the Israelites.

When Jephthah returned to his home at Mizpah, his daughter came out *of his house* to meet him; her and her alone. Besides her, he had no other children. *She celebrated the safe return of her father in the traditional way,* with tambourines and dancing.

When he saw her, he tore his clothes, and said, 'Oh my daughter. You have brought me great misery. You are the cause of my wretchedness, for I swore a solemn oath to YHWH, and I cannot break it.'

She said to him, 'My father, you have sworn an oath to YHWH. Since YHWH has given you vengeance on your enemies—the Ammonites—do to me as you have sworn.'

She then continued, 'Let me be granted this one request: Give me two months. I will roam and wander the hills. My friends and I will weep over my virginity.'

He said, 'Go!' So he sent her away for two months, and she and her friends went into the hills and wept over her virginity.

At the end of two months she returned to her father, and he did to her according to his vow. She never slept with a man.

This is why it became a custom in Israel that every year young women in Israel would go out for four days to commemorate the daughter of Jephthah the Gileadite.

Ephraim Argues with Jephthah[44]

After this, men of Ephraim were summoned *together to confront Jephthah.* They crossed *the Jordan River* to Zaphon, s*even kilometres north of Jabok.*

They said to Jephthah, 'Why did you go and fight against the Ammonites, without calling on us to go with you? We will burn your house down over your head.'

---

[44] Judges 12:1-7

But Jephthah said to them, 'My people and I were involved in a serious conflict with the Ammonites. I did call you, but you did not deliver me from their hand. When I realised you were not going to deliver me, I took my life in my hands, went up against the Ammonites, and YHWH gave them into my hand. So why have you come to me today to fight against me?'

Jephthah then gathered all the men of Gilead and fought against Ephraim.

Despite their accusations, the real reason the Ephraimites went to Gilead was to look for fugitives. Indeed, they accused the men of Gilead of being fugitives from Ephraim, living in Ephraim and Manasseh. So the Gileadites struck down the Ephraimites.

Then, to stop the Ephramites from retreating, the Gileadites captured the fords of the Jordan *River on the way back* to Ephraim. *Furthermore, they came up with a simple language test to reveal the accent of the fleeing soldiers, who were trying to pass themselves off as Gileadites.*

When any Ephraimite who had escaped *the battle* said, 'Let me cross over', the men of Gilead would ask them if they were an Ephraimite. If they said, 'No', they would ask them to say the word 'shibboleth', *knowing that the* Ephraimites were unable to pronounce the word correctly. They would say 'sibboleth'. In this way, they were seized and slaughtered at the fords of the Jordan *River*.

At that time, forty-two thousand *men from* Ephraim were killed.

Jephthah, the Gileadite, judged Israel for six years, and then he died. He was buried in *one of* the towns in Gilead.

C14. IBZAN
(c. 1170-1103 BC)

Ibzan[45]

After Jephthah, Ibzan of Bethlehem judged Israel. He had thirty sons and thirty daughters.

He was a man of great ambition; someone who was keen to widen his sphere of influence by creating political alliances. Indeed, he gave away *his daughters in marriage* to those outside *his clan*; and he brought in thirty young women from outside for his sons.

He judged Israel for seven years. Then Ibzan died and was buried in Bethlehem.

---

[45] Judges 12:8-10

C15. ELON
(c. 1153-1093 BC)

Elon[46]

After Ibzan, Elon, the Zebulunite judged Israel. He judged Israel for ten years. Then Elon the Zebulunite died and was buried in Aijalon in the land of Zebulun.

---

[46] Judges 12:11-12

C16. ABDON
(c. 1153-1085 BC)

Abdon[47]

After Elon, Abdon, son of Hillel the Pirathonite judged Israel. *He exercised something like royal power. Indeed,* he had forty sons and thirty grandsons who rode on seventy donkeys.

He judged Israel for eight years. Then Abdon, son of Hillel, the Pirathonite, died. He was buried at Pirathon in the land of Ephraim in the hill country of the Amalekites.

---

[47] Judges 12:13-15

C17. SAMSON
(c. 1115-1065 BC)

The Birth of Samson Foretold[48]

The Israelites again did evil in the eyes of YHWH. So YHWH gave them into the hands of the Philistines for forty years.

There was a certain man of Zorah, from the tribe of Dan. His name was Manoah. His wife was barren; she had been unable to bear any *children*.

An angel of YHWH appeared to the woman and said to her, 'Even though you are barren and have borne no children, you will become pregnant and bear a son. *But* because the boy is to be a Nazirite to God from birth, *there are certain things that you need to do.* Make sure that you do not drink wine or fermented drink, or eat anything unclean, from conception to the birth of your son. *Then, once he is born*, no razor is to be used on his head. He will begin to deliver Israel from the hand of the Philistines.'

After the angel had left her, immediately the woman went to her husband. She said to him, 'A man of God came to me. He had the appearance of an angel of God. I was so fearful that I didn't ask him where he came from, and he didn't tell me his name. But he said to me, "You will conceive and bear a son. You are not to drink wine or fermented drink, or eat anything unclean, as the boy will be a Nazirite to God from his birth until the day he dies."'

Manoah then prayed to YHWH. He said, 'O Lord, please let the man of God you sent come back to us again. Let him teach us what we are to do for the boy who is to be born.'

God listened to Manoah, and the angel of God returned to the woman while she was in the field. Manoah, her husband, was not with her, *so* she hurriedly ran to tell her husband. She said to him, 'The man who appeared to me the other day has returned to me.' So Manoah got up and followed his wife.

When he came to the man, he said to him, 'Are you the man who spoke to my wife?'

He said, 'I am.'

Now as the boy's father, Manoah would have had expectations regarding his role in the upbringing of the child. Of particular concern would have been the child's Nazirite vows, the training required, and the timing of particular events. So Manoah said *to the angel*, 'When

---

[48] Judges 13:1-25

your words come *true*, what is to be the boy's rule of life? What kind of work will he do?'

But as far as the angel was concerned the boy's life was to be moulded by YHWH, not Manoah. As a consequence, the angel of YHWH *simply repeated the previous instructions.*

He said to Manoah, 'Your wife is to do everything that I told her. She is not to eat anything that comes from the grapevine; she is not to drink wine or fermented drink. She is not to eat anything unclean. She is to do everything I have commanded her.'

Now custom required that Manoah should have offered the man hospitality immediately on his arrival. But his keenness to discover his role in his son's upbringing may have affected his judgement. Nevertheless, Manoah *had not totally forgotten his manners, even if he* had not realised that the man was an angel of YHWH.

So Manoah said to the angel of YHWH, 'Please let us detain you. We will prepare a young goat for you.'

But the angel of YHWH said to Manoah, You may detain me, but I will not eat your food. However, if you would like to prepare a Burnt Offering, then offer it to YHWH.'

Manoah said to the angel of YHWH, 'What is your name? We would like to honour you, when your word comes true.'

The angel of YHWH said to him, 'Why do you ask my name? It is beyond comprehension.'

So Manoah took a young goat and a grain offering and, *using* a rock, offered them to YHWH. Then while Manoah and his wife were watching, YHWH performed a wonder. A flame on the altar shot up to the heavens and the angel of YHWH ascended in the flame. *When* Manoah and his wife saw this, they fell on their faces to the ground.

When the angel of YHWH did not reappear to *either* Manoah or his wife, Manoah realised that he was an angel of YHWH.

Manoah said to his wife, 'We will surely die, for we have seen God.'

But she said to him, 'If YHWH was going to kill us, he would not have accepted the Burnt Offering and grain offering from our hands. He would not have shown us all these things. He would not have told us all this.'

The woman bore a son and named him Samson (*a variation of the Hebrew word for 'sun'*). The child grew up and YHWH blessed him. *For a while he lived at* Mahaneh Dan (*'camp of Dan'*), *twelve kilometres west of Jebus. It was* between Zorah and Eshtaol. *There* the Spirit of YHWH began to stir him.

Establishing the Kingdom

A Wife from the Philistines[49]

One day Samson went down to Timnah, *about seven kilometres from his home, on the southern side of the Valley of Sorek.* There he *took* notice *of a* local young woman, among the daughters of the Philistines. So he returned *home and* told his father and his mother.

He said, 'I have seen a *young* woman in Timnah, from the daughters of the Philistines. Get her for me as a wife.'

Now his parents knew well the ethnic and religious taboos that Samson was dismissing. So his father and mother said to him, 'Aren't there *any suitable* women among your relatives, or among all my people? Must you take a wife from the uncircumcised Philistines?'

But Samson said to his father, 'Get her for me. She is right in my eyes.'

(Now his father and mother did not know that this was from YHWH; he was seeking an opportunity *to move against* the Philistines, who at that time were ruling over Israel.)

So Sampson, with his father and mother, went down to Timnah.

When they reached the vineyards of Timnah, *his father and mother stopped, while* Samson *wandered off.* He came across a young lion, who roared *at him.* Then the Spirit of YHWH came upon him, and he tore the lion apart, as one tears a young goat. He had nothing in his hand. *He then returned to his* mother and father *and they resumed their journey.* He did not tell them what he had done.

Samson then went down and talked with the woman, and she was right in his eyes.

After some time, Samson returned to marry her. *On the way*, he turned aside to see the lion's carcass, and saw a swarm of bees and honey in its body. He scooped some honey out with his hands and ate as he walked along. When he joined up with his father and mother he gave *some* to them and they ate. But he didn't tell them that he had taken the honey from the carcass of a lion.

When they arrived, his father went down to the woman, *while* Samson prepared a feast, as was the custom among young *Philistine* men. *Then,* when the people *of the town* saw him, they provided thirty companions to be with him.

Now seven days was probably the customary period for a wedding feast among the Philistines. Entertainment, as well as food and drink, would have been expected to be provided.

So Samson said to them, 'Let me tell you a riddle. If you can solve it and tell me the answer, within the seven days of the feast, I will give you thirty linen

---

[49] Judges 14:1-20

garments and thirty changes of clothes. But if you cannot give me the answer, then you are to give me thirty linen garments and thirty changes of clothes.'

They said to him, 'Tell us your riddle. Let us hear it.'

He replied to them, 'Out of the eater came something to eat; out of the strong came something sweet.'

For *the first* three days, they couldn't answer the riddle. So *feeling very frustrated*, on the fourth day, *they approached* Samson's wife. They said to her, 'Persuade your husband to explain the riddle to us. Otherwise, we will burn you and *the members of* your father's household with fire. Have you invited us *here* to rob us or not?'

Later, when they were alone, Samson's wife wept before him. She said, 'You don't love me. Indeed, you hate me. You have given a riddle to the sons of my people, but you have not explained it to me.'

He said to her, 'I haven't explained it to my father and mother. Why should I explain it to you?'

Now Samson's wife had been upset about not being given the solution to the riddle from the very beginning. Indeed, the men may have picked up her demeanour, and used it to threaten her. As a consequence, she cried in Samson's presence *every day* of the seven days of the feast, and she pressed him *so much that* on the seventh day he explained it to her.

Then she explained the riddle to the men of her people.

So on the seventh day, before sunset, the men of the town spoke to Samson. They said, 'What is sweeter than honey? What is stronger than a lion?'

He said to them, 'You couldn't have answered my riddle, if you hadn't ploughed with my heifer.'

Then the Spirit of YHWH came upon him. He went down to Ashkelon and struck down thirty men there. He stripped them, and gave the changes of clothes to those who had answered his riddle. Burning with anger, he *then* returned *alone* to his father's house. *His father-in-law, meantime, thinking that the marriage was in ruins*, gave Samson's wife to the friend who had attended him.

Samson's Revenge on the Philistines[50]

Some time later, at the time of the wheat harvest, Samson went to visit his wife. *He took* with *him* a young goat *as a peace offering.*

Now Samson did not know that his wife had been given to another man. So he said, 'I will go into my wife in her room.' But her father would not allow him to enter.

---

[50] Judges 15:1-8

Her father said, 'I was convinced that you utterly despised her, so I gave her to your friend. *In any event*, isn't her younger sister more agreeable? Take her for a wife instead.'

But Samson *stormed out and* said to *those around*, 'This time I will be innocent in regard to the harm I am about to do to the Philistines.'

Samson then went out and caught three hundred foxes. He tied the foxes *together* in pairs by their tails, took torches, and secured a torch between *each pair* of tails. He then lit the torches and released *the foxes* into the standing grain of the Philistines. It burned up the stacks, the standing grain, the vineyards, and the olive groves.

Some of the Philistines said, 'Who has done this?'

Others said, '*It was* Samson, the son-in-law of the Timnite. The Timnite took Samson's wife and gave her to his friend.'

So the Philistines, *in order to deal with the troublesome family and take revenge on Samson*, went up *to Timnah*. They then burned Samson's wife and her father with fire.

But with this, Samson *was even more aggrieved. He* said to them, 'I will surely have my revenge on you because you have acted in this way. After that, I will stop.' So he struck them down with a great slaughter. Then he went down to Etam *in Simeon*, where he lived in a cave in the rock.

Victory at Ramath-Lehi[51]

But Samson's revenge only made the Philistines angrier still. So the Philistines went up to Judah. *They* camped *there*, spreading *themselves out at a place that would later become known as Ramath*-Lehi *('jawbone hill')*.

The men of Judah said, 'Why have you come up against us?'

They said, 'We have come to take Samson prisoner. We will do to him as he has done to us.'

Three thousand men from Judah then went down to Etam, to the cave in the rock. They said to Samson, 'Don't you know that the Philistines rule over us? What then have you done to us?'

He answered them, 'I have done to them, exactly what they did to me.'

They said to him, 'We have come to tie you up, to give you into the hand of the Philistines.'

Samson said to them, 'Swear to me that you won't kill me yourselves.'

They said to him, 'We won't. We will only tie you securely. Then we will give you into their hand. But we will definitely not kill you.' So they bound him with two new ropes and brought him from the rock.

---

[51] Judges 15:9-19

As they approached Lehi, the Philistines came shouting towards Samson.

Then the Spirit of YHWH came upon him. The ropes on his arms seemed like burnt flax, and the bonds fell from his hands. Seeing a fresh jawbone of a donkey, he reached out and grabbed it, and with it he struck down a thousand men.

Then Samson said, 'With a jawbone of a donkey, *I've made* one heap, two heaps. With a jawbone of a donkey I have killed a thousand men.'

When he had finished speaking, he threw the jawbone away. Then the place was named Ramath-Lehi.

But Samson was very thirsty, and he called to YHWH. He said, 'You have given this great victory into the hand of your servant, but must I now die of thirst and fall into the hand of the uncircumcised?' God then split open the hollow place in Lehi, so that water came out of it.

When Samson drank he revived, and his strength returned. He named the spring En Hakkore (*'caller's spring'*). It was still there *when this story was written down.*

Samson and the Prostitute[52]

One day, Samson went to Gaza, *deep in Philistine territory.* He saw a woman there—a prostitute—and went into her.

The *men of* Gaza were told, 'Samson has come here.' So they surrounded *the house. They also* lay in wait for him *at* the city gate. *They remained in place* all night, keeping quiet, having said *to each other,* 'We will kill him at dawn.'

But Samson *took the men of Gaza by surprise—he only* lay down until midnight. In the middle of the night he got up *and managed to get to the city gate.* There, seeing *the way was blocked,* he took hold of the doors of the gate of the city, *with the* two *vertical* posts and *top horizontal* bar, and tore them loose. *Then, as a way of showing the people of Judah that the Philistines were no match for YHWH,* he put them on his shoulders and carried them *some sixty-three kilometres to the east,* to the top of the hill opposite Hebron.

Samson and Delilah[53]

Another time, Samson fell in love with a woman named Delilah (*sounds like the Hebrew for 'night'*). She was from the Valley of Sorek, *between Israelite and Philistine territories.*

The leaders of the Philistines went to her. They said to her, 'Draw him in. Discover the secret to his great strength. See how we can overpower him, tie him up, and subdue him.' *Then, as an indication that they were desperate to rid themselves of Samson and that Delilah's co-operation would need to be bought, they made a very generous*

---

[52] Judges 16:1-3
[53] Judges 16:4-21

offer. 'We will each give you eleven hundred *pieces* of silver'. (*If paid in shekels, they would have given her 12.5 kilogrammes of silver each.*)

Now Delilah *was well aware that* Samson *thrived on danger. So instead of using a subtle approach, she* said to Samson, 'Tell me now, why are you so strong? With what can you be tied up and subdued?'

But Samson *was not prepared to share the secret of his great strength. Instead, he joined in 'the game' with Delilah, knowing very well who it was who wanted him subdued.* He said to her, 'If they tie me with seven fresh bowstrings that haven't been dried, I will become weak. I will be like any *other* man.'

So the leaders of the Philistines brought her seven fresh bowstrings that had not been dried, and she tied him up with them.

Now there were men lying in wait in an inner room. So she said to him, 'Samson, the Philistines are upon you.' But Samson snapped the bowstrings, as a piece of string snaps when it has been burnt with fire. So *the secret of* his strength was not discovered.

Delilah said to Samson, 'You have deceived me. You have told me lies. Now tell me with what you can be tied.'

He said to her, 'If they tie me securely with new ropes that have never been used, I will become weak. *I will be like* any *other* man.'

So again men lay in wait in an inner room, and Delilah took new ropes and tied him up with them. She said to him, 'Samson, the Philistines are upon you.' But he snapped the rope around his arms as if it were thread.

Delilah said to Samson, 'Up to this point you have deceived me. You have told me lies. So tell me with what you can be tied.'

But this time, instead of indicating the things that the Philistines could do, he suggested what Delilah could do. He particularly referred to some items used in weaving—a loom, some web (unfinished woven cloth) and fastening pins—that were around her house.

He said to her, 'If you weave the seven locks of my head into the web, and tighten it with a pin, then I will become weak. I will be like any *other* man.'

So, *later*, she put him to sleep, wove the seven locks of his head into the web, and tightened it with a pin.

She said to him, 'Samson, the Philistines are upon you.'

But he awoke from his sleep and tore himself loose from the pin, the loom, and the fabric.

She said to him, 'How can you say "I love you" when your heart is not with me? You have deceived me three times now, and you *still* haven't told me what makes you so strong.'

For many days she nagged him with the things that she said. She prodded him *so much* that he despaired of life and wanted to die. So he told her his secret.

He said, 'No razor has *ever* been used on my head. I have been a Nazirite, *dedicated* to God, from the time I left my mother's womb. If *my head* were shaved, then my strength would leave me. I would become weak. I would become like any *other* man.'

When Delilah saw that he had told her his secret, she sent for the leaders of the Philistines. She called to them, saying, 'Come back one more time. He has told me his secret.' So the leaders of the Philistines returned to her with the silver in their hands. She put him to sleep on her knees and called a man *to assist her while* she shaved off the seven locks of his head.

Then, when it was clear that his strength had left him, she began to subdue him. She said, 'The Philistines are upon you, Samson.'

He *immediately* awoke from his sleep, *and being unaware of what had taken place*, he *naturally* thought 'I'll do what I've done before. I will shake myself free.' But he didn't know that YHWH had left him.

Then the Philistines seized him and gouged his eyes out. They took him down to Gaza and bound him with bronze shackles. *Then, to complete his humiliation, they set him* to grinding *grain* in the prison house.

The Death of Samson[54]

After Samson was shaved, the hair on his head began to grow *back. However, the Philistines took no notice, because they no longer saw him as a threat.*

Some time later, the leaders of the Philistines gathered together *in Gaza* to celebrate and to offer a great sacrifice to their god, Dagon *(possibly 'grain')*. They said, 'Our god has given our enemy, Samson, into our hands.'

Then, when they were in high spirits, they said, 'Call for Samson. *Let us see this "strong man" of Israel. Let us see what mighty acts he can do now.* Let him entertain us.' So they called for Samson to be brought from the prison house, and he performed in their midst. They stood him between *the two central* pillars *of the temple.*

When the people saw him they praised their god. They said, 'Our god has given our enemy—the one who wasted our land and killed *so* many of us—into our hands.'

Samson said to the boy, who was holding his hand, 'Place my hands on the pillars that support the temple. I want to lean against them.'

Now the temple *would probably have had an antechamber and a main hall. The*

---

[54] Judges 15:20; 16:22-31

hall would have looked something like an open courtyard, with two main pillars in the centre and a supporting roof extending out from the antechamber.

On this occasion, the temple was full of men and women; all the leaders of the Philistines were present. *In addition*, there were about three thousand men and women on the roof, *trying to* get a view of Samson's performance. *Indeed, the sheer number of people on the roof, jostling for positions to see 'The Destroyer', probably made the whole structure very unstable.*

Then Samson prayed to YHWH. He said, 'Lord, YHWH, remember me. Strengthen me, God, just one more time. Let me have one final act of vengeance on the Philistines for *the loss of* my two eyes.' Samson then took hold of the two central pillars of the temple, one on his right and the other on his left, and he braced himself against them.

Samson said, 'Let my life end with *those of* the Philistines.' He then strained with all his might, so that the temple came *crashing* down on the leaders and everyone else who was in it. Samson killed more people when he died than he had the rest of his life.

When Samson's family heard what had happened, his brothers and all his father's household went down *to Gaza*. They took his *body* back and buried him in his father's tomb, located between Zorah and Eshtaol.

Samson had judged Israel for twenty years, during the time that the Philistines *ruled over Israel*

C. 18. ELI
(c. 1125-1045 BC)

Family Tensions[55]

There was a certain man from Ramathaim (*'two hills'*), in the hill country of Ephraim. He was a Zuphite from the tribe of Ephraim. His name was Elkanah (*'God created'*), son of Jeroham, son of Elihu, son of Tohu, son of Zuph. He had two wives. One was named Hannah (*'favour'*), the other named Peninnah (*'fruitful'*). Peninnah had children, but Hannah was childless.

Every year, *at the same time*, Elkanah *would join in the clan feast* at Shiloh. He would go up from his town to worship and sacrifice to Almighty YHWH there; each time he *would* make his sacrifice. He would then give *one* portion each to his wife, Peninnah, and to her sons and daughters; but he would give a double portion to Hannah. He loved Hannah *very much, even though* YHWH had closed her womb.

Now Hannah's rival used to provoke her. Indeed, she *deliberately* provoked and irritated her, because YHWH had completely closed her womb. This continued year after year. Every time Hannah went up to the house of YHWH she provoked her, and Hannah wept *so bitterly* she was unable to eat.

Her husband, Elkanah, would ask her, 'Why are you weeping? Why aren't you eating? Why is your heart *so* sad? Am I not better to you than ten sons?' *But Elkanah was unable to console her.*

Hannah's Vow[56]

(*When the Israelites had first entered the Promised Land, the Tabernacle had been set up at Shiloh. However, over the years the Tent had been abandoned, and a more temple-like structure had been built.*)

Eli *was the High* Priest in Shiloh, *and* two of his sons, Hophni and Phinehas, *assisted him as* YHWH's priests.

One particular year, Elkanah went up to Shiloh, as usual.

When they had eaten and drank, Hannah stood up. She was deeply distressed. She prayed to YHWH and wept bitterly.

She made a solemn vow. She said, 'Almighty YHWH, if only you would look upon the misery of your handmaid and remember me. Do not forget your handmaid, but give her a male offspring.'

---

[55] 1 Samuel 1:1-3a, 4-8
[56] 1 Samuel 1:3b, 9-19a

Now God had given rules for working in the Tabernacle. They included the need to be a Levite, and between thirty and fifty years of age. Furthermore, to be a priest one had to be a descendant of Aaron (although Elkanah may have been a descendant, but just living among the Ephraimites).

But whatever his background, Hannah continued, 'I will give him to YHWH all the days of his life.' Then, *as a way of indicating that this was some sort of Nazirite vow and that her child would be totally dedicated to YHWH*, Hannah concluded, 'No razor will come near his head.'

Eli, the *High* Priest, was sitting on the seat of honour by the doorpost of YHWH's Tabernacle. So as Hannah continued praying to YHWH, Eli *was able to see* her mouth. Hannah was praying silently; only her lips were moving. So because her voice could not be heard, Eli thought she was drunk.

Now, by this time, drinking at sacrificial meals had become customary. But for Eli, excessive drinking had become a real problem. So Eli said to her, 'How long will you continue to get drunk? Turn away from your drinking.'

But Hannah replied, 'No, my lord, I am a deeply troubled woman. I haven't drunk any wine or beer. I have been pouring out my soul to YHWH. Don't mistake your handmaid for a daughter of Belial (*queen of the underworld*). I have *simply* been expressing the depths of my anguish and grief.'

Then Eli answered. He said, 'Go in peace, and may the God of Israel grant your request—whatever you asked of him.'

She said, 'May your maidservant find favour in your eyes.' The woman then went on her way. She then had something to eat, and her face no longer looked sad.

In the morning, they got up and worshipped in YHWH's presence. They then returned to their home *which at the time was* in Ramah, *in Benjamin*.

The Birth and Dedication of Samuel[57]

Elkanah lay with his wife, Hannah, and YHWH remembered her. In the course of time, Hannah conceived and bore a son. She called his name Samuel (*possibly 'name of God' or 'offspring of God'*). *She said*, 'Because I asked YHWH for him.'

When *it came time for the annual festival*, the man, Elkanah, *intended* his whole family to go up *to Shiloh* to offer the annual sacrifice to YHWH. *He also intended to confirm Hannah's* vow *by making it* his own. But Hannah was reluctant to go.

She said to her husband, 'No. I will take Samuel *with me another time*. He will be presented in YHWH's presence after the boy is weaned. He will then live there the rest of his days.'

---

[57] 1 Samuel 1:19b-28

Elkanah, her husband, said to her, 'Do what is good in your eyes. Remain *here* until you have weaned *him*. May YHWH establish his word.' So *while Elkanah and the rest of the family went to Shiloh*, the woman stayed. She nursed her son until she had weaned him, *about three years later*.

After Samuel had been weaned, *at the very next annual festival*, Hannah took Samuel *to Shiloh. She took with her* a three-year-old bull, an ephah of flour, and a skin of wine, *as a dedication offering*. She brought him to the house of YHWH at Shiloh, *even though* the boy was *very* young.

After they had slaughtered the bull, they brought the boy to Eli.

Hannah said *to him*, 'Oh, my lord. As you live, my lord, I am the woman who stood here beside you praying to YHWH. I prayed for this boy and YHWH granted me my request; *he gave me* what I asked of him. So I have dedicated him to YHWH. He will be dedicated to YHWH his whole life.' Then both Elkanah and Hannah worshipped YHWH there.

Song of Hannah[58]

Then Hannah prayed. She said:

> 'My heart rejoices in YHWH;
> > my horn (*a symbol of strength*) is lifted high in YHWH.
> My mouth opens wide against my enemies,
> > for I take pleasure in your deliverance.
> There is no one as holy as YHWH.
> > Indeed there is no one except you;
> > there is no Rock like our God.
>
> 'So don't keep speaking so very proudly;
> > *don't let* arrogance come from your mouth.
> for YHWH is a God of knowledge;
> > by him *all our* deeds are measured.
>
> 'The bows of the strong are broken;
> > those who stagger are girded with strength.
> The well-fed hire themselves out for bread;
> > the starving hunger no more.
> She who was barren has borne seven *sons* (*an expression of 'perfection'*);
> > while those who have many sons pine away.

---

[58] 1 Samuel 2:1-11

'YHWH is the one who brings death and brings to life;
>   *he* brings down to Sheol and he raises up.
> YHWH sends poverty and he brings wealth;
>   he brings low and he exalts.
> He picks up the lowly from the dust;
>   he raises the poor from the ash heap to sit with princes;
>   he has them inherit seats of honour.

'For the pillars of the earth belong to YHWH;
>   he placed the world upon them.
> He will keep watch over the feet of his faithful;
>   while the wicked will be cut off in darkness.

'For no man can prevail by *his own* strength.
>   *Indeed*, those who strive against YHWH will be shattered.
> YHWH will thunder against them from the heavens;
>   he will judge the ends of the earth.
> He will make his king mighty;
>   he will exalt the horn of his anointed.

Then, at the conclusion of the festival, Elkanah returned, *with his family*, to his home at Ramah. *Samuel, however, was left in Shiloh*, and the boy ministered before YHWH in the presence of Eli the priest.

Eli's Sons[59]

Now Eli's sons were sons of Belial (*queen of the underworld*). They did not know YHWH or the duties of priests to the people. *Indeed, they abused even the most corrupted practices of the time.*

So when a man offered a sacrifice, a servant of the priest would go *to him* while the meat was being boiled. With a three-pronged fork in his hand, he would plunge it into the pan, kettle, caldron, or pot. The priest would then take everything that the fork brought up. They treated every Israelite who came to Shiloh in this way.

But *worse still*, the priest's servant would *also* come to the man who was making the sacrifice before they burned the fat. He would say, 'Give some meat to the priest to roast. He will not accept boiled meat from you, only raw.'

The man would *then* say to him, 'The fat must surely be burned first. After that, take as much as you want for yourself.' But the servant would say, 'No! Give it to me now. If not I will take it by force.'

So the young men's sin was very great in the eyes of YHWH; they treated the offerings to YHWH with contempt.

---

[59] 1 Samuel 2:12-26

In the meantime, Samuel, a boy wearing a linen ephod, served before YHWH.

His mother *made a custom of* making little robes *for him*. So when she and her husband went to Shiloh for the annual sacrifice, she would take one to him. So the boy, Samuel, grew up in YHWH's presence.

Eli would bless Elkanah and his wife. He would say, 'May YHWH give you offspring by this woman, in place of the one requested of YHWH.' They would then return to their home.

YHWH then visited Hannah; she conceived and bore three sons and two daughters.

Now Eli was very old, *and* he had heard *reports of* everything that his sons were doing to all Israel. *He had also heard* that they were sleeping with the women who served at the entrance to the temple.

So he said to them, 'I am hearing *reports* about your deeds from all these people. Why are you doing these bad things? No, my sons, the report that I have heard, that is being spread throughout YHWH's people, is not good. If *one* man sins against *another* man, then God can act as a mediator for him. But if a man sins against YHWH, who can mediate for him?'

However, they refused to listen to what their father said. *So because of the path they had chosen for themselves*, YHWH desired to put them to death.

Meanwhile, the boy, Samuel, grew in stature and favour with both YHWH and men.

The Fall of the House of Eli Prophesied[60]

A man of God came to Eli. He said to him, 'These are the words of YHWH. "I did indeed reveal myself to *Levi*, your father's house, when they were subject to the house of Pharaoh in Egypt. I chose *Aaron* from all the tribes of Israel to be a priest for me—to go up to my altar, to offer incense, *and* to wear the ephod in my presence. I also gave your father's house all the food offerings of the sons of Israel.

"'Why *then* do you treat the *sacrificial system* that I ordered for my dwelling—*my* sacrifices and my offerings—with contempt? You honour your sons more than me. You *have also* made yourself fat with the choicest parts of every offering *made by* my people Israel."

'Therefore the declaration of YHWH, God of Israel, is: "Surely I promised your house, and your father's house, that they would come before me forever." But now the declaration of YHWH is, "Far be it from me! I will honour those who honour me, but those who despise me will be treated with contempt."'

---

[60] 1 Samuel 2:27-36

Then, as an indication that none of Eli's family had been faithful, he continued, "'Behold, in coming days I will cut off your strength and the strength of your father's house. There will not be any old men in your family. Indeed, there will never be an old man in your family. All of your many male descendants will die. *But there is one* man I will not cut off *immediately* from my altar.

"'You will *also* witness a decline *in interest in my* dwelling, despite all the good *that I do* in Israel. *As a consequence,* your eyes will fail and your heart will grieve.

"'This will be a sign to you of things to come: two of your sons, Hophni and Phinehas, will both die on the same day. I will then raise up a faithful priest for myself. He will do what is in my heart and mind. I will build a firm house for him, and he will walk before my *future* anointed *king* all *his* days. Everyone who is left in your family will then come and bow down to him. *They will beg* for a piece of silver or a *small* loaf of bread. *Indeed,* they will say, 'Please attach me to one of the priests. *I will do even the most menial of tasks* to eat a morsel of bread.'"

Ministering in the Temple[61]

Now the boy, Samuel, was serving YHWH under Eli*'s direction.* He did not yet know YHWH; the word of YHWH was still to be laid bare to him. *At the time,* Eli's eyes had become very weak and he could hardly see. The word of YHWH was *also* rare in those days; visions were very scarce.

As it happened, Eli was lying down in his place, *in an area close to the sanctuary.* The lamp of God, *which lit the sanctuary between dusk and dawn,* had not yet been extinguished. Furthermore, Samuel was lying down in the Tabernacle of YHWH, *near* the Ark of God, when YHWH called to Samuel.

Samuel said, 'I am here.' He then ran to Eli and said, 'I have come, for you called me.'

Eli said, 'I didn't call you. Return *to your bed and* lie down.' So he went *back* and lay down.

YHWH called to Samuel a second time. So Samuel got up, went to Eli, and said, 'I have come, for you called me.'

But Eli said, 'I didn't call, my son. Return *to your bed and* lie down.'

YHWH called Samuel a third time. So Samuel got up and went to Eli. He said, 'I have come, for you called me.'

Eli then realised that it had been YHWH calling the boy. So Eli said to Samuel, 'Go *back.* Lie down. If he calls you *again,* say, "Speak YHWH. Your servant is listening."'

So Samuel returned to his place and lay down.

YHWH then came and stood *in Samuel's presence.* He called as previously, 'Samuel! Samuel!'

So Samuel said, 'Speak. Your servant is listening.'

---

[61] 1 Samuel 3:1-4:1a

YHWH said to Samuel, 'Look, I am going to do something in Israel. Everyone who hears it *will be shocked. Indeed*, both ears will tingle.

'On the day I have set, I will stand in opposition to Eli. *I will begin to do* everything that I said about his house, from beginning to end. I told him that I would judge his house forever, for the sins of which he was aware. *Yet he did not stop his sons*; he did not restrain them. *As a consequence*, his sons have brought a curse on themselves. *They have treated my sacrifices and my offerings with contempt.* That is why I swore to the house of Eli, "The wickedness of the house of Eli can never be atoned for by *either* sacrifice or offering."'

When YHWH had left, Samuel lay *down again, and stayed there* until morning. He then *got up and* opened the doors to YHWH's house.

Now Samuel was afraid to share the vision with Eli. But Eli called Samuel. He said, 'Samuel, my son.'

Samuel *went over to Eli, and* said, 'I have come.'

He said, 'What was the message that he gave you? Please don't hide it from me. May God be ever so severe with you, if you hide any part of the message he gave you about me.' So Samuel told him all that he had said; he hid nothing from him.

Eli said, 'He is YHWH. Let him do what is pleasing in his eyes.'

Now YHWH did not let any of his words fall to the ground. He appeared again at Shiloh *and, as* Samuel grew up, YHWH remained with him. YHWH revealed himself to Samuel in Shiloh through his word, and the word of Samuel *then* came to all Israel. Indeed, the whole of Israel, from Dan *in the north* to Beersheba *in the south*, recognised that Samuel had been confirmed as a prophet of YHWH.

The Philistines Capture the Ark[62]

One day, Israel marched out to meet the Philistines in battle. They camped at Ebenezer, *to the west of the hill country of Ephraim*, while the Philistines camped at Aphek. The Philistines then lined up against Israel.

The battle spread, and Israel was defeated by the Philistines. About four thousand *Israelite* men were killed on the field of battle, before the Israelites returned to their camp.

The elders of Israel said, 'Why did YHWH defeat us in the face of the Philistines today? Let us fetch the Ark of the Covenant of YHWH from Shiloh. Then it will be in our midst, and it may deliver us from the hand of our enemies.' So the people sent *men* to Shiloh. They then brought the Ark of the Covenant of Almighty YHWH, who was enthroned between the cherubim, from Shiloh.

---

[62] 1 Samuel 4:1b-11

Two of Eli's sons, Hophni and Phinehas, came with the Ark of the Covenant of God.

As the Ark of the Covenant of YHWH was brought into the camp the whole of Israel gave a mighty shout. Indeed, the ground shook.

The Philistines heard the noise of the shouting. So they said, 'What's all this noise coming from the Hebrew camp? Why is there so much shouting?' But they *soon* realised that the Ark of the Covenant of YHWH had come into the camp.

Now the Philistines had evidently heard many stories about the Israelites, but not all had been told, or remembered, accurately. So *at this news*, the Philistines became afraid. They said, '*Israel's* gods have come into their camp.' They then continued, 'Woe to us! Nothing like this has happened before. Now we're in trouble. Who is going to deliver us from the hand of these mighty gods? These are the gods who struck down the Egyptians in the wilderness with every *kind of* plague.'

Others said, 'Be men of courage, Philistines, otherwise you will become slaves to the Hebrews, as they have been slaves to you. Be men and fight.'

So the Philistines did battle and Israel was defeated. The Israelites fled, each *man* to his tent. It was a very great slaughter. Indeed, thirty thousand men on foot fell from Israel. In addition, the Ark of God was taken, and two of Eli's sons, Hophni and Phinehas, were killed.

Death of Eli[63]

A man *from the tribe* of Benjamin ran from the battlefront. He arrived in Shiloh that *same* day. His clothes were torn and he had dust on his head. Eli was sitting on the seat *of honour* by the side of the road when he arrived. He had been waiting anxiously, because his heart trembled for the Ark of God.

When the man came into the town and told *his news*, the whole town cried out. Eli heard the sound of the outcry, and said, 'What is this noise? Why the uproar?' (Eli was ninety eight years old. His eyesight had failed; he couldn't see.)

The man quickly came over and told Eli *the news*. The man told Eli, 'I have come from the battle. Indeed, I fled from the battlefield today.'

Eli said, '*Tell me*, what happened, my son?'

The messenger replied. He said, 'Israel fled before the Philistines. A great slaughter was inflicted upon the people. In addition, two of your sons, Hophni and Phinehas, have died, and the Ark of God has been taken.'

The moment the messenger mentioned the Ark of God, Eli fell backward off the chair by the side of the gate. He broke his neck and died, an old and heavy man. He had judged Israel for forty years.

---

[63] 1 Samuel 4:12-22

His daughter-in-law, Phinehas's wife, was with child, and close to giving birth. She also heard the news that the Ark of God had been taken, and that *both* her father-in-law and husband had died. *So, in shock,* she *went into premature labour,* crouched down, *as was the custom,* and gave birth. But her *labour* pains were too much.

As she was dying, her attendants said to her, 'Don't be afraid. You have borne a son.' But she *was too despondent* to take any notice or reply. The Ark of God had been captured and *both* her father-in-law and husband *were dead.*

So she named the boy Ichabod (*'where is glory?'*). She said, 'Glory has been removed from Israel. Glory has been removed from Israel, because the Ark of God has been taken.'

C. 19. SAMUEL
(c. 1085-1010 BC)

The Ark in Philistine Territory[64]

After the Philistines captured the Ark of God at Ebenezer, they took it to Ashdod. Entering the temple of Dagon, they took the Ark of God and placed it beside Dagon.

When the Ashdodites arose early the next morning, *they went into the temple* and saw Dagon, fallen on his face to the ground, before the Ark of YHWH. So they took Dagon and returned him to his place.

The next morning, *the same thing happened.* The Ashdodites arose early, *and went into the temple. Again*, they saw Dagon having fallen on his face to the ground before the Ark of YHWH. *However, this time*, the head of Dagon and the palms of both of his hands were broken off, *lying* on the threshold. Only Dagon's *body* remained intact. (This then explains why the priests of Dagon, or anyone else entering the temple, *adopted the custom of* not stepping on the threshold of Dagon. *It was a custom that was still practiced when this story was written down.*)

Now the hand of YHWH was heavy upon the Ashdodites. He devastated Ashdod and its *surrounding* territory; he struck them with tumours.

When the men of Ashdod realised *that Dagon was powerless to come to their aid*, they said, 'The Ark of the god of Israel must not remain with us. His hand is hard upon both us and Dagon our god.' So they sent for all the rulers of the Philistines. They gathered them *together* and asked them, 'What shall we do with the Ark of the god of Israel?'

The rulers said, 'Let the Ark of the god of Israel be moved to Gath.' So they moved the Ark of the god of Israel.

But after it had been taken *to Gath*, the hand of YHWH was against that city. YHWH struck the men of the city, young and old; they were inflicted with tumours. *The* panic *among the people was* very great, so they sent the Ark of God to Ekron.

However, as the Ark of God was entering Ekron, *a loud* cry *came from* the Ekronites. They said, 'Why have they brought the Ark of the god of Israel to us? *It will* kill us and our people.'

There was a deathly panic in the entire city; God's hand was very heavy there. Those who didn't die were struck with tumours, and the cry of the town went up to the heavens.

---

[64] 1 Samuel 5:1-12

So they sent for all the rulers of the Philistines. They gathered them *together* and said *to them*, 'Send the Ark of the god of Israel away. Let it return to its place. Then it will not kill us or our people *anymore*.'

The Philistines Return the Ark[65]

Now some of the Philistines were sceptics. Others were reluctant to admit defeat on either political or religious grounds. As a consequence, the Ark of YHWH was in the territory of the Philistines for seven months before the Philistines *finally* called *together* the priests and the diviners. They said, 'What shall we do with the Ark of YHWH? Tell us what we have to do to return it to its place.'

They said, 'If you intend to return the Ark of the god of Israel, do not send it away empty-handed. Make sure that you send YHWH a guilt offering. Then you will be healed, and it will be clear to you why his hand has not been lifted from you.'

The Philistines said, 'What shall we send him as a guilt offering?'

They said, 'There are five rulers over the Philistines, and the same plague has affected all Philistines, including your rulers. *So send* five gold tumours and five gold rats; make images of your tumours and the rats that are ruining the land. Give honour to the god of Israel. *Then*, perhaps, he will lift his hand from you, your gods, and your land.'

Now the Philistines had taken seven months to get to this point, and even now some were not convinced that YHWH was the cause of their misery. So the priests and diviners continued, 'Why do you harden your hearts as Pharaoh and the Egyptians hardened theirs? Didn't *the god of Israel* treat them harshly *too*? It was only after they *had suffered that they* sent the *sons of Israel* on their way.

'Now take a new cart. Get it ready with two cows that have *recently* calved, but have not been yoked, and hitch the cows to the cart. Then take away their calves *and place them in a* pen away from them. Take the Ark of YHWH and place it on the cart. Put the gold objects you are sending back to YHWH as a guilt offering in a chest, and place it beside the Ark. Then send it on its way. *The cows' instincts will be to return to their calves. Only the influence of a powerful god will keep them away.* Then watch *carefully which way the cart goes.* If it goes by the way to its *own* territory, to Beth Shemesh, then *it really is the god of Israel who has* brought us this great evil. But if it doesn't, then we will know that *all this has* happened to us by chance, and that it isn't YHWH's hand that has struck us *at all*.'

So the men carried out the instructions. They took two cows that had *recently* calved, and hitched them to the cart. They then took their calves and put them in a pen. They placed the Ark of YHWH on the cart and *put* the chest with the gold rats and models of tumours *by its side*. Then, *as they watched on*, the

---

[65] 1 Samuel 6:1-12, 17-18a

cows took the straight path, following the road to Beth Shemesh. They kept to the road, lowing as they went; they did not turn *either to the* right or *to the* left.

Guilt Offerings Sent by the Philistines to YHWH	
Golden Tumours:	*Five*: one each for Ashdod, Gaza, Ashkalon, Gath and Ekron
Golden Rats:	*Five*: *one for* each of the Philistine towns (the fortified towns with their surrounding villages), belonging to the five Philistine rulers

The rulers of the Philistines followed the cows all the way to the boundary of Beth Shemesh.

The Ark in Israel[66]

Now *the people* of Beth Shemesh were in the valley reaping the wheat harvest. They looked up *from their work and* saw the Ark. They rejoiced at what they saw. The cart entered the field of Joshua of Beth Shemesh, where it came to a halt by a large stone.

Now Beth Shemesh was a town belonging to the Levites. As a consequence, there were people in the town with YHWH's authority to handle the Ark. So the Levites removed the Ark of YHWH *from the cart* and placed it on the large rock. They did the same with the chest, containing the gold objects that were with it.

The people then chopped up the wooden cart, and *used the wood* to offer the cows as a Burnt Offering to YHWH. Indeed, that day, the people of Beth Shemesh offered Burnt Offerings and presented sacrifices to YHWH. Then, that same day, the five rulers of the Philistines, who had watched all *the proceedings*, returned to Ekron.

The large stone on which the people set the Ark of YHWH remained as a witness. It was still in the field of Joshua of Beth Shemesh *when this story was written down.*

Unfortunately, not everyone treated the Ark or God's laws with respect. Indeed, seventy men of Beth Shemesh looked into the Ark of YHWH. As a consequence, YHWH struck them down.

After he had struck them down, the people mourned. YHWH had struck a great blow against the people.

---

[66] 1 Samuel 6:13-16 ; 18b-7:4

The men of Beth Shemesh said, 'Who is able to stand in YHWH's presence? He is a holy God. To whom can we send him? *How can we send the Ark away* from us?'

So they sent messengers to the inhabitants of Kiriath Jearim, saying, 'The Philistines have returned the Ark of YHWH. Come down, and take it for yourselves.'

So the men of Kiriath Jearim came down. They picked up the Ark of YHWH and took it to the house of Abinadab on the hill. There they consecrated his son, Eleazar, to keep watch over the Ark.

The Ark remained at Kiriath Jearim for many years. *Indeed, it stayed there* twenty years. During that time the whole house of Israel mourned after YHWH.

Samuel spoke to the whole house of Israel. He said, 'If you wish to return to YHWH with all your heart, then put away the foreign gods and the Ashteroths in your midst. Commit your heart to YHWH. Serve only him. He will then deliver you from the hand of the Philistines.' So the Israelites turned aside from the Baals and Ashteroths and served only YHWH.

Samuel Becomes a Judge and the Philistines Are Defeated[67]

Samuel then summoned the whole of Israel to Mizpah. He said, 'I will pray to YHWH for you.'

So they gathered at Mizpah. They drew water and, *perhaps as an act of self-denial*, they poured it out before YHWH. That *same* day they fasted and admitted, 'We have sinned against YHWH.'

In this way, Samuel, *who was recognised as a prophet of YHWH, began to* judge over the Israelites; *it happened* at Mizpah.

Now when the Philistines heard that the Israelites had gathered at Mizpah, the rulers of the Philistines *assembled their troops, and began to* march on Israel.

When the Israelites heard that the Philistines were approaching, they became very fearful. So they said to Samuel, *'Pray continually to God for us*; do not stop pleading to YHWH our God for us. Then he may deliver us from the hand of the Philistines.'

So Samuel took a suckling lamb, and offered it as a whole Burnt Offering to YHWH. Samuel pleaded to YHWH for Israel, and YHWH responded to him.

The Philistines drew near while Samuel was sacrificing the Burnt Offering. They were ready to battle Israel. But YHWH thundered with a loud voice against the Philistines. That day, he threw them into confusion and they were

---

[67] 1 Samuel 7:5-17

struck down before Israel. The men of Israel then rushed from Mizpah, chased the *fleeing* Philistines to the vicinity of Beth Car, and struck them down.

When the battle was over, Samuel took a stone and positioned it between Mizpah and Shen. He called it Ebenezer (*'stone of help'*). He said, 'Up until now YHWH has helped us.'

So the Philistines were subdued; they did not enter the territory of Israel again. Indeed, the hand of YHWH was against the Philistines all the days of Samuel.

The towns that the Philistines had taken were returned to Israel, including both Ekron and Gath. Israel delivered their territories from the hand of the Philistines. There was *also* peace between Israel and *all its indigenous inhabitants, commonly known as* Amorites.

So Samuel judged Israel all the *remaining* days of his life. Every year he would travel on a circuit: from Bethel to Gilgal and to Mizpah. He would judge Israel in all those places. But he would *always* return to his house at Ramah. He judged Israel, and he built an altar to YHWH there.

The People Ask for a King[68]

When Samuel had grown old, he appointed his sons to be judges over Israel. Joel, his firstborn son, and Abijah, his second son, *both* judged at Beersheba. However, his sons did not walk in his ways. They were inclined to seek dishonest gain; they took bribes and they perverted justice.

So all the elders of Israel met together at Ramah and came to Samuel. They said to him, 'Look, you have grown old, and your sons do not walk in your ways. So give us a king to govern us, like all the *other* nations.'

The request for a king to lead the people was displeasing in the eyes of Samuel. So Samuel prayed to YHWH.

But YHWH said to Samuel, 'Listen to the voice of the people, to all that they say to you. They have not rejected you, they have rejected me from being their king. From the day I brought them up out of Egypt to today they have done such things; they have forsaken me and served other gods. Now they are treating you the same.

'So listen to their voice. But make sure you warn them; make clear to them the rights of a king who would reign over them.'

So Samuel reported all the words of YHWH to the people who had asked him for a king.

---

[68] 1 Samuel 8:1-22

He said, 'These will be the rights of the king who will reign over you: He will take your sons. He will put some *to work* with his chariot and horses; they will run in front of his chariot. He will appoint *some to be* commanders of thousands and commanders of fifties. *Others* will plough his fields, reap his harvest, and make weapons of war and equipment for his chariot. In addition, he will *also* take your daughters to make perfume, to cook, and to bake.

'He will take your best fields, vineyards, and olive groves, and will give them to his servants. He will *also* take a tenth of your *produce*—grain and wine— and give it to his officials and his servants.

'He will take your menservants and maidservants. He will use the best of your cattle and your donkeys to do his work. He will take a tenth of your flocks, and you will be his servants.

'When all this happens, you will cry out *to YHWH. However, as the oppression you face will come from* the king whom you chose for yourself, YHWH will not answer you on that day.'

But the people refused to heed Samuel's words. They said, 'No! We definitely want a king over us. We will then be like all the *other* nations. Our king will judge us. He will lead us out and he will fight our battles.'

After Samuel had listened to all the words of the people, Samuel again reported what the people had said in the hearing of YHWH.

But YHWH said to Samuel, 'Listen to their voice. Give them a king. *But not a king like those of the surrounding nations, but one of my own choosing.*'

So Samuel reported *YHWH's command* to the men of Israel *and ordered them* to return to their towns.

The Anointing of Saul[69]

There was a Benjaminite named Kish; a man of *great* power. He had a son named Saul; a young and impressive man. Indeed there was no finer man in Israel than Saul. From his shoulders upwards he was taller than any other person.

Saul's Ancestral Line

Aphiah—Becorath—Zeror—Abiel—Kish—Saul

Saul's father, Kish, had some donkeys that had wandered off. So Kish said

---

[69] 1 Samuel 9:1-10:8

Establishing the Kingdom

to his son, Saul, 'Get up! Go and search for the donkeys. Take one of the servants with you.' So *Saul searched for his father's donkeys.*

He went through the hill country of Ephraim, and through Benjamin, but they were unable to find *them. They searched* around Shalisha, *and* the district of Shaalim.

When they reached the vicinity of Zuph, Saul said to his servant who was with him, 'Come, let us return. Otherwise, my father will become so worried about us that he will stop being concerned about the donkeys.'

But his servant said to him, 'Look, there is a man of God in this town; a highly respected man. Everything he says comes true. Let us go there. Perhaps he will tell us *about our journey and* the way you should take.'

Now at that time *it was the custom* in Israel, that when a man went to inquire of God, he would say 'Come, we will go to the seer' (for prophets were formerly called seers). *It was also the custom to give gifts to honour them and to buy favours.*

So Saul said to his servant, 'But if we go, what can we give him? Our sacks are empty of food, and we don't have a gift to take to the man of God. What do we have?'

But the servant answered Saul again. He said, 'Look at what I have in my hand. I have a quarter of a shekel (*2.85 grams*) of silver. I will give it to the man of God. Then he will tell us about our journey.'

Saul said to his servant, 'Your words are good. Come let us go *to the seer.*' So they set out in the direction of the town, where the man of God *lived.*

As they were climbing the hill on which the town *stood,* they met *some* girls coming out to draw water. They asked them, 'Is the seer here?'

They replied to them. 'He is. He *arrived just* ahead of you. So hurry, because he has come to the town today for the people's feast, *which is held* at the high place.

'As you enter the town, find him before he goes to the high place to eat. He has to bless the sacrifice. *Indeed,* the people will not *start* eating until he has arrived. Only then will those invited eat. So go now, for it's about this time of day that you will find him.'

So they continued on to the town.

When they arrived at the town, they saw Samuel coming towards them, on his way up to the high place.

Now, the day before Saul arrived, YHWH had revealed to Samuel, 'Tomorrow, about this time, I will send a man from the land of Benjamin to you. You are to anoint him as ruler over my people, Israel. He will deliver them from the hand of the Philistines. Indeed, I have heard the cry of my people and seen *their affliction.*'

Then when Samuel saw Saul, YHWH told him, 'Look, the man about whom I spoke to you *is approaching*. He is the one will rule over my people.'

Just inside the *town* gateway, Saul approached Samuel.
Saul said, 'Can you please tell me where *I may find* the house of the seer?'
Samuel answered Saul, 'I am the seer. Go ahead of me to the high place. You are to eat with me today, and in the morning I will let you go. I will tell you everything that is on your heart. However, in regard to the donkeys that were lost three days ago, do not be concerned about them. They have been found.

'Now for whom is the desire of all Israel? *Is it not for a king to judge, lead, and fight for them*? Is it not for you and your father's household?'

Saul replied, 'But I am a Benjaminite, one of the smallest tribes in Israel. My clan is *the most* insignificant clan in Benjamin. Why do you say such things to me?'

When they arrived at the high place, Samuel took Saul and his servant and brought them into the hall. He then gave them seats at the head *of the table, among* about thirty invited guests.

Samuel said to the cook, 'Serve the *priestly* portion *of the sacrifice that* I gave you *to this man*; the portion I told you to keep aside. So the cook served the thigh with what was on it, and set it before Saul

Samuel said, 'See what has been kept to be set before you. Eat! For it has been kept for you for this appointed time; that is, with the people I invited.'

So that day Saul ate with Samuel.

After they returned from the high place into the town, *Samuel provided Saul with a bed for the night* on his roof. *There* Samuel talked *again* with Saul.

The next morning, about daybreak, Samuel called to Saul on the roof. He said, 'Get up, and I will send you *on your way*. So Saul got up, and the two of them, Samuel and Saul, went outside.

As they approached the town boundary, Samuel said to Saul, 'Tell your servant to go ahead of us.' So the servant went on. *Then Samuel continued*, 'You stay here for a while, then I can give you God's message.'

Samuel then took a flask of oil and poured it on Saul's head. He kissed him and said, 'YHWH has indeed anointed you as ruler over his possession.

'Today, after you leave me, you will come across two men near Rachel's tomb, at Zelzah, on Benjamin's boundary. They will say to you, "The donkeys which you set out to look for have been found. Now your father has stopped worrying about the donkeys and is worrying about you. He has said, 'What shall I do about my son?'"

'Then you will leave there and go to the great tree of Tabor. You will be met there by three men on their way up to God at Bethel. One will be carrying three young goats, another will be carrying three loaves of bread, and another will be carrying a skin of wine. They will greet you and give you two *loaves of* bread, which you will accept from their hand.

'After that you will go to Gibeah-elohim where the Philistine garrison *is located*. As you enter the town, you will meet a band of prophets coming down from the high place. They will be prophesying. They will be led by *others playing* a lyre, tambourine, flute, and harp. The Spirit of YHWH will rush upon you and you will prophesy with them. You will be transformed into another man.

'So as *each of* these signs is fulfilled, respond in the way that you see fit. God will be with you.

'So go down to Gilgal ahead of me. You are to wait seven days until I come to you, then I will tell you what you must do. I will come down to you, to offer Burnt Offerings and to sacrifice Fellowship Offerings.'

Saul Returns Home[70]

As *Saul* turned away from Samuel, God renewed his heart. Then, that day, all the signs *that Samuel foretold* came about.

As Saul, and his servant, approached Gibeah, they saw prophets coming to meet him. The Spirit of God came upon him and he prophesied in their midst.

Many, who had known him before, saw *him* prophesying with the prophets. So the people said to each other, 'What has happened to the son of Kish? Is Saul also *to be ranked* among the prophets?'

A local man interjected, '*But* who is their *spiritual* father? *Who leads this group?* Nevertheless, the saying 'Is Saul also among the prophets?' came about *because of the events of that day*.

When *Saul* had finished prophesying he continued on up the hill.

When he arrived home, Saul's uncle *came*, and asked *both* him and his servant, 'Where have you been?'

Saul replied, 'To look for the donkeys. But when we couldn't find them, we went to *consult* Samuel.'

Saul's uncle said, 'Tell me now, what did Samuel say to you?'

Saul said to his uncle, 'He convinced us that the donkeys had been found.' He did not tell him what Samuel had said in regard to the kingship.

---

[70] 1 Samuel 10:9-16

C20. SAUL
(1079-1007 BC)

a). King Saul *(c. 1049-c. 1025 BC)*

Saul Is Chosen To Be King[71]

Samuel called the people to *assemble before* YHWH at Mizpah. He said to the Israelites, 'YHWH, the God of Israel, says, "I alone brought Israel up from Egypt. I delivered you from the hand of Egypt and from the hands of all the kingdoms that have oppressed you." But today you have rejected your God—the one who delivers you from all your disasters and troubles. You have said to him, "No! Set a king over us." So present yourselves before YHWH, by your tribes and clans.'

So Samuel had all the tribes of Israel brought near. *He* then *cast the lot, and* the tribe of Benjamin was chosen. The tribe of Benjamin was then brought forward, and the clan of Matri was chosen. Finally the lot fell to Saul, son of Kish.

However, when they looked for him, he couldn't be found. So they enquired again of YHWH. *They said*, 'Has the man not yet arrived?'

But YHWH said, 'Look, he has hidden himself among the baggage.'

So they ran and took him from *where he was hiding*. He then stood *there* in the midst of the people. From his shoulders upwards, *he was* taller than all the people.

Samuel said to all the people, 'Do you see the man that God has chosen? Indeed, there is no one like him among all the people.'

Then all the people shouted, saying, 'May the king live *forever*.'

Samuel then detailed the ordinances regarding kingship to the people. He wrote them down on a scroll and *later* deposited it *in the sanctuary* before YHWH. Samuel then dismissed all the people *and each* man *returned* to his home. Saul then returned to his home in Gibeah, accompanied by valiant men, whose hearts had been touched by God.

There were some worthless men *who* said, 'How can this *man* deliver us?' *Indeed*, the men despised Saul and did not bring him any gift. Saul *heard them*, but he *simply* turned a deaf *ear*.

The Ammonite Siege of Jabesh Gilead[72]

Now Nahash, *an* Ammonite *king*, went up to Jabesh Gilead *(about 35*

---

[71] 1 Samuel 10:17-27
[72] 1 Samuel 11:1-11

Establishing the Kingdom

kilometres south of the Sea of Galilee), and encamped *against the city*. So all the men of Jabesh said to Nahash, 'Make a treaty with us, and we will serve you.'

But Nahash, the Ammonite said to them, 'I will make a treaty with you on *one condition*: that every one of you has his right eye gouged out. In this way, I will bring disgrace on all Israel.'

The elders of Jabesh said to him, 'Give us seven days, so we can send messengers throughout Israel's territory. If no one delivers us, we will give ourselves up to you.'

The messengers came to Gibeah, *where* Saul *lived*, and they relayed what had been said in the hearing of the people. Then all the people lifted up their voices and wept.

But Saul *had not been there, he had not heard the report. So when he* returned from the field, followed by an ox, he asked, 'Why are the people weeping?' They then repeated to him the words of the men of Jabesh.

When Saul heard the words, the Spirit of God came upon him, and he became very angry. So he took a pair of oxen, cut them up, and sent *the pieces with* his messengers to every part of Israel.

Every time the messengers arrived at a town or a village, they said *to the people*, 'This will be done to the ox of anyone who does not follow Saul and Samuel.' As a consequence, the terror of YHWH fell on the people and they turned out as one man.

Saul assembled the people at Bezek (*about 20 kilometres west of Jabesh Gilead*). There were three hundred thousand men from Israel and thirty thousand men from Judah.

They told the messengers who had gathered, 'This is what you are to tell the men of Jabesh Gilead, "When the sun is hot tomorrow you will be delivered."' So the messengers went and told the men of Jabesh, and they rejoiced.

The men of Jabesh *then sent a deliberately ambiguous message to the Ammonites*. They said, 'We will come out to you tomorrow. You can then do to us whatever is good in your eyes.'

The next day, Saul divided the people into three divisions. They attacked the *Ammonite* camp during the morning watch (*between 2 a.m. and 6 a.m.*). They then struck down Ammon until the heat of the day. The *Ammonites* who survived became *so* scattered, that not two of them were left together.

All Israel Confirms Saul as King[73]

The people then said to Samuel, 'Who was it who said, "Shall Saul reign over us?" Bring the men *here* and we will kill them.'

But Saul said, 'No man will be killed today, for this is the day that YHWH has delivered Israel.'

Then Samuel said to the people, 'Come! Let us go to Gilgal. We will reaffirm the kingship there.'

So all the people went to Gilgal (*about 25 kilometres north-east of Jebus*), and they confirmed Saul as king in the presence of YHWH. They *also* sacrificed Fellowship Offerings before YHWH at Gilgal, and Saul and all the men of Israel rejoiced greatly.

Samuel Speaks Out[74]

Samuel said to all Israel, 'Look, I have heard your voice. *I have heard everything you have said to me.* I have set a king over you. So *from* now *on* the king in your midst will lead you.'

But Samuel was unhappy that the people had chosen a king, and that he had effectively been deposed. So he continued, 'As for me, I am old and grey, but my sons are here with you. I have led you, myself, from my youth until today.'

Then Samuel asked the people to confirm that he had acted appropriately as their prophet, priest, and judge.

'Here *am* I. Testify against me before YHWH and before his anointed *king*. Whose ox have I taken? Whose donkey have I taken? Who have I cheated? Who have I oppressed? From whose hand have I accepted a bribe to close my eyes to *what they were doing*? *If I have done any of these things* I will make it right to you.'

They said, 'You have not cheated us. You have not oppressed us. You have not taken anything from anyone's hand.'

Samuel said to them, 'YHWH is witness against you. His anointed is *also* a witness, this day, that you have not found anything in my hand.'

They said, '*He is* witness.'

Then Samuel said to the people, 'YHWH appointed Moses and Aaron, and brought your fathers from the land of Egypt. So take your stand now. I will present evidence to you, in YHWH's presence, of the righteous acts of YHWH—all he did for you and your fathers.

'After Jacob went down to Egypt, your fathers cried out to YHWH. So YHWH sent Moses and Aaron, and they brought your fathers from Egypt and they settled in this place. They then forgot YHWH, their God, so he sold them

---

[73] 1 Samuel 11:12-15
[74] 1 Samuel 12:1-25

into the hand of Sisera, the commander of Hazor's army. *He also sold them* into the hands of the Philistines and the king of Moab. They fought against them *all*.

'*Each time* they cried out to YHWH. They said, "We have sinned, because we have abandoned YHWH and served the Baals and the Ashteroths. But now deliver us from the hands of our enemies and we will serve you."

'Then YHWH sent Bedan *(probably Barak)*, Jerub-Baal *(Gideon)*, Jephthah, and Samuel. He delivered you from the hands of your enemies, *who surrounded you* on every side. You *were then able to* live securely.

'When you saw that Nahash, king of the Ammonites, was coming against you, you said to me, "YHWH, your God, is your king, but *we want* a king to rule over us." Now here is the king that you have chosen—the one you asked for. Behold YHWH has set a king over you.

'So fear YHWH. Serve him. Obey his voice. Do not rebel against his commands. Then *all will go well with you, because* both you, and the king who reigns over you, will be following YHWH, your God. But if you do not obey the voice of YHWH, and rebel against his commands, then YHWH's hand *will be* against you, in the same way that it was against your fathers.

'Now then, present yourselves! Watch! YHWH will do a great thing before your eyes. *Isn't it the dry season?* Isn't the wheat harvest *brought in* today? I *am about to* call upon YHWH to send thunder and rain. *Perhaps then* you will understand and see the great evil you have done in the eyes of YHWH, by asking for a king.'

So Samuel called upon YHWH, and YHWH sent thunder and rain. So that day all the people were in great fear of YHWH and Samuel.

All the people said to Samuel, 'Pray to YHWH, your God, for your servants, that we will not die. We have added *this* evil to all of our sins—we have asked for a king for ourselves.'

Samuel said to the people, 'Do not fear. You, the people, have done all this evil. Only do not turn away from following YHWH. Serve YHWH with all your heart. But do not turn after worthless idols. They can neither profit nor deliver *you*, for they are useless. For the sake of his great name, YHWH will not abandon his people, for he was glad to make you a people for himself.

'As for me, I wouldn't consider sinning against YHWH, by ceasing to intercede for you. *I will continue my role as a prophet.* I will teach you what is good and what is right. But fear YHWH. Serve him faithfully with all your heart. Indeed, meditate on the great things he has done for you. But if you continue to act wickedly, both you and your king will be snatched away.'

Saul's Kingship[75]

After Saul was pronounced king, a formal record of his kingship was kept. Unfortunately, over time, some of the detail has been lost. Saul's age at becoming king, and

---

[75] 1 Samuel 13:1

the number of years he reigned, is included in some manuscripts, but there is no consensus to the numbers. All we can say is that Saul was . . . years old when he became king, and he reigned for . . . two years over Israel.

Saul's Attack on the Philistine Garrison[76]

Now there was a Philistine garrison at Geba (about 22 kilometres west of Gilgal). So Saul *gathered his army, and* picked for himself three thousand of Israel's *warriors*. He took two thousand with him to Micmash, in the hill country of Bethel (*about 2 kilometres north-east of Geba*), and one thousand went with *his son*, Jonathan, to Gibeah of Benjamin (*about 4.5 kilometres south of Geba*). He then sent the rest of the people away, each to their *own* homes.

Jonathan then attacked the Philistines garrison at Geba.

News of the attack was heard by the Philistines. So Saul had the trumpet blown throughout the land. He said, 'Let the Hebrews hear *what has happened too.*' So all Israel heard.

But the people said *to each other*, 'Saul has attacked the Philistine garrison. Now Israel has become a stench to the Philistines.'

The people were then summoned by Saul to Gilgal.

The Philistines then gathered to fight against Israel. They came up and camped at Micmash east of Beth Aven. *They had* thirty thousand chariots, six thousand horsemen, and *their* warriors were as numerous as the sand on the seashore.

When the men of Israel saw *the magnitude of the Philistines' response*, they *knew they* were in trouble; the people felt the pressure they were under. So they *scattered and* hid in caves, among brambles and rocks, in pits, and in wells. *Some* Hebrews *even went eastwards*, crossing the Jordan *River, into* the land of Gad and Gilead.

Meanwhile Saul remained at Gilgal with *his* men, who were terrified.

Now Saul had agreed to meet with Samuel at Gilgal. Samuel was to make the appropriate sacrifices to YHWH, before he took any further action. But *after* waiting seven days—the time set by Samuel—Samuel had *still* not arrived at Gilgal, and the people were scattering from Saul's side.

So Saul said, 'Bring me the Burnt Offering and the Fellowship Offerings.' He then offered the Burnt Offering. Then, as he finished offering the Burnt Offering, he saw Samuel arriving. So Saul went out to meet and greet him.

Samuel said, 'What have you done?'

Saul said, 'I saw that the people were scattering from my side, you hadn't arrived by the set time of day, and the Philistines were assembling at Micmash.

---

[76] 1 Samuel 13:2-15

So I said *to myself*, "The Philistines will attack me here at Gilgal, and *because Samuel isn't here*, I have been unable to seek the face of God." So I was forced *to act*, and offer the Burnt Offering.'

Now Saul had been given a particular commandment by YHWH. What that commandment was is not known. But with Samuel's continuing role in the affairs of Israel, it may well have been 'not to usurp the role of the High Priest'.

So Samuel said to Saul, 'You were foolish. You have not kept the commandment of YHWH, your God—*the one* he gave you. If you had, YHWH would have established your kingdom over Israel in perpetuity. But now your kingdom will not last. YHWH has therefore sought a man after his *own* heart for himself. YHWH has appointed him as ruler over his people, for you have not kept the commandment that YHWH gave you.

Samuel then stood up, and went from Gilgal to Gibeah in the land of Benjamin. Saul, *meanwhile*, counted those men who remained with him. *There were* about six hundred men.

The Philistine Monopoly on Metal Production[77]

Now Saul, his son—Jonathan—and the people who were with them, *went and* stayed in Geba of Benjamin, while the Philistines camped at Micmash.

Three companies of raiding parties came out of the Philistine camp. One company went in the direction of Ophrah in the land of Shual; one company went by the way of Beth Horon; and one company went in the direction of the border, overlooking the Valley of Zeboim, towards the wilderness. *Meanwhile*, the Philistine garrison approached the Pass of Micmash.

At that time, the Philistines were in total control of all metal production in the area. Indeed, there were no blacksmiths in the land of Israel. That was because the Philistines had said, 'The Hebrews must not make swords and spears.'

So *whenever* an Israelite *needed* to sharpen his ploughshare, mattock, axe, or sickle, *he would take them* down to the Philistines. They were charged a pim (*8 grams of silver*) to sharpen a ploughshare and a mattock, and a third *of a shekel* (*3.8 grams of silver*) for a fork, an axe, or for repointing a goad.

So on the day of battle none of the people with Saul or Jonathan had a sword or spear in their hand. Only Saul, and his son, Jonathan, had *such weapons*.

Jonathan's Attack on the Philistine Garrison[78]

That day, Jonathan, son of Saul, said to the young man who carried his armour, 'Come, let us go across to the Philistine garrison on the other side.' But he did not tell his father.

---

[77] 1 Samuel 13:16-14:1
[78] 1 Samuel 14:2-14

Establishing the Kingdom

(Saul was sitting under the pomegranate tree in Migron, on the outskirts of Gibeah. There were six hundred men with him, *including* Ahijah who was wearing the *linen* ephod. But the people were unaware that Jonathan had left.)

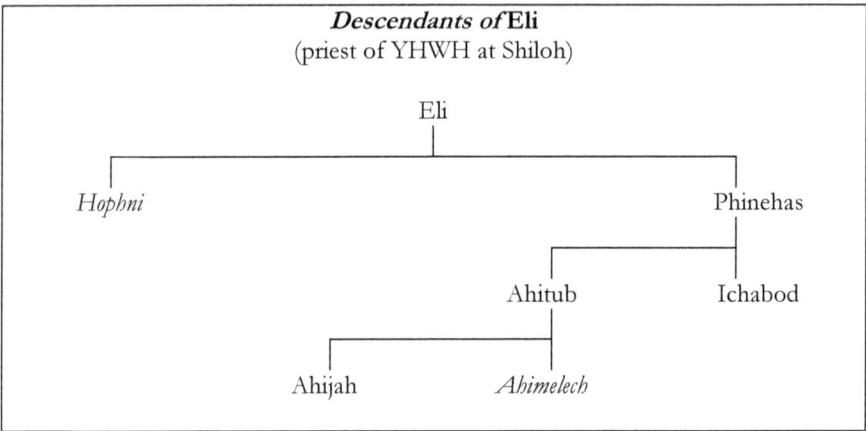

There were rocky crags on each side of the pass that Jonathan intended to cross to get to the Philistine garrison. One was called Bozez (*'shining'*), and the other Seneh (*'thorny'*). One crag rose to the north facing Micmash, the other to the south facing Geba.

Jonathan said to the young man carrying his armour, 'Come, let us go over to the garrison of the uncircumcised. Perhaps YHWH will do *something* for us. YHWH *cannot be* restrained; he can save with many or with few.'

His armour bearer said to him, 'Do everything that is on your heart. I will go with you, *for* I am of the same heart.'

Jonathan said, 'Let us go across to the men and show *ourselves to* them. If they say to us, "Remain still; we will come to you," then we will wait where we are. We will not go up to them. But if they say, "Come up to us," we will go up. For that will be our sign that YHWH has given them into our hand.' So they showed themselves to the Philistine garrison.

The Philistines said *to each other*, 'Look the Hebrews are crawling out of the holes where they were hiding.' So men from the garrison called out to Jonathan and his armour bearer. They said, 'Come on up to us. We have something to tell you.'

So Jonathan said to his armour bearer, 'Come up after me, for YHWH has given them into the hand of Israel.'

Now the Philistines did not expect Jonathan to scale the crag; indeed, they were confident that it was an impossible task. As a consequence, when Jonathan climbed up using his hands and feet, followed by his armour bearer, *the Philistines were taken by surprise. Some of* the Philistines then fell before Jonathan, while his armour bearer, *who remained* behind him, killed *others*. In that first attack Jonathan, and his armour bearer, killed about twenty men over an area *equivalent* to half a field—or a yoke of a field—*an area equivalent to a day's work ploughing with a pair of oxen*.

YHWH Delivers Israel from the Philistines[79]

Then a panic broke out in *both* the camp and the *battle* fields; all the people in the garrison and all the raiders panicked. The earth also shook. It was a panic sent by God.

Now Saul's watchmen at Gibeah in Benjamin, saw *the Philistine* multitude melting away; *indeed*, they were going here and there. *So they reported it to Saul.*

Saul then said to the people who were with him, 'Assemble the people. See who has gone from us.' So they assembled the people, *and only* Jonathan and his armour bearer were missing.

Then Saul, needing to seek YHWH's counsel, once again showed his irreverence and impatience. He said to Ahijah, *the priest*, 'Bring the Ark of God.' For the Ark of God was with the Israelites that day.

While he was talking to the priest, the roar in the Philistine camp grew louder and louder. So Saul said to the priest, '*Stop seeking YHWH's counsel*; withdraw your hand *from your ephod*.' Then Saul, and all the people with him, assembled and went into battle. *In the meantime, the Philistines* were totally confused, with each man using his sword to fight his fellow.

Now there were *some* Hebrews who had previously sided with the Philistines. They had gone up with them *and had been* around *their* camp. But *now* they turned again to side with the Israelites who were with Saul and Jonathan. Then, when all the Israelites who were in hiding in the hill country of Ephraim heard that the Philistines were fleeing, they too pursued them in battle.

So YHWH delivered Israel that day, and the battle moved on to Beth Aven (*a few kilometres west of Micmash*).

Saul's Curse[80]

Now earlier that day, Saul had made the people swear a solemn oath. He had said, 'Any man who eats food before evening, before I have avenged myself on my enemies, is cursed.' So none of the people had tasted food, and the men of Israel were in distress.

But when *the people* of the land entered *the* woods there was *some wild* honey *which had dripped down from a tree*, lying on the ground. So as the people went in,

---

[79] 1 Samuel 14:15-23
[80] 1 Samuel 14:24-48, 52

they saw the honey dripping. Yet not one put his hand to his mouth, for the people feared the oath. But Jonathan had not *been there; he had not* heard the oath by which his father had bound the people. So he reached out the staff that was in his hand, and dipped the end into the honeycomb. He then put his hand to his mouth and his eyes brightened.

One of the troops then spoke. He said, 'Your father bound the people to a solemn oath. He said, "Any man who eats food today is cursed." That is why the people are faint.'

Jonathan said, 'My father has troubled the land. See how bright my eyes have become because I have tasted a little of this honey. *Wouldn't* the slaughter of the Philistines have been even greater today, if *only* the people had eaten from the plunder they had taken from their enemies?'

That day the people struck down the Philistines from Micmash to Aijalon, and they became faint *with exhaustion. So much so, that the moment evening arrived, when the oath had expired*, the people darted greedily on the plunder. *Indeed*, they took sheep, cattle and calves, slaughtered *them* on the ground, and ate *them* with the blood.

Someone informed Saul, saying, 'Look, the people are sinning against YHWH. They are eating with the blood.'

So Saul responded, 'You have *all* acted treacherously. Roll a large stone *over to me now, so it can be used as an altar and so the blood can be drained. Then* go out among the people. Tell everyone to bring his cattle and sheep, and to slaughter and eat them here. Tell them not to sin against YHWH by eating with the blood.' So that night all the people brought their own ox and slaughtered it there. Saul built an altar to YHWH, the first altar he ever built to YHWH.

Later that night, Saul said *to the people*, 'Let us go down after the Philistines tonight. Let us plunder them until dawn tomorrow morning. Let us not leave one of them *alive*.'

They replied, 'Do all that is good in your eyes.'

But the priest said, 'Let us inquire of God *first*.'

So Saul inquired of God, 'Shall I go down after the Philistines? Will you give them into the hand of Israel?' But he did not answer them that day.

So Saul summoned all the leaders of the people, and said *to them*, '*Let us* investigate *why YHWH has not responded; let us* discover the sin that has been committed today. For as long as YHWH, who delivers Israel, lives, even if Jonathan, my son, is *guilty*, he will surely die.' But none of the people responded to his *call*.

So Saul called on the priest to use the Urim and the Thummim—decision-making tools, given by God—to decide the guilty party. Urim would mean 'condemned', and Thummim 'acquitted'.

Saul said to all Israel, 'You stand together over there, while Jonathan— my son—and I, stand together over here.'

The people said to Saul, 'Do what is good in your eyes.'

Then Saul prayed to YHWH, God of Israel, 'Give Thummim.' *In this way* the people were acquitted, and Jonathan and Saul remained. Then Saul said *to the priest*, 'Cast the lot between myself and Jonathan, my son.' *So the lot was cast* and *only* Jonathan remained.

Then Saul said to Jonathan, 'Tell me what you have done.'

So Jonathan told him. He said, 'I *put the* end of the staff that was in my hand in a little honey. I tasted it, so now I must die.'

Then Saul said, 'May God deal *with me*, and more again, if you do not surely die, Jonathan.'

But the people said to Saul, 'Should Jonathan die? He *was the one* who brought about this great deliverance in Israel. As long as YHWH lives, not a hair from his head should fall to the ground, for he did this today with God's *help*.' So the people rescued Jonathan, and he was not put to death.

Saul then withdrew from pursuing the Philistines, and the Philistines returned home.

So Saul took control over Israel, and fought his surrounding enemies. Wherever he turned he inflicted punishment. He fought valiantly, striking down the Amalekites. He delivered Israel from the hands of those who had plundered it.

Saul's Enemies	
East:	The Moabites
	The Ammonites
	The Edomites
North:	The Kings of Zobah (*an Aramean city-state*)
South:	*Amalekites*
West:	The Philistines

But the war with the Philistines continued bitterly throughout the days of Saul. So whenever Saul saw any mighty or brave man, he added him to his *service*.

Saul's Family[81]

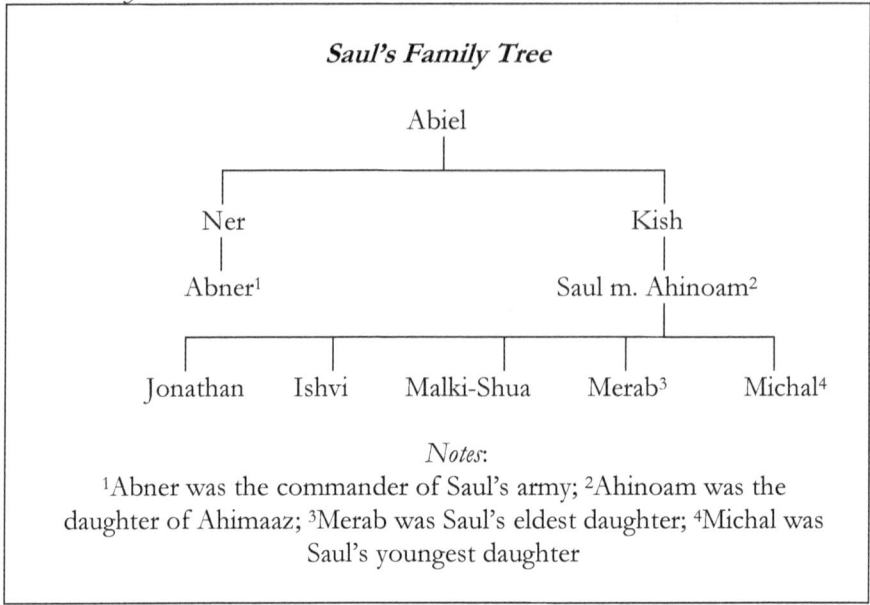

YHWH Rejects Saul's Kingship[82]

Samuel *spoke again* to Saul. He said, 'YHWH sent me to anoint you king over his people, Israel. So now listen to YHWH's words. This is what the Almighty YHWH says. "I will punish the Amalekites for what they did to Israel—how they set themselves against *my people* as they journeyed on their way from Egypt. Now go! Strike the Amalekites! Destroy everything they own. Do not spare anything. Put to death the men and women, children and babies, cattle and sheep, and camels and donkeys.'

So Saul summoned the people at Telaim (*probably in the Negev, near Amalek*). When he counted them there were two hundred thousand foot soldiers *from Israel*, and ten thousand men from Judah.

Saul approached a city *belonging to the* Amalekites and set an ambush in the valley. *He then sent a message to the* Kenites *who were in the city*. He said, 'Go! Turn away! Leave from among the Amalekites, so I do not destroy you with them. For you showed kindness to all the Israelites when they came out of Egypt.' So the Kenites turned away from among the Amalekites.

Saul then struck Amalek from Havilah to Shur, which is east of Egypt. He captured Agag, king of Amalek, alive, while he devoted the people *to YHWH*

---

[81] 1 Samuel 14:49-51
[82] 1 Samuel 15:1-35

with the edge of the sword. Indeed, Saul and the people spared Agag, and the best of the sheep, cattle, fat calves, lambs, and everything that was good. They were unwilling to devote these, but everything that was weak or despised they completely destroyed.

Then the word of YHWH came to Samuel, saying, 'I am sorry that I made Saul king. He has turned away from following me. He has not carried out my orders.' So Samuel became angry, and he cried out to YHWH all night.

The next morning, Samuel got up and went to meet Saul. But Samuel was told, 'Saul went to Carmel (*a small town in Judah*). He erected a monument for himself *there, to celebrate his victory*. He then turned around and went on his way to Gilgal.'

When Samuel reached Saul, Saul *greeted him*. He said, 'May you be blessed by YHWH.' *He then continued*, 'I have carried out YHWH's instructions.'
But Samuel said, 'Then what is this bleating of sheep in my ears. What is the lowing of cattle that I can hear?'
Saul said, 'The people brought them up from the Amalekites. They spared the best of the sheep and cattle, in order to sacrifice *them* to YHWH, your God. The rest we have already devoted *to YHWH*.'
Samuel said to Saul, 'Stop! Let me tell you what YHWH said to me *last night*.'
He said to him, 'Speak.'
Samuel said, 'You once considered yourself insignificant. Yet you are *now* the head of the tribes of Israel. YHWH anointed you king over Israel. YHWH sent you on a mission. He told you, "Go, and devote the wicked Amalekites *to me*. Fight against them until they are no more." Why then have you not obeyed the voice of YHWH? Why did you dart greedily on the plunder? You have done evil in the sight of YHWH.'
Saul said to Samuel, 'I did obey the voice of YHWH. I went on the mission that YHWH gave me. I devoted the Amalekites and brought back Agag, king of Amalek. However, *some of* the people took sheep and cattle from the plunder—the best of *all* the devoted things— to sacrifice *them* to YHWH, your God, at Gilgal.'
But Samuel said, 'Does YHWH delight *more* in Burnt Offerings and sacrifices than in obeying his voice? Obedience is better than sacrifice; having regard *is better than* the fat of rams. For rebellion is the *same as the* sin of divination, and arrogance is *like* wickedness and idolatry. Because you have rejected the word of YHWH, so he has rejected you from *being* king.'
Saul said to Samuel, 'I have sinned. Indeed, I have overlooked *both* YHWH's command and your instructions. But I was afraid of the people and I listened to their voice.

'Now, please, forgive my sin. Return with me *to the place of worship. I need you with me to pray for me there, so that I can be forgiven and* so that I may worship YHWH.'

But Samuel said to Saul, 'I will not come with you, for you have rejected the word of YHWH, and he has rejected you from being king over Israel.'

Then Samuel said, 'Bring me Agag, king of Amalek.' So Agag was brought to him in fetters.

Now Agag had said *to himself*, 'Surely the bitterness of death is passed.'

But Samuel said, 'Just as your sword has made women childless, so your mother will be childless among women.' Samuel then hacked Agag into pieces before YHWH at Gilgal.

As Samuel turned to go, Saul grabbed the hem of his robe, and it tore.

So Samuel said to him, 'YHWH has torn away the kingship of Israel from you today. He has given it to someone close by to you, to one who is better than you. Indeed, the Glory of Israel does not lie or change his mind. He is not a man *who* changes *his* mind.'

Saul said, 'I have sinned. But please honour me now before the elders of my people and before Israel. Return with me so I may worship YHWH, your God.'

So Samuel returned with Saul, and Saul worshipped YHWH. Samuel then left for Ramah, while Saul went up to his home in Gibeah of Saul.

Samuel did not see Saul *formally* again until the day he died. Despite that, Samuel mourned for Saul, and YHWH grieved that he had *ever* made Saul king over Israel.

C 20. SAUL
(1079-1007 BC)

b). Saul and David *(c. 1025-1007 BC)*

Samuel Anoints David[83]

Some time later, YHWH said to Samuel, 'How long will you mourn for Saul? I have indeed rejected him as king over Israel. As a consequence, I am sending you to Jesse the Bethlehemite. I have identified a king, for myself, among his sons. Fill your horn with oil, and go.'

But Samuel said, 'How can I go? Saul will hear *about it*, and kill me.'

YHWH said, 'Take a heifer from the herd with you. Say, "I have come to sacrifice to YHWH." Then invite Jesse to the sacrifice, and I will show you what you are to do. Anoint the one I tell you.' So Samuel did what YHWH said.

When Samuel arrived in Bethlehem, the elders of the town met him. *However, they were* terrified *that Samuel was there*. So they said *to him*, 'Have you come in peace?'

He replied, 'In peace. I have come to sacrifice to YHWH. *So* consecrate yourselves and come with me to the sacrifice.' He then consecrated Jesse and his sons, and invited them to the sacrifice.

When *Jesse's family* arrived, *Samuel took them aside, and with Jesse's help, began to examine his sons.*

He looked at Eliab and said *to himself*, 'Surely YHWH's anointed is standing in his presence.'

But YHWH said to Samuel, 'Do not look at his appearance, or his height, because I have rejected him. For I do not *see, in the same way* that a man sees. A man judges on outward appearances, but YHWH judges the heart.'

Then Jesse called Abinadab and had him pass in front of Samuel.

Samuel said, 'YHWH has not chosen this *one.*'

Then Jesse had Shammah pass.

Samuel said, 'YHWH has not chosen *one* either.'

Indeed, Jesse had seven of his sons pass in front of Samuel.

Samuel said to Jesse, 'YHWH has not chosen *any of* these.'

So Samuel said to Jesse, 'Are these all your sons?'

He said to him, '*Only* the youngest remains, but he is grazing the sheep.'

---

[83] 1 Samuel 16:1-13

Samuel said to Jesse, 'Send *someone* to get him, for we will not sit down *to eat* until he arrives.'

So Jesse sent *for his youngest son*, and had him brought *before Samuel*. He was ruddy *in complexion*, had beautiful eyes, and was good looking. Then YHWH said *to Samuel*, 'Stand up. Anoint him, for this is the one.'

So Samuel took the horn of oil and anointed him in the presence of his brothers. *Then* the Spirit of YHWH came powerfully upon David (*and was with David* from that day onward).

At the conclusion of the feast, Samuel got up, and returned to Ramah.

The Genealogy of David[84]

> **David's Family Line**
>
> Perez—Hezron—Ram—Amminadab—Nahshon—Salma—Boaz—Obed[1]—Jesse—David
>
> *Note:*
> [1] *Obed's mother was Ruth, the Moabitess*

David and Goliath[85]

The Philistines gathered their forces for battle at Socoh in Judah (*22 kilometres west of Bethlehem*). They set up camp at Ephes-Dammim, between Socoh and Azekah, while Saul and the men of Israel gathered *close by*, setting up camp in the Valley of Elah.

The Israelites then drew up for battle against the Philistines. The Philistines stood on a hill on one side *of the valley*, and Israel stood on a hill on the other side, with the valley between them.

A man came out of the Philistine camp—a champion named Goliath from Gath. He was six cubits and a span (*about 3 metres*) tall. *He wore* a bronze helmet on his head, and was clothed in a bronze coat of body armour, weighing five thousand shekels (*57 kilogrammes*). *He wore* bronze greaves on his legs, *covering his legs from his knees to his ankles, and he had* a bronze javelin *slung* on his back. The shaft of his spear was like a weaver's beam (*thick and heavy*), and the head of his

---

[84] Ruth 4:17b-22
[85] 1 Samuel 17:1-18:4

Establishing the Kingdom

spear, *which was of* iron, *weighed* six hundred shekels (*6.84 kilogrammes*). His shield-bearer went before him.

He stood and called out to the lines of Israel. He said to them, 'Why have you come and lined up in battle? Am I not a Philistine? Aren't you servants of Saul? Choose a man for yourselves. Let him come down to me. If he is able to fight me and kill me, then we will become *your* servants. But if I overpower and kill him, then you will become our servants and you will serve us.'

Then the Philistine said, 'I, personally, defy the lines of Israel this day. So give me a man, so we may fight each other.'

When Saul and all Israel heard these words of the Philistine they were dismayed and were very fearful.

For forty days, morning and evening, the Philistine came forward and took his stand.

Now in the days of Saul, Jesse, the Ephrathite from Bethlehem in Judah was *an old man*. He was advanced in years; *too old to join in the battle. But* he had eight sons, *including* David, *and had not forgotten his responsibilities to his king*. Indeed, three of Jesse's sons had gone after Saul to do battle, *while* David, the youngest, *provided the required support for his brothers. So while* the three eldest followed after Saul, David went back and forth from Saul, to tend his father's sheep in Bethlehem.

The names of Jesse's sons who went to do battle were: Eliab, the firstborn; Abinadab, the second; and Shammah, the third.

Jesse said to his son, David, 'Take this ephah (*22 litres*) of roasted grain for your brothers, with these ten *loaves* of bread, and hurry to your brothers at the camp. Take these ten pieces of cheese to the commander of their thousand. Check on the welfare of your brothers, and bring back *some* token from them. *For they are with* Saul, and all the men of Israel are in the valley of Elah fighting the Philistines.'

So David got up *early* the *next* morning and left the sheep with *another* keeper. Then he packed *the supplies on his donkey* and left, as Jesse had ordered him.

As David reached the outskirts of the camp, the army was going out to its battle line, shouting the battle cry. *Once more*, Israel and the Philistines drew up *in their* lines to face *one another*.

So David left the things that he'd brought with the keeper of supplies, and ran to the battle line. He went *in order to check* on the welfare of his brothers. But as he was talking with them, he saw the Philistine champion from Gath, named

Goliath, coming out from the Philistine lines. So David heard the same words that Goliath *had* spoken *previously.*

Whenever the men of Israel saw the man, they ran from his presence. They were very fearful. The men of Israel said *to each other,* 'Look at this man who is coming out. He is coming out to defy Israel. The king *has promised to* reward the man who kills him with great wealth. He will *also* give him his daughter, and make his father's family free*men* in Israel.'

But David hadn't heard what the men were saying. So he spoke to the men standing near him. He said, 'What will be done for the man who kills this Philistine and takes this shame away from Israel? For who is this uncircumcised Philistine that he defies the armies of the living God?'

The people then told him *what it was that was being* said. They said, 'This will be the reward for the man who kills him.'

His eldest brother, Eliab, *over*heard *David* speaking with the men, and he burned with anger against him. He said, 'Why have you come this *time*? Who have you left *in charge* of those few sheep in the wilderness? I, myself, know that you are insolent and wicked of heart. You have only come to watch the battle.'

David said, 'What have I done now? Can't I even talk?' So *David* turned away from his *brother* and *went* over to another *man*. He asked regarding the same matter, and the people *around* answered him, confirming the previous answer.

The words that David had spoken were overheard, and were reported to Saul. So Saul sent for him.

David said to Saul, 'Let no man lose their heart *over this* Philistine. Your servant will go and fight him.'

But Saul said to David, 'You are not able to go out and fight against this Philistine. You are *only* a boy, *while* he has been a fighting man since his youth.'

But David said to Saul, 'Your servant is a shepherd over his father's sheep. Whenever a lion or a bear has come and carried off a sheep from the flock, I have gone after them. I have struck them and rescued *the animal* from their mouth. When they have turned on me, I have seized them by the hair, struck them, and killed them. Your servant has killed both the lion and the bear. This uncircumcised Philistine will be like one of them, for he has defied the armies of the living God.'

David continued, 'YHWH is the one who has delivered me from the paw of the lion and the paw of the bear. He will deliver me from the hand of this Philistine.'

So Saul said to David, 'Go! May YHWH be with you.' Saul then dressed David in his *own battle* garments. He put a bronze helmet on his head and dressed him in a coat of armour. David then strapped his sword over his garments and tried to walk, because he had never tried *to walk in armour before.*

Establishing the Kingdom

But David said to Saul, 'I cannot move in these, for I have never tried *to walk* in these *before.*' So David took them off. He then took his staff in his hand and selected for himself five smooth stones from the stream. He placed them in his pouch, in the shepherd's bag he *was wearing,* and *put* the sling in his hand. David then approached the Philistine, *while* the Philistine, led by his shield bearer, came closer and closer to David.

As Saul watched David approaching the Philistine, he said to Abner, the commander of his army, 'Abner, whose son is this young man?'
Abner said, 'On your life, king, I don't know.'
The king said, 'Ask *around concerning the father of* this young man.'

When the Philistine saw David *more closely,* he looked at him with contempt. *He saw that* David was *only* a boy—ruddy but handsome in appearance.
The Philistine said to David, 'Am I a dog that you come at me with sticks?' The Philistine then cursed David by his gods. The Philistine then continued, 'Come to me, and I will give your flesh to the birds of the air and the beasts of the field.'
David said to the Philistine, 'You are approaching me with a sword, spear, and javelin. But I am approaching you in the name of Almighty YHWH, the God of Israel, whose armies you have defied. Today, YHWH will give you into my hand. I will strike you down and cut off your head. Today, I will give the carcasses of the Philistine army to the birds of the air and the beasts of the earth. The entire world will know that there is a God in Israel. All those assembled here will know that YHWH does not deliver by sword or spear, for the battle belongs to YHWH. He will give you into our hand.'
Then David ran quickly to the battle line to face the Philistine, and the Philistine drew closer to encounter David. David put his hand into the bag and drew out a stone. He *placed it in his sling and* slung *it,* and *it* struck the Philistine on the forehead. The stone sank into his forehead, and he fell on his face to the ground. David then ran over to the Philistine and stood *there.* He took the Philistine's sword, grabbed it from its scabbard, *made sure that he had* killed him, and cut off his head. In this way, David triumphed over the Philistine with a sling and a stone. There was no sword in David's hand when he struck down the Philistine and killed him.
When the Philistines saw that their champion was dead, *they did not do as Goliath had promised. They did not stay and become the servants of Israel. Instead*, they ran. So the men of Israel and Judah rose up. They shouted as they pursued the Philistines along the valley to the gates of Ekron. Dead *bodies of the* Philistines were strewn along the road to Shaaraim, as far as Gath and Ekron.

When the Israelites returned from chasing the Philistines, they plundered their camps. David took the Philistine's weapons and put them in his *victor's* tent. *He also* took the Philistine's head (*which, years later, when he had become king, he took* to Jerusalem).

When David returned from killing the Philistine, Abner took him and brought him before Saul. The head of the Philistine *was still* in his hand.
Saul said to him, 'Young man, whose son are you?'
David said, 'I am the son of your servant, Jesse, the Bethlehemite.'
Then, that day, Saul took David *and added him to his service*; he did not allow him to return *immediately* to his father. *Furthermore*, after Saul had finished talking with him, Jonathan became very attached to David. Indeed, he loved him as himself. So because he loved him as himself, he made a covenant with David. Jonathan took off the robe that he was wearing and gave it to David with his tunic, sword, bow, and belt.

A Tormented Saul[86]

In those days, it was believed that YHWH had absolute control over good and evil. Indeed, when YHWH rejected Saul as king, the Spirit of YHWH departed Saul. *But when* a spirit of evil began to torment him, *it was believed to have been* sent by YHWH *too.*

Saul's attendants said to him, 'Look, you are being tormented by God's spirit for evil. May our lord command your servants before you. Let them find someone who knows how to play the lyre. Then, when God's spirit of evil comes upon you, he can play it with his hand, and you *will feel* better.'
So Saul said to his servants, 'Find me a man who plays well. Bring *him* to me.'
One of the young men answered *him*. He said, 'Look, I have seen a son of Jesse, the Bethlehemite. He knows how to play. He is a powerful man and a warrior. He speaks wisely and is a handsome man. YHWH is with him.'
So Saul sent messengers to Jesse, saying, 'Send me your son, David, who is with the sheep.'
So Jesse *prepared some gifts for Saul. He* took a *homer* of bread (*the most that a* donkey *could carry*), a skin of wine, and a young goat. He then sent *them* to Saul by his son, David.
In this way, David came to Saul, and David served him.

Whenever the spirit from God came to Saul, David would take his lyre, and play *it* with his hand. It *brought great* relief to Saul; *it made* him *feel* better and the spirit of evil would leave him.
Saul loved him greatly, and David became an armour bearer for him. So

---

[86] 1 Samuel 16:14-23

Saul sent *a messenger* to Jesse, saying, 'Let David remain in my presence, for he has found favour in my eyes.'

Saul Tormented by Jealousy[87]

With David's return to Saul's court as a musician, he resumed his military duties. David went wherever Saul sent him, and he was *always* successful. So Saul set him over the men of war—*an appointment* that was pleasing in the eyes of both the people and Saul's officers. *However, it did not help Saul's disposition. Indeed, Saul became very jealous of him.*

The jealousy started when David killed the Philistine, as the men returned *home, and as* women from every town in Israel came out joyfully to meet Saul. The women had sung and danced, and played tambourines and lutes for the king. But as they had danced they had sung, 'Saul has slain his thousands, and David his tens of thousands.' *The refrain was not aimed as a criticism of Saul, but over time, the repeated saying of it* made Saul very angry. It was evil in his eyes.

He *came to* say *to himself*, 'They have given David *credit for* ten thousands, but they have *only* credited me *with* thousands. What else is there for him but the kingdom?' So Saul kept an eye on David from very early on.

Then, the day after *David had returned from yet another battle, and Saul heard those words just one more time*, a spirit of evil came upon Saul.

He was prophesying in the house, while David was playing *the lyre* with his hand, as previously. There was a spear—*a symbol of his kingship*—in Saul's hand, and Saul said *to himself*, 'I will pin David to the wall.' So he threw the spear. But David dodged him twice.

So Saul grew afraid of him, because YHWH was with David, but had left him. So he sent him from his presence. He made him a commander of a thousand. In this way, David went out and came in before the people.

David was successful in everything that he did, for YHWH was with him. The whole of Israel and Judah loved David, for he went out and came in before them. But when Saul saw how very successful he was, he feared him greatly.

Saul's Daughters[88]

One day, Saul said *to himself*, 'I won't *lift up* my hand against him, but *maybe I can get* the Philistines to do so.'

So Saul said to David, 'Look, *here is* my eldest daughter Merab. I will give her to you as a wife. Surely you are a brave man, and will fight YHWH's battles for me.'

---

[87] 1 Samuel 18:5-16
[88] 1 Samuel 18:17-30

But David said to Saul, 'Who am I, that I should become the son-in-law to the king of Israel? What is my life or my father's clan?' So although Merab, Saul's daughter, should have been given to David as a wife, she was given to Adriel the Meholathite *instead.*

Michal, *another of* Saul's daughters, however, loved David. So when Saul was informed, the report was *very* pleasing in his eyes.

Saul said *to himself,* 'I will give her to him, and she will become a snare to him. Then the hand of the Philistines will be against him.'

So Saul said to David a second time, *'You will* become my son-in-law, today.'

Then Saul ordered his servants, 'Speak to David in private. Tell him, "The king is pleased with you. All his servants like you. So become the king's son-in-law."' So Saul's servants spoke these words in the ears of David.

But David said, 'Is it a small thing in your eyes to become the son-in-law of the king? I am a poor man and relatively unknown.'

The servants then reported to Saul, the words that David had spoken.

Now Saul had in mind that David should fall by the hand of the Philistines. So Saul said *to his servants,* 'Say this to David. "The king does not desire a bride-price, apart from the foreskins of one hundred Philistines. The king seeks *only* vengeance on *his* enemies."' So his servants told David these words.

What they said was pleasing in the eyes of David. *But Saul had set* a deadline *for him* to become the king's son-in-law. So before the time had elapsed, David got up, and he and his men went out and killed two hundred Philistine men. Then, before the deadline had expired to become the king's son-in-law, he brought their foreskins to the king. Saul then gave Michal, his daughter, *to David,* as a wife.

Saul then became even more afraid of David. He recognised that YHWH was with David, and he saw *for himself* that Michal, his daughter, loved him. *Furthermore,* each time the commanders of the Philistines went out *to battle,* David was *more* successful than any of Saul's *other* officers. His name became well-known. So Saul became David's enemy for the rest of his days.

Saul's Plot Against David[89]

Saul spoke to his son, Jonathan, and to all his servants. *He said,* 'Kill David.' *Saul then detailed what he wanted his servants to do.*

But Jonathan, Saul's son, took great delight in David. So Jonathan warned David, saying, 'Saul, my father, is seeking to put you to death.' *Then, being aware of the arrangements, he continued,* 'In the morning be on your guard. Go *to my father's*

---

[89] 1 Samuel 19:1-8

field, and stay *there* in hiding. I, myself, will go out to the field where you are, and stand beside my father. I will then speak to my father about you. Whatever I find out, I will tell you.'

So the next day, Jonathan spoke well of David to his father, Saul. He said to him, 'May the king not act sinfully against his servant, David. He has not sinned against you. *Indeed,* his deeds have been very beneficial to you. He took his life in his hands when he killed the Philistine, when YHWH won a great victory for all Israel. You saw *what happened* and you rejoiced. So why would you sin *by shedding* innocent blood? *Why* would you kill David without reason?'

Saul listened to Jonathan's voice. Then he swore a solemn oath, 'As YHWH lives, he will not be killed.'

When Saul had gone, Jonathan called to David, and told him everything that had been said. Then Jonathan brought David to Saul, and he remained with him, as before.

War broke out again *against* the Philistines. So David went out and fought them. He *again* struck them a great blow, and they fled from his presence.

Another Attack on David[90]

A spirit of evil, *sent by* YHWH, came upon Saul *again*, while he was sitting in his house. *As previously,* he had a spear in his hand while David was playing *his lyre* with his hand. Saul *again* tried to pin David to the wall with the spear. But David dodged Saul, *and* the spear struck the wall. So David fled, and *after* that night never returned.

Saul sent *some* men to David's house to keep watch over him, *with instructions to* kill him in the morning. But Michal, David's wife, said to him, 'If you do not slip away alive tonight, tomorrow you will be killed.'

Notes:
For the *musical* director.
To the tune 'Do Not Destroy.'
A psalm.
Of David.
A miktam *(perhaps a contemplative prayer).*
When Saul sent *men* to watch David's house to kill him

---

[90] 1 Samuel 19:9-17; Psalm 59:1-17

Establishing the Kingdom

David, to YHWH

'Deliver me from those who are hostile to me, my God;
    snatch me away from those who rise up against me.
Deliver me from those who act wickedly;
    save me from bloodthirsty men.
    See how they lie in wait for me.
Mighty *men* stir up strife against me,
    but not *for any* violation or sin of mine, YHWH.
They run and make ready, *although I have done* no wrong.
    So rouse *yourself.* Help me and see.

'You, YHWH, Almighty God, *are the* God of Israel.
    So rouse *yourself* to punish all the nations.
Do not show mercy to those
    who are treacherous *and* devise evil.

                                                                Selah

'They return in the evening;
    they growl like dogs;
    they go around the town.
See *the words* that bubble up from their mouths;
    the swords that are on their lips.
    For *they say to themselves,* "Who can hear *us*?"
But you, YHWH, you laugh at them;
    you mock at all the nations.

'I will keep watch for you, my strength,
    for God is my fortress.
My loving God will go before me;
    he will let me look down on those who watch me.
Do not kill them, lest my people forget *why they were punished;*
    instead, in your might, Lord, our shield,
    make them tremble, and bring them down.
Let them be trapped by their *own* pride;
    by the sins of their mouth,
    by the words from their lips.
    For they utter curses and lies.
Consume *them* in *your* wrath, consume *them*;
    then they will be no more,
and the ends of the earth will know
    that God rules over Jacob.

                                                                 Selah

'So they return in the evening;
>they growl like dogs;
>they go around the town.
They wander about for *something* to eat;
>they howl if they are not satisfied.
But as for me, I will sing of your might;
>in the morning, I will sing of your love.
For you are my fortress;
>you are my refuge in my day of distress.
My strength, I will sing your praises;
>for *you*, God, are my fortress;
>the God of my covenant love.'

Then Michal let David down through the window.

In this way, David left *the house* and slipped away, fleeing *from Saul*. Michal then took *a household* idol and laid *it* on the bed. She placed material made of goat's hair at the head and covered *it* with a garment.

When the men *arrived—the ones* Saul had sent to take David—she told *them*, 'He is ill.' *So they reported this to Saul*. But Saul sent the men back to see David *in person*.

He told *them*, 'Bring him in his bed up to me, *so that I might* kill him.' But when the men entered *the house*, they saw the idol in the bed with the material of goat's hair at the end.

When Saul *heard what had happened, he had* Michal *brought to him*. He said to *her*, 'Why have you deceived me this way? You have sent my enemy away. He has escaped *from me*.'

Michal said to Saul, '*He threatened to kill me if I didn't help him escape*. He, himself, told me, "Let me go, or I will kill you."'

David Flees to Ramah[91]

So David fled; he escaped *from Saul*. He went to Samuel at Ramah (*about 5 kilometres north of Saul's home town of Gibeah*). He told him everything that Saul had done to him. Then he went with Samuel and stayed at Naioth (*possibly a shepherd's camp outside the town*).

Saul was told, 'Look, David is in Naioth in Ramah.' So Saul sent messengers to capture David.

---

[91] 1 Samuel 19:18-24

The messengers saw a company of prophets prophesying, with Samuel standing in charge of them. Then, immediately, the Spirit of God came over Saul's messengers and they began to prophesy as well.

When news of what had happened was reported to Saul, he sent more messengers. They prophesied too. So Saul sent a third *group of* messengers, and they also prophesied.

Finally, he too went to Ramah. When he came to the great well at Secu, he asked, 'Where are Samuel and David?'

The people replied, 'In Naioth, at Ramah.' So he went to Naioth at Ramah. But as he was walking along, the Spirit of God came upon him too, and he prophesied until he came to Naioth at Ramah.

When he arrived, he stripped off his garments and prophesied in the presence of Samuel. He lay naked all that day and all that night. This *then reinforced* the saying, 'Is Saul also among the prophets?'

David and Jonathan[92]

David then fled Naioth, at Ramah, and went to *see* Jonathan. He said *to him*, 'What have I done? What crime have I *committed*? How have I sinned against your father, that he is seeking my life?'

Jonathan said to him, 'It is not *true*. You are not *going to* die. Look, my father does nothing, *either* great or small, without disclosing *it* in my ear. So *if it were true*, why would my father hide this thing from me? It is not so.'

But David swore again. He said, 'Your father surely knows that I have found favour in your eyes. He has said *to himself*, "Jonathan must not become aware of this or he will be distressed." Yet as YHWH lives, and as you live, *there is* indeed only a step between me and death.'

Jonathan said to David, 'Whatever you ask, I will do for you.'

So David said to Jonathan, 'Look, tomorrow is the *festival of the* new moon. I am required to sit with the king to eat. But let me go, and I will hide in the field for the next three evenings. If your father genuinely misses me, say, "David pleaded with me *for permission* to rush to Bethlehem, his home town. The annual sacrifice for his whole clan *is being held* there." If he says, "Good," your servant is safe. But if he gets very angry, note well that he is consumed with evil.

'So act kindly with your servant, for the covenant you made with your servant was made in YHWH's presence. But if I am guilty, kill me yourself. Why would you need to take me to your father?'

Jonathan said, 'Far be it *from me to harm you*. If I was sure that my father was determined to do evil against you, wouldn't I tell you about it?'

---

[92] 1 Samuel 20:1-42

David said to Jonathan, 'Who will tell me if your father answers you angrily?'

So Jonathan said to David, 'Come, let us go *to* the field.' So the two of them went to the field.

When they arrived, Jonathan said to David, 'May YHWH, God of Israel, *be my witness*. I will sound out my father. Within three days *I will know* if he is favourable to you. If he isn't, I will send *a messenger* to you. Whatever I discover, I will let you hear.

'If it pleases my father to do you evil, may YHWH do *the same* to Jonathan, and more so, if I do *not* let you know. I will then send you away, so that you may go in peace. May YHWH be with you, as he was with my father.

'*As for me*, show me the loving kindness of YHWH, while I *am* alive, Then, when I am dead, *promise me that you will* never cut off your kindness from my family. Not even when YHWH cuts off each of David's enemies from the face of the earth.'

Jonathan then made a covenant with the house of David. *He said*, 'May YHWH call to account the enemies of David.' Then Jonathan made David swear again regarding his love for him, for he loved him as he loved himself.

Jonathan said to him, 'Tomorrow is the New Moon *festival*. You will be missed, as your seat will be empty. On the third day go down quickly to the place where you hid that day. Wait by the stone of Ezel. I, myself, will shoot three arrows *to one* side of it; I will shoot in your direction at a target. Then watch. I will send the boy, "Go! Find the arrows." If I say to the boy, "Look, the arrows are on this side of you. Get them," then come. For as YHWH lives, you are safe and in no danger. But if I say to the boy, "Look, the arrows are beyond you," go! For YHWH is sending you away. Regarding the matter that you and I have spoken about, YHWH is witness between you and me forever.'

So David hid in the field.

When *it* came *time for* the New Moon *festival*, the king sat down at the feast to eat. The king sat in his usual place at the seat by the wall, *while* Jonathan took his position, and Abner *sat* at Saul's side. But David's place was empty. *Despite that*, Saul didn't say anything that day. He said *to himself*, '*Something* has happened. He cannot be clean; he must surely be *ceremonially* unclean.' But the next day, the second of the new moon, David's place was *also* empty.

Saul said to Jonathan, his son, 'Why has the son of Jesse failed to come to the meal both yesterday and today?'

Jonathan answered Saul, 'He pleaded with me to *let him go* to Bethlehem. He said, "Let me go now, for our family sacrifice *is being observed* in the town. My brother has personally ordered me *to attend*. So if I have found favour in your eyes, let me slip away now. Let me *go and* see my brothers." This is the reason why he has not come to the king's table.'

Then Saul's anger burned against Jonathan. He said to him, 'You son of a twisted, rebellious woman. *Do you think that* I am unaware that you have allied yourself with the son of Jesse? You disgrace yourself. You are a disgrace to your mother's nakedness. For as long as the son of Jesse lives on earth, neither you nor your kingdom will be established. Now send *for him*. Bring him to me, for he is a dead man.'

But Jonathan responded to his father, Saul. He said to him, 'Why should he die? What has he done?' But Saul hurled the spear at him, to strike him. Then Jonathan knew that his father was determined to put David to death.

So Jonathan, burning with anger, got up from the table. He did not eat the meal on the second day of the New Moon *festival*. He had been humiliated by his father, and he grieved for David.

In the morning, Jonathan went out to the field as agreed with David. *He took* with him a small boy. He said to the boy, 'Run *across the field, then you will* find the arrows that I'll shoot.' *Then as* the boy was running, Jonathan shot arrows *in the air, intending them to land* beyond him. *In this way*, the boy came to the place where *one of* the arrows that Jonathan shot had *rested*.

Jonathan called after the boy. He said, 'Isn't *there an* arrow beyond you?' Then Jonathan continued, 'Hurry. Make haste. Don't *just* stand *there*.' So Jonathan's boy gathered the arrows and returned to his master.

Now the boy knew nothing *about the* matter *between Jonathan and David*, only Jonathan and David knew. Jonathan then gave his weapons to the boy who was with him, and said to him, 'Go, take them back to the town.' *So* the boy left.

David then stood up from the southern side *of the stone, where he had been hiding*, and fell on his face to the ground. He bowed three times, they kissed each other, and they wept together. David *wept* the most.

Jonathan said to David, 'Go in peace. We have both sworn *an oath to one another* in the name of YHWH. *We have* said, "YHWH is *witness* between you and me, and between my descendants and yours forever."' Then David got up and left, while Jonathan returned to the town.

David and the Priest at Nob[93]

David went to Nob, to Ahimelech the priest. *Suspecting something was wrong*, Ahimelech was trembling when he met David. He said to David, 'Why are you alone? *Apart from your servants*, why is no *other* man with you?'

David said to Ahimelech, the priest, 'I have been ordered by the king on a *secret* matter. He said to me, "No man is to know anything *about* the mission I'm sending you on, or the orders I've given you." So I've told the men *to meet me* at a certain place.

---

[93] 1 Samuel 21:1-10a

'Now then, what *food* do you have in your possession? Give me five *loaves of* bread or whatever can be found.'

The priest answered David. He said, 'There is no ordinary bread on hand. But there is consecrated bread. If only *your* servants have kept themselves from women.'

David replied to the priest. He said to him, 'Indeed, women have been kept from us, as is usual before I set out. *Furthermore*, the young men's vessels are *always* holy, *even* when *we are* not *on* a sacred mission. So *how much* more would their vessels be holy today?'

So, since there was no *ordinary* bread, the priest gave him the consecrated. *He gave them* the Bread of the Presence that had been removed from YHWH's presence, which had been replaced by fresh bread *earlier* in the day.

David said to Ahimelech, 'Do you have a sword or a spear in your possession? The king's business was urgent, so I have brought neither my sword nor *any other* weapon with me.'

The priest replied, '*I have* the sword of Goliath, the Philistine—the *man* you killed in the valley of Elah. Look, it is wrapped in cloth behind the ephod. If you would take it for yourself, *then* take *it*. For *there are* no other *weapons* here except that one.'

David said, '*There are* no *others* like it. Give it to me.'

Then David stood up, *and* that *same* day left Saul's *territory*.

One of Saul's servants was there that day—the head of Saul's shepherds. His name was Doeg, the Edomite. *For ceremonial reasons*, he had been detained before YHWH.

David at Gath[94]

David then *went to the territory of the Philistines, where he was seized.*

Notes:
For the *musical* director.
To the *tune* 'The Dove of Far Away *Lands*'.
Of David.
A miktam *(perhaps a contemplative prayer)*.
When the Philistines seized him in Gath.

David, to YHWH
'Show me *your* favour, God, for men trample *over* me;
all day *long*, I am oppressed by those who attack me.

---

[94] 1 Samuel 21:10b-22:1a; Psalms 34:1-22; 56:1-13

Those who slander me, crush me all day *long*;
indeed many *take* pride in attacking me.

'When I am afraid,
I *put my* trust in you.
I boast in the word of God;
in God I *put my* trust.
I will not be afraid;
indeed what can *mere* flesh do to me?

'All day *long* they twist my words;
all their thoughts *are aimed* at harming me.
They stir up strife, they hide, they observe my steps,
as they *eagerly* wait *to take* my life.
Repay them in accordance *with their* evil;
bring down the peoples in your anger, God.

'You have taken note of my wanderings *as a fugitive*,
you have put my tears in your skin bottle.
Are *all these things* not *recorded* in your book?
So those who are hostile to me will retreat on the day I call;
I know this, because God is with me.

'I boast in the word of God;
I boast in the word of YHWH.
In God I put my trust.
I will not be afraid;
Indeed, what can a *mere* man do to me?
I will fulfil my vows to you, God;
I will offer thank-offerings to you.
For you have delivered my soul from death;
you have kept my feet from stumbling,
so I can walk in the presence of God,
in the light of life.'

David was brought to Achish, king of Gath.
The servants of Achish said to the king, 'Isn't this David, the king of the land? Don't they sing about him as they dance, saying, "Saul has killed his thousands, and David his tens of thousands"?'
As David pondered those words in his heart, he became very fearful. *His life was in danger in the* presence of Achish, king of Gath. So *while* he was in their

presence, he changed his behaviour. He *began* to boast, he put marks on the doors of the gate, and he let his saliva run down his beard.

Achish said to his servants, 'Look, you are watching a mad man. Why did you bring him to me? Do I need *more* mad *men* that you brought this *one*, to act madly in front of me? *Do you really want this man to* come into my house *to be a mercenary?*'

So David left there, and slipped away to the cave of Adullam (*'refuge'*), near Bethlehem in Judah.

Later, a psalm was written. It was an acrostic psalm, with each verse beginning with a different letter of the Hebrew alphabet. Over time, though, the psalm has been corrupted; there is no letter waw (ו), and it finishes with a second letter pe (פ). The reference to 'Abimelech' ('my father is king'), and not Achish, suggests that a Hebrew title is being used in preference to the king's name.

Notes:
Of David.
When David changed his behaviour before Abimelech,
so that Abimelech drove him out, and he went on his way.

David, to those with him

א 'I will bless YHWH at all times;
     praise of him will always be on my lips.
ב My soul will boast in YHWH;
     let those who are afflicted hear and be glad.
ג Ascribe glory to YHWH with me;
     let us exalt his name together.

ד 'I sought YHWH, and he responded to me;
     he rescued me from all my fears.
ה Those who look to him are radiant;
     their faces will never *show* shame.
ז This humble man called out and YHWH heard *him*;
     he delivered him from all his afflictions.
ח The angel of YHWH encamps around those that fear him,
     so that he might rescue them.

ט '*So* taste and see that YHWH is good;
     for the man who seeks refuge in him will be blessed.
י Show reverence *to* YHWH, *you*, his holy *people;*
     for those who fear him lack nothing.

| כ | Young lions suffer *from* want and hunger;
| | but those who seek YHWH will not lack any good thing.

| ל | 'Come children, hear my *words*;
| | I will teach you to revere YHWH—
| מ | *to* any man who delights in life,
| | *and* desires to enjoy many good days.

| נ | '*So* keep your tongue from evil;
| | your lips from speaking treachery.
| ס | Turn aside from evil and do good;
| | seek peace and chase after it.
| ע | The eyes of YHWH watch those who are righteous;
| | his ears *are alert* to their cry.
| פ | The face of YHWH is opposed to those who do evil;
| | *he will* cut off *all* memory of them from the earth.
| צ | *When the righteous* cry *out*, YHWH hears;
| | he delivers them from all their afflictions.
| ק | YHWH is near to those who are shattered;
| | he delivers those who are crushed in spirit.
| ר | A righteous *man may face* many afflictions;
| | but YHWH will deliver him from all of them.
| ש | *Indeed*, he will keep watch over all his bones;
| | not one of them will be broken.'

| ת | 'But *doing* evil will bring death to the wicked;
| | those who hate the righteous will be condemned.
| פ | YHWH will redeem the souls of his servants;
| | no one taking refuge in him will be condemned.'

David in the Cave at Adullam[95]

There are two psalms that refer to David hiding from Saul in caves. But whether they relate to the events at Adullam, or some other occasions, as Saul chased David around the strongholds of southern Judah, is not known.

Notes:
For the *musical* director. *To the tune* 'Do Not Destroy'.
Of David. A miktam *(perhaps a contemplative prayer)*.
When *David had* fled from Saul into the cave.

---

[95] Psalms 57:1-11; 142:1-7

Establishing the Kingdom

David, to God
'Show me *your* favour, God; show me *your* favour,
    for my soul seeks refuge in you.
I seek refuge in the shadow of your wings,
    until the storms of destruction have passed by.

David, to others with him
'I will call to God Most High,
    to God who fulfils *his purposes* for me.
He will send *help* from the heavens and deliver me;
    he will rebuke those who trample over me.

                                                        Selah

'God will send his loving-kindness and his faithfulness.

'As for me, *I am* surrounded by lions;
    I lie down with ravenous sons of men.
Their teeth *are like* spears and arrows;
    their tongues *are like* sharp swords.

David, to God
'Be exalted above the heavens, God;
    let your glory *be* over all the earth.

They have spread a net for my feet;
    my soul is bowed down.
They have dug a pit for me;
    but they have fallen into it.

                                                        Selah

'My heart is firm, God, my heart is firm;
    I will sing, I will make music.

David, to himself
'Wake up, my soul; wake up, harp and lyre;
    I will wake up the dawn.

David, to God
'I will give thanks to you, Lord, among the nations;
    I will make music to you among the peoples.
For your covenant love reaches to the heavens;
    your faithfulness *stretches* to the clouds.

'Be exalted above the heavens, God;
>   *let* your glory *be* over all the earth.'

Notes:
A maskil (*possibly a contemplative poem*).
Of David.
When he was in the cave.
A Prayer.

> *David, to others with him*

'*With* my voice I cry out to YHWH;
>   *with* my voice I ask YHWH for mercy.

Before him I pour out my complaint;
>   before him I tell *him* my trouble.

> *David, to YHWH*

'When my spirit is faint within me,
>   you will *still* know my way.

'Along the path that I walk,
>   they have concealed a trap for me.

Look to the right and see,
>   *for* there is no one who has any regard for me.

There is no place of refuge for me;
>   no one cares for my life.

'YHWH, I cry out to you;
>   I say, "You are my refuge,
>   *you are* my portion in the land of the living."

Incline your ear to my cry,
>   for I am very low.

Deliver me from those who chase me;
>   for they are stronger than I.

Bring me out of *this* prison,
>   *so that I can* give thanks to your name.

Those who are righteous will *then* gather around me,
>   because you have been good to me.'

Establishing the Kingdom

David in Judah and Moab[96]

David's family were in as much danger from Saul as David himself. So when his brothers, and his father's entire household, heard *where he was*, they went down to him. *But so did* all who were distressed, in debt, and discontented. *They* gathered around him, and he became their leader. Those with him *grew to* about four hundred men.

David *left* there and went to Mizpah, in Moab. *He knew that being on the run, would not suit his elderly parents. In addition, as his great-grandmother, Ruth, had come from Moab, he probably felt that the king would be sympathetic to any request.*

So he said to the king of Moab, 'Please let my father and mother stay with you, until I find out what God intends to do for me.'

The king agreed, so he left them in the presence of the king of Moab, and they stayed with him all the time that David stayed in *another* stronghold, *probably also in Moab.*

Later Gad, the prophet, said to David, 'Do not remain at the stronghold. Come, return to the land of Judah.' So David left *the stronghold* and went to the forest of Hereth, *in the south of Judah.*

Saul's Revenge on Nob[97]

But *the location* of David, and the men who were with him, was discovered and reported to Saul. At the time, Saul was sitting under the tamarisk tree on the hill at Gibeah. He had *his royal* spear in his hand, and all his servants were standing around him.

This is how it happened.

Knowing that David was still popular with the people, Saul had said to his servants, standing around him, 'Listen, Benjaminites, will the son of Jesse give you all fields and vineyards? Will he make you all commanders of thousands and commanders of hundreds?

'All of you have conspired against me. *Indeed,* not one *of you* revealed in my ear that my son had made a covenant with the son of Jesse. None of you *has shown any* concern for me, or *even* told me that my son has stirred up my servant against me, to lie in wait *for me,* as *he does* today.'

Then Doeg, the Edomite, who was standing with Saul's servants, spoke. He said, 'I have seen the son of Jesse. He came to Nob, *and spent time with* Ahimelech, son of Ahitub. Ahimelech enquired of YHWH for him and gave him provisions and the sword of Goliath, the Philistine.'

---

[96] 1 Samuel 22:1b-5
[97] 1 Samuel 22:6-23; Psalm 52:1-9

So the king sent for Ahimelech, the son of Ahitub, the priest. He summoned *him*, with all his father's family, who were priests at Nob.

> They all came *and presented themselves* to the king.
> Saul said, 'Listen, now, son of Ahitub.'
> Ahimelech said, 'I am here, my lord.'
> Saul said to him, 'Why have you and the son of Jesse conspired against me? You have given him bread and a sword, and have enquired of God for him. *You have* rebelled against me *and he* lies in wait *for me*, as *he does* today.'
> But Ahimelech answered the king. He said, 'Who among all your servants is as faithful as David? *He is* the king's son-in-law, and a commander of your guard. He is *well*-respected in your household.
> 'Was this the first time I had consulted God for him? No! *So do* not let the king bring *such* accusations against his servant, or against any of his father's family. For your servant knows nothing—big or small—about this whole affair.'
> But the king said, 'You will surely die, Ahimelech, you and all you father's house.'
> The king then said to *his* guards who were standing with him, 'Go around, and put the priests of YHWH to death. Their hands are with David too. They knew that he was fleeing, but they did not reveal it to me.' But the king's servants were unwilling to raise their hands against the priests of YHWH.
> So the king said to Doeg, 'Turn around. Strike the priests.' So Doeg, the Edomite, turned around and struck the priests himself. On that day, he put to death eighty-five men who wore the linen ephod.

> *Doeg then went to* Nob, the town of the priests, and put it to the edge of the sword. He put to the sword every man, woman, child, and baby, *together with all the* cattle, donkeys, and sheep.
> But one of the sons of Ahimelech, son of Ahitub, escaped. His name was Abiathar, and he fled to David.
> Abiathar informed David that Saul had slain the priests of YHWH.
> Then David said to Abiathar, 'I knew that day, when Doeg the Edomite was there, that he would surely tell Saul. I am personally responsible for every one of your father's family. Stay with me. Do not be afraid, for whoever seeks my life seeks yours. Indeed, you will be under my protection.'

> *Notes:*
> For the *musical* director.
> A maskil (*possibly a contemplative poem*).
> Of David.
> When Doeg the Edomite went and spoke to Saul, he said to him,
> 'David went to the house of Ahimelech.'

David, to Doeg (in Doeg's absence)
'Why do you boast of evil, ruthless one?
    Don't you know that God's goodness *continues* all day *long*?
You plan destruction;
    your tongue is like a sharpened razor;
    you are a worker of deceit.
You love evil more than good;
    you prefer deception to speaking what is right.

                                                      Selah

'You love every word that devours,
    y*our* tongue *speaks* treachery.
But, *like a wall*, God will pull you down, never *to be rebuilt*;
    he will pluck you up, and remove you from *your* tent;
    he will uproot you from the land of the living.

                                                      Selah

David, to YHWH
'The righteous will see, and be filled with awe;
    they will laugh at him, *saying*,
"Here *is* the man who did not take refuge in God;
    he trusted in the abundance of his wealth.
    He grew strong through his destructive *ways*."

'As for me, I am like an olive tree, thriving in the house of God;
    I trust in the covenant love of God, forever and ever.
I will thank you forever, for *what* you have done;
    I will wait on your name, for *it is* good,
    in the presence of your faithful *people*.'

David Rescues Keilah[98]

Now it was reported to David that the Philistines had attacked Keilah (*in Judah, near the border with the Philistines*), and they were plundering the threshing floors.

So David enquired of YHWH, saying, 'Shall I go? Shall I strike against these Philistines?'

YHWH answered David, 'Go, strike against the Philistines. Deliver Keilah.'

But David's men said to him, 'Look, we are afraid *for our lives*, here in *the*

---

[98] 1 Samuel 23:1-5

midst of Judah. How much more then, if we should go into *the disputed territory around* Keilah, against the ranks of the Philistines?'

So David enquired again of YHWH, and YHWH gave him his answer.

He said, 'Rise up. Go down to Keilah. I will give the Philistines into your hands.'

So David, with his men, went to Keilah. He fought the Philistines, and took away their livestock. *Indeed*, David struck them a heavy blow, and in doing so delivered those who were living in Keilah.

Saul's Pursuit of David[99]

When Saul *was* told that David had gone to Keilah, he said, 'God has given him into my hand, for by entering a town *with* bars and gates he has shut himself in.' So Saul summoned all the people for battle to march to Keilah and besiege David and his men.

> Now *by this time, the linen ephod, had taken on a secondary role. Originally designed, like an apron, for the High Priest to wear while conducting his priestly duties, an ephod was also now carried by a priest, and used for enquiring of YHWH. It may also have been accompanied by an Urim and a Thummim, which would previously have only been carried in the High Priest's breastplate.* So when Abiathar, son of Ahimelech, had fled to David, he had taken an ephod with him, *and he had brought it to* Keilah.

Now David knew that Saul would be plotting evil against him. So he said to Abiathar, the priest, 'Bring the ephod *here, so that I may enquire of YHWH.'* So *he did.*

Then David said to YHWH, 'God of Israel, your servant has indeed heard that Saul is intending to come to Keilah. He will destroy the town because of me. Will the leaders of Keilah deliver me into his hand? Will Saul come, as your servant has heard? YHWH, God of Israel, tell your servant now.'

YHWH said, 'He will come down.'

Then David said, 'Will the leaders of Keilah deliver *both* me and my men into the hand of Saul?'

YHWH said, 'They will deliver.'

So David and his men, about six hundred men, got up, left Keilah, and travelled from one place to another.

When Saul was told that David had slipped away from Keilah, he cancelled *his plans* to go *there*. David then stayed among the *various* strongholds in the wilderness; he remained in the hills of the wilderness of Ziph (*about 20 kilometres south-east of Keilah*). Saul sought for him for many days, but God did not give him into his hand.

---

[99] 1 Samuel 23:6-29; Psalm 54:1-7

Establishing the Kingdom

One day, while David was at Horesh in the wilderness of Ziph, he learned that Saul had come to seek his life.

Jonathan, son of Saul, arose and went to David at Horesh, and he encouraged him in God. He said to David, 'Do not be afraid, for the hand of my father, Saul, will not find you. You are the one who will be king over Israel, *while* I, myself, will be second to you. My father, Saul, knows this well.'

The two of them made a covenant before YHWH. Then Jonathan returned to his home, while David remained at Horesh.

Then the Ziphites went to Saul at Gibeah. They said *to him*, 'Isn't David hiding among us? *He is* amongst the strongholds at Horesh, on the hill of Hakilah, south of Jeshimon. Now, king, whenever you desire to come down, we will deliver him into your hand.'

Saul said, 'May you be blessed by YHWH, for you *have shown* compassion to me. Now go! Confirm *what you have told me*. Watch his place *and* his movements. *Check* who has seen him there, because I am told he is very crafty. So look, discover all the places where he hides, and return to me with specific details. Then I will go with you. If he is there in the land, I will search for him among all the thousands of *men in* Judah.' They then got up and left for Ziph, ahead of Saul.

Now David and his men were in the wilderness of Maon, in the Arabah, south of Jeshimon. So when Saul and his men came to search *for him*, it was reported to David. David remained in the wilderness of Maon, but headed down to *what was known as* 'the rock'.

When Saul heard *where David was*, he pursued David into the wilderness of Maon. Saul traversed one side of the mountain, while David and his men traversed the other. David hurried to get away from Saul, while Saul and his men *tried to* encircle David and his men, to capture them.

Then a messenger came to Saul. He said, 'Come! Make haste! The Philistines have raided the land.' So Saul turned away from pursuing David, and he went to encounter the Philistines. For this reason the place was called 'Sela Hammahlekoth' (*'rock of escape' or 'rock of parting'*). Then David left there and went to live in the strongholds of En Gedi (*on the western shore of the Salt Sea*).

Notes:
For the *musical* director.
With stringed instruments.
A maskil (*perhaps a contemplative poem*).
Of David.
When the Ziphites said to Saul, 'Isn't David hiding among us?'

David, to YHWH
'By your name, God, save me;
    By your might, defend me.
Hear my prayer, God;
    listen to the words that I say.

'For strangers have taken a stand against me;
    men of violence seek my life.
They do not put God before themselves.

                                              Selah

David, to others around him
'Look, God is my helper;
    the Lord is the one who sustains my life.
He will rebound the evil on my enemies.

David, to YHWH
'In your faithfulness,
    put an end to them.
I will sacrifice a freewill offering to you;
    I will praise your name, YHWH, for *it is* good.

David, to others around him
'For he has delivered me from every trouble,
    and my eye has seen *what God has done to* my enemies.'

David and Saul at En Gedi[100]

After Saul had returned from pursuing the Philistines, it was reported to him, 'David is in the wilderness of En Gedi.' So Saul took three thousand chosen men from all of Israel and went to search for David and his men, in the vicinity of the rocks of the wild goats. Along the way, he came to the sheep folds, with a cave *nearby*. Saul then went in*to the cave* to relieve himself.

Now David and his men were staying in the back of the cave. So the men said to David, '*Remember* the day when YHWH *spoke* to you. He said, "I will give your enemy into your hand." So do to him as is pleasing in your eyes.' So David stood up and secretly cut off the corner of Saul's robe.

But as soon as he had cut off the corner of Saul's robe, his conscience began to trouble him. So he *returned to the back of the cave and* said to his men, 'YHWH forbid that I should do this thing to my lord, to the anointed of

---

[100] 1 Samuel 24:1-22

YHWH. *I cannot* raise my hand against him, for he is YHWH's anointed.' With *these* words, David disagreed with his men, and he refused them permission to rise up against Saul. Saul then left the cave and went on *his* way.

But before Saul had gone very far, David stood up and came out of the cave. He called after Saul, saying, 'My lord, king!' When Saul looked behind him, David bowed down with his face to the ground, and he submitted himself *to Saul*.

David said to Saul, 'Why do you listen to the words of men who say, "Look, David is seeking to harm you"? This very day you have seen with your *own* eyes how YHWH delivered you into my hand in the cave. *Someone* said *I should* kill you, but I have spared you. *Indeed*, I said, "I will not raise my hand against my lord, for he is YHWH's anointed."

'Now, my father, look carefully at the piece of your robe *that I have* in my hand. For I cut it from the corner of your robe. However, I didn't kill you. *So* realise and see that I am not responsible *for any* evil or rebellion. I have not wronged you, but you lie in wait to take my life.

'May YHWH judge between me and you. May YHWH take vengeance on you, for *what you have done to* me. Despite that, my hand will not be against you. Just as the old proverb says, "From the wicked comes wickedness," so my hand will not be against you.

'Who *is it that* the king of Israel *has* come out against? Who are you pursuing—a dead dog or a single flea? So may YHWH judge; may he decide between me and you. May he see *what has happened* and plead my cause. May he deliver me from your hand.'

When David had finished speaking these words to Saul, Saul said, 'Is that your voice, David, my son?' Then Saul lifted his voice and wept.

Then he said to David, 'You are more righteous than I. For in our dealings, you have been good to me, while I, myself, have treated you wickedly. You, yourself, have told me just now of the good that you have done to me; that YHWH delivered me into your hand. Yet you didn't kill me. When a man finds his enemy, does he *normally* send him safely away? May YHWH reward you with good things, for what you have done for me this day.

'Now look, I know for certain that you will be king, and that the kingdom of Israel will flourish by your hand. So swear to me, by YHWH, that you will not cut off my descendants *who will follow after* me; that you will not destroy my name from my father's house.'

So David swore *an oath* to Saul. Saul then went back to his home, while David and his men went up to the stronghold *at Adullam*.

Establishing the Kingdom

David, Nabal, and Abigail[101]

Samuel died, and all Israel gathered together. They mourned for him and buried him by his home in Ramah. Then, *as all future hope of reconciliation between Saul and David was probably lost*, David got up and moved to the wilderness of Maon, *in the south-east of Judah*.

Now there was a man in Maon, who worked *nearby in the hill country* in Carmel. The man was very wealthy—he owned three thousand sheep and a thousand goats. The man's name was Nabal (*'fool'*), and his wife's name was Abigail (*'my father's joy'*). The woman was intelligent and beautiful, but the husband was harsh and dishonest in his dealings. He was a descendant of Caleb.

One day, Nabal was in Carmel shearing his sheep—*a time when it was customary for a wealthy man to give to his needy neighbours*. So when David, in the wilderness, heard that Nabal was shearing his sheep, he sent ten *of his* young men *to Nabal*.

David said to the men, 'Go up to Carmel and go to Nabal. Greet him in peace in my name. Say *to him*, "*May you have a long* life. Peace be to you and your household, and to everything that is yours.

"'I have heard that you are shearing. *Some of* your shepherds were with us *for a while. During that time*, we did not mistreat them; and all the time they were at Carmel, nothing of theirs went missing. Ask your young men, and they will tell you.

"'So let *my* young men find favour in your eyes, for *this is* a festive day for us. *So* give, I pray, whatever your hand finds, to your servants and to David, your son."'

When David's men arrived, they repeated to Nabal every word in the name of David. They then waited *for a reply*.

But Nabal answered David's servants. He said, 'Who is David? Who is the son of Jesse? There are many servants today who are breaking away from their masters. Should I take my bread and water, and the meat that I slaughtered for my shearers, and give them to *other* men? *Particularly, when* I don't know where they have come from.'

So David's young men turned away, and went on their way back *to David*.

When they arrived they told him everything that had been spoken.

David said *to his men*, 'I have surely kept watch in vain over everything that this *man* owns in the wilderness. Nothing that he owned went missing. But now he has returned my good with evil.' *David then continued with a crude and foolish oath*, 'May God do *evil* to David's enemies, and more so, if by morning I have left anything alive that belongs to him. *They are just* urinators against a wall.'

---

[101] 1 Samuel 25:1-42

Then David ordered his men, '*Every* man, put on your swords!' So they all put on their swords, while David put on his. Then about four hundred men went with David *to Nabal*, while two hundred remained with the equipment.

One of Nabal's *servants went and* spoke to Abigail, Nabal's wife. He said, 'Look, David sent messengers from the wilderness to greet our master. But he *simply* shouted *insults* at them. Yet the men have been very good to us. They did not mistreat us, and nothing we had went missing all the time we were with them in the fields. They were a wall around us, both night and day, all the time they were with us, while we were herding the sheep.

'So consider! Examine what you should do, for our master and his whole household are facing complete ruin. He is *such a* worthless man *that no one can talk to him*.'

On hearing this news, Abigail *immediately* rushed *to protect her household*. She gathered together *a variety of produce* and loaded *it* on donkeys.

Abigail's Gift to David

200 loaves of bread
2 skins of wine
Five dressed sheep
5 seahs (*36.6 litres*) of roasted grain
100 bunches of raisins
200 pressed figs

She said to her young men, 'Go on ahead of me. I will follow after you.' But she said nothing to her husband, Nabal.

As she was riding *her* donkey, she descended through the mountain ravine. There she saw David and his men *on the other side of the ravine*, descending to meet her. So she met them.

When Abigail saw David, she hurriedly got off *her* donkey and fell on her face before him. Falling at his feet, she bowed to the ground.

She said, 'Let the blame fall upon me, my lord. Let your maidservant speak, I pray, into your ears; hear the words of your maidservant. Please, my lord, take no notice of this worthless man, Nabal. For as his name *means 'fool'*, *so* he is a fool. Foolishness is with him. As for me, your servant, I did not see my lord's men whom you sent.

'So now, my lord, as YHWH lives and as you live, YHWH has held you back from committing bloodshed from avenging yourself with your *own* hand. So, my lord, may *all* your enemies who intend to harm you, be like Nabal.

'Now let this gift, which your maidservant has brought to my lord, be given to the young men who are with my lord.

'Forgive, I pray, the transgression of your maidservant. YHWH will surely make a lasting house for my lord, for my lord fights YHWH's battles. So let no evil be found in you all your days. Should someone stand up to pursue you to take your life, my lord's life will be tied up in the bundle of life by YHWH your God. But your enemies' lives will be hurled away, as from the cradle of a sling.

'So when YHWH does for my lord, all the good things that he has spoken *about concerning* you and appoints you ruler over Israel, do not let this *situation become the cause for* grief or a stumbling of the heart for my lord. *Do not* shed blood needlessly or, my lord, take vengeance for yourself.

'When YHWH blesses my lord, remember your maidservant.'

David said to Abigail, 'Blessed is YHWH, God of Israel, who has sent you to meet me this day. You are blessed; so too are your judgements. For you have restrained me from shedding blood today; from avenging myself with my *own* hand. YHWH, the God of Israel, who lives, has held me back from harming you. *Indeed*, if you had not been quick to come to me by daybreak, none of those who urinate against a wall, who belong to Nabal, would have been left *alive*.'

Then David took from her hand what she had brought for him. He said, 'Go to your home in peace. Look, I have heeded your words and have granted your requests.'

Then Abigail returned home.

When Abigail came to Nabal, he was holding a feast in his *own* house—a feast fit for a king. Nabal was in good heart, for he had had much to drink. So she didn't tell him anything, great or small, until the light of the morning.

Then in the morning, when the effects of the wine had left Nabal, his wife told him what had happened. *Immediately*, his heart died within him and he became like stone. Then, about ten days *later*, YHWH struck Nabal and he died.

When David heard that Nabal had died, he said, 'Blessed be YHWH. He has upheld *my* dispute against Nabal. He has held back his servant from doing evil. YHWH has returned Nabal's evil on his *own* head.'

Then David *arranged for* a message to be sent to Abigail, *telling her* that he would take her for himself as a wife.

Indeed, David's servants went to Abigail at Carmel. They said to her, 'David has sent us to you, to take you as a wife for himself.'

Then she rose and bowed her face to the ground, *as though David himself were present.*

She said, 'Look, your maidservant is a maid, *fit only* to wash the feet of my lord's servants.'

Abigail then quickly rose and got on the donkey. Then, with her five handmaidens following, she went with David's messengers and became a wife to him.

David's Wives[102]

> ### David's Wives
>
> *Michal, daughter of Saul*
> *Abigail, widow of Nabal*
> Ahinoam, from Jezreel

While David was in hiding, Saul took measures to reduce David's popularity and weaken his political position.

Saul took his daughter, Michal (David's wife), and gave her to Palti, the son of Laish, from Gallim (*possibly a town north of Jebus*).

Cush the Benjaminite[103]

Saul was not the only one chasing David. He was also being pursued by Cush. But being a Benjaminite, from the same tribe as Saul, Cush may simply have been working for his king.

Nevertheless, the existence of a psalm—the only record of anyone named Cush chasing David—indicates that David needed to be on the alert, even when Saul was at home in Gibeah.

Notes:
A shiggaion (*perhaps a lamentation*).
Of David.
He sang this to YHWH regarding Cush the Benjaminite.

David, to YHWH

'YHWH, my God, in you I have taken refuge;
    save me and deliver me from all who chase after me.
Otherwise, he will tear me like a lion;
    he will tear me apart,
    and there will be no one to rescue *me*.

'YHWH, my God, if I had done this,
    there would be injustice on my hands.

---

[102] 1 Samuel 25:43-44
[103] Psalm 7:1-17

Establishing the Kingdom

So, if I have dealt evil to those who are at peace with me,
>or if I have robbed my enemy, without cause,
then let my enemy chase after me and overtake me.
>Let him trample my life to the ground;
>let my honour sleep in the dust.

Selah

'Rise up, YHWH, in your anger;
>rise up against the arrogance of my enemies.
>Awake for me the justice you have decreed.
Let the assembly of the peoples surround you;
>sit *in judgement* over them from on high.

David, to others with him

'YHWH judges the peoples;
>so may YHWH judge my righteousness,
>may the Most High *judge* my integrity.
Let the evil of the wicked end,
>and the righteous *man* be secure.
For the righteous God
>searches the hearts and minds.

'God is my shield;
>he saves the upright in heart.
God is a righteous judge;
>he is provoked to wrath every day.
If *a man* doesn't repent, *God* will sharpen his sword;
>he will bend and string his bow.
For he has prepared his deadly weapons;
>he has made ready his burning arrows.

'Look, he who conceives wickedness
>becomes pregnant with mischief,
>and gives birth to deception.
He digs a pit, digging it out;
>but he falls into the pit that he makes.
The trouble he causes rebounds on his *own* head;
>on his *own* head, his violence descends.

'I will give thanks to YHWH because of his righteousness.
>I will sing praise to the name of the Most High, YHWH.'

Establishing the Kingdom

David Spares Saul Again[104]

The Ziphites went to Saul at Gibeah. They said, 'Isn't David hiding on the hill of Hakilah, south of Jeshimon?' So Saul arose and went down to the wilderness of Ziph, with three thousand chosen men of Israel, to search for David in the wilderness.

When he arrived, Saul set up camp beside the road, on the hill of Hakilah, south of Jeshimon. David, meanwhile, remained in the wilderness.

When David heard that Saul had come after him into the wilderness, he sent out spies to learn where Saul had set up base.

Then David set out and came to the place where Saul had set up camp. David saw the place where Saul and Abner, son of Ner, the commander of his army, had laid down. Indeed, Saul was lying down inside the camp, with the people camped around him.

Then David spoke to Ahimelech—the Hittite—and Abishai, son of Zeruiah, brother of Joab. He said, 'Who will go down with me, into the camp, to Saul?'

Abishai said, 'I myself will go with you.' So *that* night David and Abishai went down to the people. They saw Saul lying down, asleep, inside the camp, with his spear stuck in the ground by his head, with Abner and the people lying around him.

Abishai said to David, 'Today God has delivered your enemy into your hand. Now, I pray, let me pin him to the ground. It will *take only* one thrust of *his* spear; I will not *need to strike* him twice.'

But David said to Abishai, 'Do not kill him. For who can stretch out his hand against YHWH's anointed and remain innocent?' David *continued*, 'As YHWH lives, surely YHWH will strike him down; his day will come and he will die, or he will go into battle and perish. YHWH forbid that I should raise my hand against his anointed.

'Now get the spear and jug of water that are by his head, and let us go.' So David took the spear and the jug of water by Saul's head, and they left. No one saw or knew *what had happened*, nor did anyone wake up. They all *remained* asleep, for a deep sleep from YHWH had fallen upon them.

David then crossed over to the other side *of the valley*.

When David reached the top of the hill, with some distance between him and Saul, he *turned and* stood *there*. David called out to the people and to Abner, son of Ner. He said, 'Abner, will you not answer?'

Abner replied, 'Who are you, that you have called to the king?'

David said to Abner, 'Aren't you a man? *Indeed*, who is like you in all Israel?

---

[104] 1 Samuel 26:1-25

So why have you failed to watch over your lord, the king? For *tonight* someone came *into the camp* to kill your lord, the king. This thing you have done is not good. As YHWH lives, you should be dead men, because you did not keep watch over your lord, YHWH's anointed.

'Now look, where is the king's spear, and *where is* the jug of water that was by his head?'

Saul recognised David's voice. So he said, 'Is that your voice, David, my son?'

David said, '*It is* my voice, my lord the king.' Then he said, 'Why is my lord chasing after his servant? What have I done? What evil *have I committed* by my hand? Now, I pray, let my lord the king hear the words of his servant.

'If YHWH has incited you against me, then *maybe* he *will* accept an offering *to resolve this matter instead*. But if the sons of men *are responsible, let them be* cursed before YHWH, for this day they have cast me out from a share in the inheritance of YHWH. They have said, "Go, serve other gods!"

'However, do not let my blood fall to the ground, away from YHWH's presence. For the king of Israel has come out seeking a single flea, like he would hunt a partridge in the mountains.'

Then Saul said, 'I have done wrong. Come back, David, my son. My life was precious in your eyes today, so I will never do *anything* evil to you again. I can see I have been foolish; I have strayed considerably.'

But David answered *him*. He said, 'Look, the king's spear *is in my hand*. Let one of the young men come across and get it.

'YHWH rewards each man *according to* his righteousness and faithfulness. YHWH delivered you today into *my* hand, but I would not stretch out my hand against YHWH's anointed. As surely as your life was valued in my eyes today, so may my life be valued in the eyes of YHWH. May he deliver me from every danger.'

Then Saul said to David, 'You are blessed, David, my son. You will surely succeed in everything you do; you will become very powerful.' Then David went on his way, and Saul returned to his place.

David and Achish[105]

But David said to himself, 'One day Saul's hand will snatch me away. Nothing good *will happen* to me *if I stay in Israel*; I must surely escape to the land of the Philistines. Then Saul will give up searching for me within the borders of Israel, and I will slip away from his hand.'

So David arose and he, and the six hundred men who were with him, crossed *Judah into the land of the Philistines, and* went to Achish, son of Maoch, the king of Gath. David settled with Achish in Gath.

---

[105] 1 Samuel 27:1-28:2

Establishing the Kingdom

When Saul was told that David had fled to Gath, he stopped seeking him.

Those Who Went To Gath With David

David's *six hundred* men
The men's households
David's two wives: Ahinoam the Jezreelite and
Abigail, widow of Nabal, the Carmelite

After David had been in Gath some time, David said to Achish, 'If I have truly found favour in your eyes, let a place be given to me in one of the towns in the land. I can live there instead. Why should your servant remain in the royal city with you?' So that day Achish gave him Ziklag *near the border with Judah. That is why* Ziklag *still* belonged to the kings of Judah *when this story was first written down.* (The length of time that David lived in the land of the Philistines was a year and four months.)

David, and his men, went up and raided the Geshurites, the Girzites, and the Amalekites—*all peoples that the Israelites should have devoted to YHWH when they had entered the Promised Land.* They had been living in the land *south of the Philistines,* between Shur and Egypt, since ancient times. Each time David struck the land, he left no one alive—man or woman. However he took the sheep, cattle, donkeys, camels, and clothes, and returned *to Ziklag.*

After David had been on a raiding party, he would go to Achish, *no doubt to give him a share of the spoils. Each time* Achish *would* enquire, 'Where have you been raiding today?'

David would *typically* say, 'Against the Negev of Judah, or against the Negev of Jerahmeelite, or against the Negev of the Kenites.' *Each time he would indicate raids against Judah or its allies. But* David did not leave *any* man or woman *alive* to bring to Gath, for he said *to himself,* 'They would inform on us, by saying, 'David did this . . .' Such was his practice all the days that he lived in the land of the Philistines.

So Achish believed David. He said *to himself,* 'He has surely made *himself* a stench to his *own* people, Israel. He will be my servant forever.'

About that time, the Philistines assembled their camp to wage war, to do battle against Israel.

Achish said to David, 'You must surely know that you, and your men, need to join me in the camp.'

David said to Achish, 'Then you will personally find out what your servant can do.'

Achish said to David, 'I will then make you my bodyguard, all *your* days.'

Saul and the Necromancer[106]

The Philistines then marched north and set up camp at Shunem, *north of Jezreel*, while Saul assembled all Israel, and set up camp *on Mount* Gilboa, *to the south*.

Now when Samuel had died, the whole of Israel had mourned for him. They had buried him in Ramah, his home town. *Furthermore*, Saul had driven away *all the* necromancers and spiritists from the land. *So, as YHWH had rejected his kingship, he was no longer able to enquire of YHWH.*

So when Saul saw the Philistine camp *from the mountain* he became fearful, his heart was terrified. So he enquired of YHWH, but YHWH refused to answer him either by dreams, by the Urim *and Thummim* or through the prophets.

So Saul said to his servants, 'Search for a woman for me, a mistress of the spirit *world*. Then I can go to her, and enquire of her.'

His servants said to him, 'Look, *there is a* woman, a spirit mistress in Endor, *just north of Jezreel*.' So Saul disguised himself; he put on other clothes. Then he, with two of his men, went *to see her*.

When they arrived, at night, at the woman's *house*, Saul said *to her*, 'Consult a spirit for me please. Conjure up the one I tell you.'

But the woman said to him, 'You must know what Saul has done. He has cut off the necromancers and spiritists from the land. So why are you striking at my life? *Do you wish* me to die?'

Saul then swore to her by YHWH. He said, 'As YHWH lives, no punishment will fall upon you regarding this matter.'

Then the woman said, 'Whom shall I bring up for you?'

He said, 'Bring up Samuel for me.' *So the woman conjured up Samuel*. But as soon as the woman saw Samuel, she cried out in a loud voice.

The woman said to Saul, 'Why have you deceived me? You are Saul.'

The king said to her, 'Do not fear! Now what do you see?'

The woman said to Saul, 'I see *what looks like* a god coming up out of the ground.'

He said to her, 'What does he look like?'

She said, 'An old man is coming up. He is wrapped in a robe.'

Then Saul knew that it was Samuel. So he bowed his face to the ground, and showed him honour.

---

[106] 1 Samuel 28:3-25

Samuel said to Saul, 'Why have you disturbed me by bringing me up?'

Saul said, 'I am greatly disturbed. The Philistines *have drawn up* to fight against me, and God has turned away from me. He doesn't answer me anymore, either through the prophets or by dreams. So I have called on you. Let me know what I should do.'

Samuel said, 'If YHWH has turned away from you and become your adversary, why do you enquire of me? YHWH has dealt *with you*, as he told *you* through me. YHWH has torn the kingdom from your hand. He has given it to David, your neighbour. YHWH has done this thing to you today, because you did not obey the voice of YHWH. You did not put into force his burning anger against Amalek. So YHWH will give both Israel and you into the hand of the Philistines.

'Tomorrow you and your sons *will be* with me. YHWH will also give the Israelite camp into the hand of the Philistines.'

When Samuel had finished speaking, Saul immediately fell flat to the ground. He greatly feared the words of Samuel. *Furthermore*, he had not eaten food all that day and night, so he was devoid of strength.

After Samuel had left, the woman approached Saul. She saw that he was greatly disturbed. So she said to him, 'Look, your maidservant obeyed your voice. I took my life in my hands. I heard the words that you spoke to me. Now listen, I pray, to your maidservant's voice. Let me set a morsel of bread before you. *Then* eat, so *you can regain* your strength. Then you can go on your way.'

He refused. He said, 'I will not eat.' But the men who were with him, with the woman, urged *him to eat*. So he listened to their voices. He then got up from the ground and sat on the couch.

Now the woman had only offered a morsel of bread, but she had *been* fattening a calf. So she rushed out of the house and slaughtered it. She took flour, kneaded *it*, and baked him *some* bread without yeast. *It was a very generous meal, possibly intended to place an obligation on Saul regarding her welfare. The time required to prepare such a meal would have also delayed Saul returning to his camp by a considerable time.* She then set *the meal* before Saul and his men. So that night they ate, then they got up and went *on their* way.

David Is Sent Back to Ziklag[107]

Now the Philistines *had moved their forces* to Aphek (*about half-way between Gath and Shunem*). They had set up camp there. Meanwhile, Israel *had also moved*; they had set up camp by the spring in Jezreel. The rulers of the Philistines then advanced by their hundreds and by their thousands.

---

[107] 1 Samuel 29:1-11

David and his men advanced, at the rear, with Achish. But the rulers of the Philistines said, 'What *are* these Hebrews *doing in our midst?*'

Achish said to the rulers, 'Isn't this David? He *was* a servant of Saul, king of Israel. He has been with me for over a year. From the day he abandoned *Saul* until now, I have not found anything *wrong* with him.'

But the rulers of the Philistines were angry. They said to Achish, 'Send the man back. Let him return to his place—the one you designated for him—for he must not go down into the battle with us. He will *turn* against us in battle; *he will be* an adversary. What *better way* could he make himself favourable to his lord than with the heads of our men?

'Isn't this *the same* David they sang about as they danced? They said, "Saul has slain his thousands, and David his tens of thousands"?'

So Achish called for David. He said to him, 'As YHWH lives, you have indeed been upright *to me*. Now it would be pleasing in my eyes *for you* to go out and come in with me from the camp. For since the day you came to me until now, I have found no evil in you. But you are not pleasing in the eyes of the rulers. So go back! Go in peace. Do not *do anything* that may be displeasing in the eyes of the rulers of the Philistines.'

David said to Achish, 'What have I done? From the day I came to you until now, what have you found against your servant? *Why* can't I go and fight against the enemies of my lord, the king?'

But Achish answered David. He said, 'I know that you are as pleasing in my eyes as an angel of God. Despite that the rulers of the Philistines have said, "He must not go up with us to the battle."

'So rise early in the morning, with the servants of your lord who came with you. Rise early in the morning, and as soon as it is light go on your way.'

So David, and his men, rose early in the morning. They then went on their way back to the land of the Philistines, while the Philistines went up to Jezreel.

David Takes Revenge on the Amalekites[108]

David and his men arrived at Ziklag on the third day. However, the Amalekites had made a raid on the Negev and had struck Ziklag. They had taken the women and all who were in it—young and old—into captivity. They had not killed anyone, but had burned Ziklag with fire, carried off *the people*, and gone on their way. So when David, and his men, came to the town, they saw that it had been destroyed by fire, and that their wives, sons, and daughters had been taken captive.

So David, and the people who were with him, raised their voices and wept until they no longer had the strength to weep. David's two wives, Ahinoam the

---

[108] 1 Samuel 30:1-31

Jezreelite and Abigail widow of Nabal, the Carmelite, *were among those* who had been taken captive. Furthermore, David was greatly troubled because the people *began* talking about stoning him. All the people were bitter in spirit—each *one* because of his sons and daughters. However David found strength in YHWH, his God.

David said to Abiathar, the priest, the son of Ahimelech, 'Please bring me the ephod.' So Abiathar brought the ephod to David. David then enquired of YHWH. He said, 'Should I chase after this band *of raiders*? Should I overtake them?'

YHWH said to him, 'Chase after *them*, for you will indeed overtake *them* and rescue *your people*.' So David left, with the six hundred men who were with him.

When they arrived at the brook at Besor, two hundred *of the* men were *too* exhausted to cross the brook. *So* they remained at Besor, while David and *the other* four hundred men *continued their* pursuit.

Some of David's men found an Egyptian man in a field—*an abandoned slave*. He had not eaten *any* bread or drunk *any* water for three days and nights. So they brought him to David and gave him food *to eat* and water to drink, *which he ate and drank*. They gave him a piece of cake of pressed figs and two bunches of raisins. *Then, once* he had eaten, his spirit returned to him.

David said to him, 'To whom do you belong? Where are you from?'

He said, 'I am a young man from Egypt, a slave of an Amalekite man. My master left me *behind* three days *ago*, because I was ill.

'We raided the Negev of the Kerethites, the land of Judah, and the Negev of Caleb, and we burned Ziklag with fire.'

David said to him, 'Can you take me down to this band *of raiders*?'

He said, 'Swear to me, by God, that you will not kill me or deliver me into the hand of my master. Then I will take you down to this band.'

So he led him down.

When they arrived, the raiders were spread out over the land. They were eating, drinking, and celebrating because of the large *quantity of* plunder they had taken from the land of the Philistines and from Judah. So David fought them from dusk until the following evening. None of the men escaped. However four hundred young men got away from them, and fled by riding off on their *own* camels.

In this way, David rescued everything that the Amalekites had taken; he even rescued his two wives. Nothing of theirs was missing, whether small or great, sons or daughters, plunder or anything *else* they had taken. David took it all back. *In addition*, David took all the sheep and cattle *that had belonged to the*

Amalekites and drove them ahead of the *other live*stock. *David's men* said *this about the livestock*: 'This is David's plunder.'

Then David returned to the two hundred men who had remained at the brook at Besor, the ones who had been *too* exhausted to follow him *any further*.

The men came out to meet him and the people who were with him, so David drew near to the men and asked after their welfare.

But all the evil and worthless men who had gone with David said, 'Every man may take his wife and children and leave, but we will not give them any of the plunder we recovered, because they did not go with us.'

But David said, 'My brothers, you must not act this *way* with what YHWH has given us, for he has kept watch over us. He has given the band *of raiders*, who came against us, into our hands.

'Who *do you think* will listen to these words of yours? The share of those who stayed with the equipment will be the *same* as the share of those who went down into battle. They will *all* share alike.' So from that day onwards David made *this principle* a statute, an ordinance for Israel, *which was still in effect when* this story was written down.

After David had returned to Ziklag, he sent some of the plunder to the elders of Judah, to his friends. He said, 'Look, *here is* a present for you, from the plunder of YHWH's enemies.

The Places Where David Sent His Plunder

Bethel	Jerahmeelite towns
Ramoth in the Negev	Kenite towns
Jattir	Hormah
Aroer	Bor Ashan
Siphmoth	Athach
Eshtemoa	Hebron
Racal	

Everywhere that David and his men had been

The Death of Saul[109]

While David was pursuing the band of Amalekites, the Philistines began their fight against Israel. But the Israelites fled from them and many fell pierced on

---

[109] 1 Samuel 31:1-13; 1 Chronicles 10:1-14

Mount Gilboa. The Philistines pursued Saul and his sons, and the Philistines killed Saul's sons Jonathan, Abinadab, and Malki-Shua.

The fighting became very intense around Saul, and *some of the* archers *among the Philistines* found their target. He was critically wounded by their arrows.

Saul said to his armour bearer, 'Draw your sword! Thrust me through with it! Otherwise these uncircumcised will come, run me through, and deal ruthlessly with me.' But his armour bearer refused, for he was very afraid. So Saul took the sword and fell on it.

When his armour bearer saw that Saul was dead, he also fell on his sword, and died with him. So Saul, three of his sons, his armour bearer, and all the men (the men of his house) died together that day.

When the Israelites, who *lived* on *the northern side of* the *Jezreel* valley and across the Jordan *valley*, realised that the men of Israel had fled, and that Saul and his sons were dead, they left their towns and fled. The Philistines then came and occupied them.

The following day, the Philistines returned to Mount Gilboa to strip the pierced. They found Saul and his three sons who had fallen *there*. They cut off Saul's head, stripped off his armour, and took his head and his armour *away*. *They* impaled his body, *and his sons'* bodies on the wall at Beth Shan (*about 8 kilometres east of Mount Gilboa*) *in full view of the Israelites*. They then sent *a report* throughout the land of the Philistines, for proclamation in the temple of their idols and among the people. *Then, as tributes to their gods*, they placed Saul's weapons in the house of their gods—in the temple of Ashteroth—and impaled his head in the temple of Dagon.

The inhabitants of Jabesh Gilead (*19 kilometres south east of Beth Shan*) heard how the Philistines had treated Saul's *body*, so all their valiant men stood up *as one*, and walked all night to Beth Shan. They took down the bodies of Saul and his sons from the wall, and returned to Jabesh.

Now it was not normal for a body to be burnt. But the bodies of Saul and his sons had been mistreated, and there was always a chance that the Philistines would come and mistreat them again. So they burned the bodies. They then took *the remains of* their bones and buried them under the tamarisk *tree* in Jabesh. They *then showed the customary respect for their former leader by* fasting for seven days.

So Saul died for his unfaithfulness. He was unfaithful to YHWH by not keeping the word of YHWH; he sought guidance by consulting with a necromancer; and he failed to enquire of YHWH. So YHWH put him to death and turned the kingdom over to David, son of Jesse.

David Responds to Saul's Death[110]

Shortly after Saul's death, David returned to Ziklag. He had been there for two days following his attack on the Amalekites, when on the third day a man from Saul's camp was seen coming *towards them*. His clothes were torn, and he had dust on his head.

When he came to David he fell to the ground and bowed down *before him—effectively acknowledging David as king*.

However, David knew nothing about what had happened. So David said to him, 'Where have you come from?'

He said to him, 'I have escaped from the Israelite camp.'

David said to him, 'Tell me, I pray, what has happened?'

He said, 'The people fled from the battle. In addition, many of the people fell and died. Saul and Jonathan, his son, also died.'

Then David said to the young man, who was reporting to him, 'How do you know that Saul and his son, Jonathan, have died?'

Now the young man was seeking a reward for himself. So he embellished the facts. He did so, believing it would put him in a very positive light. The young man giving the report said to him, 'By chance, I was there on Mount Gilboa. I saw Saul leaning on his spear. I saw the chariots and the horseman closing in on him. He turned in my direction, and saw me.

'He called to me, and I said, "Here I am."

'He said to me, "Who are you?"

'I said, "I am an Amalekite."

'Then he said to me, "Come! Stand over me! Kill me, for I am seized with pain, yet life still remains in me."

'So I stood over him and killed him, for I knew that he had fallen and was not going to live. Then I took the crown that was on his head, and the *royal* bracelet from his *upper* arm, and I have brought them to my lord here.'

David *immediately* took hold of his *own* clothes and tore them. So did every man who was with him. They then wailed and wept and fasted until evening, because Saul, his son—Jonathan—YHWH's people, and the house of Israel had fallen by the sword.

David said to the young man, who had reported to him, 'Where are you from?'

He said, 'I am the son of a temporary resident, *who lives in your land*. I am an Amalekite.'

David said to him, 'Why is it that you were not afraid to stretch out our hand to kill YHWH's anointed?' David then said to him, 'Your blood is on your *own* head; your mouth has testified against you. You have said, "I have killed YHWH's anointed."'

---

[110] 2 Samuel 1:1-16

Then David summoned one of *his* young men. He said, 'Come here! Strike him down!' So he struck him down and he died.

David's Lament[111]

Then David chanted this elegy for Saul and his son, Jonathan. He ordered that the Lament of the Bow be taught to the men of Judah. *It can be* seen written in the Book of the Upright, *among the collection of songs.*

Lament of the Bow

'*Your* honour, Israel, *has been* slain on your mountains;
    how the mighty have fallen.

'Don't tell it in Gath;
    don't announce it in the streets of Ashkelon.
Otherwise the daughters of the Philistines will rejoice;
    the daughters of the uncircumcised will leap for joy.

'Mountains of Gilboa, let no dew or rain *fall* on you
    or on the fields of first fruits.
For the shield of the mighty was abhorred there;
    the shield of YHWH will no longer be anointed with oil.

'Jonathan's bow did not retreat
    from the blood of the slain.
Saul's sword did not return empty
    from the fat of the strong.
Saul and Jonathan—beloved and dear—
    undivided in death!
They were swifter than eagles;
    they were stronger than lions.

'Daughters of Israel, weep for Saul,
    the one who dressed you in luxury, in scarlet;
    the one who put golden ornaments on your clothing.'

'How the mighty have fallen in the midst of battle;
    Jonathan has been slain on your mountains.
I mourn for you, Jonathan, my brother.
    You were *very* dear to me.

---

[111] 2 Samuel 1:17-27

> Your love for me was greater
>> than the love of women.
>
> 'How the mighty have fallen,
>> and the weapons of war lost.'

David's Men[112]

David had gathered many supporters during his time in the wilderness in southern Judah and at Ziklag in the land of the Philistines. They had come from all over Israel, and over time some of them had become very well-known.

This is a list of Gadites who had defected to David *while he was* at the stronghold in the wilderness (*possibly at En-Gedi*). They were mighty *men*, strong, and trained for battle. They could handle both shield and spear. Their faces were the faces of lions, and they were as swift as gazelles on the mountains.

From the Tribe of Gad

1. Ezer
2. Obadiah
3. Eliab
4. Mishmannah
5. Jeremiah
6. Attai
7. Eliel
8. Johanan
9. Elzabad
10. Jeremiah
11. Macbannai

Note: These Gadites, *in rank order,* were the leaders of the army. The lowest *ranked man could hold off* a hundred *men*, and the highest a thousand men. *Indeed,* these are the ones who crossed the Jordan *River* in the first month, when all its banks were in flood, and all the valleys to the east and west were unpassable

---

Some Benjaminites and *men from* Judah *had also come* to David at the stronghold. David had come out to meet them, and had spoken *to them.*

He had said to them, 'If you have come in peace to help me, my heart will be as one with you. But if *you have come* to betray me to my adversaries, even

---

[112] 1 Chronicles 12:1-22

Establishing the Kingdom

though my hands are free of wrong, may the God of our fathers see *it*, and make judgement.'

Then the spirit of God had come upon Amasai, a leader of the Thirty. *He had said*, '*We are* with you, David; *we are* with you, son of Jesse. Peace will surely be to you, and peace *will be with* anyone who helps you. For your God will help you.' So David had accepted them and made them as leaders of *his* band.

This *is a list of* those who had come to David at Ziklag, while he was hiding from the presence of Saul, son of Kish. They were among the mighty *men* who had helped in battle. They were skilled with the bow *and with the sling*, being able to use both right and left hands to *sling* stones and *shoot* arrows. They were Saul's kinsmen, from *the tribe of* Benjamin

---

Saul's Kinsmen from the Tribe of Benjamin

Ahiezer, son of Shemaah the Gibeathite[1]
Joash, son of Shemaah the Gibeathite
Jeziel, son of Azmaveth
Pelet, son of Azmaveth
Beracah
Jehu, the Anathothite
Ishmaiah, the Gibeonite[2]
Jeremiah
Jahaziel
Johanan
Jozabad, the Gederathite
Eluzai
Jerimoth
Bealiah
Shemariah
Shephatiah, the Haruphite
Elkanah
Isshiah
Azarel
Joezer, the Korahite
Jashobeam, the Korahite
Joelah, son of Jeroham from Gedor
Zebadiah, son of Jeroham from Gedor

Notes: [1] *Ahiezer, son of Shemaah was* their leader; [2] *Ishmaiah, the Gibeonite was* a mighty man among the Thirty—a leader of the Thirty

This is a list of those from Manasseh who had defected to David at Ziklag, when he went with the Philistines to fight against Saul. However, they had been unable to help him because, after consultation, the rulers of the Philistines had sent him away.

The rulers had said *to Achish, king of Gath*, 'He will desert to his master, Saul, at *the cost of* our *own* heads.'

From the Tribe of Manasseh

Adnah
Jozabad
Jediael
Michael
Jozabad
Elihu
Zillethai

Note: These men were all leaders of thousands in Manasseh. They helped David against the band of raiders, for they were all strong leaders and commanders in the army

---

In addition to those listed, many more had defected to David. Indeed, day after day *men had* come to David to help him, until his camp had grown so big that it was like the army of God.

C21. ISHBAAL/ISHBOSHETH
(c. 1047-1003 BC)

The Kings of Judah and Israel[113]

After *Saul's death*, David *considered it might be safe to return to his homeland*. So he enquired of YHWH. He said, 'Shall I go up to one of the towns of Judah?'

YHWH said to him, 'Go up!'

David said, 'Where shall I go?'

YHWH said, 'To Hebron.'

So David went to Hebron, with his two wives, Ahinoam the Jezreelite, and Abigail the widow of Nabal the Carmelite. He took with him his men, and their families, who settled in the surrounding settlements.

Then the men of Judah came together and anointed David king over the house of Judah.

When the men told David that the men of Jabesh Gilead had buried Saul, he sent messengers to the men of Jabesh Gilead.

He said to them, 'May you be blessed by YHWH, because you have done this *great* kindness to your lord, Saul, by burying him. May YHWH show *his* covenant love and faithfulness to you. In addition, I will personally do good things for you, because you have done this deed. May your hands be strong, and *your* men brave, for your lord, Saul, is dead.'

Now Jabesh Gilead was some distance away, north of Judah, and David had not been made king over all Israel. So perhaps, as a way of suggesting that they align themselves with his kingship, David concluded, 'The house of Judah has anointed me king over them.'

But one of Saul's sons had survived the battle. His name was Ishbaal ('man of the Lord'), but he also became known as Ishbosheth ('man of shame'), because the Semitic rendering of his name as 'man of Baal' was seen to be shameful.

Furthermore, Abner, son of Ner, the *former* commander of Saul's army, *was keen for the kingship to remain in Saul's family*. So he took Ishbosheth, the son of Saul, *to a place outside the reach of both the Philistines and David*. He took him to Mahanaim, *on the eastern side of the Jordan River, and there* he made him king over Gilead, Ashuri, Jezreel, Ephraim, and Benjamin—all of Israel.

Ishbosheth, son of Saul, was forty years old when he became king over Israel, and he was king *in Mahanaim* for two years *before hostilities with David began*. The house of Judah, however, followed David. Indeed, David ruled in Hebron,

---

[113] 2 Samuel 2:1-11

over the house of Judah, for *all the* seven years and six months *that the kingdom was divided.*

War Between Ishbosheth and David[114]

Abner, son of Ner, and the servants of Ishbosheth, son of Saul, left Mahanaim *and went* to Gibeon *in Benjamin.* Joab, son of Zeruiah, and David's servants went there *too.* They met together by the pool of Gibeon. Abner's group sat on one side of the pool and Joab's group sat on the other.

Abner said to Joab, 'Let the young men stand up and perform in front of us.'

So Joab said, 'Let them stand up.'

So the young men stood up and were counted as they took their positions. Twelve *men represented the tribe* of Benjamin and Ishbosheth, son of Saul; twelve servants *represented* David. Each *one* grabbed his opponent by the head, and *thrust* his sword into his opponent's side, so they fell together. For this reason that place in Gibeon was called Helkath Hazzurim (*possibly 'field of sides'*).

With no apparent winner in the mock fight, the two groups began fighting one another. Indeed, there was a very fierce battle that day, and Abner and the Israelites were struck down by David's servants.

The three sons of Zeruiah were there: Joab, Abishai, and Asahel. Asahel was fleet-footed, like a gazelle in the wild. He chased after Abner. He turned neither to the right or the left from pursuing him.

As Asahel was closing in, Abner *stopped and* turned. He said, 'Is that you, Asahel?'

He answered, 'It is I.'

Abner said to him, 'Turn away to your right or to your left. Grab hold of one of the young men and take what he has as your *share of the* spoils.' But Asahel refused to turn away from chasing him.

Again Abner said to Asahel, 'Turn away from following me. Why should I strike you to the ground? How could I lift my face to your brother, Joab?' But he refused to turn. So Abner struck him in the stomach with the butt of the spear, until the spear came out through his back. Asahel fell there and died. *So it became a custom for* everyone who came to the place where Asahel had fallen and died *to stand still and reflect on the events of that day.*

Then Joab and Abishai chased after Abner. As the sun was going down they came to the hill of Ammah, facing Giah, on the road to the wilderness of Gibeon. The Benjaminites gathered together to support Abner. They became one band, and they stood as one on top of a hill.

---

[114] 2 Samuel 2:12-3:5

Abner called to Joab. He said, 'Must the sword devour forever? Don't you know how bitter it will be in the end? How long will you hold back from telling your people to turn away from their brothers?'

Joab said, 'As God lives, if you hadn't spoken, all the people would have continued to chase their brothers until morning.' So Joab blew on the trumpet and all the people halted. They stopped chasing after Israel; they ceased to engage them in further battle.

All that night Abner, and his men, went through the Arabah. They crossed the Jordan *River* and walked all morning until they came to Mahanaim. Meanwhile, Joab turned back from following Abner and assembled all the people. Nineteen of David's servants were missing, plus Asahel. But David's servants had struck down *many of the* Benjaminites and Abner's men. *Indeed*, three hundred and sixty *of their* men had died.

Joab and his men took Asahel's *body* and buried him in his father's tomb in Bethlehem. They then continued *walking* all night, arriving at Hebron at daybreak.

The war between the house of Saul and the house of David continued for a long time. *All the while* David grew stronger, while the house of Saul grew weaker.

David's Sons Born in Hebron
In order of birth

Son	Mother
1. Amnon[1]	Ahinoam, the Jezreelite
2. Kileab (*or Daniel*)	Abigail, widow of Nabal of Carmel
3. Absalom	Maacah, daughter of Talmai, king of Geshur
4. Adonijah	Haggith
5. Shephatiah	Abital
6. Ithream	Eglah

Note: [1] *Amnon was David's* firstborn

Abner Defects to David[115]

During the war between the house of Saul and the house of David, Abner strengthened his *position* in the house of Saul. *So much so, that Ishbosheth became very suspicious of Abner's motives.*

---

[115] 2 Samuel 3:6-21

Indeed, Saul had had a concubine. Her name was Rizpah, daughter of Aiah. *But Ishbosheth believed that Abner had been sleeping with her. As a consequence, and as Aiah had been the mother of two of Saul's children, Ishbosheth believed that Abner was making a claim for his throne.*

So Ishbosheth said to Abner, 'Why did you go in to my father's concubine?'

But Abner responded very angrily to Ishbosheth's accusation. He said, 'Am I a dog's head from Judah *that you accuse me of such a disgraceful act? Up until this very* day I have shown kindness to the house of Saul: *to* your father, his brothers, and his friends. I have not given you into the hand of David. Yet today you accuse me of an offence concerning *this* woman.

'So may God deal with Abner and continue *to punish* him, if I do not do for David as YHWH has sworn to him. *That is*, to pass the kingdom over from the house Saul and set up David's throne over *both* Israel and Judah—from Dan *in the north* to Beersheba *in the south*.'

When Abner had finished speaking, Ishbosheth *had nothing to say. He* was unable to respond to Abner's words. He was afraid of him *and what he was about to do.*

Abner sent messengers to David on his *own* behalf. He said, 'To whom does the land *belong?*' He said, 'Make your covenant with me. Look, my hand will be with you to bring all Israel over to you.'

David *then sent messengers back to Abner,* saying, 'Good! I will make a covenant with you. However, I ask one thing from you: to bring Michal, Saul's daughter *with you* when you come to see me. You will not see my face until *you* do.'

At the same time, David sent messengers to Ishbosheth, son of Saul. He said, 'Give me my wife, Michal. I was betrothed to her for a hundred Philistine foreskins.' So Ishbosheth, *no longer wishing to pursue his conflict with David,* sent *for her* and had her taken from her husband, Paltiel, son of Laish. But her husband travelled with her, weeping as he went.

When they reached Bahurim, *in Benjamin,* Abner said to him, 'Go! Go back!' So he returned *home.*

Now Abner had *already* spoken with the elders of Israel. He had said, 'You have previously sought David to be king over you. So make it so, for YHWH made a promise to David. He said, "I will deliver my people, Israel, from the hand of the Philistines and from all their *other* enemies, by the hand of my servant, David."' Abner spoke in the hearing of the Benjaminites too. Then he went on to Hebron, to tell David everything that was good in the eyes of both Israel and the house of Benjamin.

When Abner, and the twenty men who were with him, came to David at Hebron, David prepared a feast for them.

Afterwards, Abner said to David, 'Let me arise and go. Let me assemble all Israel for my lord, the king. They will then make a covenant with you, and you will be king over everything your heart desires.' So David sent Abner on his way, and he went in peace.

Joab's Revenge on Abner[116]

A short time later, David's servants, *led by* Joab, returned from a raid. They brought with them much plunder. However, Abner was no longer in Hebron with David, because he had sent him away, and he had gone in peace.

When Joab, and all the army that was with him, arrived, Joab was told *what had happened*. It was reported, 'Abner, son of Ner, came to the king, but the king sent him away. He has gone in peace.'

So Joab went to the king, and said, 'What have you done? Look, Abner came to you, so why did you send him away? He has already gone. You know that Abner, son of Ner, came to deceive you. He came to take note of your going out and your coming in—to learn everything you are doing.' Then Joab left David's *presence*.

Joab sent messengers after Abner, and they brought him back from the well of Sirah. But David knew nothing *of this*.

Then, as Abner returned to Hebron, *at the gateway into the town*, Joab took him aside to speak with him in private. There Joab stabbed him in the stomach and he died. *So Joab was avenged* for the blood of Asahel, his brother. Joab and his brother, Abishai, killed Abner, because Abner had killed their brother, Asahel, in the battle at Gibeon.

Later, David heard *the news concerning* the *shedding of* blood. So he said, 'I, and my kingdom, are without guilt before YHWH regarding Abner son of Ner— *now and* forever. May *the guilt* fall upon Joab's head and all his father's house. May there never be *a time when someone in his house isn't suffering* from a discharge, leprosy, requires a crutch to lean on, has fallen by the sword, or lacks food.'

Then David, *having arranged a funeral procession*, said to Joab, and to all the people who were with him, 'Tear you clothes! Put on sackcloth and wail before Abner. *Then the procession began with* King David walking behind the *funeral* bed.'

Abner was buried in Hebron. The king raised his voice and wept at Abner's tomb. All the people wept. Then the king sang a lament for Abner. He said:

> 'Should Abner have died
>   as a fool dies?

---

[116] 2 Samuel 3:22-39

> Your hands were not tied,
>> nor were your feet in fetters.
> As one falls before the unrighteous,
>> *so* you have fallen.'

Then all the people wept over him again.

While it was still day*light*, all the people came to persuade David to eat *some* bread. But David had sworn *an oath*, saying, 'May God deal with me, and may he continue to do so, if I taste bread or anything *else* before the sun goes down.'

All the people regarded *David's response*, and it was pleasing in their eyes. *Indeed*, everything that the king did was pleasing in the eyes of all *the people*. So all the people, and all Israel, knew that day that the king *had not been behind* the murder of Abner, son of Ner.

The king said to his servants, 'Don't you know that a prince—a great man—has fallen today in Israel? I am weak today, even though I am the anointed king. But these men, the sons of Zeruiah—*Joab and Abishai*—are too hard for me. May YHWH repay anyone who does evil, in accordance with their wicked *deeds*.'

David's Forces at Hebron[117]

These are the numbers of armed men, *ready* for war, which came to David at Hebron. *They came* to turn the kingdom of Saul over to David, as YHWH had promised.

(See table on next page)

All these fighting men, who could draw in battle, were whole of heart and came to Hebron to make David king over all Israel. The rest of Israel were also of one mind to make David king.

They were there with David three days eating and drinking, for their families had provided *food* for them. In addition, their neighbours, even as far away as Issachar, Zebulun, and Naphtali brought food on donkeys, camels, mules, and oxen. *There was a great* quantity of flour, fig cakes, bunches of raisins, wine, oil, cattle, and sheep. There was great joy in Israel.

---

[117] 1 Chronicles 12:23-40

The Number of Armed Men, Ready for Battle

Tribes	Description	Number
Sons of Judah	Armed for war, carrying shields and spears	6,800
Sons of Simeon	Strong and ready for war	7,100
Sons of Levi	4,600 men, *plus* Jehoida, leader of *the family of* Aaron with 3,700 *men, plus* Zadok, a strong man ready for war, with 22 leaders from his father's family	*unknown*
Sons of Benjamin	Saul's kinsmen, most of whom had previously been loyal to the house of Saul	3,000
Sons of Ephraim	Well-known men in their fathers' households, who were strong and ready for war	20,800
Half of the tribe of Manasseh	Handpicked *men sent* to make David king	18,000
Sons of Issachar	*Men* who understood the times, who knew what Israel needed to do: 200 leaders, with all their kinsmen at their command	*unknown*
Sons of Zebulun	Seasoned fighters, who could draw up in battle with all the weapons of war. *Men* of undivided loyalty.	50,000
Sons of Naphtali	1,000 leaders, with 37,000 carrying shields and spears	*38,000*
Sons of Dan	*Men* ready for battle	28,600
Sons of Asher	Seasoned fighters, who could draw up in battle	40,000
Those from the east of the Jordan River:	*Men from* Reuben, Gad and the *other* half of the tribe of Manasseh, with every kind of weapon of war	120,000

Ishbosheth Murdered[118]

When *Ishbosheth*, son of Saul, heard that Abner had died in Hebron, his courage fell. The whole of Israel was dismayed *at his murder*.

Now Saul's son had two men, who were the leaders of raiding bands. One

---

[118] 2 Samuel 4:1-12

was named Baanah and the other Recab; they were the sons of Rimmon the Beerothite. They were Benjaminites, as Beeroth was considered to be part of Benjamin. Indeed, the Beerothites had fled to Benjamin, to Gittaim, where they still lived as aliens *when this story was written down.*

Now Recab and Baanah, the sons of Rimmon the Beerothite, set out *from Gittaim*, and came in the heat of the day to the house of Ishbosheth, while he was taking his midday rest. Indeed, they entered the house as if to get some wheat, while he was lying on his bed in his bedroom. They then stabbed him in the stomach and killed him. Recab and his brother, Baanah, then cut off his head and, taking his head, slipped away. They then travelled all night by the way of the Arabah and brought Ishbosheth's head to David at Hebron.

They said to the king, 'Look! The head of Ishbosheth, son of Saul! *Here is* your enemy who sought your life. YHWH has given my lord, the king, vengeance against Saul and his offspring today.'

David answered Recab and his brother, Baanah, the sons of Rimmon the Beerothite. He said to them, 'As YHWH lives, he has delivered my life from every danger.

'When someone told me, "Saul is dead," it was good news in his eyes. But I took hold of him and killed him in Ziklag. That was my reward to him for the news. *So* when wicked men kill a righteous man on his bed, in his *own* house, shouldn't I seek his blood from your hand? *Shouldn't* I destroy you from the earth?'

So David commanded *his* young men and they killed them. They cut off their hands and their feet and hung *their bodies* by the pool in Hebron. But they took Ishbosheth's head and buried *it* in Abner's tomb at Hebron.

Now Ishbosheth had not been the only survivor of Saul's family.

Jonathan, son of Saul, *also* had had a son, whose feet were crippled. He had been five years old when the report had come from Jezreel *that* Saul and Jonathan *had been killed.*

His nurse had picked him up and fled. But as she had hurried to leave, he had fallen and become crippled. His name was *Merribbaal ('from the mouth of the Lord')*, or as he was also known, Mephibosheth *('from the mouth of shame')*.

At the time of Ishbosheth's death he was about twelve years old.

C22. DAVID
(1040-970 BC)

a). King of Israel and Judah *(1003-991 BC)*

David, King of Israel[119]

Every tribe of Israel came to David at Hebron. They said, 'Look at us! We are your bone and your flesh. In times past, when Saul was king over us, it was you who led Israel out and lead *Israel* in. YHWH, your God, said to you, "You will be the one to shepherd my people, Israel. You will become ruler over my people."' That is why all the elders of Israel came to the king at Hebron, and King David made a covenant with them before YHWH.

There they anointed him as king over Israel, as YHWH had promised through Samuel.

David had been thirty years old when he was made king *over Judah, and he was thirty seven when he became king over all of Israel.*

A Victory over the Philistines[120]

Now the Philistines heard that the people had anointed David king over all Israel, so they all went in search of him. But David heard *that they were coming* and went down to the stronghold *at Adullam in Judah.*

When the Philistines arrived, they spread out in the valley of Rephaim, *north of Adullam.* They raided *the land and cut off the connection between Israel and Judah.*

Now it was harvest time, and three of the thirty mighty *men* had gone down to David at the cave of Adullam, while a band of Philistines were encamped in the valley of Rephaim. So David was in the stronghold, and a garrison of the Philistines was in Bethlehem, *sixteen kilometres away.*

Now no doubt the proximity of Bethlehem, and the special qualities of the water there inspired David to desire *some of its water. But not expecting to be taken seriously,* David said, 'Who will get me water to drink from the well by the gate in Bethlehem?'

So the three mighty *men went*, broke through the Philistine camp, and drew water from the well by the gate in Bethlehem. They then carried it *back and* brought *it* to David.

But he was unwilling to drink it, and poured it out to YHWH. He said, 'Far be it from me, YHWH, that I should drink this. *Can I drink* the blood of

---

[119] 2 Samuel 5:1-4a; 1 Chronicles 11:1-3
[120] 2 Samuel 5:17-21; 23:13-17; 1 Chronicles 11:15-19; 14:8-12; Psalm 124:1-8

the men who risked their lives, for they brought it *to me* at the risk of their *own* lives?' So he refused to drink it.

These were the *sorts of* deeds that the three mighty *men* did.

David enquired of YHWH. He said, 'Shall I go against the Philistines? Will you give them into my hand?'

YHWH said to David, 'Go, for I will certainly give the Philistines into your hand.' So David went out against them; he went to Baal Perazim and he defeated them there.

David said, 'As water breaks out, so YHWH has burst forth against my enemies, in my presence, and by my hand.' This is why the place was named Baal Perazim (*'Lord of the breaches'*).

Now the Philistines had fled in such a hurry that they had left their gods behind, and *as it was customary for the victors to carry off the gods of the enemy*, David and his men carried them away. But David commanded that they burned with fire.

One of the psalms 'of David' picks up the theme of water and floods in the context of battle. It may well have been written with this battle in mind. It is also noted as being a 'song of ascents'. So it was probably used later by pilgrims on their way to Jerusalem.

It begins with an introduction encouraging others to join in.

Notes:
A song of ascents (*possibly a devotion for those on a pilgrimage to Jerusalem*).
Of David.

David, to those with him
'If YHWH had not been for us . . .
    Now let Israel say . . .

Those with David, to each other
"'If YHWH had not been for us,
    when men rose up against us,
then when their anger burned against us
    they would have swallowed us alive.
Then the waters would have washed over us;
    the torrent would have gone over us;
    the raging waters would have swept over our bodies.

"'Blessed be YHWH,
    who has not let us be prey for their teeth.

We have slipped away, like a bird,
> from a baited bird trap.
The trap has been broken,
> and we have slipped away.
Our help is in the name of YHWH,
> the one who made the heavens and the earth.'"

David Conquers Jebus[121]

Now *David needed a base that would be acceptable to both Israel and Judah; a city between the two, but which did not belong to either. So* the king, and his men, and all Israel, went to Jebus *(later to be known as* Jerusalem [*'foundation of peace'*]) *to fight* the Jebusites who were living in the land.

The Jebusites said to David, 'You cannot enter here. Even the blind and the lame could turn you away.' *Indeed,* they said *to each other,* 'David will not be able to enter here.'

But David had a seen a weakness in their defences. So that day, David said *to his men,* 'Anyone who wants to strike *against* the Jebusites will need to reach *them* through the water tunnel. The first to strike a Jebusite will be made commander and chief. *Let him attack* "the lame and the blind"—those who hate David's life.' (That is the origin of the saying, 'The blind and lame will not enter the house'.)

So Joab, the son of Zeruiah, *who had previously been in charge of David's men, took up the challenge.* He was the first, so he became commander *of all Israel.*

So David captured the stronghold of Zion *(possibly 'fortress')*, and he named the city 'the City of David', and it became known as that, because he began to live there.

David built up the area around the city, from the Millo *(possibly an embankment)* inward. *Or rather,* David built up the city around the Millo and surrounding area, and Joab rebuilt the remainder of the city.

David then continued to increase in power, for YHWH, Almighty God, was with him.

The Father of Hiram, King of Tyre[122]

Abibaal, king of Tyre, *the father of* Hiram, sent messengers to David. *They brought with them* cedar trees, carpenters, and stonemasons. They built a palace for David.

Then David knew that YHWH had established him as king over Israel; that he had raised up his kingdom on account of his people, Israel.

---

[121] 2 Samuel 5:6-10; 1 Chronicles 11:4-9
[122] 2 Samuel 5:11-12; 1 Chronicles 14:1-2

Moving the Ark[123]

David, again, gathered together all the chosen *men* of Israel—thirty thousand *troops*. He consulted with the commanders of thousands and hundreds, with every leader.

David then spoke to the whole Israelite assembly. 'If the idea is pleasing to you and YHWH our God, let us send *a message* to our brothers everywhere. *Let it be sent* to *everyone who* remains throughout the territories of Israel. Let the priests and Levites, who live in the towns with pasture lands, also assemble with us. Then let us take the Ark of God and bring it with us *into the city*, because we paid no attention to it in the days of Saul.'

The whole assembly said, '*We should* do this. It is right in the eyes of all the people.' So David gathered all of Israel from Shihor of Egypt *in the south*, to Lebo Hamath *in the north*, to bring the Ark of God from Kiriath Jearim.

Then David, and all those with him—all Israel—arose and set out to Baalah (*also known as* Kiriath Jearim), in Judah (*23 kilometres north-west of the City of David*). They went to bring the Ark of God from there *into the city—the Ark which* is called by the Name, the name of Almighty YHWH, who is enthroned between the cherubim.

When they arrived, they mounted the Ark of God on a new cart. They then took it from the house of Abinadab, which was on the hill, with Uzzah and Ahio, sons of Abinadab, driving the new cart. Indeed, they took the Ark from the house of Abinadab, which was on the hill, with Ahio walking ahead of it.

Now David and all the house of Israel were celebrating, before YHWH, with all their might and with songs. *They played* wooden instruments, harps, lyres, tambourines, sistrums (*a type of rattle*), cymbals, and trumpets. *However, they ignored YHWH's ordinance, given on Mount Sinai, on how to move such a sacred object.* Then, when they came to the threshing floor that belonged to Nacon (*also known as* Kidon), the oxen made the Ark of God slip.

When Uzzah reached out his hand and grasped it, YHWH's anger burned against him. So God struck him down there, because of *his* disregard *for YHWH*, by placing his hand on the Ark. So he died there beside the Ark of God, before God.

But David's anger *also* burned, because YHWH had broken out against Uzzah. So he called that place Perez Uzzah ('*Uzzah's breach*'), *and it was still called that when this story was written down*.

That day, David was *very* fearful of God, of YHWH. He said, 'How can I bring the Ark of YHWH with me *into the city*?' As a consequence, David was unwilling and did not take the Ark of YHWH with him into the City of David. Instead, David took it to the house of Obed-Edom, the Gittite, nearby.

---

[123] 2 Samuel 6:1-11; 1 Chronicles 13:1-14

The Ark of God of YHWH stayed in the house of Obed-Edom, the Gittite, for three months. *During that time*, YHWH blessed Obed-Edom, his entire house, and everything that was his.

The Ark Is Brought to Jerusalem[124]

Now David had constructed houses for himself in the City of David. He had also established a place for the Ark of God and pitched a tent for it.

So when King David heard that YHWH had blessed the house of Obed-Edom and all that was his, because of the Ark of God, he said, 'Only the Levites will carry the Ark of God—no one *else*—because YHWH chose them to carry the Ark of YHWH and to minister to him forever.'

David then gathered all of Israel to Jerusalem, *so that* the Ark of YHWH could be brought to the place he had prepared for it. Descendants of Aaron and the Levites *were included in those* he assembled.

Descendants of Aaron and Levites Assembled by David

Descendants of:	Leader	No. of kinsmen
Kohath	Uriel	120
Merari	Asaiah	220
Gershom	Joel	130
Elizaphan	Shemaiah	200
Hebron	Eliel	80
Uzziel	Amminadab	112

Then David called *together* Zadok and Abiathar—the priests—and the *leaders of the* Levites: Uriel, Asaiah, Joel, Shemaiah, Eliel, and Amminadab. He said to them, 'You are the leaders of *your* fathers' *houses* among the Levites. Consecrate yourselves, you and your kinsmen, so you can bring up the Ark of YHWH, the God of Israel, to *the place* I have prepared for it.

'The first time you were not *with us, and* YHWH, our God, broke out against us, for we had no regard to him; *we didn't* keep *his* ordinance.'

So the priests and the Levites consecrated themselves to bring up the Ark of YHWH, God of Israel.

David *also* told the leaders of the Levites to appoint singers from their kinsmen, with the accompanying musical instruments: lyres, harps, and

---

[124] 2 Samuel 6:12-15; 17-19a; 1 Chronicles 15:1-28;16:1-6

cymbals. They were to lift up their voices with the sound of joy. So the Levites appointed *the various singers and musicians.*

Levitical Appointments

Leaders	Heman, son of Joel *from the Kohathites*
	Asaph, son of Berekiah *from the Gershomites*
	Ethan, son of Kushaiah, from the Merarites
Assistants	Zechariah, Jaaziel, Shemiramoth, Jehiel, Unni, Eliab, Benaiah, Maaseiah, Mattithiah, Eliphelehu, Mikneiah,
Assistants and porters	Obed-Edom, Jeiel

Musicians

Sounding the bronze cymbals	Heman, Asaph, Ethan
Playing lyres, tuned to the voices of young women	Zechariah, Aziel, Shemiramoth, Jehiel, Unni, Eliab, Maaseiah, Benaiah
Playing harps, directed by the eight-stringed lyre	Mattithiah, Eliphelehu, Mikneiah, Obed-Edom, Jeiel, Azaziah

Other Roles

Leader of the singing	Kenaniah (the head Levite), because he was so skilful
Gatekeepers of the Ark	Berekiah and Elkanah, Obed-Edom, Jehiah
Priests blowing the trumpets before the Ark	Shebaniah, Joshaphat, Nethanel, Amasai, Zechariah, Benaiah, Eliezer

So David, the elders of Israel, and the commanders of thousands went down to the house of Obed-Edom to bring the Ark of the Covenant of YHWH up *to the city* with *great* joy.

This time, the Ark was carried correctly. The Levites carried the Ark of God, just as Moses had commanded, according to the word of YHWH. *They carried it* on their shoulders, by the *two carrying* poles *inserted in the chest's rings.*

After those who were carrying the Ark had taken six steps, *they stopped*. David then sacrificed a bull and a fattened calf. *Indeed*, because God was helping the Levites who were carrying the Ark, they sacrificed seven bulls and seven rams *too*.

Now David, the Levites who were carrying the Ark, the singers, and Kenaniah, the leader of the singers, were all dressed in robes of fine linen. David was also wearing a linen Ephod. *It was not as ornate as that worn by the High Priest, but it showed that the role of the king was somehow linked with that of a priest.*

David danced with all his might before YHWH. Then, *as he continued to dance, and with the addition* of shouting and the sound of a ram's horn, trumpets, cymbals, lyres, and harps, David and the whole house of Israel brought the Ark of YHWH *into the City of David*. Indeed, they brought the Ark of YHWH *into the city*, and put it down in its place, inside the tent that David had had erected for it. David, and all Israel, then sacrificed Burnt Offerings and Fellowship Offerings before YHWH.

When David had finished sacrificing the Burnt Offerings and Fellowship Offerings, he blessed the people in the name of Almighty YHWH. Then, *as part of the festivities*, he distributed to everyone in the crowd—every man and woman—a loaf of bread, a cake of dates, and a raisin cake.

That day, he also appointed Levites to serve before the Ark of YHWH: to remember, to thank, and to praise YHWH, the God of Israel.

Levites Appointed to Serve before the Ark of YHWH

Names	*Roles*
Asaph	Leader, and to play the cymbals
Zechariah	Second-*in-charge*
Jeiel, Shemiramoth, Jehiel, Mattithiah, Eliab, Benaiah, Obed-Edom, Jeiel	To play lyres and harps
Benaiah, Jahaziel (priests)	To blow trumpets regularly before the Ark of YHWH

David's Song of Thanksgiving[125]

That was the day that David first put Asaph and his kinsmen *in charge* of giving thanks to YHWH.

---

[125] 2 Samuel 6:19b; 1 Chronicles 16:7-43

Establishing the Kingdom

Asaph and his kinsmen, to all Israel
'Give thanks to YHWH, call upon his name;
    make his deeds known among the peoples.
Sing to him, make music to him;
    speak of all his wonderful acts.
Praise his holy name;
    let the hearts of those who seek YHWH rejoice.
Seek YHWH and his might;
    continually seek his face.
Remember the wonderful acts he has done;
    his miracles and the judgements he has proclaimed.

'Offspring of Israel, his servant,
    YHWH is our God.
Sons of Jacob, his chosen ones,
    his judgements *can be seen* throughout the earth.
Remember his covenant forever;
    the word he commanded for a thousand generations.
Remember the covenant he made with Abraham,
    and his oath to Isaac
He confirmed it to Jacob as a decree;
    to Israel as an everlasting covenant.
He said, "I will give you the land of Canaan;
    I will give you the territory as an inheritance."

'You were a people, few in number,
    and strangers in the land.
Then your *fathers* wandered from one nation to another,
    from one kingdom to another people.
But he did not allow any man to oppress them;
    he *even* rebuked kings on their behalf.
He said, "Do not touch my anointed ones;
    do not hurt my prophets."'

Asaph and his kinsmen, to all creation
'Sing to YHWH, all the earth;
    proclaim his salvation from day to day.
Make known his glory among the nations;
    his wonderful deeds among all the peoples.
For YHWH is great and *is worthy of* great praise;
    he is to be feared above all gods.

Establishing the Kingdom

For all the peoples' gods are *mere* idols;
  but YHWH made the heavens.
Majesty and honour *go* before him;
  strength and joy *are* in his dwelling place.

'Credit to YHWH, families of the peoples,
  credit YHWH *with* glory and strength;
  credit to YHWH the glory of his name.
Bring an offering, and come before YHWH;
  worship YHWH in the glory of *his* holiness.
Tremble before him, all the earth;
  for the world is sound, it cannot be shaken.
Let the heavens be glad and the earth rejoice;
  let them say among the nations, "YHWH is king."
Let the sea, and everything in it, thunder;
  let the field, and everything in it, rejoice.
Then the trees of the forest will give a ringing cry before YHWH,
  when he comes to judge the earth.

Asaph and his kinsmen, to all Israel
'Give thanks to YHWH for he is good;
  for his covenant love is forever.
Say, "Save us, God of our salvation;
  gather and deliver us from the nations."

Asaph and his kinsmen, to YHWH
'*Then we can* give thanks to your holy name,
  and we can boast in your songs of praise.
Blessed is YHWH, the God of Israel.
  He is from everlasting to everlasting.'

All the people said, 'Amen,' and praised YHWH. Then *David* left Asaph, and his kinsmen, there before the Ark of the Covenant of YHWH. *They then commenced their duties, continually* serving before the Ark, as each day required.

Additional Appointments to Serve before the Ark

Names	Roles
Obed-Edom and 68 kinsmen	*Assistants*
Obed-Edom, son of Jeduthun and Hosah	Gatekeepers

Appointments for YHWH's Tabernacle at the High Place in Gibeon	
Names	*Roles*
Zadok, the priest and his fellow priests	To present the Burnt Offerings on the Altar of Burnt Offering regularly, morning and evening, as it is written in YHWH's laws, which he gave to Israel.
Heman, Jeduthun, and the rest of those who were chosen, designated by name	To give thanks to YHWH for his everlasting love
Heman, Jeduthun	*To play* trumpets, cymbals, and *other* instruments for God's songs
Sons of Jeduthun	Gatekeepers

When the celebrations were over all the people dispersed, each to his *own* house. Then David returned *home* to bless his *own* family.

Celebrating Unity[126]

Many of the psalms 'of David' were written in reference to specific events. As a consequence, it is not unrealistic that one would have been written regarding the uniting of the people, under one king, and in Jerusalem.

While it is not known, whether the following psalm was written for this occasion, the references to anointing with oil, and the people being united, fits the circumstances well. It is also fitting that the psalm could be used later by pilgrims on their way to Jerusalem.

Notes:
A song of ascents (*possibly a devotion for those on a pilgrimage to Jerusalem*).
Of David.

David, to those around him
'See how agreeable and delightful it is
    for brothers to live united together.
It is like the precious oil *that is poured* upon the head,
    that runs down the beard.

---

[126] Psalm 133:1-3

> *Indeed, at* Aaron's *ordination* it ran down *his* beard,
> onto the collar of his robes
> It is like the *heavy* dew of *Mount* Hermon *in Syria*,
> falling on Mount Zion.
> For here, *in Jerusalem*, YHWH commands his blessing:
> life for evermore.'

Michal's Contempt for David[127]

When the Ark of YHWH had been brought into the City of David, Michal, Saul's daughter, had been looking out of the *palace* window. She had seen King David leaping and dancing and laughing before YHWH *in his linen ephod*, and *she had come to* despise him in her heart.

So when David returned *home* to bless his *own* house, Michal, daughter of Saul, came out to meet him. She said, 'How the king of Israel has dignified himself today. He has uncovered *himself* in *full* sight of his servants' handmaidens, in the same way that a fool reveals *himself*.'

But David said to Michal, '*It was* before YHWH. He chose me over your father and over all your father's house. He appointed me ruler over the people of YHWH, over Israel. So I will laugh in YHWH's presence. I will become more contemptable than this. I will be brought low *even* in my *own* eyes. But I will be held in honour by the maidservants you have spoken about.'

Michal, Saul's daughter, did not have any children to the day she died.

The Gibeonites Avenged[128]

In the days of David, there was a famine year after year, for three years. So David sought YHWH's presence.

YHWH said, 'It is because of Saul and the blood guilt that is on his house, because he put the Gibeonites to death.' So the king summoned the Gibeonites to speak to them.

Now the Gibeonites were not Israelites, but a remnant of the Amorites. But *while* the Israelites had made a solemn vow to *spare* them, Saul, in his zeal for the sons of Israel and Judah, had sought to strike them down.

David said to the Gibeonites, 'What can I do for you? How can I correct *the injustice of the past* so *that you may* bless YHWH's inheritance?'

The Gibeonites answered him, 'We do not require silver or gold from Saul or his family, and it is not up to us to put anyone to death in Israel.'

So David continued, '*So* what do you ask that I should do for you?'

They said to the king, 'The man, *Saul*, the chosen one of YHWH, plotted

---

[127] 2 Samuel 6:16; 20-23 ; 1 Chronicles 15:29
[128] 2 Samuel 21:1-14

against us and persecuted us. *He wanted to* eliminate us from within the borders of Israel. So from his sons, let seven men be given to us. We will then "alienate" them before YHWH at Gibeah, Saul's *home town*.'

The king said, 'I will personally give *them to you*.' So the king took *seven of Saul's male descendants* and gave them into the hand of the Gibeonites. However, because of a solemn oath before YHWH, between David and Jonathan, son of Saul, the king spared Jonathan's son, Mephibosheth. The Gibeonites then *went* and 'alienated' them on the mountain before YHWH; the seven of them fell together.

The Seven Descendants of Saul Given to the Gibeonites

Sons	*Parentage*
Two sons: Armoni and Mephibosheth	Saul and Rizpah, daughter of Aiah
Five sons	Adriel, son of Barzillai the Meholathite and Merab, daughter of Saul

They were put to death in the first days of the harvest, at the beginning of the barley harvest.

But Rizpah, daughter of Aiah, *concerned that the bodies would be attacked by birds and wild animals*, took *some* sackcloth and spread it out on a rock. She *then sat on it* from the beginning of the harvest until the rains poured down on the bodies from the heavens. *Indeed*, she did not allow the birds of the air to rest on *the dead bodies* by day, or the wild animals *to attack* by night.

Now the Philistines had struck down Saul on *Mount* Gilboa, and that same day had hung the bodies of Saul and Jonathan, his son, *on the wall* at Beth Shan. *Furthermore*, men from Jabesh Gilead had stolen the *bodies* from the square at Beth Shan.

So when David was told what Rizpah, daughter of Aiah, Saul's concubine, was doing, he went to Jabesh Gilead. He took the *remains of the* bones of Saul and Jonathan from the people. He then took them to Benjamin, with the bones he had collected of those who had been 'alienated'.

The bones of Saul, his son Jonathan, *and the seven descendants*, were then buried at Zela, in the land of Benjamin, in the tomb of Kish, *Saul's* father.

Then, once the king's orders had been completely carried out, God answered *David's* prayer for the land.

Another Victory over the Philistines[129]

The Philistines came on another raid of the valley of Rephaim. They spread out in the valley. So David, again, enquired of God, of YHWH.

But YHWH said, 'Do not go after them *and confront them face-to-face. Instead,* circle around them *so you can* attack them from behind, in front of the balsam trees. When you hear the sound of marching in the tops of the balsam trees, look sharp. Then go out to battle, for YHWH will go ahead of you to strike against the Philistines' camp.'

David did just as YHWH had commanded him. He *and his men* struck down the Philistine army from Gibeon to Gezer.

David's name became well-known throughout the lands. Indeed, YHWH put the fear of David on all the nations.

David's Wars[130]

After this, David struck the Philistines. He humbled them and took control of Gath, the main city, and its surrounding villages.

He defeated Moab, *and although it was normal for all captured troops to be put to death, David let a third of them live.* He made the *troops* lie down on the ground and measured them with a cord. Every two lengths *of the cord* that were measured, *he had the men* killed. *Then, every third and* full length, he let *the men* live. So the Moabites became David's servants and brought tribute *to him.*

When David went to regain control of his *territory* along the River Euphrates, he also fought Hadadezer, son of Rehob, king of Zobah (*north of Damascus*). David captured one thousand chariots, seven thousand horsemen, and twenty thousand foot soldiers from him. He then hamstrung all the chariot horses, except for the hundred chariot horses that he kept for himself.

Arameans from Damascus came to help Hadadezer, king of Zobah, but David struck down twenty-two thousand men. David then placed garrisons in *the* Aramean *territory* of Damascus. Aram became David's servants and brought tribute *to him.*

David then took the gold shields that Hadadezer's servants had carried and brought them to Jerusalem. He *also* took a very large *quantity* of bronze from Betah and Berothai (*also known as* Tibhath and Cun), towns in Hadadezer's *kingdom.* (*This would be later used by* Solomon to make the bronze Sea, and the pillars and the articles of bronze *for the Temple.*)

---

[129] 2 Samuel 5:22-25; 1 Chronicles 14:13-17
[130] 2 Samuel 8:1-14; 1 Chronicles 18:1-13

Now Toi (*also known as* Tou), king of Hamath (*north of Zobah*), had been at war with Hadadezer. So when he heard that David had struck against Hadadezer's entire army, he sent his son, Joram (*also known as* Hadoram), to King David to seek peace with him. Toi congratulated David because he had fought against Hadadezer and defeated him. *Joram then gave David the* articles of silver, gold, and bronze that he had brought *him*.

Abishai, son of Zeruiah, *also* struck down eighteen thousand Edomites in the Valley of Salt. So garrisons were placed throughout the land. Indeed, garrisons were put everywhere in Edom. So the Edomites become David's servants *too*.

By the time that David returned from striking down eighteen thousand Edomites in the Valley of Salt, he had made a name *for himself*.
In this way, YHWH delivered David *from his enemies* everywhere he went.
King David then dedicated the articles *from Toi* and the plunder of Hadadezer, son of Rehob, king of Zobah, to YHWH. *Indeed*, he dedicated all the silver and gold from all the nations he had subdued: Aram, Edom, Moab, the Ammonites, the Philistines, and Amalek.

Set Backs[131]

Now not all of David's battles went well; some had to be fought many times. Indeed, the following psalm indicates that there were times when it was believed that YHWH had deliberately withdrawn his support. Nevertheless, bit by bit, with YHWH's guidance and support, David was able to reclaim the land that God had given his people.

Notes:
For the *musical* director.
To *the tune* 'Lily of the Covenant'.
A miktam (*perhaps a contemplative prayer*).
Of David.
For teaching.
When he struggled against Aram Naharaim and Aram Zobah.
When Joab returned and struck twelve thousand Edomites in the Valley of Salt.

David, to YHWH
'God, you have spurned us;
   you have broken through our *defences*;
   you have been angry—*so* turn back to us.

---

[131] Psalm 60:1-12

You have shaken the land, you have split it open.
>   Heal its breaches, for it is quaking.
You have made your people face harsh *times*;
>   you have given us wine that sends us reeling.
But for those who fear you, you have given a banner,
>   *that it might be* unfurled *to display* the truth.

>>>>>>> Selah

'Deliver with your right hand;
>   help us, so that your loved ones may be rescued.

>>>>> *David, to those around him*
'God has spoken from his sanctuary,
>   "I will rejoice. I will divide up Shechem;
>   I will measure out Succoth.
Gilead and Manasseh are mine;
>   Ephraim is the helmet on my head;
>   Judah is my sceptre.
Moab is my wash basin (*a possible reference to the Sea of Salt*);
>   I will fling my sandal upon Edom (*claiming ownership*).
>   I shout in triumph over Philistia."

>>>>>>> *David, to YHWH*
'Who will conduct me into the fortified city?
>   Who will guide me into Edom?
Is it not you, God, who spurned us?
>   Will you not go out with our armies?
Give us help against the foe,
>   for deliverance by man is useless.

>>>>>> *David, to those around him*
'With God we will achieve victory;
>   and he will trample over our foes.'

David's Song of Praise[132]

David spoke the words of this song to YHWH, on the day that YHWH delivered him from the hand of all his enemies, and from the hand of Saul. He said:

---

[132] 2 Samuel 22:1-51; Psalm 18:1-50

Establishing the Kingdom

Notes:
For the *musical* director.
Of David, a servant of YHWH.

David, to YHWH
'I love you, YHWH;
 you are my strength.

David, to those around him
'YHWH is my cliff, my *hillside* fortress,
 and my deliverer.
My God is my rock, in whom I seek refuge;
 he is my shield and the horn of my salvation.
He is my stronghold, my refuge, and my saviour.

David, to YHWH
'You deliver me from violence.

David, to those around him
'I call upon, and boast about, YHWH,
 and I am saved from those who are hostile to me.

'The breakers of death surrounded me;
 the flood waters of the worthless terrified me.
The cords of Sheol were tied around me;
 I was faced with the snares of death.
So in my distress I called, "YHWH";
 to my God I called out.
He heard my voice from his temple;
 my cry for help *reached* his ears.

'Then the earth shook and trembled;
 the foundations of the mountains (*or* heavens) became agitated.
 They were shaken, because he burned with anger.
Smoke rose from his nostrils;
 devouring fire from his mouth;
 out of him came burning coals.
He made an opening in the heavens and came down;
 heavy clouds were under his feet.
He mounted a cherub and flew;
 he appeared on the wings of the wind.

He made darkness a pavilion around him;
    dark clouds and a mass of water.
In the brightness of his presence,
    his clouds, hailstones, and coals of fire passed by.
YHWH thundered from the heavens;
    the Most High sent forth his voice,
    hailstones, and coals of fire.
He sent out arrows, and scattered his enemies;
    he flashed his lightning and confused them.
The channels of the sea *became* exposed;
    the foundations of the world were revealed.

'At the rebuke of YHWH,
    he reached down from above and took me.
At the blast of the breath of his nostrils,
    he drew me out of mighty waters.
He delivered me from my powerful enemy;
    from those who hate me,
    for they were too strong for me.
They confronted me on the day of my distress,
    but YHWH supported me.
He brought me out to *the safety of* an open place;
    he withdrew me *from where I was hemmed in*,
    because he delighted in me.

'YHWH has dealt with me
    in accordance with my righteousness;
He has repaid me
    in accordance with the cleanness of my hands.
For I have observed the ways of YHWH;
    I have not acted wickedly against my God.
Indeed, all his laws were before me;
    I did not turn away from his statutes.
I was blameless before him;
    I kept myself from sin.
So YHWH repaid me in accordance with my righteousness;
    in accordance with my cleanness before his eyes.

David, to YHWH

'With the devout you show yourself devout;
    with the blameless you show yourself blameless.
With the pure you show yourself pure;
    but with the perverted you show yourself perverted.

You deliver people who are humble;
> but your eyes are on the proud to bring them down.

Indeed, you light my lamp, YHWH;
> *you*, YHWH, shine in my darkness.

Indeed, with you I can run against a troop;
> with my God I can jump over a wall.

David, to those around him

'As for God, his way is perfect,
> the word of YHWH has been tested *in the furnace*;
> he is a shield to all who seek refuge in Him.

For who is God, but YHWH?
> Who is a rock, but our God?

God is my strength *and* my refuge;
> he makes my way complete.

He makes my feet like those of a deer;
> he enables me to stand on high places.

He trains my hands for battle,
> so that my arms can bend a bow of bronze.

David, to YHWH

'You gave me your shield of salvation;
> your right hand sustains me
> and your lowliness has made me great.

You widened my steps beneath me;
> my ankles didn't get twisted.

I chased after my enemies,
> overtook *them*, and destroyed them;
> I did not turn back until they were consumed.

I crushed them, I shattered them;
> they were unable to rise, they fell under my feet.

You equipped me with strength for battle;
> you bowed down those who took a stand against me.

You gave me the necks of my enemies;
> I put an end to those who hate me.

David, to those around him

'They gazed, crying out for help, but there was no one to deliver *them*;
> *they cried out* to YHWH, but he did not answer them.

I beat them as fine as the dust of the earth before the wind;
> I crushed *and* stamped *on them*, like mud in the streets.

David, to YHWH

'You have delivered me from the strife of my *own* people;
    you have preserved me as head of the nations.
People I have not known *now* serve me.
Foreigners fawn obedience to me;
    when they hear *me*, they obey me.
Foreigners have lost heart;
    they gird themselves *before leaving* their strongholds.

David, to those around him

'As YHWH lives, blessed is my rock;
    may God, the rock of my salvation, be exalted.
He is the God who gives me vengeance;
    he is the one who puts people under my *authority*.
He has brought me out and saved me
    from those who are hostile to me;
he has raised me up above my foes;
    he has delivered me from men of violence.

David, to YHWH

'For this, YHWH, I will raise you up among the nations;
    I will make music to your name,
        to the one who gives great victories to his king.

David, to those around him

'YHWH is a tower of salvation to his king;
    he shows his unfailing love to his anointed,
        to David, and his offspring forever.'

David's Plans for a Temple [133]

After King David had settled in his house and YHWH had given him rest from all his surrounding enemies, the king spoke to Nathan the prophet. *He said*, 'Look, I am now living in a house of cedar, while the Ark of God remains within curtains.'

So Nathan said to the King David, 'Go ahead! Do all that you have in mind, for God. YHWH, is with you.'

But that night the word of YHWH came to Nathan, saying, 'Go! Tell my servant David, "This is what YHWH says: 'Will you build me a house to dwell in? I have not dwelt in a house since the day the sons of Israel brought me out

---

[133] 2 Samuel 7:1-17; 1 Chronicles 17:1-15

of Egypt. Even to this day I have moved about in a tent; *I have lived* in a Tabernacle. Wherever I have gone with all the Israelites, have I *ever* said a word to any of the rulers of Israel? *Have I ever* said *to those* I have charged with shepherding my people, Israel, "Why have you not built me a house of cedar?"?"'

'Now then, tell this to my servant, David. "This is what Almighty YHWH says: 'I myself took you from the pasture, from tending the flock, to be ruler over my people Israel. I have been with you everywhere you have gone. I have cut off all your enemies from your presence. But now I will make your name great, like the names of the great *men* on the earth. I will establish a place for my people, Israel. I will plant them so they may settle in their place; they will not be disturbed again. The wicked will no longer afflict them, as they have done since the day I appointed judges over my people Israel. I will humble all your enemies. I will give you rest from everyone who is hostile to you.

"'YHWH declares to you, that he will make you a house. When your days come to an end and you lie down with your fathers, I will raise up your offspring to follow *in your footsteps*. He will be *one* of your sons. He will come forth from your body and I will establish his kingdom. He will build a house for my name and I will establish the throne of his kingdom forever. I myself will be a father to him and he will be a son to me. When he does wrong, I will discipline him with a rod *like* men *use*, with the strokes *inflicted by* mankind. But I will not turn my covenant love away from him, as I turned it away from Saul, whom I removed from your presence. I will set him over my house and my kingdom forever. Your house and your kingdom will endure before me forever; your throne and his throne will be established forever.""'

So Nathan told David everything that was said and revealed *to him*.

David's Prayer[134]

King David went *to the tent* and sat before YHWH. He said, 'Who am I, Lord God YHWH? What is my house? *Why have you blessed me so much* that you have brought me to this point? Yet what you have done is insignificant in your eyes, Lord YHWH. You have also spoken of the future of your servant's house. You have seen me as man of high rank, YHWH God. *You have given* this man direction.

'What more can David say to you for honouring your servant, for you know your servant, Lord YHWH?

'For the sake of your servant and your promise, and in accordance with your will, you have done this great thing. You have made known all these great things; you have made them known to your servant. For this reason *alone* you

---

[134] 2 Samuel 7:18-29; 1 Chronicles 17:16-27

are great, Lord YHWH. *There is* no one like you. According to everything that we've heard with our ears, *there is* no God except you.'

He thought to himself, 'Israel is the one nation on earth that God came and redeemed for himself as a people, to make a name for himself. He performed great and fearful wonders in the presence of his people, whom he redeemed for himself from Egypt. He drove out nations, and their gods, from his people's presence.'

Then he continued to YHWH, 'Who is like your people, Israel? You established your people Israel for yourself, as a people forever. You yourself, YHWH, have become their God.

'So now, YHWH God, you have made this promise concerning your servant and concerning his house. Let it stand forever! Do as you have said, so that your name will be great forever. *People will* say, "Almighty YHWH, the God of Israel is God to Israel." So may the house of your servant David be established before you, for you are Almighty YHWH, God of Israel. You, my God, have revealed in your servant's ear, "I will build a house for you." For this *reason,* your servant has found the courage to pray this prayer in your presence.

'So now Lord YHWH, you are God. Your words are true and you have promised these good *things* for your servant. So, I pray, may it please *you* to bless the house of your servant. May it continue forever in your presence. For you yourself, Lord YHWH, have spoken. You, YHWH, have blessed, and with your blessing the house of your servant will be blessed forever.'

David's Officials[135]

David reigned over all Israel; he administered justice and equity for all his people.

David's Officials	
Name	*Position*
Joab, son of Zeruiah	In charge of the army
Jehoshaphat, son of Ahilud	Recorder
Zadok, son of Ahitub	Priest
Ahimelech, son of Abiathar	Priest
Seraiah (*or* Shavsha)	Secretary
Benaiah, son of Jehoiada	In charge of the Kerethites and Pelethites (*foreign mercenaries*)
David's sons	Priests *and/or* the king's officials

---

[135] 2 Samuel 8:15-18; 1 Chronicles 18:14-17

Establishing the Kingdom

David and Mephibosheth[136]

After he had established his kingship in Israel and had achieved a time of relative peace with his neighbours, David's focus shifted to the succession of the throne. He was particularly concerned that some of Saul's relatives may have survived to reclaim it. Indeed, he wanted to know where they were, so he could keep an eye on them.

So David said, 'Is there anyone remaining from the house of Saul, that I may show him kindness for Jonathan's sake?'

Now there was a servant from Saul's household, whose name was Ziba. So they summoned him to David.

The king said to him, 'Are you Ziba?'

He replied, '*I am* your servant.'

The king said, 'Is there anyone from the house of Saul to whom I can show God's kindness?'

Ziba said to the king, 'There is still one of Jonathan's sons; he is crippled in both feet.'

So the king said to him, 'Where is he?'

Ziba said the king, 'He *lives* in the house of Makir, son of Ammiel, in Lo Debar.' So King David sent *for him*, and had him brought from the house of Makir, son of Ammiel, in Lo Debar.

When Mephibosheth, son of Jonathan the son of Saul, came to David, he fell on his face; he bowed down *before the king*.

David said, 'Mephibosheth!'

He said, '*I am* here. *I am* your servant.'

David said to him, 'Don't be afraid. I am going to treat you with great kindness for the sake of your father, Jonathan. I will return all the land of your grandfather, Saul, to you. Furthermore, you will regularly eat food at my table.'

He bowed and said, 'Who is your servant, that you take notice of a dead dog like me?'

Then the king summoned Ziba, Saul's servant, who had fifteen sons and twenty servants. He said to him, 'I have given to your master's *grand*son everything that belonged to Saul and his family. You and your sons and your servants are to work the land for him. You are to bring in *the produce*, so that your master's *grand*son may have food. But Mephibosheth, your master's *grand*son, will eat regularly at my table.'

Ziba said to the king, '*I am* your servant. Everything that my lord, the king, commands, so his servant will do.'

---

[136] 2 Samuel 9:1-13

David thought to himself, 'Mephibosheth *will be* eating at my table, like one of the king's sons. *There I can keep an eye on him.*'

Mephibosheth *also* had a young son named Mica.

Everyone who lived in the house of Ziba was a servant of Mephibosheth. But Mephibosheth lived in Jerusalem, because he was *not only* crippled in both feet but ate regularly at the king's table.

Battles Against Ammon and Aram[137]

Some time later, Nahash, king of the Ammonites, died, and Hanun, his son, became king in his place.

David said, 'I will be good to Hanun, son of Nahash, just as his father was good to me.' So David sent *some of* his servants *to deliver a message*, to console him concerning his father.

When David's servants arrived in the land of the Ammonites, the Ammonite officials spoke to their lord, Hanun.

They said, 'Is David *really* honouring your father by sending you messengers to console you? *Is that what* you see? Hasn't David sent his servants to you in order to search the city *and* the land, to spy it out *so that he can* overthrow it?' So, *as a serious insult to David and Israel, and symbolic of castration*, Hanun took David's servants, shaved off half of their beards, cut their garments in half at their buttocks, and sent them away.

When David was told *what had happened, and* how humiliated the men were, he sent *messengers* to meet them. The king said, 'Stay in Jericho until your beards grow back. Then return *to Jerusalem.*'

The Ammonites then saw that they had become a stench to David. So they sent for and hired *soldiers from among the* Arameans; Hanun and the Ammonites sent one thousand talents of silver to hire chariots and charioteers. So they came and set up camp near Medeba (*32 kilometres south of Rabbath-bene-ammon*). Meanwhile the Ammonites were gathered from their towns.

Aramean Soldiers (from 2 Samuel)

From	Number
Beth Rehob, Zobah	20,000 foot soldiers
King of Maacah	1,000 men
Tob	12,000 men

---

[137] 2 Samuel 10:1-19; 1 Chronicles 19:1-19

> **Aramean Soldiers (from 1 Chronicles)**
>
> | From | Number |
> |---|---|
> | Naharaim, Maacah, Zobah | 32,000 chariots |
> | King of Maacah | *unspecified number of* people |

When David heard, he sent Joab and the entire army of mighty men *to face them*.

The Ammonites came out *of their city* and drew up in battle formation outside the city gates, *and the* Aramaean kings *from* Zobah, Rehob, Tob, and Maacah *positioned* themselves in the fields.

When Joab saw that the battlelines were against him, in front and behind, he selected the best from Israel and readied *them* against the Arameans. He then put Abishai, his brother, in charge of the rest of the people and positioned them against the Ammonites.

Joab said, 'If Aram is too strong for me, then you are to come and save me. But if the Ammonites are too strong for you, then I will come to your aid. Be strong! Let us be strong for our people and for the cities of our God. YHWH will do *what is* good in his eyes.' So Joab, and the people who were with him, approached to fight against Aram.

But the Arameans fled before him, and when the Ammonites saw that the Arameans were fleeing, they also fled from Abishai into the city.

Then Joab returned from *fighting* the Ammonites and came to Jerusalem.

When the Arameans saw that they had been struck down by Israel, they gathered *themselves* together. *Indeed,* Hadadezer sent for and brought *together* Arameans who lived beyond the River *Euphrates*. They came to Helam, led by Shobach (*or* Shophach), the commander of Hadadezer's army.

When David was told, he gathered all Israel and crossed the Jordan *River*. He then came to them at Helam and drew up in formation against them. The Arameans lined themselves up against David and they fought him.

David killed seven hundred charioteers and forty thousand horsemen. He also struck down Shobach the commander of the army, who died there. So the Arameans fled from Israel's presence.

When all the kings, servants of Hadadezer, saw that they had been struck down by Israel, they made a covenant of peace with David and with Israel; they became their servants. So the Arameans were afraid, and were unwilling to assist the Ammonites again.

Wars Against the Philistines[138]

There was another war—the Philistines against Israel. So David, with his servants, went down and fought the Philistines. Ishbi-Benob, a descendant of the Rapha (*'giants'*), *was there*. The weight of his spearhead was three hundred *shekels* (*3.42 kilogrammes*) of bronze. He was also girded with a new *sword*.

David was very tired, *and unable to defend himself*, so the Philistine said, 'I will strike David down.' But Abishai, son of Zeruiah, came to his aid. He struck down the Philistine and killed him.

Then David's men swore to him, 'You will never come into battle with us again. That way the lamp of Israel will not be extinguished.'

After that, there was another battle with the Philistines at Gob (*or* Gezer). There Sibbecai the Hushathite struck down Saph (*or* Sippai), *another* descendant of the Rapha (*or* Rephaites), and the Philistines were humiliated.

Then there was another battle at Gob with the Philistines. Lahmi, the brother of Goliath the Gittite, had a spear whose shaft was like a weaver's beam. But Elhanan, son of Jaare-Oregim (*or* Jair) the Bethlehemite, struck him down.

Then there was another battle, at Gath. *This time they faced* a man, a giant, with six fingers on each hand and six toes on each foot—twenty four *digits* in total. He was also descended from the Rapha. He defied Israel, but Jonathan, the son of Shimeah, David's brother, killed him.

All four *opponents* were descendants of the Rapha in Gath. They *all* fell by the hands of David and his servants.

Bathsheba and the War with the Ammonites[139]

Spring was the dry season—the time when kings went off *to war*. So the following spring, David sent Joab with his servants, and the whole of Israel, *to fight the Ammonites*. So Joab led out the army and they destroyed the land of the Ammonites and besieged Rabbah. But David remained in Jerusalem.

Late one afternoon David got up from his bed, and *began* walking about on the roof of the king's house.

Now it was normal for people to wash and bathe on their roofs, particularly in the heat

---

[138] 2 Samuel 21:15-22; 1 Chronicles 20:4-8
[139] 2 Samuel 11:1-27a; 12:26-31; 1 Chronicles 20:1-3

of the day, and from the roof he saw a woman bathing. The woman was very beautiful in appearance, so he sent *one of his servants* to find out about the woman.

The servant reported *back*, 'It is Bathsheba, the daughter of Eliam, the wife of Uriah the Hittite.' David then sent messengers to get her. So she came to him and he lay with her. Then she returned to her home.

Now Bathsheba had been purifying herself from the uncleanness *of her menstrual period, so there was an increased possibility of pregnancy,* and the woman conceived. She then sent *a message* to David to tell him that she was pregnant.

So David sent *a message* to Joab, 'Send Uriah, the Hittite, to me.' So Joab sent Uriah to David.

When Uriah arrived, David asked regarding the welfare of Joab and the people, and *for a* report about the war. David said to Uriah, 'Go down to your house, and "wash your feet".' So Uriah left the king's house.

A gift from the king was sent after him. But Uriah did not go to his house. *Instead*, Uriah lay down at the entrance of the king's house with all his master's servants.

When David was told, 'Uriah did not go down to his house,' *he summoned him*.

David said to him, 'Haven't you come a long way? Why didn't you go down to your house?'

Uriah said to David, 'The Ark, Israel, and Judah are *all* living in tents; *indeed*, my master Joab and my lord's men are camping on the *battle* field. How then could I go to my own house to eat, drink, and lie with my wife? As surely as you live, I cannot do such a thing.'

David said to Uriah, 'Stay here today and tomorrow, *then* I will send you back.' So Uriah stayed in Jerusalem that day.

The following day, David invited him to eat and drink in his presence. *He* got him drunk. But in the evening when he left, Uriah didn't go back to his house, but lay down on his mat with his master's servants.

In the morning, David wrote a letter to Joab, *sealed with the king's seal*, and sent it by Uriah's hand. In the letter he wrote, 'Place Uriah at the front, facing the fiercest *part of* the battle, then pull back from him. Then he will be struck down and die.'

So while Joab kept watch on the city, he placed Uriah in the position where he knew the enemy was strongest. When the men of the city came out and fought against Joab, some of the people, David's servants, fell. Uriah the Hittite

Establishing the Kingdom

also *died*. Joab then sent *a message* telling David everything that had occurred in the battle.

He ordered the messenger, 'When you have finished telling the king everything that occurred in the battle, the king may be very angry. He may say, "Why did you get *so* close to the city? Didn't you know that they would shoot *arrows* from the wall? *After all,* who killed Abimelech, son of Jerub-Besheth (*Gideon*)? Wasn't it a woman who threw an upper millstone on him from the wall? *That's why* he died at Thebez. Why did you get so close to the wall?" If he does, say, "Your servant Uriah, the Hittite, is also dead."' So the messenger set out.

When the messenger arrived *in Jerusalem*, he reported to David everything that Joab had sent him *to say*. The messenger said to David, 'The men were too strong for us. They came out *of the city* and attacked us in the open. But we drove them back to the entrance, to the *city* gate. Then archers shot *arrows* at your servants from the wall. So some of the king's servants died; your servant Uriah the Hittite also died.'

David said to the messenger, '*Give* Joab this message, "Do not consider this matter to be evil in your eyes, for the sword devours one as it devours another. Fight harder against the city. Throw it down." Encourage him *with these words.*'

When Uriah's wife heard that her husband had died, she mourned for her husband. But after the *customary* period of mourning was over (*possibly seven days*), David sent *for her*. He had her brought to his house, and she became a wife for him.

Meanwhile, Joab fought against the Ammonites at Rabbah. Joab sent messengers to David, saying, 'I have fought against Rabbah, and have even taken the city's water *supply*. So gather the rest of the people; encamp against the city and capture it. *If you don't*, I will take the city myself and it will be named after me.'

So David gathered all the people and went to Rabbah. He fought against it and captured it. *He also captured the ceremonial* crown *which* weighed a talent (*34.2 kilogrammes*) of gold, which was *set with* a precious stone. *In this way*, he removed the *ceremonial* crown from their king's head. *Then, with assistance, it was placed* on David's head.

He then took a great amount of plunder from the city. He brought out the people *who lived* in the city, and set them to work, using saws, iron picks, and iron axes. He *also* set them to work making bricks.

He did this in every town belonging to the Ammonites. Then David, and all the people, returned to Jerusalem.

In this way, Joab struck Rabbah, the royal city, and threw it down.

Nathan's Parable[140]

But what David had done was evil in the eyes of YHWH. So YHWH sent Nathan to David. He went to him and said, 'There were two men *living* in the same city, one rich and the other poor. The rich *man* had a great many sheep and cattle, but the poor *man* had nothing except one small ewe lamb. He had bought it and raised it, and it had grown up with him and his children. It ate from his meagre scraps, drank from his cup, and slept on his chest. It was like a daughter to him.

'Now a traveller came to the rich man. But the man was reluctant to take from his *own* sheep or cattle to prepare *a meal* for his visitor. Instead, he took the poor man's ewe lamb and prepared it for the man who had come to him.'

At this, David's anger burned greatly against the man. He said to Nathan, 'As YHWH lives, the man who did this thing deserves to die. He must pay for the lamb four times *over*, because he did this thing, and because he *acted* without compassion.'

Nathan said to David, 'You are this man. YHWH, the God of Israel, says, "I am the one who anointed you king over Israel. I am the one who delivered you from the hand of Saul. I gave you your master's house; *I gave* your master's wives to your breast. I gave you the houses of Israel and Judah. But if that had not been enough, I would have given you much, much more.

'"Why have you despised the word of YHWH, by doing evil in my eyes? You have struck down Uriah the Hittite with the sword; you killed him with the sword of the Ammonites. You have *also* taken his wife to be one of your own. So because you have despised me and taken the wife of Uriah the Hittite to be your own wife, the sword will never depart from your house."

'This is what YHWH says, "Look, I will bring trouble upon you from *within* your *own* house. I will take your wives away while you are looking on, and I will give them to someone close to you. He will lie with your wives in broad daylight. Indeed, *what* you *have done* you have done in secret. But what I *am about to do* I will do openly before all Israel."'

David said to Nathan, 'I have sinned against YHWH.'

Nathan said to David, 'Yes, but YHWH has taken away your sin. You will not die. However, by your actions *you have given* YHWH's enemies *grounds* to show their utter contempt *for him*. The son *that is* to be born to you will surely die.'

Then Nathan went to his house.

But David was contrite for what he had done. He recognised the serious position he had put himself in with his God, and he realised that he needed to be ritually cleansed before God.

---

[140] 2 Samuel 11:27c-12:15a; Psalm 51:1-19

Notes:
For the *musical* director.
A psalm of David.
When Nathan the prophet had come to him,
after he had gone into Bathsheba.

David, to YHWH
'According with your covenant love,
    have mercy on me, God.
As is fitting with your abundant compassion,
    wipe out my transgressions.
Wash away my many iniquities;
    cleanse me from my sin.

'For I know my offences;
    my sin is continually before me.
I have sinned against you, *and* you alone;
    I have done *what is* evil in your eyes.
As a consequence, when you speak you are just;
    when you judge, you are without blame.
Surely I was brought into this world in iniquity;
    my mother conceived me in sin.
But you delight in truth in the innermost being;
    you teach me wisdom in *my* hidden parts.

'Purify me with hyssop and I will be clean;
    wash me and I will be whiter than snow.
Let me hear joy and gladness;
    let the bones that you crushed rejoice.
Conceal your face from my sins;
    wipe out all my wrongful acts.

'Create a pure heart within me, God;
    renew an unshakeable spirit in my inmost parts.
Do not have me removed from your presence;
    do not take your holy spirit away from me.
Restore the joy of your deliverance to me;
    sustain me with a noble spirit.
I will *then* teach those who rebel against your ways,
    so the sinful will turn back to you.

'Deliver me from *my own* bloodshed, God;
>   *for you are the* God of my salvation.
> My tongue will cry out your righteousness.
> Open my lips, lord,
>   that my mouth may declare your praise.
> For you take no delight in sacrifice;
>   if I were to offer a Burnt Offering,
>   you would take no pleasure it.
> *Rather*, the sacrifice *acceptable to* God is a shattered spirit;
>   God does not despise a shattered and crushed heart.

'In your benevolence be good to Zion;
>   build the walls of Jerusalem.
> Then you will delight in righteous sacrifices—
>   Burnt Offerings (*that is*, whole *Burnt* Offerings);
>   then bulls will be offered on your altar.'

David's Vigil[141]

In due time, Bathsheba bore David a son. But YHWH struck the child that the wife of Uriah the Hittite had born to David; the child became very weak.

So David enquired of God regarding the child. He went on a special fast, and *even* lay on the ground when he went in to spend the night. The elders of his household stood beside him to get him up off the ground, but he refused to eat food with them. Then on the seventh day the child died.

David's servants were afraid to tell him that the child was dead, for they thought, 'Look, while the child was *still* alive we spoke to him and he refused to listen to us. How now can we tell him that the child is dead? He might do something rash.'

But David saw that his servants were whispering; he realised that the child was dead. So David said to his servants, 'Is the child dead?'

They said, 'He is dead.'

So David got up from the ground, washed, perfumed *himself*, and changed his clothes. He then went to the house of YHWH and bowed down *before God*. He then returned to his house and requested *food*.

So his servants set food before him, and he ate. His servants said to him, 'What is it you are doing? While the child was alive, you fasted and wept. But now the child is dead, you get up and eat food.'

He said, 'While the child was still alive, I fasted and wept. I said *to myself*, "Who knows, YHWH may be gracious to me. He may let the child live." But

---

[141] 2 Samuel 11:27b; 12:15b-24a

now he has died, why should I *continue to* fast? Can I bring him back *to life* again? I can go to him, but he cannot return to me.'

Then David comforted Bathsheba, his wife. He went to her and lay with her.

The Birth of Solomon[142]

Bathsheba bore a son, and she named him Solomon (*'peace' or 'replacement'*). YHWH loved him, and he sent *a message* by Nathan the prophet. So David called him Jedidiah (*'beloved of YHWH'*), because of YHWH.

David's Wives in Jerusalem[143]

After he had left Hebron and came to Jerusalem, David took more concubines and wives, and more sons and daughters were born to him.

The Names of Children Born to David in Jerusalem
Shammua
Shobab
Nathan
Solomon
Ibhar
Elishua
Elpelet
Nogah
Nepheg
Japhia
Elishama
Eliada (*or* Beeliada)
Eliphelet

The Mighty Men of David[144]

These are the names of the mighty men, who supported David. They, with all Israel, had made him king over Israel, as YHWH had promised.

(See table on next page)

---

[142] 2 Samuel 12:24b-25
[143] 2 Samuel 5:13-16; 1 Chronicles 14:3-7
[144] 2 Samuel 23:8-12, 18-39; 1 Chronicles 11:10-14; 20-47

Establishing the Kingdom

The Three Mighty Men of David

Chief of the three: Josheb-Basshebeth, a Tahkemonite (*also known as* Jashobeam, son of Hacmoni)

On one occasion he wielded his spear, and pierced three hundred *men* (*1 Chronicles*) *or* eight hundred *men* (*2 Samuel*).

Next *in line*: Eleazar, son of Dodai, the Ahohite

One of the three mighty men who were with David when they defied the Philistines gathered at Pas Dammim for battle. They took their stand in a field of barley. When the men of Israel fled, the mighty men remained in the middle of the field. They defended it and struck down the Philistines. Eleazar's hand grew weary, although his hand clung to the sword. YHWH brought a great victory that day. The people then returned to Eleazar, *but* only to strip *the dead*.

Next *in line*: Shammah, son of Agee, the Hararite

The Philistines had gathered at Lehi, in a plot of land filled with lentils. The people fled from the Philistines, but he took his stand in the middle of the field. He defended it and struck down the Philistines. YHWH brought about a great victory

Two Other Mighty Men

Chief of the thirty: Abishai, brother of Joab, son of Zeruiah

On one occasion, he used his spear against three hundred *men and* killed *them*. So his name *was as well-known* as the three, but he did not become one of them. However he was the most honoured by the thirty and became their commander

In charge of David's bodyguard (appointed by David): Benaiah, son of Jehoiada, from Kabzeel

A strong man, *known for his* mighty deeds. He struck down two sons of Ariel of Moab; he went into a pit, on a snowy day, and killed a lion; and he struck down an impressive Egyptian man, five cubits tall (*2.3 metres*). The Egyptian may have had a spear, like a weaver's beam, in his hand, but Benaiah attacked him with a club. He then tore the spear from the Egyptian's hand, and killed him with his spear. These were the *sort of* things that he did, and *he made a* name *for himself* among the three mighty *men*. He was greatly honoured by the thirty, but did not become one of the three

The 'Thirty'

The List from 2 Samuel[1]	*The List from 1 Chronicles[1]*
Asahel, brother of Joab	Asahel, brother of Joab
Elhanan, son of Dodo, from Bethlehem	Elhanan, son of Dodo, from Bethlehem
Shammah, the Harodite	Shammoth, the Harodite
Elika, the Harodite	
Helez, the Paltite	Helez, the Pelonite
Ira, son of Ikkesh, the Tekoaite	Ira, son of Ikkesh, the Tekoaite
Abiezer, the Anathothite	Abiezer, the Anathothite
Mebunnai, the Hushathite	Sibbecai, the Hushathite
Zalmon, the Ahohite	Ilai, the Ahohite
Maharai, the Netophathite	Maharai, the Netophathite
Heleb, son of Baanah, the Netophathite	Heled, son of Baanah, the Netophathite
Ithai, son of Ribai, from Gibeah in Benjamin	Ithai, son of Ribai, from Gibeah in Benjamin
Benaiah, the Pirathonite	Benaiah, the Pirathonite
Hiddai, from the brooks of Gaash	Hurai, from the brooks of Gaash
Abi-Albon, the Arbathite	Abiel, the Arbathite
Azmaveth, the Barhumite	Azmaveth, the Baharumite
Eliahba, the Shaalbonite	Eliahba, the Shaalbonite
The sons of Jashen	Sons of Hashem the Gizonite
Jonathan *son of* Shammah the Hararite	Jonathan, son of Shagee the Hararite
Ahiam, son of Sharar the Hararite	Ahiam, son of Sacar the Hararite
Eliphelet, son of Ahasbai, son of the Maacathite	Eliphal, son of Ur
Eliam, son of Ahithophel the Gideonite	
	Hepher, the Mekerathite
	Ahijah, the Pelonite
Hezro, the Carmelite	Hezro, the Carmelite
Paarai, the Arbite	Naarai, son of Ezbai
Igal, son of Nathan from Zobah	
	Joel, brother of Nathan

(Continued on next page)

> *(Continued from previous page)*
>
> | | |
> |---|---|
> | The son of Haggadi | Mibhar, son of Hagri |
> | Zelek, the Ammonite | Zelek, the Ammonite |
> | Naharai, the Beerothite[2] | Naharai, the Berothite[2] |
> | Ira, the Ithrite | Ira, the Ithrite |
> | Gareb, the Ithrite | Gareb, the Ithrite |
> | Uriah, the Hittite | Uriah, the Hittite |
> | | Zabad, son of Ahlai |
> | | Adina, son of Shiza the Reubenite[3] |
> | | Hanan, son of Maacah |
> | | Joshaphat, the Mithnite |
> | | Uzzia, the Ashterathite |
> | | Shama, son of Hotham the Aroerite |
> | | Jeiel, son of Hotham the Aroerite |
> | | Jediael, son of Shimri |
> | | Joha, the Tizrite, *son of Shimri,* brother of Jediael |
> | | Eliel, the Mahavite |
> | | Jeribai, son of Elnaam |
> | | Joshaviah, son of Elnaam |
> | | Ithmah, the Moabite |
> | | Elial |
> | | Obed |
> | | Jaasiel, the Mezobaite |
>
> *Notes:*
> [1]*There are more than 30 names in each of the lists. That suggests that the number of Mighty Men may have been fairly fluid. These lists would include both casualties and their replacements*; [2]Naharai was the armour bearer of Joab, son of Zeruiah; [3]Adina was chief of the Reubenites, and had thirty Reubenites with him

Including Joab, there were *normally* a total of thirty-seven *mighty men*.

C22. DAVID
(1040-970 BC)

b). A Problem of Succession *(991-975 BC)*

Amnon's Violation of Tamar[145]

Absalom, son of David, had a beautiful sister named Tamar and, over time, Amnon, David's *eldest* son, fell in love with her. But, even though she was a virgin, Amnon could not see how a relationship with her could be possible. Indeed, Amnon became so tormented regarding Tamar, his *half*-sister, that he became ill.

Now Amnon had a friend named Jonadab, the son of Shimeah, David's brother. He was a very crafty man.

Jonadab said to him, 'King's son, why are you so downcast morning after morning? Won't you tell me?'

So Amnon said to him, 'I am in love with Tamar. *She is* the sister of my brother Absalom.'

Jonadab said to him, 'Lie down on your bed and pretend to be ill. When your father comes to see you, ask him, "Please let Tamar, my sister, come and give me food to eat. Let her prepare food in my presence, so that I may see it. Then I can eat it from her hand."'

So Amnon lay down *on his bed* and pretended to be ill.

When the king came to see him, Amnon said to the king, 'Please let my sister, Tamar, come and make *some* cakes in my presence; two cakes that I can eat from her hand.' So David sent *a message* to Tamar at *Absalom's* house.

He said, 'Go now to the house of Amnon, your brother. Prepare him *some* food.' So Tamar went to the house of Amnon, her brother. *She found him* lying down. So she took *some* dough, kneaded *it*, and made cakes while he watched on. She then baked the cakes, took the pan, and served him. But he refused to eat.

Amnon said, 'Dismiss all my servants from my presence.' So all his servants left him. Then Amnon said to Tamar, 'Bring the food into the *bed* chamber, so that I may eat from your hand.' So Tamar took the cakes that she had prepared and brought them to her brother, Amnon, in his *bed* chamber.

As she was drawing near to him with the food, he grabbed her. He said to her, 'Come! Come lay with me, my sister!'

But she said, 'No, my brother, do not violate me, for such *things* should

---

[145] 2 Samuel 13:1-22

not be done in Israel. Don't do this disgraceful thing. *Where would it leave* me? Where would I go in my shame. *Furthermore, where would it leave* you? You would be *treated* like one of the fools in Israel. Please speak to the king; he will not withhold me from you.' But he was unwilling to heed her voice. *Then, as* he was stronger than she was, he violated her.

But *as soon as he had done so*, he felt a hatred for her—a very great hatred. Indeed, the hatred he felt was greater than the love he had *previously* felt for her.

Amnon said to her, 'Get up! Get out!'

But she said to him, 'No! Don't send me away! That would be a greater wrong than what you have just done to me.' But he was unwilling to listen to her.

So he called to the young man who attended him. He said, 'Remove this woman from my presence. *Put her* outside and bolt the door behind her.' So the attendant put her outside and bolted the door behind her.

Now the daughters of kings, who were virgins, wore long-sleeved robes. *So* Tamar put ash on her head, and tore the long-sleeved robe she was wearing. She then put her hand on her head and returned weeping *to her brother's house*.

Her brother, Absalom, *saw her, and realised what had happened. But he didn't offer any comfort. Indeed, he seemed more concerned with protecting the family name.*

He said to her, 'Has Amnon, your brother, been with you? Now be silent, my sister, he is your brother. Do not take this matter to heart.'

Despite that, from that day onwards Absalom refused to speak to Amnon, either good or bad. Absalom hated Amnon because he had violated his sister, Tamar.

In due course, King David heard all that had happened, and became very angry. But Tamar lived *the rest of her life*, a lonely *woman*, in the house of Absalom, her brother.

Absalom's Revenge on Amnon[146]

Two years later, Absalom *was* at Baal Hazor, near Ephraim, (*possibly 19 kilometres north east of Jerusalem*). He *was there with his sheep* and his shearers—*a traditional time for a feast*. So Absalom invited all the king's sons *to a feast*.

Absalom went to the king and said, 'Look, your servant is shearing, so will the king and his officials please come *and join in the feast* with your servant?'

But the king said to Absalom, 'No, my son, we cannot all go. We would be a burden to you.'

Although Absalom urged him, he would not go. But he blessed him *instead*.

So Absalom said, 'If *you will* not, please let Amnon, my brother, go with us.'

---

[146] 2 Samuel 13:23-39

The king said to him, 'Why should he go with you?' But Absalom urged him. So David sent Amnon with all the king's sons *to the feast.*

When Absalom *returned to Baal Hazor, he* ordered his servants, 'Look, when Amnon's heart is merry with wine, I will say to you, "Strike down Amnon!" Then *you are to* kill him. Do not be afraid, I have personally ordered you *to do so.* So be strong! Be brave!'

So Absalom's servants did to Amnon as Absalom had ordered.

Then the king's sons, *fearing for their lives,* stood up, mounted their mules, and fled. Absalom also fled, *but in the opposite direction.*

As the king's sons were returning *to Jerusalem,* a report was given to David. *He was told* that Absalom had struck down all the king's sons; not one of them was left. So the king stood up, tore his clothes, and lay down on the ground. Then all his servants tore their clothes, but remained standing.

But Jonadab, the son of Shimeah, David's brother, said, 'My lord should not say that all the young men have been killed; of *all* the king's sons, only Amnon will be dead. Absalom has been set on this since the day Amnon violated his sister, Tamar. So now, my lord the king, do not take this report to heart—the one that says that all the king's sons are dead—because Amnon, and only Amnon, will be dead.'

Now there was a young man, *a city* watchman, and he looked up. He saw many people coming from the road behind him by the side of the mountain.

Jonadab said to the king, 'Look, the king's sons are coming. As your servant has said, so it has happened.'

Immediately he finished speaking, the king's sons arrived, raising their voices and weeping. The king and all his servants *also* wept—a very bitter weeping.

David mourned for his son every day.

Now *when* Absalom had fled, he had gone to Talmai, son of Ammihud, king of Geshur *(near Damascus).* He remained in Geshur for three years. *Meanwhile,* King David was consoled over the death of Amnon, but longed to go to Absalom.

Reconciliation with Absalom[147]

Joab, son of Zeruiah, realised that the king's heart *yearned* for Absalom, so he sent *a message* to Tekoa and had a wise woman brought from there.

He said to her, 'Please *act as if* you are in mourning. Put on mourning

---

[147] 2 Samuel 14:1-33

clothes, don't use any perfume, and pretend to be a woman who has been grieving for the dead for many days. Then go to the king and speak to him the words *I will give you*.' Then Joab put words into her mouth.

So the woman from Tekoa *went* to the king to speak *to him*.

She fell on her face to the ground, and bowed down *before him*.
She said, 'Help, King!'
The king said to her, 'What *is* your problem?'
She said, 'Truly, I am a widow; my husband is dead.

'Your maidservant had two sons, and the two of them wrestled in a field; there was no one to keep them apart. Then one of them struck the other and killed him. But now the whole clan has risen up against your maidservant. They have said, "Give us the one who struck his brother. We will put him to death for the life of his brother; we will get rid of the *remaining* heir." *But if they do*, they will put out the remaining embers within me. They would leave my husband without name or descendant on the face of the earth.

'Now I came to tell my lord the king these words, because the people have made me fearful. Your maidservant said *to herself*, "I will speak to the king. Perhaps the king might respond to the words of his maidservant. Perhaps the king might listen. *He might* deliver his maidservant from the hand of the man who wants to cut off both myself and my son from the inheritance of God."

'So now your maidservant says, "Please let the word of my lord, the king, *bring me* comfort. For my lord, the king, is like an angel of God. He discerns good and evil. May YHWH, your God, be with you."'

The king said to the woman, 'Go to your house. I will personally give an order concerning you.'

But continuing the pretence, the woman from Tekoa said to the king, 'My lord *and* king, let the guilt be on me and my father's house. But let the king and his throne *be* without guilt.'

The king said, 'If someone speaks to you, bring him to me. He will not touch you ever again.'

Then she said, 'Let the king, I pray, call on YHWH, your God. *Let the* avenger of blood *be stopped from* adding to the destruction. Let them not destroy my son.'

He said, 'As YHWH lives, not a hair on your son's *head* will fall to the ground.'

Then the woman said, 'Please, let your maidservant say a word to my lord, the king.'

He said, 'Speak.'

The woman said, 'Why then have you considered such a thing against the people of God? By speaking this way, the king *has shown himself to be just as* guilty. The king has not brought his banished *son* back *home*. We will *all* surely die, like water spilled on the ground, which cannot be recovered. But God does not take life away. He works out ways so that anyone who has been banished may not remain distant from him.'

Then the king responded. He said to the woman, 'Please do not conceal the answer to what I am about to ask you.'

The woman said, 'Please speak, my lord the king.'

The king said, 'Has the hand of Joab been with you in all this?'

The woman answered. She said, 'As you live, my lord the king, no one can turn to the right or to the left regarding anything that my lord the king says. Your servant Joab did indeed command me. He put all these words into the mouth of your maidservant. Your servant, Joab, did this in order to reverse the present order. My lord is wise. *He has the* wisdom of an angel of God. *He knows* everything *that happens* in the land.'

David then dismissed the woman and summoned Joab.

The king said to Joab, 'Look, I will do this thing. So go, bring back the young man, Absalom.'

Joab fell on his face to the ground. He bowed down and blessed the king. Joab said, 'My lord the king, your servant knows that today I have found favour in your eyes. The king has granted your servant's request.'

But the king said, 'He is to go to his *own* house; he is not to come into my presence.' Then Joab got up *and left*.

So Joab went to Geshur and brought Absalom *back* to Jerusalem. *Indeed*, Absalom went to his *own* house and did not go into the king's presence.

Now there was no man as handsome as Absalom in all Israel. He was highly praised from the soles of his feet to the crown of his head. He was without blemish. He cut his hair at the end of each year, *but only* because it became too heavy for him. *When he did*, the hair from his head weighed two hundred shekels (*2.3 kilogrammes*) by the royal standard.

Absalom had three sons and one daughter. The daughter's name was Tamar (*possibly named after her aunt*), and she *grew up to be* a beautiful woman.

Absalom lived in Jerusalem for two years without *once* going into the king's presence. He then sent for Joab, *so* he could send him to the king. But Joab refused to come. So Absalom sent for him a second time. But again Joab did not come.

So Absalom said to his servants, 'Look, Joab's field is close by, *and he is growing* barley. Go and light it! Set it on fire!' So Absalom's servants *went and* set the field on fire.

Then Joab arose and came to Absalom's house. He said to him, 'Why have your servants set my field on fire?'

Absalom said to him, 'Look, I sent for you, saying, "Come here, so I can send you to the king." *I want you to* ask *him*, "Why have I come from Geshur? It would have been better for me to have remained there." I want to see the king's face. If there is *any* guilt in me, let him put me to death.' So Joab went to the king.

After *Joab* had reported to David *what Absalom had said*, the king summoned Absalom. So Absalom came to the king and bowed down to the ground before him. The king then kissed him.

Absalom's Conspiracy[148]

Some time later, Absalom acquired for himself a chariot, horses, and fifty men to run ahead of him. He used to rise early and stand beside the road to the *city* gate. When any man *came along*, who had a dispute to put before the king for judgement, Absalom would call out to him. He would say, 'What town are you from?' The man would reply, 'Your servant is from one of the tribes of Israel.' Then Absalom would say to him, 'Look, what you say is good and right, but there is no one to hear *your case* on the king's behalf.' Absalom *would then* say, 'If only I had been appointed judge in the land, then every man who has a dispute or judgement could come to me. Then I could give him justice.'

Now, as the king's son, it would have been normal for people to acknowledge his position. However, when someone came near to bow down before him, Absalom would *stop him. Instead, he would* stretch out his hand, take hold of him, and kiss him. Absalom behaved this way to every Israelite who came to the king seeking justice. So Absalom stole the hearts of the men of Israel.

At the end of four years, Absalom *went* to the king. He said, 'Please let me go to Hebron. Let me fulfil my vow—*the one* that I made to YHWH. For while your servant was living at Geshur, in Aram, I made a solemn vow. I said, "If YHWH will indeed take me back to Jerusalem, then I will serve YHWH."'

The king said to him, 'Go in peace.' So he arose and went to Hebron, *but not before* he had sent *messengers* on foot to all the tribes of Israel, saying, 'When you hear the sound of the trumpet, say, "Absalom is king in Hebron."'

Two hundred men then went with Absalom from Jerusalem. They knew nothing *of Absalom's plans*; they had been invited *as guests*, and went in *all* innocence. *They certainly didn't know they would be used as apparent supporters of his cause.* Then, while he was offering sacrifices, he sent for Ahithophel, the Gilonite, David's counsellor (*or, perhaps, former counsellor, as he was at* his *home* town of Giloh [*10 kilometres north of Hebron*] *and not with the king*).

In this way, the conspiracy grew in strength and the *number of* people with Absalom continued to increase.

---

[148] 2 Samuel 15:1-12

David's Flight from Jerusalem[149]

A messenger came to David, saying, 'The hearts of the men of Israel are with Absalom.' So David spoke to all his servants who were with him in Jerusalem.

He said, 'Come, we must take flight, otherwise there will be no escape for us from Absalom. We must go in haste; *we must* leave or he will quickly overtake us. He will bring misery down upon us and will strike the city with the edge of the sword.'

The king's servants answered the king, 'As all that my lord, the king, chooses, *we are* your servants.' So the king, with his entire household at his feet, set out. But the king left behind ten women—concubines—to look after the house.

So the king, and all the people at his feet, set out. They halted at the last house. There, all his servants paraded before him. In addition, all the Kerethites, Pelethites, and Gittites who had followed him from Gath—six hundred men—paraded before the king.

The king said to Ittai the Gittite, 'Why are you coming with us? Turn back! Remain with the *new* king. You are an alien and an exile from your home. *It seems like only* yesterday that you came *here*. So will I make you wander about with us today? I will only know where I am going, when I get there. So turn back, take your brothers, and may love and faithfulness be with you.'

But Ittai responded to the king. He said, 'As YHWH lives, and as my lord, the king, lives, *I make this solemn vow*. Wherever my lord, the king, finds himself, whether for death or life, there your servant will surely be.'

So David said to Ittai, 'Go! March on!' So Ittai, the Gittite, with all his men and all the children who were with him, marched on.

The whole land wept with a loud voice as all the people passed by.

Then the king crossed the Kidron brook *outside the city*, as all the people continued towards the road to the wilderness.

Zadok also *went with David, as did* all the Levites with him. They carried the Ark of the Covenant of God. But they *stopped and* set the Ark of God down, so that Abiathar could offer sacrifices until all the people had finished passing out of the city.

Then the king said to Zadok, 'Take the Ark of God back to the city. If I find favour in the eyes of YHWH, he will bring me back. Then he will let me see himself and his dwelling. But if he says, "I take no pleasure in you," then here I am. Let him do to me as is good in his eyes.'

The king then continued to Zadok, the priest, 'Are you *not* a seer? Go back

---

[149] 2 Samuel 15:13-37; Psalm 3:1-8

Establishing the Kingdom

to the city in peace. *Take* your son, Ahimaaz, and Abiathar's son, Jonathan. *Indeed*, both *you and Abiathar take* your sons with you. Look, I will wait at the fords in the wilderness until word comes from you letting me know *what is happening*.' So Zadok and Abiathar took the Ark of God back to Jerusalem and they remained there.

David then ascended the Mount of Olives, weeping as he went. His head was covered and he walked barefoot. All the people who were with him had their heads covered too. They wept as they went.

It was then reported to David that Ahithophel, *his former counsellor*, was among Absalom's conspirators. So David prayed, 'Please, YHWH, make Ahithophel's counsel foolishness.'

When David arrived at the summit, where God was worshipped, he saw that Hushai, the Arkite, had come to meet him. His robe was torn and he had dust on his head. David said to him, 'If you come with me, you will be a burden to me. But if you go back to the city, tell Absalom, "*My* king, I am your servant. In the past, I was your father's servant. But now I am your servant," then you can frustrate Ahithophel's counsel for me. Won't Zadok and Abiathar, the priests, be there with you? Tell Zadok and Abiathar, the priests, anything that you hear in the king's house. Their two sons, Ahimaaz, *son* of Zadok, and Jonathan, *son* of Abiathar, will be there with them. Send me anything that you hear by their hand.' So Hushai, David's friend, returned to the city.

Then Absalom entered Jerusalem.

Notes:
A psalm of David.
When he fled from the presence of his son, Absalom.

David, to YHWH
'How many adversaries *do I have*, YHWH?
    How many have risen up against me?
Many say about me,
    "There is no salvation for him in God."

                                                                 Selah

'But you, YHWH, are a shield around me;
    you are my glory, the one who lifts my head.

David, to those with him
'*With* my voice I cry to YHWH;
    he answers me from his holy mountain.

                                                                 Selah

'I lie down and sleep;
  I wake up, because YHWH provides for my needs.
I will not fear the multitude of people
  who circle against me on every side.

David, to YHWH

'Arise, YHWH!
  Deliver me, my God!
For you have struck on the cheek all those who are hostile to me;
  you have shattered the teeth of the wicked.
Deliverance *comes* from YHWH;
  your blessing *is* on your people.'

Selah

David and Ziba[150]

After David had travelled a little way from the summit, he saw Ziba, Mephibosheth's servant, coming to meet him. He was leading two donkeys, laden with two hundred *loaves of* bread, one hundred bunches of raisins, a hundred fig cakes, and a skin of wine.

The king said Ziba, 'Why *do you have all* this with you?'

Ziba said, 'The donkeys are for the king's household to ride. The bread and the fruit are for the young men to eat, and the wine is for those who get weary in the wilderness to drink.'

Then the king said, 'Where is your master's *grand*son?'

Ziba said to the king, '*As you can* see, he has remained in Jerusalem. He has persuaded himself, "That the house of Israel will return my *grand*father's kingdom to me today."'

The king said to Ziba, 'Look, all that belongs to Mephibosheth is yours.'

So Ziba said, 'I bow myself down *to you*. May I *always* find favour in your eyes, my lord the king.'

David and Shimei[151]

When King David reached Bahurim, *east of Jerusalem*, he saw a man coming out of the town. His name was Shimei, the son of Gera, from the clan of the house of Saul. He was coming in a determined manner, cursing. *When he got close enough*, he threw stones at David, the king's servants, and all the people and mighty men who were on David's right and left.

Then Shimei cursed him. He said, 'Get out! Go away, man of bloodshed,

---

[150] 2 Samuel 16:1-4
[151] 2 Samuel 16:5-14; Psalm 63:1-11

Establishing the Kingdom

you worthless fellow. YHWH has paid you back for all the bloodshed in the house of Saul, in whose place you have ruled. YHWH has given the kingdom into the hand of Absalom, your son. Now you yourself are facing misery, because you are a man of bloodshed.'

Abishai, son of Zeruiah, said to the king, 'Why should this dead dog curse my lord the king? Let me go over now and cut off his head.'

But David knew he was being punished by God for his sins; he accepted that the punishment was just. He also knew that if he approached his punishment with humility, God might ease his burden. So the king said, 'What *is it* to me and to you, sons of Zeruiah? He may be cursing because YHWH told him, "Curse David." Who then can ask, "Why are you cursing"?'

David then spoke to Abishai and all his servants. *He said*, 'Look, my son, the produce of my loins is seeking my life. How much more, then, this Benjaminite? Leave him alone. Let him curse, for YHWH *has* told him *to do so*. Perhaps YHWH will see my affliction. *He may then* repay me with good for the Benjaminite's curse today.'

Then David and his men *continued their* journey along the road, with Shimei following on the hillside opposite them. As he went, Shimei cursed and threw stones and dust at David.

In this way, the king, and all the people who were with him, arrived *at the Jordan River very* weary. So the king refreshed himself there.

Notes:
A psalm of David.
When he was in the wilderness of Judah.

David, to God

'God, my God,
    I constantly search for you.
My soul thirsts for you;
    my whole being faints for you,
    in a dry and weary land without water.

'I have seen you in the sanctuary,
    I have seen your might and your glory.
So my lips will praise you,
    because your covenant love is better than life.
For *as long* as I live, I will praise you;
    I will raise my hands *in prayer* in your name.
My soul will be refreshed, as with the choicest of foods;
    my mouth will boast with joyful lips.'

'I think of you on my bed;
    I meditate on you, through the watches of the night.
For you are my help,
    and in the shadow of your wings I sing for joy.
My soul clings to you;
    your right hand supports me.'

'But those who seek to destroy my life,
    will go down to the depths of the earth.
They will be delivered into the power of the sword;
    they will be prey for jackals.'

'But the king will rejoice in God;
    all who swear by God will boast of him.
Meanwhile, the mouths of those who tell lies
    will be shut.'

Conflicting Advice to Absalom[152]

Absalom, and all the people—the men of Israel—arrived in Jerusalem. Ahithophel was with him.

So Hushai, the Arkite, David's friend, went to Absalom.

Hushai said to Absalom, '*Long* live the king. *Long* live the king.'

Absalom said to Hushai, 'Why didn't you go with your friend? Is this the loyalty you show him?'

Hushai said to Absalom, 'No! *My loyalty is* to the one YHWH choses, to this people, and to all the men of Israel. I will be with him, and remain with him. In addition, whom should I serve if not his *father's* son? Just as I served in your father's presence, so I will *serve* in yours.'

Absalom *needed to consolidate his position,* so *he* said to Ahithophel, 'Give *us* your counsel. What shall we do?'

Now Ahithophel realised that Absalom needed to confirm his kingship; he needed to give the people reason for their support. He also realised that if Absalom had sexual relations with David's concubines, the people would accept that as his claim to the kingdom. So Ahithophel said to Absalom, 'Go into your father's concubines, the ones he left to maintain the house. All Israel will hear that you have made yourself a stench to your father. But the hands of all who are with you will be strengthened.' So they pitched a tent on the roof *of the king's house, so that* Absalom *could* go in to his father's concubines, in full view of all Israel.

---

[152] 2 Samuel 16:15-17:29

Now the counsel Ahithophel provided in those days was like one who enquired of the word of God. All Ahithophel's counsel to David and Absalom was like this. But YHWH had decided to frustrate Ahithophel's good counsel, so that he might bring Absalom ruin.

Then Ahithophel, *knowing that David would be tired and disorganised*, said to Absalom, 'Please let me choose twelve thousand men. I will then set out and pursue David tonight. I will come upon him while he is weary and disheartened. I will terrify him and all the people with him will flee. I will strike down the king alone, and I will bring all the people to you. When the man you are seeking is dead, all the men will return to you. *Then* all the people will be at peace.'

Now the plan seemed good in the eyes of both Absalom and all the elders of Israel. *However*, Absalom *was keen to seek further advice*. So he said, 'Summon Hushai, the Arkite. Let us hear *words* from his mouth too.'

When Hushai arrived, Absalom spoke to him telling *him* everything that Ahithophel had said. *He then said*, 'Should we do as he has said? If not, speak.'

Then Hushai said to Absalom, 'The counsel that Ahithophel has provided, this time, is not good.'

He then continued, 'You know that your father and his men are mighty men. They are fierce of spirit, like a bear robbed of *its* cubs in an open field. Your father is a man of war; he will not spend the night with the people. Look, *even* now he *will be* hiding in one of the caves or in some *other* place. So if your men should fall at the first *attack*, whoever hears the report will say. "There has been a slaughter among the people who follow Absalom." Then even the bravest *man*, whose heart is like the heart of a lion, will completely dissolve. All Israel will know that your father is a mighty *man*, and that brave men are with him.

'So I counsel that all Israel, from Dan *in the north* to Beersheba *in the south*, be gathered to you in the one place. *Then*, as numerous as the *grains of* sand that are by the sea, you yourself lead *them* into battle. Then we can go against him, wherever he may be found. We can fall on him, as dew falls on the ground. Then not one will be left alive; neither him nor any of the men that are with him. If he escapes into a town, all of Israel can bring ropes to that city. We can then drag the city into the valley until not one pebble can be found there.'

Then Absalom and all the men of Israel said, 'The counsel of Hushai, the Arkite, is better than the counsel of Ahithophel.'

Later, Hushai spoke to Zadok and Abiathar, the priests. *He told them* what Ahithophel had counselled Absalom and the elders of Israel. *He also told them* what he had advised them. *Then he continued*, 'Send a message immediately to David. Tell him, "Do not spend the night at the fords of the wilderness. Make sure you cross over *the Jordan River*, otherwise the king and all the people who are with him will be swallowed up.'"

Now Jonathan and Ahimaaz were waiting at En Rogel *close by*, so they wouldn't be seen entering *and exiting* Jerusalem. A maidservant was sent to inform them, so they could go and tell King David. But *they were seen*—a young man saw them and *went to* tell Absalom, *while* the two men, *knowing they had been seen*, rushed *off*.

They came to the house of a man in Bahurim who had a well in his courtyard. They climbed down it. The *man's* wife then took a covering and spread it over the mouth of the well. She then scattered grain *on the covering*, so that the existence of the well would be hidden.
Later, Absalom's servants came to the woman at the house. They said, 'Where are Ahimaaz and Jonathan?'
The woman said to them, 'They crossed the brook of water.' So they searched, but when they didn't find anyone they turned back to Jerusalem.
Then, once they had gone, the two men climbed out of the well, and left.

When they arrived at King David, they informed *him of everything that had happened*. They said 'Set out! Cross the water immediately, Ahithophel has counselled against you.'
So David, and all the people who were with him, set out and crossed the Jordan *River*. Indeed, by the break of day, *everyone* had crossed the Jordan *River*; not one person was left.

When Ahithophel saw that his counsel had not been acted upon, *he realised his dilemma. Faced with Absalom's coming defeat, and not wishing to face David again, he saw only one option*. So he saddled a donkey and left *Jerusalem*. He went to his *home* town, to his house, and put his house in order. Then he hanged himself. So he died and was buried in his father's tomb.
Meanwhile, David continued on to Mahanaim (*48 kilometres north east of the river crossing*).

On their arrival, *supplies* were brought *by the local people* for David and the people who were with him to eat. They said, 'The people are hungry, tired and thirsty *from being* in the wilderness.'

(See table on next page)

Now Absalom had set Amasa over the army in place of Joab. Amasa was the son of a man named Ithra. He was *an Ishmaelite, but considered* an Israelite,

Establishing the Kingdom

who had *in some way* gone in to Abigail, Nahash's daughter. *He was a cousin of both David and Joab.* Abigail, *however*, was Joab's mother's sister.

So *with Amasa leading them*, Absalom and all the men of Israel who were with him, crossed the Jordan *River,* and camped in the land of Gilead.

Supplies Given to David at Mahanaim

Providers	*Supplies*
Shobi, son of Nahash from Rabbah of the Ammonites	Beds, basins, articles of pottery, wheat, barley, flour, roasted grain, beans, lentils, honey, curds, sheep, cow's cheese
Makir, son Ammiel from Lo Debar	
Barzillai, the Gileadite from Rogelim	

The Death of Absalom[153]

David gathered the people who were with him. He then put commanders of thousands and commanders of hundreds over them.

Commanders *of David Army*

Commander	*Number under command*
Joab	One third
Abishai, son of Zeruiah, Joab's brother	One third
Ittai, the Gittite	One third

The king said to the people, 'I am determined to come with you.'

But the people said, 'You must not come, for if we have to flee, their hearts will not be set on us. Even if half of us die, their hearts will not be set on us. You are like ten thousand of us. It would be better that you remain in the city, where you can give us support.'

The king said to them, 'I will do what is good in your eyes.' The king, however, then gave an order to each of the commanders, in the hearing of the

---

[153] 2 Samuel 18:1-18

people, concerning Absalom. He commanded Joab, Abishai and Ittai, 'Treat the young man, Absalom, gently for my sake.' David then sent the people out.

So the king stood beside the gate, while all the people went out in their hundreds and thousands. So the people went out into the field to fight against Israel.

The battle began in the forest of Ephraim, but it spread over the whole countryside. Nevertheless, the forest devoured more people that day than the sword.

During the battle, Absalom was riding his mule when he came across *some of* David's servants. *He sped up to get away*, but as the mule went under the branches of a large oak tree, his head became caught in the tree. He was then left *hanging* between the heavens and the earth, while the mule that had been under him continued on.

One *of David's* men, who had seen, *went* and told Joab. He said, 'I have seen Absalom hanging in the oak.'

Joab said to the man, 'You saw him? Why, then, did you not strike him to the ground *right* there? If you had, I would have given you ten *shekels* (*114 grams*) *of* silver and a belt.'

But the man said to Joab, 'Even if a thousand *shekels* (*11.4 kilogrammes*) *of* silver were weighed into my hands, I would not have stretched out my hand against the king's son. The king commanded you, Abishai, and Ittai, in our hearing, "Keep the young man, Absalom, safe." Now nothing is hidden from the king. So *if I had killed him*, I would have been disloyal, risking my *own* life. Then even you would be keeping your distance from me.'

But Joab said, 'I will not wait *around* with you like this.' So he took three javelins in his hand *and went over to the* tree. Then, because Absalom was still alive in the heart of the tree, he thrust the spears into Absalom's heart. Ten young men, Joab's armour bearers, then gathered around Absalom. They struck him and killed him.

Joab then sounded the trumpet, halting the troops. So the people *immediately stopped their chase and* returned from pursuing Israel. They took Absalom's *body* and *gave it a burial fit for someone who was cursed*. They threw it into a deep pit in the forest and piled a heap of very large stones over it. Meanwhile, all the *remaining* Israelites fled, each to his *own* home.

So the Israelite army was defeated by David's servants in the forest of Ephraim. There was a great slaughter; *indeed*, twenty thousand men *were killed* that day.

Now it wouldn't have taken long for Absalom's grave to have become unidentifiable. However, while he was alive, Absalom had taken a pillar and erected it for himself in the Valley of the King. He had said *to himself*, 'I don't have a son to carry on my name.' So he had given the pillar his own name, and *even when this story was written down* it was still known as Absalom's Monument.

The Report of Absalom's Death[154]

Ahimaaz, son of Zadok, said, 'Let me run; let me bear the news to the king that YHWH has delivered him from the hand of his enemies.'

However, Joab knew how David would react to such news. Indeed, he was concerned for the welfare of any Israelite he might send. So he said to Ahimaaz, 'You are not the man *to carry* the news today. You may bear news another day. But you are not to take the news today, because the king's son is dead.'

Then Joab said to a Cushite *with the troop*, 'Go! Tell the king what you have seen.' So the Cushite bowed before Joab and ran off.

But Ahimaaz, son of Zadok, repeated his request to Joab, 'Whatever may happen, please let me run too. *Let* me *run* after the Cushite.'

Joab said, 'Why do you want to run, my son? You will receive nothing for bearing the news.'

But he said, 'Whatever happens, I want to run.'

So Joab said, 'Run!'

So Ahimaaz ran *the longer but easier route* by the way of the plain, and he outran the Cushite *who had taken the shorter route through the forest*.

When the watchman went onto the roof of the gate, by the wall, David was sitting between *the outer and inner* gates. The watchman raised his eyes, looked out, and saw a lone man running *towards them*. The watchman called out and reported *it* to the king.

The king said, 'If he is alone, he must be the bearer of good news.'

The runner got closer and closer. Then the watchman saw another man running.

The watchman called to the gatekeeper. He said, 'Look, *there is another* man running on his own.'

The king said, 'He too must be the bearer of good news.'

But the watchman said, 'I can see the first runner *a little better now*. He is running like Ahimaaz, son of Zadok.'

The king said, 'He is a good man. He is coming with good news.'

As Ahimaaz approached, he called out to the king. He said, 'Peace.' He then bowed before the king with his face to the ground. He said, 'Blessed be YHWH, your God. He has delivered up the men who raised their hand against my lord, the king.'

The king said, 'What of the welfare of the young man, Absalom?'

---

[154] 2 Samuel 18:19-33

Ahimaaz said, 'When the king's servant, Joab, sent your servant, I witnessed a great commotion. But I don't know what *it was about.*'

He then saw that the Cushite had arrived.

So the king said *to Ahimaaz*, 'Move aside! Wait over there!' So he moved aside and stood *there*.

The Cushite *then approached the king and* said, 'Let my lord, the king, hear the good news. YHWH has delivered *you*, today, from the hand of everyone who rose up against you.'

The king said to the Cushite, 'What of the welfare of the young man, Absalom?'

The Cushite said, 'May *all* the enemies of my lord, the king, be like that young man. *Indeed*, all who rise up against you to do you harm.'

At this news, the king was overcome *with grief*. So he went up to the room over the gate and wept. As he went, he said, 'My son, Absalom, my son. My son, Absalom. If only I myself had died, instead of you. Absalom my son, my son.'

David Mourns for Absalom[155]

Now it was reported to Joab, 'The king is weeping. He mourns for Absalom.' Indeed, all the people heard that the king was grieving for his son. So the victory was turned into mourning for the people. Indeed, later that day, as the people returned, they stole into the city. They stole in, like people who have been humiliated because they had fled from battle. Meanwhile, the king kept his face covered and cried out in a loud voice, 'My son, Absalom. Absalom, my son, my son.'

Joab went to the king's house. He said *to the king*, 'Today you have covered the faces of all you servants in shame. Today they saved your life, the lives of your sons and daughters, and the lives of your wives and concubines. *But you are acting as though* you love those who hate you and hate those who love you. You have demonstrated today that your commanders and servants mean nothing to you. Indeed, I know that if Absalom was still alive today, and all the rest *of us were* dead, then it would be pleasing in your eyes.

'So get up! Go! Speak to the hearts of your servants. For I swear by YHWH, that if you don't go, not one man will remain with you tonight. This will be worse for you than all the evil that you have faced, from your youth until now.' So the king got up and sat in the gateway.

All the people were then told, 'Look, the king is sitting in the gateway.' So all the people came before the king.

---

[155] 2 Samuel 19:1-8a

Establishing the Kingdom

Encounters at the Jordan River[156]

After Israel had fled, each to his *own* home, all the people in every tribe of Israel *then began* arguing.

They said *to their leaders*, 'King *David* delivered us from the hand of our enemies; he saved us from the hand of the Philistines. But he had to flee from the land because of Absalom, whom we anointed over us. But now Absalom has died in battle, why do you remain silent about bringing King *David* back?'

Word of what Israel was saying reached the king at his house *in Mahanaim*. So David sent *a messenger* to Zadok and Abiathar, the priests.

He said, 'Ask the elders of Judah, "Why will you be last to bring the king back to his house *in Jerusalem*? You are my brothers, my bone and my flesh. Why would you be the last to bring the king back?"'

He then made a move to reconcile the followers of Absalom with his own supporters— a move which recognised Joab's involvement in the death of his son. He said, 'Tell Amasa, "You are my bone and my flesh. May God deal with me, and continue to do so, if you are not the commander of my army from now on, instead of Joab."'

The hearts of all the men of Judah were turned; *they were* as one man. So they sent *a message* to the king, for him and his servants to return.

So the king *began his* return, and came as far as the *eastern side of the* Jordan *River*, while Judah came to Gilgal, *near the ford on the western side of the river*. They intended to meet the king and bring him *safely* across the Jordan *River*. *There were also a number of* Benjaminites with the men of Judah, who hurried to the meet the king.

Shimei, son of Geza, the Benjaminite from Bahurim, rushed to the Jordan, to the king, with the thousand men who were with him. So too did Ziba, the servant of the house of Saul, with his fifteen sons and his twenty servants. They *all* crossed the ford to *the eastern side, so they could help* bring the king's household over *the river*, and do what was good in his eyes.

As soon as Shimei, son of Gera, reached the *eastern side of* the Jordan, he fell down before the king.

He said to the king, 'My lord, do not hold me guilty. Do not remember the wrong your servant committed the day my lord the king left Jerusalem. May the king not take it to heart, for your servant knows that I am the one who sinned. *That is why*, of all the house of Joseph, *of all the northern tribes*, I am the first to come to meet my lord the king today.'

Abishai, son Zeruiah, replied, 'Shimei should be put to death for this. He cursed YHWH's anointed'

---

[156] 2 Samuel 19:8b-43

Establishing the Kingdom

But David said, 'What *is it* to me and to you, sons of Zeruiah? You come to me today as *though you were* an adversary. Should anyone in Israel be put to death today? Don't I know, today, that I am king over Israel?' Then the king said to Shimei, 'You will not be put to death.' The king then swore a solemn oath concerning him.

Mephibosheth, Saul's *grand*son, *also* came to meet the king. He had not *looked after himself* from the day the king had left *Jerusalem* until the day he returned in peace. He had not taken care of his feet, trimmed his moustache, or washed his clothes.

So when he came from Jerusalem to meet the king, the king said to him, 'Why didn't you come with me, Mephibosheth?'

He said, 'My lord, the king, my servant betrayed me. *As you know* your servant is lame. *Despite that*, your servant instructed, "Saddle my donkey for me; I will ride on it. Then I can go with the king." My servant has slandered your servant to my lord, the king. But my lord, the king, is like an angel of God. So do what is good in your eyes. For all my *grand*father's house are nothing but dead men before my lord, the king. Despite that, you set your servant a place with those who eat at your table. What right, then, do I have to make any other appeals to the king?'

Then the king, *clearly understanding that there was an element of truth in what Mephibosheth had said*, said to him, 'Why say anything further? I say to you that you and Ziba are to divide the land.'

Mephibosheth said to the king, 'Because my lord, the king, will be returning in peace to his house, let him take it all.'

Now Barzillai, the Gileadite, was a very wealthy man. *He was one of the men who had* provided *food* for the king during his stay at Mahanaim. *He* had *also* come from *his home at* Rogelim and had accompanied the king to the Jordan, to give him a send-off. But Barzillai was very old; he was eighty years of age.

But the king, *wishing to reward him*, said to him, 'Cross over with me. I will provide for you. *Stay* with me in Jerusalem.'

Barzillai said to the king, 'How many years have I left to live, that I should go with the king to Jerusalem? I am currently eighty years old. I *no longer* know right from wrong. Can your servant taste what he eats and drinks? Can he still hear the sound of men and women singing? Why should your servant be another burden to my lord, the king? Your servant will *come* a short *distance; he will* cross the Jordan with the king. But why should the king honour me *with* this reward?

'Let your servant return *home*. Let me die in my *own* town, near the grave of my father and mother.'

Then, presenting Kimham, probably one of his own sons, and hoping that David would give him the reward that he had promised, he continued, 'However, here is your servant

Kimham. Let him cross the Jordan *River* with my lord, the king. Do for him what is good in your eyes.'

The king said, 'Kimham will cross with me. I will personally do for him what is good in your eyes. Everything that you would want from me, I will do for you.' Then all the people crossed the Jordan *River* with the king.

The king then kissed Barzillai and blessed him. Then Barzillai returned to his home.

The king then went on to Gilgal, with Kimham. He was accompanied by all the people from Judah and half of the people from Israel. Soon, however, all the men of Israel had come to the king.

But tensions remained high between the people of Judah and Israel. So the men of Israel said to the king, 'Why have our brothers—the men from Judah—stolen you *from us*? They have brought the king, his house, and all the men who were with you, across the Jordan *River*.'

But the men of Judah answered the men of Israel. *They said, 'We brought* the king *across* because *he* is a close *relative* of ours. Why do you burn with anger about this? Have we eaten from the king's *supplies*? Have we taken anything for ourselves?'

But the men of Israel answered the men of Judah. They said, 'We have ten shares in the king. We *have a* greater *share* in David than you. Why then do you dishonour us? Weren't we the first to talk about bringing our king back?'

But the words of the men of Judah were harsher than the words of the men of Israel.

Sheba's Revolt[157]

Now there was a worthless fellow there, named Sheba, son of Bicri, a Benjaminite. He sounded the trumpet and shouted, 'We want no share in David. We want no part of the son of Jesse. Everyone to his *own* home, Israel!'

So all the men of Israel abandoned David *and* followed Sheba son of Bicri. Meanwhile, the men of Judah kept close to their king *on the journey* from the Jordan to Jerusalem.

So David arrived at his house in Jerusalem. The king then took the ten women, the concubines he had left to take care of his house, and put them in a house under guard. He provided for them, but did not go into them. They were confined, living as widows, until the day they died.

David then turned his attention to the problem of Sheba, son of Bicri.

The king said to Amasa, 'Summon the men of Judah. *Let them appear* before me *in* three days' time. Be here yourself too.' So Amasa went to summons *the*

---

[157] 2 Samuel 20:1-26

Establishing the Kingdom

men of Judah. But *the people were used to Joab leading them, and* it took him longer than the time that had been set. *However the task was urgent, and David needed to consider another plan.*

So David said to Abishai, 'Sheba, son of Bicri, will harm us more than Absalom. So take your lord's servants and chase after him. Otherwise he will find fortified cities for himself and disappear from sight.' So Joab's men, the Kerethites, the Pelethites, and all the mighty *men* went after him. They left Jerusalem to chase after Sheba son of Bicri, and Amasa caught up with them at the great rock in Gibeon (*10 kilometres north of Jerusalem*).

Now Joab was dressed in his tunic. He wore a belt strapped around his waist over his clothing, with a *short dagger-like* sword in its sheath *attached to his belt. But* as he stepped forward *to greet Amasa, he* slipped the sword out *of its sheath*.

Joab said to Amasa, 'Are you well, my brother?' Joab then grabbed Amasa's beard with his right hand *in order to* kiss him. Amasa did not see the sword in Joab's *left* hand. So Joab struck him with it in the belly and his intestines spilled out onto the ground. He did not need *to strike* him a second time.

So Amasa died.

One of Joab's men stood beside Amasa's *body*. He said, 'Whoever delights in Joab and whoever is for David, *let him* follow Joab.' Then Joab and Abishai, his brother, *continued their* pursuit of Sheba son of Bicri.

Amasa's *body* was left lying in a *pool of* blood in the middle of the road. So when Joab's man saw that people were stopping *to have a look*, he removed Amasa's *body* from the road *and put it in a* field. *Indeed*, realising that those who came to the body would stop, he threw a garment over the body. Then, once the body had been removed from the road, all the men continued with Joab to chase after Sheba, son of Bicri.

Now Sheba had travelled through all the tribes of Israel to Abel Beth Maacah, *near Dan, in the far north*. All of *his clan*, the Berites, had gathered together and joined him. So when Joab and his men arrived, they besieged Abel Beth Maacah. They built a ramp up to the city; it stood by the rampart. Then all the people who were with Joab began battering down the wall.

A wise woman called out from the city. *She said*, 'Listen! Listen! Tell Joab, "Come here, so I can speak to you."' So Joab came near to her.

She said, 'Are you Joab?'

He said, 'I am.'

She said to him, 'Listen to the words of your maidservant.'

He said, 'I am listening.'

She said, 'In former times *this city was well-known for its wisdom. Indeed*, it was said, "If you want a definitive answer, ask at Abel" *In this way, disputes would be settled. Now* I am someone who is peaceful and faithful in Israel. But you are trying to destroy a city, even a mother in Israel. Why would you swallow up the inheritance of YHWH?'

But Joab replied. He said, 'Never! I would never swallow up or destroy *the inheritance of YHWH*. Furthermore, that is not the case *here*. Rather a man from the hill country of Ephraim has raised his hand against the king, against David. His name is Sheba, son of Bicri. Give him, *and* him alone, *into my hand* and I will withdraw from the city.'

The woman said to Joab, 'Look, his head will be thrown over the wall to you.'

Then the woman went *and spoke* wisely to all the people. They cut off the head of Sheba, son of Bicri, and threw *it over the wall* to Joab. Joab then sounded the trumpet, and the men withdrew from the city. Each *man returned* to his *own* home, while Joab returned to Jerusalem, to the king.

David's Leading Men

Name	Position
Joab	The commander of Israel's whole army
Benaiah, son of Jehoiada	The commander of the Kerethites and Pelethites
Adoram	In charge of the forced labour
Jehoshaphat, son of Ahilud	Recorder
Sheva	Secretary
Zadok	Priest
Abiathar	Priest
Ira the Jairite	David's Priest

David's Census[158]

Now, in David's time, it was normal to attribute all things, good and bad, to YHWH. So when David decided to count the people, it was deemed that YHWH was the instigator of the decision. However, by the time of the Chronicler, people were far more sensitive about how God was portrayed. As a consequence, the story of David's census to gauge the military strength of Israel (rather than rely on God), has two alternative introductions.

We can read with the people of David's time: once again YHWH's anger burned against Israel. He incited David against them, saying, 'Go, count Israel and Judah.' *Or we can read with the Chronicler*: Satan rose up against Israel. He incited David to take a census of Israel.

---

[158] 2 Samuel 24:1-17; 1 Chronicles 21:1-17; 27:23-24

King David spoke to Joab and to the commanders of the army who were with him. *He said*, 'Go through all the tribes of Israel, from Dan *in the north* to Beersheba *in the south*. Register the people, and report back to me, so that I may know how many people there are.'

Joab said to the king, 'May YHWH, your God, add to the people. *May there be a hundred times more men in your army, and may* the eyes of my lord, the king, see *them*. But isn't everyone servants of my lord? Why, then, does my lord, the king, want to do this thing? Why should he bring guilt on Israel?' (YHWH had said that he would make Israel as numerous as the stars in the heavens.)

But the king's word took precedence over Joab and the commanders of the army. So David *ordered* that anyone who was aged twenty years or less be excluded from the count.

Joab, and the commanders of the army, then left the king's presence to register the people of Israel.

They crossed the Jordan *River* and *began by* setting up camp near Aroer, *in the east. Then* Joab son of Zeruiah began to count, and they went *from town to town* throughout the whole land of Israel.

Path of the Census

Aroer
South of the town in the gorge
Gad
Jazer
Gilead
The region of Tahtim Hodshi
Dan Jaan
Sidon
The fortress of Tyre
All the towns of the Hivites
All the towns of the Canaanites
Beersheba, in the Negev of Judah

But Joab didn't finish *the job*. At the end of nine months and twenty days they returned to Jerusalem. Joab then reported the number of people registered to the king. However, Joab did not include *anyone from the tribes of* Levi or Benjamin, because the king's command was abhorrent to him. He also refused to enter any numbers in the annals of King David.

> ### *Census*
> (Valiant men who could handle a sword)
>
> | | *2 Samuel*[1] | *1 Chronicles*[1] |
> |---|---|---|
> | Israel | 800,000 | 1,100,000 |
> | Judah | 500,000 | 470,000 |
>
> Note:
> [1] *The Hebrew term 'thousand' can be used to refer to either military units (e.g. 800 units) or the number of men (e.g. 800,000). This may well help explain the high numbers, and the differences between the two sources*

But having registered *most of* the people, David was stricken in *his* heart. He said to YHWH, 'I have sinned greatly in what I have done. I have been very foolish. Now, YHWH, I pray that you will take away the guilt of your servant.'

But what had been done was evil in the eyes of God, so God *was determined* to punish Israel.

By morning, when David arose, the word of YHWH had come to Gad the prophet, David's seer. He told *him*, 'Go and say to David, "This is what YHWH says: 'I am offering you three *choices*. Choose one of them, and I will do it to you.'"'

So Gad went to David, and told him. He said to him, 'Shall three years of famine come upon you in your land? Or will you flee from your enemies for three months, while your enemies' swords overtake you? Or shall there be three days of YHWH's sword—a plague in the land, with an angel of YHWH bringing destruction on every part of Israel? Now consider *the options*. See what *your* response *is*, so I can give it to the one who sent me.'

But David said to Gad, 'I am in great anguish. But YHWH's mercy is great. So let us leave it in his hands. But do not let me fall into human hands.'

So beginning that morning, *YHWH's* wrath fell upon Israel because of what David had done. YHWH sent a plague on Israel *for* the time indicated. From *all* the people, from Dan to Beersheba, seventy thousand men died.

When the angel *reached Jerusalem*, David looked up and saw the angel of YHWH who was striking down the people. The angel was at the threshing floor of Araunah (*otherwise known as* Ornan), the Jebusite. He was standing between the heavens and the earth, with his sword drawn; his hand was reaching out over Jerusalem. So David and the elders, dressed in sackcloth, fell on their faces.

David said to YHWH, 'I am the one who ordered that the people be counted. I am the one who has sinned; I am the one who has done wrong. What have these sheep done? YHWH, my God, let your hand be against me and my father's house. But do not *continue to inflict* your people with the plague.'

Then, as the angel stretched out his hand to destroy Jerusalem, YHWH *had a change of heart. He felt* sorrow concerning the misery *that had been caused.* So he said to the angel who was destroying the people, 'Enough! Withdraw your hand.'

The Threshing Floor[159]

The angel of YHWH said to Gad, 'Tell David that he is to go and build an altar on the threshing floor of *Araunah* (*or* Ornan) the Jebusite.'

So that *same* day, Gad came to David. He said to him, 'Go up! Build YHWH an altar on the threshing floor of Araunah the Jebusite.' So David went up, as Gad had instructed in the name of YHWH, just as YHWH had commanded.

Now Araunah had been threshing wheat and had turned and seen the angel. So he had hidden with the four sons who were with him.

But Araunah looked down *from the threshing floor* as David approached him. He saw King David and his servants coming toward him. So Araunah left the threshing floor and bowed down before the king with his face to the ground.

Araunah said, 'Why has my lord, the king, come to his servant?'

David said, 'To buy the site of the threshing floor from you. Sell it to me at its full price, so I can build on it an altar to YHWH. Sell it to me, so that the plague on the people may be restrained.'

But Araunah said to David, 'Let my lord, the king, take *it*. Let my lord, the king, offer *sacrifices* and do *whatever is* good in his eyes.

'Look, *here is* the ox for the Burnt Offering, and the threshing sledges and ox yokes for the wood. *Here is* the wheat for the Grain Offering. *My* king, Araunah gives it all to you.'

Araunah then continued to the king, 'May YHWH, your God, respond favourably to you.'

But the king said to Araunah, 'No! I must buy it from you at its full price. I will not take what is yours for YHWH. I will not offer Burnt Offerings to YHWH, my God, *that* have cost *me* nothing.' So David bought the site of the threshing floor and the oxen.

---

[159] 2 Samuel 24:18-25; 1 Chronicles 21:18-27

> **Cost of the Threshing Floor**
>
> 2 Samuel   50 shekels *(570 grams)* of silver
> 1 Chronicles   600 *shekels (6.84 kilogrammes)* of gold
>
> *Note:*
> *There is a discrepancy in the two accounts of the cost of the threshing floor. However it has been suggested that: Samuel's version may be restricted to the purchase of the threshing floor itself, whereas the Chronicler was concerned with the whole site; the price in 2 Samuel may represent 50 shekels per tribe (i.e., 600 shekels in total); or that silver was more valuable than gold in David's time, and that the Chronicler has substituted gold for silver which by then had become more valuable*

David then built an altar to YHWH there. He offered Burnt Offerings and Fellowship Offerings. He then called on YHWH, and YHWH answered him with fire from the heavens on the altar of Burnt Offering.

YHWH then answered *David's* prayer for the land. YHWH commanded the angel, and the angel put his sword back into his sheath and the plague was withdrawn from Israel.

David Orders the Construction of the Temple[160]

Now at that time, YHWH's Tabernacle, and the Altar of Burnt Offering which Moses had made in the wilderness, were located in the high place at Gibeon. But David was unwilling to go there to enquire of God. He was terrified because of the sword of the angel. So when David realised that YHWH had answered him on the threshing floor of Araunah, the Jebusite, he *began to* offer *his own* sacrifices there. *Indeed*, David said, 'This is the house of YHWH, *our* God. This is the Altar of Burnt Offering for Israel.'

But having two sites where sacrifices could be made, contradicted YHWH's commands to Moses. As a consequence, David realised that his dream of a temple in Jerusalem, to replace the Tabernacle in Gibeon, needed to come to fruition. He may not have been the one to build it, but at least he could begin the preparations.

But who would do the work? Even the preparations would require a substantial workforce—and YHWH's laws stated that the Israelites were not to be subjected to forced labour. In any event, he did not want to antagonise the tense relationship between Israel and Judah, or his monarchy.

So David said, 'My son, Solomon, is a boy of tender *years*, and the house

---

[160] 1 Chronicles 21:28-22:19

to be built for YHWH is to be exceedingly great. *It is to be* renowned and *known for its great* beauty through all the nations. So I will make preparations for it.'

David then gave the command for *all* aliens living in the land of Israel to assemble. He then assigned stonecutters to prepare blocks of stone to build the house of God. David provided a large quantity of iron. *This was used* for *making* nails for the doors of the gateways and for clamps. *He also provided* more bronze than could be weighed and more cedar logs than could be counted. Indeed, great quantities of cedar logs were brought to David by the people of Sidon and Tyre. In this way, David made great preparations *for the Temple* before he died.

David then called for his son, Solomon, and commanded him to build a house for YHWH, God of Israel.

David said to Solomon, 'My son, I myself wanted to build a house to the name of YHWH, my God. But the word of YHWH came to me, saying, "You have shed much blood; you have fought great wars. You are not to build a house to my name because you have shed much blood on the land in my presence. But a son will be born to you. He will be a man of rest. Indeed, I will give him rest on every side from all his enemies. Solomon will be his name, and I will grant Israel peace and quiet *all* his days. He will build a house to my name. He will be a son to me, and I will be a father to him. I will establish the throne of his kingdom over Israel forever."

'Now, my son, may YHWH be with you. May you succeed; may you build the house of YHWH your God, just as he said you would. May YHWH also give you discernment and understanding when he gives you charge over Israel. *May you* keep the laws of YHWH your God. If you are careful to observe the statutes and laws, that YHWH gave Moses for Israel, you will prosper. Be strong! Be bold! Do not fear or get discouraged.

'Now look! In my poverty I have provided for the Temple of YHWH. *I have given* a hundred thousand talents *(3,420 metric tonnes)* of gold, a million talents *(34,200 metric tonnes)* of silver, and so much bronze and iron that they are beyond weight. *I have also* provided timber and stone. You may add to them *as you wish.* You *will* have many workmen with you. *You will have* stonecutters, stonemasons, carpenters, and any number of people skilled in every *type* of work *involving* gold, silver, bronze, and iron. *So* arise! *Start* work! May YHWH be with you.'

David then charged all the leaders of Israel to help Solomon, his son. *He said*, 'Isn't YHWH your God with you? Hasn't he given you rest on every side? He has given the inhabitants of the land into my hand; the land has been subdued before God and his people.

'Now set your heart and your soul to seeking YHWH your God. Arise, and build the sanctuary of YHWH *your* God. *Then* take the Ark of the Covenant of YHWH, and the sacred articles of God, into the house that is being built for YHWH's name.'

C22. DAVID
(1040-970 BC)

c). King Solomon and the Temple *(975-970 BC)*

Abishag the Shunammite[161]

King David was old, advanced in years, and couldn't keep warm *in bed*, even when his servants covered him with *bed* clothes.

So his servants said to him, 'Let your servants seek a maiden, a virgin for my lord, the king. Let her attend the king, so she may be of benefit to him. Let her lay in your bosom, so my lord, the king, can keep warm.'

So they searched throughout the territory of Israel for a beautiful maiden and found Abishag, the Shunammite. They brought her to the king, and she became of *great* benefit to the king and served him. *But even though* she was a very beautiful maiden, the king did not have sexual relations with her.

Adonijah's Claim to the Throne[162]

Now Adonijah *was David's* son *through* Haggith. He was *his fourth* born, next after Absalom. *He was also the eldest surviving son, and would normally have been considered next in line to the throne. Adonijah* was also a very handsome man *and, like Absalom, had captured the people's hearts. Despite that*, his father never reproached him by asking him why he behaved as he did.

So realising David's state of health, and with Solomon being so young, Adonijah decided to assert himself. He said, 'I am the one who will become king.' He then had words with *a number of David's supporters, some of whom* agreed to help him, *while others* refused support. He then arranged chariots and horsemen for himself, with fifty men to run ahead of him.

Adonijah's Support Base

Those Who Gave Support	*Those Who Refused Support*
Joab, son of Zeruiah; Abiathar, the priest	Zadok, the priest; Benaiah, son of Jehoiada; Nathan, the prophet; Shimei; Rei; David's mighty *men*

---

[161] 1 Kings 1:1-4
[162] 1 Kings 1:5-27

Then, having invited all his brothers (the king's sons) and all the men of Judah (the king's servants) *to gather more support*, he left for the Stone of Zoheleth, near En Rogel, *not far from the city*. There, he sacrificed sheep, cattle, and fattened calves *for his guests*. However, he did not invite Nathan the prophet, Benaiah, the mighty *men*, or Solomon, his brother.

Nathan *went and* spoke to Bathsheba, Solomon's mother. He said, 'Have you not heard that Adonijah, son of Haggith, has become king? Yet our lord, David, doesn't know it. So come now, let me counsel you. *Let me* advise *you, and* save your life and the life of your son, Solomon.
'Go to King David! Say to him, "My lord, the king, did you not swear to your servant, saying, 'Surely your son Solomon will be king after me. He will sit on my throne.' So why has Adonijah become king?" Then, while you are still speaking, I will come in, and confirm your words to the king.' So Bathsheba went to the king.

The king was in *his* chamber, for he was very old, and Abishag the Shunammite was serving him.
Bathsheba bowed down and showed honour to the king.
The king said, 'What *can I do* for you?'
She said to him, 'My lord, you swore to your servant, by YHWH, "Surely Solomon your son will be king after me. He will sit on my throne." But look, Adonijah has become king, yet my lord, the king, is not aware of it. He invited all the kings' sons, Abiathar the priest, and Joab, the commander of the army. He sacrificed a multitude of cattle, fattened calves, and sheep. But he did not invite your servant, Solomon.
'So, my lord, the king, the eyes of all Israel are on you. You need to tell them who will sit on the throne of my lord, the king, after him. If you don't, when my lord, the king, lies down with his fathers, then I—I and my son Solomon—*will be* deemed guilty *of plotting against Adonijah*.'
While she was still speaking with the king, Nathan the prophet entered *the room*.
David's servants told the king, 'Here is Nathan the prophet.' So Nathan came into the king's presence and bowed down before the king with his face to the ground.
Nathan said, 'My lord, the king, have you said, "Adonijah will be king after me. He will sit on my throne"? For today he has gone and sacrificed many cattle, fattened calves, and sheep. He invited all the king's sons, the commanders of the army, and Abiathar the priest, and now they are eating and drinking with him. They are saying, "*Long* live King Adonijah."
'As for me, I, your servant, was not invited. *Neither were* Zadok the priest, Benaiah son of Jehoiada, or your servant Solomon. So has this thing been done

by my lord, the king? Have you not let your servant know who would be sitting on the throne of my lord, the king, after him?'

Solomon Anointed King[163]

A little while later, King David responded *to what he had been told.* He said, 'Call Bathsheba to me.' So she came into the king's presence and stood before him. Then the king swore *an oath.* He said, 'I did indeed swear to you by YHWH, God of Israel, "Surely Solomon your son will be king after me. He will sit on my throne in my place." So as YHWH lives, who has redeemed my life from every trouble, I will certainly make it so today.'

Bathsheba then bowed down with her face to the ground and showed him honour. She said, 'May my lord, the king, live forever.'

Then King David said, 'Call to me, Zadok the priest, Nathan the prophet, and Benaiah son of Jehoiada.' So they came before the king.

The king said to them, 'Take your lord's servants with you. Set my son, Solomon, on my mule and take him down to Gihon *on the eastern slope of the city.* Zadok the priest and Nathan the prophet are to anoint him king over Israel there. Afterwards, blow on the trumpet and shout, '*Long* live King Solomon.' Then follow him back *here, where* he will sit on my throne. He will be king instead of me, *for* I have appointed him ruler over Israel and Judah.'

Benaiah, son of Jehoiada, answered the king. He said, 'Amen! So says YHWH, the God of my lord, the king. Just as YHWH has been with my lord, the king, so may he be with Solomon. May he make his throne greater than the throne of my lord, King David.'

So Zadok the priest, Nathan the prophet, Benaiah son of Jehoiada, the Kerethites, and the Pelethites, went and mounted Solomon on King David's donkey. They then went with him to Gihon. Zadok the priest took the horn of oil, *which he had taken* from the tent *that housed the Ark of the Covenant*, and anointed Solomon. They then blew the trumpet and all the people shouted, '*Long* live Solomon.' Then all the people followed him back *to the city*—some playing flutes, others expressing great joy. Indeed, the ground shook with the noise *that they made.*

Adonijah, and all those he had invited who were with him, heard *the noise.* They had *just* finished their feast when Joab heard the sound of the trumpet. He said, 'What is that roar coming from the city?'

He was still speaking when Jonathan, the son of Abiathar the priest, arrived.

Adonijah said, 'Come in. You are a brave man. You *must be* bringing good news.'

---

[163] 1 Kings 1:28-53

But Jonathan answered. He said to Adonijah, 'No! Our lord, King David, has made Solomon king. He sent Zadok the priest, Nathan the prophet, Benaiah son of Jehoiada, the Kerethites, and the Pelethites and they mounted Solomon on the king's mule. Zadok the priest and Nathan the prophet anointed him as king at Gihon. From there, they returned with great joy to the city. The roar *of the people* is the noise you are hearing. Furthermore, Solomon is sitting on the royal throne.

'The king's servants also went to bless our lord, King David. They said, "May God make Solomon's name more famous than yours. May he make his throne greater than yours." Then the king bowed *in worship* on the bed.

'King *David* said this, "Blessed be YHWH, God of Israel, who has given me *the privilege* of seeing *Solomon* sitting on my throne today."'

At this news, everyone who had been invited, who was with Adonijah, trembled. They stood up, and each went on his way. Adonijah, however, was afraid of Solomon. *But he knew something about the laws concerning the Cities of Refuge; he knew the rules relating to the protection of the innocent. So in the hope that Solomon would overlook his deliberate attempt to usurp the throne*, he got up, went *to the sanctuary, and* took hold of the horns of the altar.

Solomon was told, 'Look, Adonijah is afraid of King Solomon. He has taken hold of the horns of the altar. *He is* saying, 'Let King Solomon swear to me today, that he will not kill his servant with the sword.'

But Solomon said, 'If he *proves* to be worthy, not *a single* hair *on his head* will fall to the ground. But if he proves to be evil, he will die.'

Then King Solomon sent *for him*.

They brought him down from the altar, and he came and bowed down before King Solomon.

Solomon said to him, 'Go to your house!'

The Levites[164]

So when David was old and had lived a full life, he made his son Solomon king over Israel. He then gathered all the leaders of Israel, with the priests and Levites. *All* the Levites thirty years of age or older were counted, and the total number was thirty-eight thousand men.

(see tables on next two pages)

---

[164] 1 Chronicles 23:1-32

Establishing the Kingdom

Classification of the Levites

Task	Number
Supervisors for the work of YHWH's Temple	24,000
Officials and judges	6,000
Gatekeepers	4,000
Musicians (offering praise to YHWH with the instruments that David made to praise YHWH)	4,000
TOTAL	*38,000*

David then organised them into divisions *corresponding to the three* sons of Levi: Gershom, Kohath, and Merari.

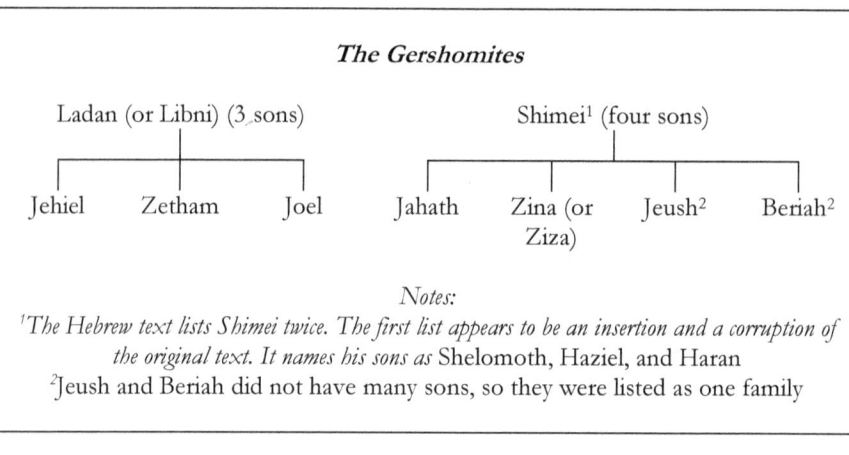

The Gershomites

Ladan (or Libni) (3 sons): Jehiel, Zetham, Joel

Shimei[1] (four sons): Jahath, Zina (or Ziza), Jeush[2], Beriah[2]

Notes:
[1] The Hebrew text lists Shimei twice. The first list appears to be an insertion and a corruption of the original text. It names his sons as Shelomoth, Haziel, and Haran
[2] Jeush and Beriah did not have many sons, so they were listed as one family

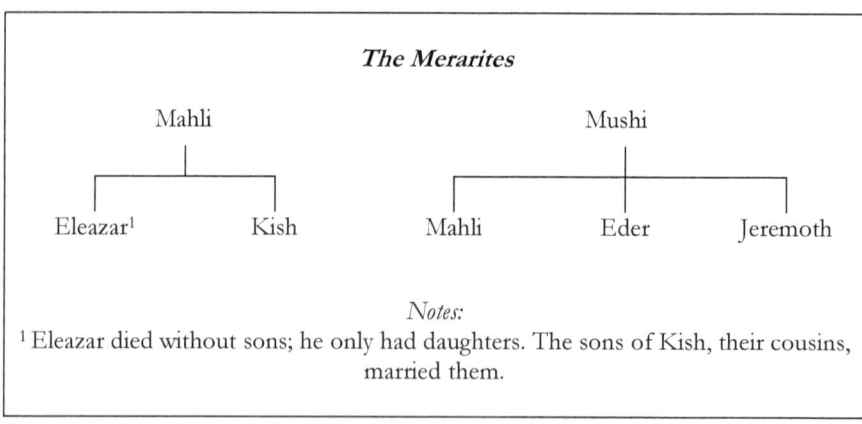

The Merarites

Mahli: Eleazar[1], Kish

Mushi: Mahli, Eder, Jeremoth

Notes:
[1] Eleazar died without sons; he only had daughters. The sons of Kish, their cousins, married them.

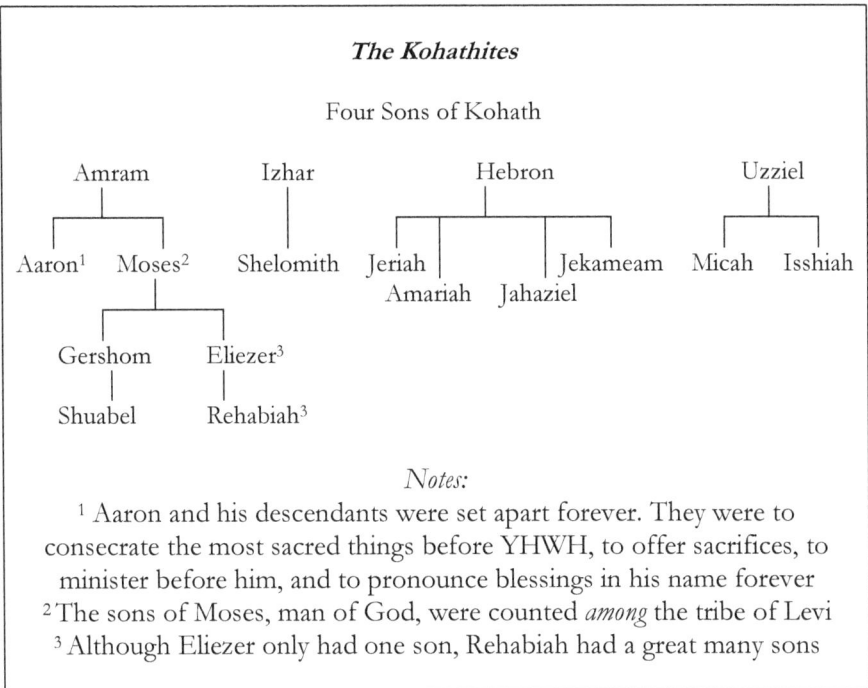

These were the sons of Levi according to their fathers' houses. *They were the heads of families who were counted, twenty years of age or older. They were listed by name, in the census, to do the work for the service of the house of YHWH.* Indeed, according to the last instructions of David, *which may have recognised that the minimum age needed to be lowered to provided enough workers*, the sons of Levi twenty years of age and older were counted.

David said, 'YHWH, God of Israel, has given his people rest. He has come to dwell in Jerusalem for ever. The Levites no longer need to carry the Tabernacle and all its utensils for his service.' So their duties *were changed*.

(See table on next page)

So the Levites kept watch over the Tent of Meeting and the Holy Place; they assisted the descendants of Aaron, their brothers, in the service of the house of YHWH.

> ### *The Revised Duties of the Levites*
>
> *Principal Duty*
> To assist Aaron's descendants in the service of the house of YHWH
>
> *Specific Areas of Responsibility*
> The courtyards
> The chambers
> The purification of all sacred things and the work of service in the house of God
> The bread set out *on the table*
> The flour for the Grain Offerings, unleavened wafers, for what was baked and what was mixed *with oil – including responsibility* for measuring all the quantities and size
> To stand every morning to thank and to praise YHWH
> To stand every evening to thank and to praise YHWH
> *To stand whenever* Burnt Offerings are presented to YHWH, i.e., on Sabbaths, New Moons, and appointed festivals
> *To carry out duties* with the number *required*, and in the way *set* for them, *regularly before YHWH*

The Priests[165]

This is how Aaron's sons were divided:

Aaron had had *four* sons: Nadab, Abihu, Eleazar, and Ithamar. But Nadab and Abihu had died in their father's presence, without having had any sons of their own. So Eleazar and Ithamar had served as priests *in their stead, and* more leaders of men were found among Eleazar's descendants than amongst the descendants of Ithamar.

So David, with Zadok (a descendant of Eleazar), and Ahimelech (a descendant of Ithamar), divided them according to their prescribed duties.

They divided Eleazar's descendants into sixteen heads of family houses, and Ithamar's into eight. They divided them by lot, treating *both families* alike, because the descendants of *both* Eleazar and Ithamar were *to be* officials of the sanctuary and officials of God.

Shemaiah, son of Nethanel, a Levite, acted as scribe. He recorded their *names* in the presence of the king, the officials, Zadok the priest, Ahimelech son of Abiathar, and the heads of the families of *both* the priests and the Levites.

---

[165] 1 Chronicles 24:1-19

Establishing the Kingdom

One of the heads was from *the descendants of* Eleazar, and another from *the descendants of* Ithamar.

The Division of Aaron's Sons

Lot	Head of Family	Lot	Head of Family	Lot	Head of Family
1	Jehoiarib	9	Jeshua	17	Hezir
2	Jedaiah	10	Shecaniah	18	Happizzez
3	Harim	11	Eliashib	19	Pethahiah
4	Seorim	12	Jakim	20	Jehezkel
5	Malkijah	13	Huppah	21	Jakin
6	Mijamin	14	Jeshebeab	22	Gamul
7	Hakkoz	15	Bilgah	23	Delaiah
8	Abijah	16	Immer	24	Maaziah

Their prescribed duties were to enter the house of YHWH *and carry out their work* in accordance with the regulations *given* them through their ancestor Aaron, just as YHWH, God of Israel had commanded.

The Remaining Levites[166]

The remaining descendants of Levi *were also divided.*

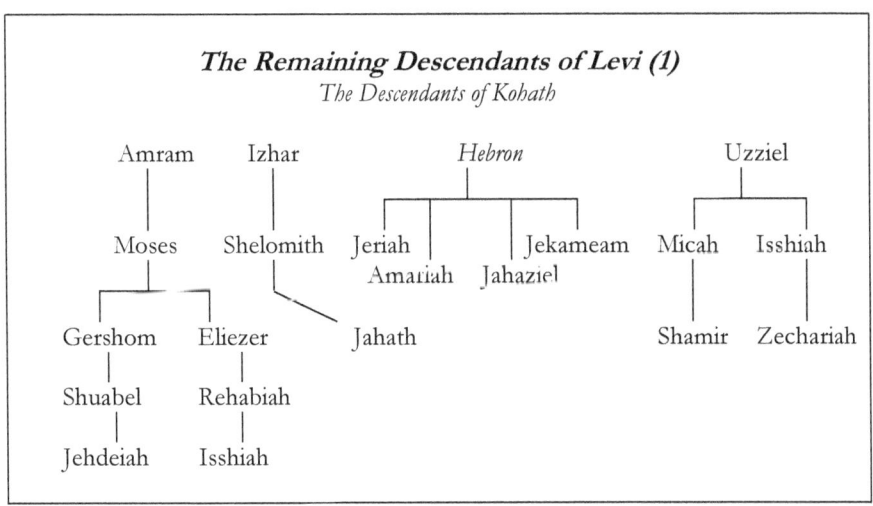

The Remaining Descendants of Levi (1)
The Descendants of Kohath

---

[166] 1 Chronicles 24:20-31

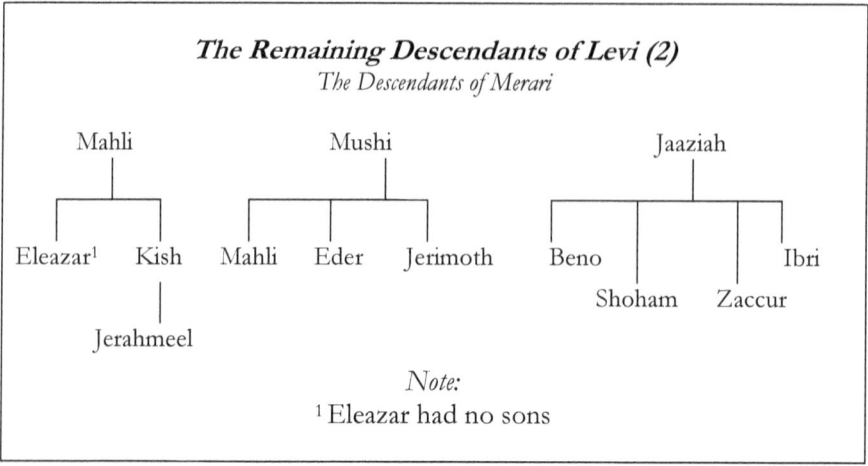

These were sons of Levites, according to their father's houses. Lots were cast for them in the same way *they had been for* their brothers, the descendants of Aaron. *That is*, in the presence of King David, Zadok, Ahimelech, and the heads of the families of *both* the priests and the Levites. *Both* family head and younger brother were treated alike.

The Musicians[167]

David, and the commanders of the army, set apart *those* for the ministry of prophesying. *They were chosen* from the sons of Asaph, Heman, and Jeduthun. *They were to be* accompanied with harps, lyres, and cymbals.

(See table on next page)

They were all to sing in the house of YHWH, under the direction of their fathers; *they were to sing* accompanied by cymbals, lyres, and harps in the service of the house of God. Asaph, Jeduthun, and Heman, *however, remained* under the direction of the king.

The total number of skilled *musicians* in YHWH's service totalled two hundred and eighty eight. These included their relatives who were trained in music. Lots were cast for their duties, in which young and old, teacher and student, were treated alike.

---

[167] 1 Chronicles 25:1-31

The List of Workers in Their Service

Families	*Sons*	*Comments*
From the sons of Asaph	Zaccur, Joseph, Nethaniah, Asarelah,	Under the direction of Asaph, who prophesied under the direction of the king
Six sons of Jeduthun	Gedaliah, Zeri, Jeshaiah, *Shimei*, Hashabiah, Mattithiah	Under the direction of their father Jeduthun, who prophesied with a harp in thanks and praise to YHWH
From the sons of Heman	Bukkiah, Mattaniah, Uzziel, Shubael, Jerimoth, Hananiah, Hanani, Eliathah, Giddalti, Romamti-Ezer, Joshbekashah, Mallothi, Hothir, Mahazioth	All of these were sons of Heman, who by the word of God was the king's seer. To exalt Heman God gave him 14 sons and 3 daughters

List of Musicians[1]

Lot	Name	Lot	Name	Lot	Name
1	Joseph	9	Mattaniah	17	Joshbekashah
2	Gedaliah	10	Shimei	18	Hanani
3	Zaccur	11	Azarel	19	Mallothi
4	Izri	12	Hashabiah	20	Eliathah
5	Nethaniah	13	Shubael	21	Hothir
6	Bukkiah	14	Mattithiah	22	Giddalti
7	Jesarelah	15	Jerimoth	23	Mahazioth
8	Jeshaiah	16	Hananiah	24	Romamti-Ezer

Note:
[1] *Each lot was cast for 12 people*--the person and his sons and relatives. *Total number: 288*

The Gatekeepers[168]

These were the divisions of the gatekeepers:

---

[168] 1 Chronicles 26:1-19

Establishing the Kingdom

The Gatekeepers (1)
Korahites

Meshelemiah, son of Kore, son of Asaph

- Zechariah
- Jediael
- Zebediah
- Jathniel
- Elam
- Jehohanan
- Elieoenai

Meshelemiah's sons and relatives—able men. *Total* 18

Obed-Edom[1]

- Shemaiah[2]
  - Othni
  - Rephael
  - Obed
  - Elzabad
- Jehozabad
- Joah
- Sacar
- Nethanel
- Ammiel
- Isaachar
- Peullethai

The descendants of Obed-Edom, their sons and relatives—able men with the strength to do the work. *Total* 62

Notes:
[1] God blessed him *with many sons*
[2] Shemaiah's sons were leaders in their father's house, because they were men of valour. His relatives Elihu and Semakiah were also able men

The Gatekeepers (2)
Merarites

Hosah

- Shimri[1]
- Hilkiah
- Tabaliah
- Zechariah

Hosah's sons and relatives. Total 13

Note:
[1] Shimri was not Hosah's firstborn, but his father put him first

These were the divisions of the gatekeepers by their head men. *They were given their* duties for ministering in the house of YHWH in the same way as their relatives. Lots were cast, gate by gate, according to their father's house, for young and old alike.

Lots Cast for Each Gate

Gates	*Lots*
East Gate	Shelemiah
North Gate	Zechariah[1], son of Shelemiah
South Gate	Obed-Edom[2]
West and Shalleketh[3] Gates	Shuppim and Hosah

Notes:
[1] *Zechariah was* a prudent counsellor; [2] The lot for the storehouse fell to Obed-Edom's sons; [3] The Shalleketh gate was on the upper road

---

Daily Watches[1]

Location	*No of Levites*
East Gate	6
North Gate	4
South Gate	4
Storehouses (2)	2 at each
Western Colonnade	2
Western Colonnade (on the road)	4

Note:
[1] Each guard was side by side with *another* guard

These were the divisions of the gatekeepers, descendants of the Korahites and Merarites.

The Treasuries[169]

As for the responsibilities of other Levites:

---

[169] 1 Chronicles 26:20-28

Other Responsibilities of the Levites

Clans	Person	Responsibilities
Unknown	Ahijah	In charge of the treasuries of the house of God and of the treasuries of sacred gifts
Gershomites	Zetham and his brother Joel, and sons of Jehieli[1]	In charge of the treasuries of the house of YHWH
Amramites, Izharites, Hebronites and Uzzielites	Shubael, descendant of Gershom son of Moses	Officer in charge over the treasuries
	The sons of Eliezer: Rehabiah, Jeshaiah, Joram, Zicri, and Shelomith[2]	Shelomith and his brothers were in charge of all the treasuries of sacred gifts that had been dedicated[3]

Notes:
[1] Zetham and Joel were descendants of Ladan the Gershomite. They were heads of their father's house, belonging to Ladan the Gershomite
[2] Relatives of Shubael through Eliezer, *Gershom's brother*
[3] Shelomith and his brothers were in charge of all things dedicated by Samuel the seer, Saul son of Kish, Abner son of Ner, Joab son of Zeruiah, King David, the heads of the fathers' *houses*, the commanders of thousands and hundreds, and the commanders of the army. Some of the plunder taken in battle was set apart for the repair of the house of YHWH

Civil Officials[170]

(See table on next page)

---

[170] 1 Chronicles 26:29-32

Civil Officials

Clan/People	Responsibilities
Izrahites: Kenaniah, and his sons	Duties away from *the house of YHWH*, as officials and judges over Israel
Hebronites: Hashabiah and his relatives – 1700 able men	Oversight of Israel west of the Jordan *River*, in regards to all the work of YHWH and for the service of the king
Hebronites: Jeriah and his relatives – 2,700 able men	*Oversight of Israel east of the Jordan River*, in charge of the Reubenites, Gadites and half of the tribe of Manasseh, in regard to all matters concerning God and the king[1]

Notes:

[1] In the fortieth year of David's reign the records of the fathers of the Hebronites were searched. In them, able men at Jazer in Gilead were found. Jeriah had 2,700 able men among his relatives, heads of the fathers. So King David appointed them overseers.

Military Divisions[171]

This is a list of the Israelites, by the heads of their fathers' houses—the commanders of thousands and hundreds. *It is a list of* the officers serving the king in all matters concerning the divisions. Each division of twenty four thousand *men* came in and went out, month by month, through all the months of the year.

Army Divisions

Division	Month	Commander	Number
1	1	Jashobeam, son of Zabdiel, a descendant of Perez. The chief of all the army officers for the first month	24,000
2	2	Dodai, the Ahohite. Mikloth the chief officer	24,000
3	3	Benaiah[1], son of Jehoiada the priest, was chief. Ammizabad his son was in charge of his division	24,000
4	4	Asahel, brother of Joab, and following him, Zebadiah his son	24,000

(Continued on next page)

---

[171] 1 Chronicles 27:1-15

(Continued from previous page)

5	5	Shamhuth the Izrahite	24,000
6	6	Ira, son of Ikkesh the Tekoite	24,000
7	7	Helez the Pelonite, an Ephraimite	24,000
8	8	Sibbecai the Hushathite, a Zerahite	24,000
9	9	Abiezer, the Anathothite, a Benjamite	24,000
10	10	Maharai the Netophathite, a Zerahite	24,000
11	11	Benaiah the Pirathonite, an Ephraimite	24,000
12	12	Heldai, the Netophathite, *a descendant* of Othniel	24,000

Notes:
[1] Benaiah was *one of* the mighty *men, one of* the Thirty. He was also in charge of the Thirty.

Officers of the Tribes[172]

The officers over the tribes of Israel:

The Officers of the Tribes of Israel

Tribe[1]	*Officer*
Reuben	Eliezer, son of Zicri
Simeon	Shephatiah, son of Maacah
Levi	Hashabiah, son of Kemuel[2]
Judah	Elihu, brother of David
Issachar	Omri, son of Michael
Zebulun	Ishmaiah, son of Obadiah
Naphtali	Jerimoth, son of Azriel
Ephraim	Hoshea, son of Azaziah
Half of the tribe of Manasseh	Joel, son of Pedaiah
Half of the tribe of Manasseh, in Gilead[2]	Iddo, son of Zechariah
Benjamin	Jaasiel, son of Abner
Dan	Azarel, son of Jerohaam

Notes:
[1] *The tribes of Gad and Asher are absent from this list. Responsibility for the two tribes may have fallen to the other tribes or, over time, the list may have become corrupted and the names lost*
[2] Zadok was *the officer over the house* of Levi

---

[172] 1 Chronicles 27:16-22

Establishing the Kingdom

Public and Private Overseers[173]

The Overseers of David's Property

Person	Responsibility
Azmaveth, son of Adiel	The king's storehouses
Jonathan, son of Uzziah	The storehouses in the field, towns, villages, and towers
Ezri, son of Kelub	The workers in the field, farming the land
Shimei, the Ramathite	The vineyards
Zabdi, the Shiphmite	The produce of the vineyards, and the wine cellars
Baal-Hanan, the Gederite	The olive and sycamore trees in the Shephelah (*foothills south-west of Jerusalem*)
Joash	The supplies of olive oil
Shitrai, the Sharonite	The herds grazing in Sharon (*a coastal plain to the north west of Jerusalem*)
Shaphat, son of Adlai	The herds in the valleys
Obil, the Ishmaelite	The camels
Jehdeiah, the Meronothite	The donkeys
Jaziz, the Hagrite	The flock

The King's Personal Counsellors

Person	Responsibility
Jonathan, David's uncle	A counsellor, a man of discernment, and a scribe
Jehiel, son of Hacmoni	*The upbringing and tutoring of* the king's sons
Ahithophel[1]	A counsellor to the king
Hushai, the Arkite	A friend of the king
Joab	The commander of the king's army

Note:
[1] Ahithophel was succeeded by Jehoiada, son of Benaiah, and Abiathar

---

[173] 1 Chronicles 27:25-34

Establishing the Kingdom

David's Plans for the Temple[174]
Now David summoned all the officials of Israel to Jerusalem.

Officials Gathered in Jerusalem

The leaders of the tribes
The commanders of the divisions that served the king
The commanders of thousands and hundreds
The overseers of all property and livestock belonging to the king
The overseers of the king's sons
Eunuchs
The Mighty *Men* and all the brave warriors

When they were assembled, King David rose to his feet and said, 'Listen to me, my brothers and my people. I *had it* in my heart to build a house of rest for the Ark of the Covenant of YHWH; a footstool for the feet of our God. I *even* made plans to build *it*. But God said to me, "You will not build a house for my name because you are a man of war; you have shed blood." Yet YHWH, God of Israel, chose me from all my father's house to be king over Israel forever. Indeed, he chose Judah to lead, and from the house of Judah *he chose* my father's house. Then, from my father's sons, he took pleasure in me and made *me* king over all Israel.

'Now YHWH has given me many sons. But of all my sons he has chosen my son, Solomon, to sit on the throne of YHWH's kingdom over Israel. He said to me, "Your son, Solomon, is the one who will build my house and my courts, for I have chosen him to be as a son to me, and I will be as a father to him. If he continues to be resolute in keeping my commands and laws as *is being done* today, I will establish his kingdom forever."

'So now, in the sight of all Israel, YHWH's assembly, and in the hearing of our God, observe and pursue all the commandments of YHWH, your God. Then you will *continue to* possess the good land, and your sons may inherit it after you forever.'

Then addressing Solomon directly, he continued, 'Now you, Solomon, my son, know the God of your father. Serve him with a whole heart and a willing mind. For YHWH searches every heart and discerns every intention behind *a man's* thoughts. If you seek him, you will find him; but if you abandon him, he will reject you forever. Think about it, for YHWH has chosen you to build a house

---

[174] 1 Chronicles 28:1-21

as *his* sanctuary. *So* be of courage! Do *the work*!' Then David gave Solomon, his son, *the* plans *and other instructions for the Temple*—all that he had in mind.

A List of the Plans for the House of YHWH

The porch	The house of atonement
The houses	The courts
The storehouses	The surrounding rooms
The chambers	The treasuries of the house
The inner rooms	The treasuries of sacred gifts

A List of Other Instructions Given for the House of YHWH

The divisions of the priests and Levites
All the work of service
All the articles used in service
The weight of gold to be used in all gold articles used in service
The weight of silver to be used in all silver articles used in service
The weight of *all* the gold lampstands and their gold lamps
The weight *of each gold* lampstand and its lamps
The weight *of each* silver lampstand and its lamps, according to its purpose
The weight of gold for each table, for the rows *of consecrated bread*
The weight of silver for each silver table
The amount of pure gold for the forks, sprinkling bowls, and pitchers
The weight of gold for each *gold* bowl
The weight of silver for each silver bowl
The weight of refined gold for the Altar of Incense
The design of the chariot, i.e., the gold cherubim spreading *their wings*, covering the Ark of the Covenant of YHWH

David then said to all his officials, 'All *of these plans are* in writing. YHWH's hand has been upon me; he has given *me* understanding of every aspect of the plan.

Then David said to Solomon, his son, 'Be strong and courageous! Do the work! Don't be afraid or become discouraged, for YHWH God, my God, is with you. He will not fail you, or leave you *in this task,* until all the work for the service of the house of YHWH is completed.

'Now look, the divisions of the priests and the Levites *are waiting. They will do* all the work on the house of God. Every willing man, skilled in any kind of service will be with you in all the work. The officials and all of the people will also be totally at your command.'

Contributions for the Construction of the Temple[175]

Then King David said to the whole assembly, 'My son, Solomon, is the one whom God has chosen *to build his house*. He is young and inexperienced, but the task is great. For the Temple is not for man, but for YHWH God.

'But I have *also* provided for the house of my God, using all the resources *available* to me.

David's Provision for the Temple

Gold for the gold *work*
Silver for the silver *work*
Bronze for the bronze *work*
Iron for the iron *work*
Wood for the wood *work*
Onyx stones and settings
Turquoise stones
Coloured stones
All sorts of precious stones
Great quantities of marble

'Besides, *because of* my devotion to the house of my God, I give my *own* treasures of gold and silver for the house of my God. *This is* over and above all that I have *already* provided for the holy house.

David's Personal Contribution to the Temple

Gold (gold of Ophir)	3,000 talents (*102.6 metric tonnes*)
Refined silver[*1]	7,000 talents (*239.4 metric tonnes*)

Note:
[*1]To overlay the walls of the buildings

---

[175] 1 Chronicles 29:1-9

'The gold *is* for the gold *work, and* the silver *is* for the silver *work. It is* for all the work *done* by the hands of craftsmen. Who then is willing to consecrate himself this day to YHWH?'

Then the leaders of the fathers' *houses*, the officers of tribes of Israel, the commanders of thousands and hundreds, and the overseers of the king's work, gave willingly.

The Gifts for the Work of the House of God

Gold	5,000 talents (*171 metric tonnes*)
Gold	10,000 darics (*84 kilogrammes*)
Silver	10,000 talents (*342 metric tonnes*)
Bronze	18,000 talents (*615.6 metric tonnes*)
Iron	100,000 talents (*3,420 metric tonnes*)

Anyone who possessed *precious* stones gave them to the treasury of the house of YHWH, into the hand of Jehiel, the Gershomite.

Then the people rejoiced *because their leaders had given so* willingly; for they had whole heartedly given freely to YHWH. King David also rejoiced, *being filled with* great joy.

David's Prayer of Thanksgiving[176]

Then David blessed YHWH in the sight of the whole assembly. David said,

David, to YHWH

'Blessed are you, YHWH,
    God of our father Israel, for ever and ever.
To you, YHWH, *belong* greatness and might,
    and glory and eminence and majesty;
    for everything in the heavens and the earth *are yours*.
The kingdom, YHWH, is yours;
    you are exalted as head over all.
Riches and honour *come* from you;
    you rule over everything.
In your hand are power and might;
    it is in your hand to make great and give strength to all.
But now, our God, we give thanks to you;
    we boast in your glorious name.'

---

[176] 1 Chronicles 29:10-20

David then continued to YHWH, 'But who *am* I, and who *are* my people that we are able to give as willingly as this? For all things *come* from you. We have given you *only what we have received* from your hand. For we are aliens in your presence; *we are* strangers, as *were* all our fathers. Our days on the earth are like a shadow; there is no hope. YHWH, our God, all this abundance that we have provided, to build you a house for your holy name, is from your hand. All of it *belongs* to you.

'My God, I know that you examine the heart and take pleasure in integrity. I, in the uprightness of my heart, have given willingly all my share. But now, I have seen, with joy, that your people here have given willingly to you *as well*.

'YHWH, *you are the* God of our fathers, Abraham, Isaac, and Israel. Keep these thoughts and desires in the hearts of your people forever; direct their hearts to you. Give to Solomon, my son, an undivided heart, *so he may* keep your commandments, your decrees, and your statutes; to keep them all, and to build the Temple for which I have provided.'

Then David said to the whole assembly, 'Now bless YHWH, your God.' So the whole assembly blessed YHWH, the God of their fathers. They bowed down and paid honour to YHWH and the king.

Solomon's Accession[177]

The next day they slaughtered sacrifices to YHWH. They offered Burnt Offerings, *Drink Offerings, and other sacrifices* to YHWH, for all Israel.

Sacrifices to YHWH	
Offering	*Quantity*
Bulls	1,000
Rams	1,000
Drink Offerings	In abundance
Other Sacrifices	In abundance

So that day they ate and drank in the presence of YHWH with great joy. They then made Solomon, son of David, king a second time. In YHWH's presence, they anointed Solomon ruler, and Zadok priest. So Solomon sat on the throne of YHWH as king instead of his father, David.

---

[177] 1 Chronicles 29:21-23a

Establishing the Kingdom

David's Last Words[178]

These are the last words of David.

David, to all the people

'An oracle of David son of Jesse;
    an oracle of the man raised up on high.
The anointed of the God of Jacob;
    the singer of the songs of Israel.

'The spirit of YHWH spoke through me;
    his word was on my tongue.
The God of Israel spoke to me;
    the rock of Israel *said,*
"Anyone who rules over men *is to rule* justly;
    anyone who rules *is to* fear God.
Then they will be like the light of dawn,
    when the sun rises on a cloudless morning,
or the sunshine after the rain
    that brings forth the grass from the land."

'Surely, so is my house with God;
    for he made an everlasting covenant with me—
    everything in order and secure.
So will he not care for my every need,
    and my every *godly* desire?
As for the worthless *rulers*, they will be discarded,
    like thorns which cannot be collected in the hand.
Whoever touches them *will need to* use iron
    and the wooden *shaft* of a spear.
They will be totally consumed with fire
    on *their* thrones.'

David's Charge to Solomon[179]

When the time for David to die was approaching, he laid a charge on Solomon, his son. He said, 'I am going the way of all the earth. So be strong and be a man. Keep the requirements of YHWH your God, and walk in his ways. Keep his statutes, his commandments, his laws, and his regulations, as written in the Law of Moses. Then you will succeed in all that you do and everywhere you go. Indeed, YHWH will be able to keep the promise that he

---

[178] 2 Samuel 23:1-7
[179] 1 Kings 2:1-9

made to me. He said, "If your descendants watch their ways, *and* walk before me faithfully with all their heart and all their soul, none of your successors will be cut off from the throne of Israel."

'Now you know what Joab, son of Zeruiah, did to me; you *know* what he did to two of the commanders of Israel's armies—to Abner son of Ner, and Amasa son of Jether. He killed them; he shed the blood of battle in a time of peace. As a consequence, he stained the belt around my waist and the sandals on my feet with that blood. So deal *with him*, in accordance with your wisdom. But do not let his grey head go down to Sheol in peace.

'Show kindness, however, to the sons of Barzillai the Gileadite. Let them be among those who eat from your table. For they certainly helped me when I was fleeing from your brother Absalom.

'Shimei son of Gera, the Benjaminite from Bahurim, is also with you. He was the one who cursed me with a bitter curse, the day I went to Mahanaim. He was the one who came down to meet me at the Jordan *River*. I swore to him then, by YHWH, "I will not kill you with the sword." But now, do not hold him guiltless. You are a wise man; you will know what you should do to him. *So* bring his grey head down to Sheol in blood.'

The Death of David[180]

David then died at a good old age, full of days, wealth, and honour. He lay down with his fathers and was buried in the City of David. David, son of Jesse, had been king over all Israel, and had reigned over Israel for forty years. He had reigned for seven years in Hebron over Judah, and thirty-three years in Jerusalem over all Israel and Judah. Then Solomon, his son, *aged twenty one*, became king in his place. So Solomon sat on the throne of his father, David, and his kingdom became firmly established.

Now the words of King David, from first to last, are written in the records of Samuel the seer, Nathan the prophet, and Gad the seer. *The records include details* of his reign and his might, as well as the events that came upon him, Israel, and all the kingdoms of the earth.

---

[180] 2 Samuel 5:4b-5; 1 Kings 2:10-12; 1 Chronicles 29:26-30

C23. SOLOMON/JEDIDIAH
(991-930 BC)

a). Establishing the Throne *(970-967 BC)*

Adonijah, Abiathar, and Joab[181]

Adonijah, son of Haggith, went to Solomon's mother, Bathsheba.

She said, 'Have you come in peace?'

He said, '*Yes*, in peace.' Then he continued, 'I have something *to ask* you.'

She said, 'Ask.'

He said, 'You yourself know that the kingdom was mine. Indeed, the whole of Israel looked in my direction to be *their* king. But the kingdom has turned and gone to my brother, for it has come to him from YHWH. So now I have one request to ask of you. Do not turn me *down*.'

She said to him, 'Ask!'

He said, 'Please ask Solomon, the king, *on my behalf. Let him* give me Abishag, the Shunammite, as a wife. He will not refuse you.'

Bathsheba said, '*That is* good. I will personally speak to the king for you.' So Bathsheba went to King Solomon to speak to him on Adonijah's behalf.

The king stood up to greet her, bowed to her, and sat on his throne. He then had a throne brought for the mother of the king, and she sat on his right.

She said, 'I have one small request to ask you. Do not refuse me.'

The king said to her, 'Ask, my mother, for I will not refuse you.'

She then said, 'Let Abishag, the Shunammite, be given to your brother, Adonijah, as a wife.'

King Solomon answered. He said to his mother, 'Why are you asking for Abishag, the Shunammite, for Adonijah? *Why not* ask for the kingdom for him *as well?* He is my older brother. *Perhaps you would also like* Abiathar the priest and Joab son of Zeruiah for him, *so they can anoint him king over Israel.*'

Then King Solomon swore by YHWH. He said, 'May God do to me, and more so, *if I don't deal with Adonijah*. For Adonijah has spoken this word *at the cost* of his life. *God* has established me; he has sat me on the throne of David my father; he has made me a house, just as he promised. So now, as YHWH lives, Adonijah will be put to death today.' King Solomon then sent *the order* by the hand of Benaiah, son of Jehoiada, who found Adonijah, and killed him.

Then the king said to Abiathar the priest, 'Go back to Anathoth, to your

---

[181] 1 Kings 2:13-37

fields. You are a dead man. But I will not kill you today, for you carried the Ark of the Lord YHWH before my father David, and you suffered *with* my father in all his hardships.' So Solomon expelled Abiathar from being priest of YHWH, thus fulfilling the word of YHWH that he had spoken at Shiloh, concerning the house of Eli.

Now Joab had supported Adonijah, but not Absalom. So when *Adonijah's death was* reported to Joab, Joab fled to YHWH's tent. *There*, he took hold of the horns of the altar.

King Solomon was told that Joab had fled to YHWH's tent, and *that he could be* found beside the altar, so he sent Benaiah son of Jehoiada *after him*. He said, 'Go! Strike him down!' So Benaiah *went and* entered YHWH's tent.
He said to Joab, 'This is what the king says, "Come out!"'
But Joab said, 'No! I will die here.'
Benaiah then sent a report to the king, detailing what Joab had said and how Joab had answered him.
Then the king said to him, 'Do as he has said. Strike him down and bury him. *By doing* so, you will remove *the guilt* from me and my father's house, *caused* by the blood that Joab shed without cause. He fell on two men, more righteous than himself. He killed with the sword: Abner son of Ner, the commander of Israel's army, and Amasa son of Jether, the commander of Judah's army. My father knew nothing *about either death*. So YHWH will repay their blood on his head. May their blood turn back on the heads of Joab and his descendants forever. But may YHWH's peace be forever on David, his descendants, his house, and his throne.'
So Benaiah son of Jehoiada went and fell upon Joab and killed him. Joab was then buried by his house in the wilderness. The king then put Benaiah, son of Jehoiada, over the army instead of Joab, and Zadok the priest in place of Abiathar.

Shimei[182]

Then the king sent and called for Shimei. He said to him, 'Build a house for yourself in Jerusalem. Live there! Do not go from one place to another. Because the day you go and cross the Kidron Valley you can be certain that you will die. Your blood will be on your *own* head.'
Shimei said to the king, '*Your* word is good. Your servant will do just as my lord, the king, has said.' So Shimei remained in Jerusalem many days.

Three full years later, two of Shimei's servants fled to Achish, son of

---

[182] 1 Kings 2:38-46

Maacah, king of Gath. Shimei was told, 'Look, your servants are in Gath.' So Shimei arose, saddled his donkey, and went to Gath; he went to look for his servants. So he went to Gath and brought back his servants.

Solomon was told that Shimei had left Jerusalem *to go to* Gath and had *now* returned. So the king sent and called for Shimei. He said to him, 'Didn't I make you swear by YHWH? Didn't I warn you, saying, "The day you leave to go here or there, you can be certain that you will die?" Didn't you say to me, "I have heard *your* word *and it* is good."? So why have you not kept the oath *that you swore* to YHWH, or the command that I gave you?'

The king then continued to Shimei, 'In your heart, you yourself know all the evil that you did to my father, David. So now YHWH will turn your evil back on your head. But King Solomon will be blessed, and the throne of David will be established before YHWH forever.' Then the king gave charge to Benaiah, son of Jehoiada, so he went out and fell upon Shimei so that he died.

In this way, the kingdom became established in the hand of Solomon.

A Political Alliance[183]

Solomon made an *alliance through* marriage with Pharaoh, king of Egypt. He married Pharaoh's daughter and brought her to the City of David, *where she lived* until Solomon finished building his *own* house, YHWH's house, and the wall around *all of* Jerusalem.

Solomon Seeking Wisdom[184]

Solomon loved YHWH; he walked in the statutes of David, his father. However, he slaughtered his sacrifices and burnt incense on the high places. Indeed, *all* the people slaughtered their sacrifices on the high places, because no house for the name of YHWH had been built in those days.

David had brought up the Ark of God from Kiriath Jearim to Jerusalem, *and had put it in the place* he had prepared for it, in a tent he had pitched for it. But the Tent of Meeting of God, which Moses, servant of YHWH, had made in the wilderness *was still at Gibeon. Indeed,* David had placed the bronze altar that Bezalel, son of Uri, son of Hur had made in front of the Tabernacle. Gibeon, then, was the most important *of all the* high places, and it was where Solomon and the assembly enquired of YHWH.

So Solomon spoke to all Israel: to the commanders of thousands and hundreds, to the judges, and to all the leaders, the heads of the fathers' *houses* in all Israel. Then Solomon, and all the assembly who were with him, went to the

---

[183] 1 Kings 3:1
[184] 1 Kings 3:2-15; 2 Chronicles 1:2-13a

high place at Gibeon. The king went there to offer his sacrifices. Solomon went to the bronze altar before YHWH, in the Tent of Meeting, and offered a thousand Burnt Offerings on the altar.

While there, during the night, YHWH appeared to Solomon in a dream.
God said, 'Tell *me*, what I should give you?'
Solomon said to God, 'You are the one who treated your servant, my father David, with great kindness. He walked before you in faithfulness and righteousness; he was upright in heart towards you. You have maintained this great kindness to him, by giving him a son to sit on his throne, as *it is* this day.

'Now YHWH, my God, you are the one who made your servant king, in place of David, my father. But I am a small boy; I don't know *how* to go out or to come in. So YHWH God, confirm your promise to my father, David. Your servant is in the midst of your people—*the people* you have chosen. They are a great people, like the dust of the earth, too numerous to be counted or numbered. So give to your servant a mind *that can* listen, *so I can* judge your people and distinguish between right and wrong. Give me wisdom and knowledge so that I may go out and come in before the people. For who is able to govern this great people of yours?'

The words that Solomon spoke were pleasing in the eyes of YHWH. So God said to him, 'You have asked for *one* thing: discernment, wisdom, and knowledge *so you can* administer justice and govern my people over whom I have made you king. You have not asked for a long life, wealth, or the life of your enemies. Because of that, I will do as you have asked: I will give you a wise and discerning mind; I will give you wisdom and knowledge. No one like you has come before you, and no one like you will arise after you. In addition, I will give you what you have not asked for—riches, wealth, and honour. While you live, there will be no one like you among the kings. *Indeed,* no king before you or any after will enjoy *such wealth and honour.* Then, if you walk in my ways, keeping my statutes and commandments, as your father David did, I will lengthen your days.'

Then Solomon awoke, and realised *that it had been* a dream.

Solomon *left the high place at Gibeon,* returned to Jerusalem, and stood before the Ark of the Covenant of the Lord. He sacrificed Burnt Offerings, offered Fellowship Offerings, and gave a feast for all his servants.

Wood and Stone for the Temple[185]

Solomon then ordered that a house for the name of YHWH be built, with a royal palace for himself.

---

[185] 1 Kings 5:1-18; 2 Chronicles 2:1-18

He took a census of all alien men who were *living* in the land of Israel, as his father, David, had previously done, and there were found to be one hundred and fifty-three thousand six hundred men. So Solomon conscripted *them to work with stone.*

Additional Labour Force

Workers	*Numbers*
Burden bearers	70,000
Stone cutters in the hill	80,000
Supervisors[1]	3,300 or 3,600[2]

Notes:
[1] The supervisors were appointed by Solomon to oversee the project and direct the workers; [2] 1 Kings notes 3,300, and 2 Chronicles 3,600

At the king's command they quarried large, heavy stones, *so that* the foundation of the house *could be laid with* dressed stone.

Now Hiram, king of Tyre had been a friend to David all *his* days. So when he heard that Solomon had been appointed king in his place, *he was concerned. He wanted the friendly relationship to continue and the trade routes through Israel to remain open. So* he sent his servants to Solomon.

Solomon then sent *a message* to Hiram, king of Tyre.

He said, 'You know that my father, David, could not build a temple for the name of YHWH, his God. He was surrounded with wars until YHWH put his enemies under the soles of his feet. But now YHWH, my God, has given me peace on every side; *there is* no adversary or bad circumstance. So I am planning to build a house for the name of YHWH, my God, just as YHWH told David, my father. *YHWH* said *to him*, "I will set your son on your throne in your place. He will build the house for my name."

'*The house will be* set apart to YHWH. Fragrant incenses will be burnt before him, and consecrated bread *will be set out* regularly. *There will be* Burnt Offerings in the mornings and evenings, on the Sabbaths, at the New Moons, and at the appointed feasts of YHWH, our God. This *will continue on* forever in Israel.

'The Temple that I am building will be great, because our God is greater that all the gods. But who is able to build a house for him, since the heavens and the highest heavens cannot contain him? Who then am I, that I should build a house for him, except as a place to burn sacrifices before him?

'So just as you did for my father, David, by sending him cedar, *so he could* build himself a house to live in, *do the same for me.* Give the order for cedars, from the cedars of Lebanon, to be cut down for me. Send me cedars, cypress, and algum trees from Lebanon, for I know that your men are skilled to cut down the trees of Lebanon. My servants will *work* with your servants. I will need much timber, because the Temple I am building *will be* great and magnificent.

'I will pay the wages of your servants to you, whatever amount you set. For you yourself know that there is no one among us who is as skilled as the Sidonians to fell timber. I will give your servants, the woodsmen who cut down the trees, *the following supplies*:

Solomon's Supplies to the Woodsmen

Type	*Quantity*
Ground wheat	20,000 cors (*4,400 kilolitres*)
Barley	20,000 cors (*4,400 kilolitres*)
Wine	20,000 baths (*440 kilolitres*)
Pressed olive oil	20,000 baths (*440 kilolitres*)

'Send me a man, skilled in working in gold, silver, bronze, and iron, as well as in crimson and violet cloth; *someone* who is experienced in engraving. *Someone who can work* with the skilled *men* who are with me in Judah and Jerusalem, whom my father, David, provided.'

When Hiram heard the words of Solomon, he was very pleased. He said, 'Blessed be YHWH today. He has given David a wise son *to rule* over this great nation.'

So Hiram sent a letter to Solomon, saying, 'Because YHWH loves his people, he has made you king over them.' He then continued, 'Blessed be YHWH, God of Israel, who made the heavens and the earth. He has given King David a wise son, endowed with prudence and understanding. He will build a house for YHWH and a palace for his kingdom.

'I have heard *the message* that you sent me. I will personally carry out everything that you wish concerning the cedar, cypress, *and algum* trees. My servants will take them from Lebanon to the sea. I will *then* make them into rafts to go by sea to the place that you have indicated to me. There I will have the rafts broken up, and you can take *the timber* away.

'I will send *you* Huram-Abi, a skilled man endowed with understanding. His mother is from Dan' (*or more likely, Naphtali*) and his father is from Tyre. He has been trained to work in gold, silver, bronze, iron, stone, and wood, as well as purple, violet, fine linen, and crimson *cloth*. He *can do* all kinds of engraving, and can work out any design given to him. *He will work* with your craftsmen, and with the craftsmen of my lord, David, your father. You, however, can grant my wish by giving food for my house.

'So now let my lord send to his servants the wheat, barley, oil, and wine that he promised to his servants. We will then cut down as many trees as you need from Lebanon. We will send them to you as rafts by sea to Joppa. You can then take them up to Jerusalem.'

So Hiram supplied Solomon with as many cedar and cypress trees as he wished. Solomon *in turn* gave *these supplies* to Hiram year after year.

Solomon's Annual Supplies to Hiram

Type	*Quantity*
Wheat, as food for his house	20,000 cors (*4,400 kilolitres*)
Barley	*20,000 cors* (*4,400 kilolitres*)
Wine	20,000 baths (*440 kilolitres*)
Pressed olive oil	20,000 baths (*440 kilolitres*)

YHWH gave Solomon wisdom, just as he promised him, and there was peace between Hiram and Solomon. The two of them made a treaty.

So King Solomon conscripted a labour force of thirty thousand men from all of Israel and sent them off to Lebanon in shifts of ten thousand. *Each shift spent* a month in Lebanon, *followed by* two months at home. *He put* Adoniram in charge of the forced labour.

So Solomon's builders and Hiram's builders, with *the help of* the Gebalites *from north of Tyre*, cut the stone and prepared the timber and the stone to build the house.

Solomon's Reign[186]

So Solomon, son of David, established himself over his kingdom, for YHWH his God *was* with him and made him exceedingly great. Solomon

---

[186] 1 Chronicles 29:23b-25; 2 Chronicles 1:1; 13b

prospered and all Israel listened to him. All the officials, the Mighty *Men*, and all King David's sons swore allegiance to Solomon, the king. *Indeed*, YHWH raised up Solomon in the eyes of all Israel and bestowed him with such royal splendour that no king of Israel had ever had before.

So Solomon reigned over Israel.

Two Prostitutes[187]

Two women—prostitutes—came to the king and stood before him. One of the women said, 'Please, my lord, this woman and I live in the same house, and I gave birth while she was in the house. On the third day, *after* I had given birth, this woman also gave birth. *There were* the two of us in the house; we *were* together. There was no stranger with us.

'Now this woman's son died in the night, because she lay on him. So she got up in the middle of the night and, while your maidservant was asleep, took my son from my side. She then put her dead son to my breast, *went back to bed*, and put my son to her breast. In the morning, I got up to nurse my son and *I* saw *that he was* dead. However, when I looked *more* closely at him in the morning *light*, I saw that he was not my son whom I had borne.'

Then the other woman said, 'Not so. The one that is alive is my son, and the one that is dead is yours.'

But the first one said, 'Not so. The one that is dead is your son, and the one that is alive is mine.' In this way, they spoke before the king.

The king said, 'This one says, "My son is the living *one*, and your son is the dead *one*." But this one says, "Not so, your son is the dead *one*, and my son is the living *one*."'

Then the king said *to his servant*, 'Get me a sword!' So they brought the sword before the king. The king said, 'Cut the living child in two. Give half to one and half to the other.'

The woman, whose son was alive, burned with compassion for her son. She said to the king, 'Please, my lord, give her the one that was born, *that is still* alive. Do not kill him under any circumstances.'

But the other one said, 'He will be neither yours nor mine. He will be cut *in two*.'

Then the king answered. He said, 'Give the first woman the boy that was born that is still alive. Make sure not to kill him, for she is his mother.'

The whole of Israel heard the judgement the king had given. They were in awe of him, because they saw that he had God's wisdom inside him to administer justice.

---

[187] 1 Kings 3:16-28

Establishing the Kingdom

Solomon's Officials and Governors[188]

So King Solomon was king over all Israel. These were his officials:

Solomon's Officials	
Person	*Position*
Azariah, son Zadok	Priest
Elihoreph and Ahijah, sons of Shisha	Secretaries
Jehoshaphat, son of Ahilud	Recorder
Benaiah, son of Jehoiada	In charge of the army
Zadok and Abiathar	Priests
Azariah, son of Nathan	In charge of the officials
Zabud, son of Nathan	Priest, and friend of the king
Ahishar	In charge of the *king's* house
Adoniram, son of Abda	In charge of the forced labour

Solomon *also* had twelve governors over all Israel. They provided for the king and his house. Each provided for one month in the year.

The Twelve Governors of Israel	
Name	*District*
Ben-Hur	The hill country of Ephraim
Ben-Deker	Makaz, Shaalbim, Beth Shemesh, Elon-Beth-hanan
Ben-Hesed	The Arubboth, including Socoh and all the land of Hepher
Ben-Abinadab[1]	All of Naphoth Dor
Baana, son of Ahilud	Taanach and Megiddo and all of Beth Shan, which is beside Zarethan below Jezreel. From Beth Shan to Abel Meholath, beyond Jokmeam
Ben-Geber	Ramoth Gilead, including the settlements of Jair son of Manasseh in Gilead, and the district of Argob in the Bashan with its 60 large walled cities with barred bronze *gates*
Ahinadab, son of Iddo	Mahanaim
Ahimaaz[2]	Naphtali
(Continued on next page)	

---

[188] 1 Kings 4:1-19

Establishing the Kingdom

	(Continued from previous page)
Baana, son of Hushai	Asher and Aloth
Jehoshaphat, son of Paruah	Issachar
Shimei, son of Ela	Benjamin
Geber, son of Uri	The land of Gilead (land of Sihon king of the Amorites and Og king of Bashan). He was the only governor in that land

Notes:
[1] He took Taphath, Solomon's daughter as a wife;
[2] He took Basemath, Solomon's daughter as a wife

Provisions for the Court[189]

Now the people of Judah and Israel were as numerous as the sand by the sea. They ate and drank and were happy. Solomon ruled over all the kingdoms from the River *Euphrates, to the* land of the Philistines, and to the border with Egypt. *Indeed,* Solomon ruled over everything west of the River *Euphrates,* from Tiphsah to Gaza. *He ruled* over all the kings west of the River and he had peace on every side. *Furthermore,* tribute was brought *and people* served Solomon all the days of his life.

During the whole of Solomon's lifetime, Judah and Israel, from Dan to Beersheba, lived in safety, *each* man under his vine or fig tree.

The daily provisions *required* for Solomon for one day, *were as follows*:

Solomon's Provisions for One Day

Items	*Quantities*
Fine flour	30 cors (*6.6 kilolitres*)
Meal	60 cors (*13.2 kilolitres*)
Cattle (fat)	10
Cattle (pasture fed)	20
Sheep	100
Deer, gazelle, roebucks, and fattened fowls	*unknown*

---

[189] 1 Kings 4:20-28

In addition, Solomon had four thousand stalls for his chariot horses and twelve thousand horses.

So the twelve governors, each in his month, provided for King Solomon and all who came to his table. They left nothing lacking. They also provided barley and straw for the horses and chariot horses—each according to his measure.

The Wisdom of Solomon[190]

God gave Solomon wisdom and exceedingly good insight. His breadth of understanding was *as vast* as the sand on the sea-shore. Solomon's wisdom exceeded that of the wisdom of all the men of the east; it was greater than all the wisdom of Egypt. He was wiser than any man, including Ethan the Ezrahite, and Heman, Calcol, and Darda (sons of Mahol). His name was *known* by all the surrounding nations.

The Wisdom of Solomon

He wrote 3,000 proverbs
He *composed* 5,000 songs
He could describe plants (from the cedar in Lebanon, to the hyssop that grows on the wall)
He could teach about animals, birds, things that creep, and fish

---

People came from all the nations to hear the wisdom of Solomon. *They were sent* from all the kings of the earth, who heard *about* his wisdom.

---

[190] 1 Kings 4:29-34

C23. SOLOMON/JEDIDIAH
(991-930 BC)

b). Building the Temple *(967-940 BC)*

The Main Temple Structure[191]

Four hundred and eighty years after the Israelites came out from Egypt, Solomon began building the house of YHWH. He began in the fourth year of his reign over Israel, on the second day of the second month, the month of Ziv.

He began building the *main* Temple *structure* and completed it. He *then* roofed the Temple and built rooms against *the* side *walls*.

The word of YHWH came to Solomon. He said, 'You are building this house *for me*. So if you walk in my statutes, obey my ordinances, and keep all my commandments by walking in them, I will fulfil the promise that I gave to David, your father, through you. I will live among the Israelites; I will not forsake my people, Israel.'

After Solomon *had* completed *the basic structure* of the Temple, he then lined it. He partitioned *off an area* at the rear of the Temple, to form an inner sanctuary for the Most Holy Place. He then prepared the inner sanctuary within the house, so he could put the Ark of the Covenant of YHWH within it.

He overlaid the interior with gold until the whole house was finished. He also overlaid the altar in the inner sanctuary. He then made a pair of cherubim in the inner sanctuary, and carved engravings on all the walls in both the inner and outer *rooms* around the Temple. He made doors for the entrance to the inner sanctuary and for the main hall.

He then built the inner courtyard, *the outer courtyard, and the priests' courtyard*.

The foundations for the house of YHWH had been laid in the fourth year *of Solomon's reign*, in the month of Ziv, and in the eleventh year, in the month of Bul, the eighth month, the house was finished. It had taken seven years to build, following every detail and all of the plans.

---

[191] 1 Kings 6:1, 9a, 11-15a, 16a, 19, 22-23a, 29a, 31a, 36a, 37-38; 2 Chronicles 3:1a, 2, 8a, 10a; 4:9a

Other Temple Structures and Fittings[192]

During this time, King Solomon had sent and brought Huram-*Abi* from Tyre. He was the son of a widow from the tribe of Naphtali *(or Dan)*; his father was a man from Tyre. He was a worker in bronze, and was filled with *great* knowledge and experience in working in bronze. So he came to King Solomon, and carried out all his work.

Solomon *ordered* pillars *to be* made for the front of the Temple. So Huram-*Abi* cast two bronze pillars, two capitals, and pomegranates. The pillars were then set up by the porch of the *east-facing* Temple: one on the right *(or south)*, and one on the left *(or north)*. So the work of the pillars was completed. He then made the Sea *(a settling tank)*, ten bronze Stands and ten bronze Basins. He then positioned the Stands *and the Sea in their places around the Temple*. Huram-*Ali* also made *pots, shovels, and bowls*.

So Huram-*Ali* completed all the work that he was doing for King Solomon in the house of YHWH.

The Work of Huram-Ali

The 2 pillars
The bowl shaped capitals for the top of the pillars
2 sets of latticework to decorate the two bowl-shaped capitals
400 pomegranates for the two sets of latticework
10 basins on their ten stands
10 gold lampstands
A bronze altar
The Sea with the 12 bulls underneath it
Pots, shovels, bowls, forks, and all the utensils

All the *utensils* that Huram-*Ali* made for King Solomon for the house of YHWH *were made of burnished bronze*. The king had them cast in clay moulds at the clay ground on the Jordan plain between Succoth and Zarethan. There were so many that Solomon didn't weigh them; the weight of the bronze was never determined.

Solomon also had all the furnishings in the house of YHWH made.

When King Solomon had finished doing all the work on the house of YHWH, he brought in all the dedicated things of his father, David. He placed

---

[192] 1 Kings 7:13-15a, 16a, 18a, 21a, 22b-23a, 27a, 38a, 39a, 40a, 40c-42a, 43-45a, 46-48a, 51; 2 Chronicles 3: 15a, 17a; 4:1a, 2a, 6a, 7a, 8a, 11a, 11c-13a, 14-16a, 17-19a; 5:1; 8:16

the silver, gold, and all the furnishings in the treasuries of the house of YHWH. Then all the work of Solomon had been carried out, from the foundation day of the Temple until its completion. The house of YHWH was finished.

The Gathering in Jerusalem[193]

Eleven months after the completion of the Temple, King Solomon assembled the elders of Israel, *and* all the heads of the tribes—the leaders of the fathers' houses of the Israelites. He *called them* to himself in Jerusalem to bring up the Ark of the Covenant of YHWH from the City of David (*also* known as Zion). So all the men of Israel gathered to King Solomon in the seventh month, the month of Ethanim, at the Feast *of Tabernacles*.

When all the elders of Israel arrived, the priests *and* Levites picked up the Ark of YHWH, and brought the Ark, the Tent of Meeting, and all the sacred utensils that were in the Tent *to the Inner Courtyard of the Temple*. Priests, who were Levites, carried them. Then King Solomon, and the entire assembly of Israel, who gathered with him before the Ark, sacrificed so many sheep and cattle that they couldn't be counted or numbered.

Then the priests took the Ark of the Covenant of YHWH to its resting place, underneath the wings of the cherubim in the Most Holy Place, the inner sanctuary of the house. There, the cherubim's wings were spread out over the Ark, with the cherubim overshadowing the Ark and its *carrying* poles from above.

The poles were long, and the ends of the poles could be seen from the Holy Place, in front of the inner sanctuary, but they could not be seen from outside. They were still there *when this story was written down*. The Ark contained only the two stone tablets that Moses had placed there. (*He had done so* at Horeb, where YHWH had made a covenant with the sons of Israel after they had come out from Egypt.)

Then the priests came out of the Holy Place.

All the priests who were present had consecrated themselves, regardless of what work they performed.

The Levites who were musicians—all of them, including Asaph, Heman, and Jeduthun, with their sons and relatives—were *there* dressed in fine linen. They were standing on the east side of the Altar *of Burnt Sacrifice* playing cymbals, harps, and lyres. With them were one hundred and twenty priests sounding trumpets.

The trumpeters and singers made *themselves* heard *with* one voice. They praised and thanked YHWH; they raised their voices, accompanied by

---

[193] 1 Kings 8:1-21; 2 Chronicles 5:2-6:11; 7:2

trumpets, cymbals, and musical instruments. They praised YHWH, 'For *he is good; his loving-kindness is forever.*'

Then a cloud filled the house of YHWH. *Indeed*, the priests were unable to stand to minister because of the cloud; they could not enter the house, for the glory of YHWH filled the house of YHWH.

Then Solomon said *to the people*, 'YHWH said that he would dwell in a dense cloud.' *He then addressed YHWH directly*, 'I have surely built a noble house for you; a place for you to dwell in forever.' Then the king turned *to the people* and blessed the whole assembly of Israel who were standing *before him*. He said, 'Blessed be YHWH, God of Israel. With his hand he has fulfilled the words that he spoke to my father, David. He said, "I brought my people Israel out of Egypt. Since then, I have not chosen a city among any of the tribes of Israel for a house to be built for my name. Nor have I chosen any man to be leader over my people, Israel. But *now* I have chosen Jerusalem, *that* my name will be there, and I have chosen *you*, David, to be *king* over my people, Israel."

'It was in my father, David's, heart to build a house for the name of YHWH, God of Israel. But YHWH said to my father, David, "It is in your heart to build a house for my name. *Indeed*, you have done well to have it in your heart. Nevertheless, you yourself are not *the one* to build it. But your son who will be born to you, he is the one who will build the house for my name."

'Now YHWH has kept the word that he made. I have followed my father, David; I sit on the throne of Israel, just as YHWH promised. I have *also* built a house for the name of YHWH, God of Israel. I have set a place there for the Ark, which contains the covenant that YHWH made with our fathers when he brought them out of the land of Egypt.'

The Dedication of the Temple[194]

Now Solomon was standing before the altar of YHWH, in front of the whole assembly of Israel. His hands were spread out to the heavens. However, he had made a platform of bronze. It was five cubits *(2.29 metres)* long, five cubits *(2.29 metres)* wide, and three cubits *(1.37 metres)* high. It was placed in the centre of the outer court. So he *went* and stood on it. Then he knelt down before the whole assembly of Israel, with his hands spread to the heavens.

He said, 'YHWH, God of Israel, there is no God like you in the heavens above or on the earth beneath. You have kept your covenant and *you have shown your* love to your servants who continue to walk before you with all their heart. You have kept the word that you gave to your servant David, my father; the word that you spoke, you have fulfilled with your hand today.

'So now YHWH, God of Israel, keep *the other word* that you spoke to your servant David, my father. *You* said to him, "Your sons are to be careful in their

---

[194] 1 Kings 8:22-61; 2 Chronicles 6:12-7:1, 3

ways. They are to walk according to my law; *they are* to walk before me, as you walked before me. *If they do*, then none of your successors will be cut off from sitting before me on the throne of Israel." So, I pray, God of Israel, let the word that you spoke to your servant David, my father, be confirmed.

'But will God really dwell with man on earth? Look, the heavens and the highest heavens cannot contain you, so how much less this Temple I have built. Yet you take notice of your servant's prayer and his humble request, YHWH, my God. Hear the cry and the prayer that your servant is praying before you today. May you watch over this house, night and day. *May you look towards* the place of which you have said, "My name will be there." Then you will hear the prayers that your servant prays *as I* face this place. So hear the prayers and requests of your servant and your people Israel, when they pray facing this place. Hear from your dwelling place, from the heavens, *and* forgive.

'When a man wrongs his neighbour, he may be required to swear a solemn oath. So if he comes to swear an oath before your altar in this Temple, then you will hear in the heavens and act. You will judge your servants. *You will* condemn the wicked and bring his deeds on his head. But you will justify the righteous and reward him according to his righteousness.

'Your people, Israel, may be defeated in the face of an enemy because they have sinned against you. But if they turn back to you and confess your name, and pray and make requests to you in this Temple, then hear *them* in the heavens. Forgive the sin of your people, Israel, and bring them back to the land that you gave to them and to their fathers.

'The heavens may get shut up; there may be no rain because your people have sinned against you. But if they pray facing this place, confess your name, and turn from their sin for which you have afflicted them, then hear *them* in the heavens. Forgive the sin of your servants, your people, Israel. Indeed teach them the right way, so they can walk in it, and send rain on your land that you gave your people to possess.

'Famine or plague may come on the land. *So too might* blight, mildew, locusts, and grasshoppers. Enemies may besiege your people in the cities of their land. There may be any kind of plague or disease. But a man, or *even* all your people, Israel, may become aware of the afflictions of their hearts and their pain. Then, *should* he spread out his hands in the direction of this holy Temple and *should* any prayer or request come, you would hear in your dwelling place in the heavens. Then you can forgive and act. You can deal with every *man* according to his deeds. For you know his heart, as you alone know the hearts of all the sons of men. They will then fear you, and walk in your ways, all the days that they live in the land that you gave to our fathers.

'Furthermore, foreigners, who are not from your people, Israel, have come from distant lands because of your name. They have heard of your great name, your mighty hand, and your outstretched arm. So when they come and pray facing this Temple, you will hear in your dwelling place, in the heavens. You will do everything that the foreigner asks of you. That way all the peoples of the earth will know your name. They will fear you as *do* your people, Israel. They will know that this house that I have built is called by your name.

'Your people will go out to fight against their enemies, whichever way you send them. They will pray to YHWH, facing the city you have chosen and the Temple that I have built in your name. But when you hear their prayers and requests in the heavens, *you will* uphold their cause.

'Your people will sin against you (for there is no man who doesn't sin). You will be angry with them and give them over to an enemy. They may be taken captive to the land of their enemy, far away or near. But their hearts *may* turn back *to you* in the land where they have been taken captive; they *may* repent and seek your favour in the land of their captors. They may say, "We have sinned. We have done wrong. We have acted wickedly." They *may* turn back to you, with all their heart and all their soul, in the land of their enemies who took them captive. They *may* pray to you facing towards the land that you gave to their fathers, the city you have chosen, and the Temple that I have built for your name. Then you will hear their prayer and their requests in your dwelling place in the heavens, and you will uphold their cause. Then you can forgive your people who sinned against you; all the transgressions that they committed against you. You can show them compassion in the presence of their conquerors. Then their conquerors will have compassion on them. For they are your people and your inheritance, whom you brought out of Egypt from the midst of the iron furnace.

'Now, my God, I pray that your eyes be open and your ears be attentive to the prayers of this place. Hear the requests of your servant and your people, Israel. May you listen to them in all their cries to you, for you yourself separated them out for yourself, as an inheritance, from all the nations of the earth. *It was what* you promised, Lord YHWH, through Moses your servant, when you brought our fathers from Egypt.

> 'Now arise, YHWH, God,
> *come* to your resting place;
> *the resting place of* you and your mighty Ark.
> May your priests, YHWH God, be clothed in salvation;
> let your godly people rejoice in goodness.
> YHWH God, do not turn away from the face of your anointed;
> remember *your* kindness to your servant, David.'

When Solomon had finished praying all *his* prayers and requests to YHWH, he stood before the altar of YHWH. Then fire came down from the heavens and consumed the Burnt Offerings and the sacrifices. When all the Israelites saw the fire coming down and the glory of YHWH upon the Temple, they bowed down on the pavement with their faces to the ground. They worshipped and praised YHWH, 'For he is good; for his love is forever.'

Solomon then blessed the whole assembly of Israel in a loud voice. He said, 'Blessed be YHWH. He has given his people, Israel, rest. *Indeed*, not one word has failed from all the good promises he made, through the hand of Moses, his servant. May YHWH, our God, be with us, just as he was with our fathers. May he not leave us or abandon us. May he incline our hearts to him to walk in his ways and to keep his commandments, laws, and regulations that he gave to our fathers. May these words of mine, seeking YHWH's favour, be near to YHWH, our God, day and night. May he uphold the cause of his servant and the cause of his people, Israel, day by day. Then all the peoples of the earth will know that YHWH is God; *there is* no other.

'But your hearts are to be at peace with YHWH, our God. You are to walk in his statutes, and keep his commandments, as at this day.'

The Dedication Sacrifices[195]

Then the king, and every Israelite who was with him, offered sacrifices in YHWH's presence. Solomon slaughtered *many* Fellowship Offerings which he offered to YHWH. So the king and all the Israelites dedicated the house of YHWH.

Solomon's Fellowship Offerings	
Cattle	22,000
Sheep	120,000

Then the priests and the Levites took their stand, opposite *each other*. The priests blew their trumpets, while the Levites played YHWH's musical instruments. (These were the ones that King David had made, to be played when he was giving thanks to YHWH, 'For his loving kindness endures forever'.)

That day the king consecrated the centre of the courtyard in front of the house of YHWH, because the bronze altar was too small to hold all the offerings. So he offered Burnt Offerings, Grain Offering and the fat of the Fellowship Offerings there.

Solomon, and all the Israelites who were with him, *dedicated the altar for seven*

---

[195] 1 Kings 8:62-66; 2 Chronicles 7:4-10

days, then they celebrated the festival, before YHWH their God. There was a great assembly—*people* from Lebo Hamath to the brook of Egypt. *They celebrated for* seven days, and *then* seven days *more—a total of* fourteen days: seven days for the dedication of the altar, and seven days for the Feast *of Tabernacles*. Then on the fifteenth day they held a solemn assembly, before sending the people away. So on the twenty-third day of the seventh month he sent the people to their homes.

The people blessed the king. They went to their homes full of joy and glad of heart, for all the good that YHWH had done for his servant, David, for Solomon, and his people, Israel.

The Construction of Solomon's Palace[196]

After completing the Temple, Solomon took *a further* thirteen years to build his palace.

The House of the Forest of Lebanon

Purpose	*An armoury and treasury*
	It may also have been a place of assembly
Size	Length: 100 cubits (*45.72 metres*)
	Width: 50 cubits (*22.86 metres*)
	Height: 30 cubits (*13.72 metres*)
Columns	4 rows of cedar columns
Beams	Cedar beams (supported by the columns): 45 (15 per row)
Roof	Cedar over the beams that rested on the columns
Windows	3 rows of 3 windows, facing each another *on each side of the building*
Doorways	Three doors at the front facing one another
Doorframes	Square frames

The Hall of Pillars

Purpose	*Perhaps a porch to the Hall of the Forest*
Size	Length: 50 cubits (*22.86 metres*)
	Width: 30 cubits (*13.72 metres*)
Porch	In front of hall
Pillars, with canopy	In front of porch

---

[196] 1 Kings 7:1-12

The Throne Hall *or* Hall of Justice

Purpose: Where Solomon judged
Panelling: Cedar, from floor to floor

The King's House

Purpose: Where Solomon was to live
Location: In the other court, back from the hall
Design: Similar to the hall

The Palace for Pharaoh's Daughter

Purpose: A Palace for Pharaoh's daughter whom Solomon married
Design: Similar to the hall

Materials Used

Location	*Material*
All buildings (from foundations to the eaves, including the great courtyard)	Costly blocks of stone, cut to size with a saw inside and out
Foundations	Costly blocks of large stone 10 cubits (*4.57 metres*) and *other* stone 8 cubits (*3.66 metres*)
Above foundations	Costly stone, cut to size and cedar
The wall surrounding the great courtyard	3 rows of dressed stone and one row of cedar (as were the porch and the inner courtyard of YHWH's Temple)

When it was completed, Solomon brought Pharaoh's daughter up from the City of David to the house that he had built for her. He said, 'My wife shall not live in the house of David, king of Israel, for the places that the Ark of YHWH has entered are holy.'

YHWH Appears to Solomon[197]

When Solomon had finished building *both* the house of YHWH and the king's house, he had done everything he had desired to do regarding YHWH's Temple and his palace. Then YHWH appeared to Solomon a second time, at night, as he had appeared to him at Gibeon.

YHWH said to him, 'I have heard your prayer and your request that you made before me. I have chosen this place for myself as a house of sacrifice. I may shut up the heavens, so it does not rain. I may command locusts to devour the land. I may send a plague among my people. But if my people, who are called by my name, humble themselves and pray, seek my face and turn back from their wicked ways, then I will hear *them* in the heavens. I will then forgive their sin and heal their land.

'My eyes will be open, and my ears attentive to the prayers *offered* in this place; my eyes and my heart will always be there. So I have chosen and have consecrated this Temple that you have built, setting my name there forever.

'But you, walk before me with integrity and an upright heart, as your father, David, did. Do everything that I command you; observe my statutes and ordinances. Then I will establish your royal throne over Israel forever, as I promised your father, David. I said *to him*, "None of your successors will be cut off from the throne of Israel."

'However, you or your sons may well turn away from following me. You may cease to observe my commandments and laws that I gave you. You may go and serve other gods and worship them. Then I will pluck them from my land which I have given them; I will cut off Israel from the face of the land. I will reject the Temple, that I have consecrated for my name, from my presence. Then Israel will become a proverb *depicting disaster; it will be an object of* taunt among all the peoples. This Temple will become a heap of ruins, and all who pass by it will be appalled. They will whistle and say, "Why has YHWH done this to this land and to this Temple?" Then they will say, "They abandoned YHWH, their God, the God of their fathers, who brought their fathers from the land of Egypt. They embraced other gods *instead*; they worshipped them and served them. This is why YHWH, their God, has inflicted this calamity."'

Solomon and the King of Tyre[198]

Twenty years after *the beginning of the construction of the Temple*, Solomon had

---

[197] 1 Kings 9:1-9; 2 Chronicles 7:11-22; 8:11
[198] 1 Kings 9:10-14; 2 Chronicles 8:1-3

built two buildings: the house of YHWH, and the king's house. Furthermore, Hiram, king of Tyre, had provided Solomon with cedar and cypress trees, and as much gold as he had wanted. Indeed, Hiram had sent one hundred and twenty talents (*4.1 metric tonnes*) of gold to the king. So King Solomon gave Hiram twenty towns in the land of Galilee. But when Hiram came from Tyre to see the towns that Solomon had given to him, they were not pleasing in his eyes.

Hiram said *to Solomon*, 'What sort of towns are these that you have given me, my brother?' Then he called them the Land of Cabul (*'good for nothing'*), which *they were still known as when this story was written down.*

As for the towns that Hiram had given to Solomon, Solomon rebuilt and settled Israelites in them. Solomon then went to Hamath Zobah (*north of Damascus*) and captured it.

Forced Labour[199]

This is the account of the forced labour that King Solomon had conscripted *to build the Temple and his palace. The original projects took twenty years to complete. However, his ongoing projects took many more years.* Indeed, everything that Solomon desired *to build*, he built, *whether* in Jerusalem, in Lebanon, and anywhere *else* in the land that he ruled.

Work Constructed with Solomon's Forced Labour

The House of YHWH
Solomon's Palace
The supporting terraces
The wall of Jerusalem
Hazor
Megiddo
Gezer[1]
Upper Beth Horon[2]

Lower Beth Horon[2]
Baalath
Tadmor in the wilderness in the land *of Judah*
All Solomon's store-cities, including in Hamath
The towns for his chariots
The towns for his horses

Note:

[1] Pharaoh, king of Egypt had attacked and captured the Canaanite city of Gezer (*30 kilometres north-west of Jerusalem*). *He had then* burnt it with fire, killed the inhabitants, and given it to his daughter, Solomon's wife, as a wedding present. So Solomon rebuilt Gezer; [2] Fortified cities, with walls, gates, and bars

---

[199] 1 Kings 9:15-24; 2 Chronicles 8:4-10

The people, whom Solomon conscripted, were not Israelites but the remnants of *the other nations who lived in Israel*. They were the descendants of those who remained in the land, whom the Israelites had been unable to devote *to YHWH*. So Solomon conscripted them to forced labour, and they were still slaves *when this story was written down*.

Solomon did not make slaves of any of the Israelites, because they were men of war, his servants, and his chiefs, officers, commanders of his chariots, and horsemen. *They were also* the officials supervising those doing the work on Solomon's projects.

Number of Supervisors	
According to 1 Kings	550
According to 2 Chronicles	250

Solomon's Forced Labour Force
Amorites
Hittites
Perizzites
Hivites
Jebusites

Only after Pharaoh's daughter had come from the City of David to *live in* the palace that Solomon had built for her, did Solomon build the supporting terrace.

Solomon's Ongoing Temple Obligations[200]

Solomon *ordered* Burnt Offerings to be offered to YHWH, on the altar that he had built in front of the porch. They were offered according to the day to day requirements, *and as otherwise required*, as commanded by Moses.

(See table on next page)

---

[200] 1 Kings 9:25; 2 Chronicles 8:12-15

> **Events on which variations in the daily Sacrifices were required**
>
> Sabbaths
> New Moons
> The three annual feasts: Unleavened Bread, Weeks, and Tabernacles

In keeping with what his father, David, had prescribed, Solomon appointed *the various priests and Levites to their duties*; for that is what, David, the man of God, had ordered. Solomon did not deviate from the command of King David in any matter concerning the priests and Levites, or regarding the treasuries.

> **Solomon's Appointments at the Temple**
>
> | *Divisions* | *Functions* |
> |---|---|
> | The priests | For their service |
> | The Levites | For their praise, and for assisting the priests in their daily duties |
> | The gatekeepers | For the gates |

Solomon *himself* sacrificed Burnt Offerings and Fellowship Offerings, on the altar that he had built for YHWH, three times a year. He made smoke sacrifices with them before YHWH. In this way, he fulfilled *his obligations to* the Temple.

C23. SOLOMON/JEDIDIAH
(991-930 BC)

c). Love Songs *(c. 940 BC)*

Introduction[201]

Solomon's Song of Songs, *is a series of linked dramas about the relationship of King Solomon with a Shulammite woman (origins unknown). It includes tales of their courtship, wedding, and their continuing love for each another.*

In the original Hebrew, there are no indications of who is speaking at any given time. As a consequence, each interpreter has needed to identify the particular speakers.

The Story Begins[202]

The story begins with the Shulammite's pursuit of the king.

Woman to Friends	Let him kiss me with kisses of his mouth.
Woman to King	Your love is better than wine. Your oils have a pleasing fragrance; your name is *like* oil poured out. Because of this, maidens love you. Haul me after you; let us run.
Woman to Friends	The king brought me into his chambers.
Friends to Woman	We will rejoice and be glad with you. We will praise your love greater than wine.
Woman to King	The *maidens* rightly love you.
Woman to Friends	Daughters of Jerusalem, I am dark, but comely. *I am the colour of the* tents of Kedar and the curtains of Solomon. Do not stare at my blackish complexion; I have been caught by the sun. My mother's sons were angry with me; they made me keeper of the vineyards. *But* my *own* vineyard, *my own body*, I have ignored.

---

[201] The Song of Solomon 1:1
[202] The Song of Solomon 1:2-6

Establishing the Kingdom

A Date with Love[203]

The Shulammite may have attracted the king's interest, but there was still a long way to go. So, in order to pursue the relationship, the Shulammite arranged a meeting outside of the city, where they could spend some time on their own.

Woman to King	Tell me, *you* whom I love, where do you graze? Where do you lie *your sheep* down at noon? Why should I be like a woman who has to cover herself, *like a whore, trying to find you* among your companions' flocks?
King to Woman	If you do not know yourself, most beautiful of women, follow the tracks of the flock. Graze your young goats by the shepherds' tents.
	My darling, I liken you to a mare among the *stallions* of Pharaoh's chariots. Your cheeks are enhanced with ornaments, your neck with strings of beads. We will make earrings of gold, with drops of silver, for you.
Woman to Friends	While the king was on his couch, my nard gave off its scent. My beloved *also gave off his scent* to me—*like* a sachet of myrrh, as I cradled *his head* between my breasts. My beloved is *as pleasing* to me as a cluster of henna blossoms, in the *oasis of the* vineyards of En Gedi.
King to Woman	Look, my darling, how beautiful you are; how beautiful you are. Your eyes *are as enchanting as* doves.
Woman to King	Look, my beloved, how handsome you are; how charming *you are*. Our couch is green.
King to Woman	The beams of our houses are *made of* cedar; our rafters *made of* fir.
Woman to King	I am *like a flower in spring*, a rose of Sharon, a lily of the valleys.
King to Woman	My darling is among the maidens, as a lily among thorns.
Woman to King	My beloved is among the young men, like an apple tree

---

[203] The Song of Solomon 1:7-2:7

	among the *common* trees of the forest. I take pleasure and sit in his shade; his fruit is sweet to my taste.
Woman to Friends	He brought me to the house of wine; he *flew* his banner over me *announcing his* love. Sustain me with raisins; refresh me with apples, for I am faint with love. His left *hand* is under my head and his right *hand* embraces me. But, daughters of Jerusalem, *do not be envious*. Swear to me, by the gazelles and does of the field, that you will not arouse or awaken love *for yourselves* prematurely.

The Lovers in Spring[204]

The Shulammite had attracted the king's attention. Now the king took the initiative.

Woman to Friends	The sound of my beloved! Look, here he comes leaping over the mountains; bounding over the hills. My beloved is like a gazelle or young stag. Look, he is standing there behind our wall. *He is* gazing through the windows, peering through the lattices. My beloved speaks. He says to me, 'Arise, my darling, my beautiful one. Come! Look! Winter has passed and the rains have come and gone. Flowers can be seen in the land. The time of singing has arrived and the cooing of turtledoves can be heard in our land. Fig trees have put forth their first fruit; the vines are blossoming and producing their fragrance. Arise! Come, my darling, my beautiful one. Come!'
King to Woman	My dove, *you are like a dove that hides* in the clefts of the rock, in the steep hiding places. Let me see you, let me hear your voice; for your voice is sweet and your appearance is comely.
Woman to King	Catch the foxes *that threaten our relationship*—the little foxes that are wrecking the vineyards—for our vineyards are in blossom.

---

[204] The Song of Solomon 2:8-17

Establishing the Kingdom

Woman to Friends	My beloved is mine and I am his; he pastures *his flock* among the lilies.
Woman to King	Stay around, my beloved, until the day breaks and the shadows flee. Be like a gazelle or a young stag on cleft mountains.

Lonely at Night[205]

The Shulammite may have won the heart of the King, but he wasn't hers yet. Indeed, there were still many lonely nights to come.

Woman to Friends	On my bed at night I sought the one my heart loves. I sought him but did not find him. *So I said to myself,* 'I will get up and go around the city, through the streets and squares. I will search for the one my heart loves.' *Then* I sought him, but did not find him.
	Watchmen found me as they made their rounds of the city. *I said,* 'Have you seen the one my heart loves?' I had hardly left them, when I found the one my heart loves. I held him. I didn't let him go until I had brought him to my mother's house, into the room where I had been conceived.
	Daughters of Jerusalem *do not be envious.* Swear, by the gazelles and does of the field, that you will not arouse or awaken love *for yourselves* prematurely.

The Wedding Procession[206]

The time for the wedding arrived, and it began with the royal procession of the groom.

Narrator	Who is this *who is* coming up from the wilderness, like a column of smoke? *Who is this who is* perfumed with myrrh and incense, from all the powders of the merchant?
	Look, it is Solomon's carriage. *It is* surrounded by sixty Mighty *Men* from the Mighty *Men* of Israel. They are all

---

[205] The Song of Solomon 3:1-5
[206] The Song of Solomon 3:6-11

> wearing swords. *They are all* experts in war. Each *one* has his sword at his side, ready for the terrors of the night.
>
> King Solomon has made himself a sedan from the trees of Lebanon. He has made its posts from silver, its base from gold, and its seat from purple. Its interior has been inlaid with love by the daughters of Jerusalem.
>
> Come out, daughters of Zion. Look at King Solomon! *He is wearing the* wreath *with which* his mother crowned him. *This is* the day of his wedding; *this is* the day of his gladness of heart.

The Wedding Night[207]

The official celebrations were over, and the bride and groom were on their own. Despite that the bride, who had never before been frightened of taking the initiative, was a little distant.

King to Woman	Look, my darling, how beautiful you are; you look beautiful. Your eyes behind your veil are *as enchanting as* doves. Your *dark wavy* hair is like a flock of goats descending Mount Gilead. Your teeth are *as white as a* flock of *newly* shorn sheep after they've been washed. Each of them has its twin; not one of them is missing. Your lips are *as red* as a scarlet thread; your mouth is comely. Your *reddish* cheeks behind your veil are like halves of a pomegranate. Your neck is like the tower of David; it is built in courses; *it is adorned with necklaces. It is as if* a thousand shields are hung on it; all the shields of the Mighty *Men*. Your two breasts are *as attractive and youthful as* two fawns; *they are like* twins of a gazelle *which frolic about while they* graze among the lilies. Until the day breaks and the shadows flee I will take myself to the mountain of myrrh, to the hill of frankincense. You are altogether beautiful my darling. You are without blemish. *But you are a little distant. So come* with me from Lebanon, *my* bride; come with me from Lebanon. Descend the summits of Amana, Senir, and Hermon. *Come down* from

---

[207] The Song of Solomon 4:1-5:1

	the dens of lions and from the mountains of leopards. You stole my heart, my sister, *my* bride. You stole my heart with one *glance of* your eyes, and with one jewel of your necklace.
	How beautiful is your love, my sister, *my* bride. Your love is more pleasing than wine; the fragrance of your oils is better than any spice. Your lips *are as sweet as the* honeycomb, *my* bride; milk and honey are under your tongue. The fragrance of your garments is like the fragrance of Lebanon.
	But you are *as inaccessible as* a locked garden, my sister, *my* bride. *You are a* locked pool, a sealed up spring. *Yet your garden is filled with exotic fruits. You have* an orchard of pomegranates with choice fruits. You have henna with nard, nard and saffron, calamus and cinnamon, all *kinds of* incense trees, myrrh, aloes, and all the finest spices. *You are* a garden spring, a well of living water, flowing down from Lebanon.
Woman to King	Rouse yourself, north wind! Come, south wind! Blow upon my garden, so that its fragrances may spread. Let my beloved come into his garden. Let him taste its choice fruits.
King to Woman	I have come into my garden, my sister, *my* bride. I have gathered my myrrh with my spice. I have eaten my honeycomb and my honey. I have drunk my wine and my milk.
Friends to Lovers	Eat, friends! Drink, and be drunk, *you* lovers.

Life in a Harem[208]

Being married to a king involved living in a harem. It meant there were other queens and concubines competing for the king's attention. So being able to respond quickly to the demands of the king was a very important aspect of palace life, and failure to do so had serious consequences.

---

[208] The Song of Solomon 5:2-6:3

Woman to Friends	I was asleep, but my heart was awake. *I heard* a noise! My beloved was knocking.
King to Woman	Open to me, my sister, my darling, my dove, my perfect one. For my head is drenched with dew; my locks *are wet* with the dew of the night.
Woman to Friends	I took off my robe *to go to bed*, but must I now put it on *to answer the door*? I washed my feet, must I now soil them?
	My beloved has put his hand through the hole in the door. My inmost being is stirred for him.
	I got up to open *the door* for my beloved. My hands were dripping with myrrh, and my fingers passed myrrh onto the handles of the bolt. I opened *the door* myself for my beloved, but my beloved had turned away; he had gone.
	My heart had gone out *to him* when he had spoken. I looked for him, but couldn't find him; I called to him, but there was no reply. Watchmen found me as they made their rounds of the city. The guards on the walls struck me, bruised me, and took my cloak from me.
	Daughters of Jerusalem, swear to me. If you find my beloved, what will you tell him? *Tell him* that I am faint with love.
Friends to Woman	Fairest among women, how is your beloved better than *any other*? How is your beloved better than *any other*, that you *tell* us to swear?
Woman to Friends	My lover is radiant and ruddy; he stands out in *a crowd of* ten thousand men. His head is *like* gold, refined gold; his locks are wavy, as black as a raven. His eyes are like *wet* doves *glistening* beside streams of water; like being bathed in milk, with a jewel mounted *in the centre*. His cheeks are like beds of spices growing perfume; his lips are lilies dripping with myrrh. His arms are cylinders of gold set with gems from Tarshish; his body is an ivory tusk, inlaid with sapphires. His legs are pillars of marble set

	on bases of refined gold; his appearance is like Lebanon, as choice as its cedars. His mouth is sweetness; he is totally desirable. This is my beloved; this is my friend, Daughters of Jerusalem.
Friends to Woman	*So* where has your beloved gone, fairest among women? Where has your beloved turned to, that we may seek him with you?
Woman to Friends	My beloved *would have* gone down to his garden, to the spice beds. There he would graze in the gardens and gather lilies. I am my beloved's and my beloved is mine. *But* he is grazing among the lilies.

A King's Reflection[209]

Although the Shulammite had not answered the door to him, the king still held strong feelings for her.

King to himself	My darling, you are as beautiful as Tirzah *in the north*, as comely as Jerusalem *in the south*, and as overpowering as an army with banners. Look away from me, for your eyes overwhelm me. Your *dark wavy* hair is like a flock of goats descending *Mount* Gilead. Your teeth are *as white as* a flock of sheep after they've been washed. Each of them has its twin; not one is missing. Your *reddish* cheeks behind your veil are like halves of a pomegranate.

The King's Favourite[210]

Of all the king's wives and concubines, the Shulammite was his favourite.

King to Friends	There *are* sixty queens, eighty concubines, and virgins without number *within the royal harem. But* my dove, my perfect one *stands* alone. She is her mother's darling; to the one who bore her she is perfect. Maidens have seen her and called her blessed; queens and concubines have

---

[209] The Song of Solomon 6:4-7
[210] The Song of Solomon 6:8-10

	also praised her.
Friends to King	Who is this that appears like the dawn, is as fair as the moon, is as bright as the sun, and is as overpowering as an army with banners?

In the Nut Grove[211]

After failing to open her door to the king, the Shulammite went to the king's garden, where she found him.

Woman to Friends	I went down to the nut grove to see the fresh shoots in the valley; to see if the vines had budded *and* the pomegranates were in bloom. Before I knew it, my soul put me in a chariot with my royal prince.
Friends to Woman	Turn around! Turn around, Shulammite! Turn around! Turn around, so that we may look at you.
Woman to Friends	Why would you look at *me*, a Shulammite? *Why do you find me as mesmerising* as the dance between two army camps?

A Love Song[212]

The king was totally besotted with the Shulammite, and continually sang her praise.

King to Woman	How fair are your sandalled feet, noble daughter? The curves of your thighs are like jewels, the work of a craftsman's hands. Your navel *is like a* round bowl that never lacks mixed wine. Your belly *is like a* heap of wheat encircled by lilies. Your two breasts are *as attractive and youthful as* two fawns; *they are like* twins of a gazelle. Your neck is *as grand as* an ivory tower; your eyes *glisten like* the pools of Heshbon at the gate of Bath Rabbim; your nose is *as grand and dignified* as the tower of Lebanon, which faces Damascus. Your head is as majestic as *Mount* Carmel. The flowing locks of your head are like purple; the king is held captivated by *your* tresses.

---

[211] The Song of Solomon 6:11-13
[212] The Song of Solomon 7:1-10

	How beautiful you are. How pleasing you are, *my* love, with *your* delights. You are as tall and slim as a palm tree; your breasts are like clusters *of dates*. I said, 'I will climb the palm tree, I will take hold of the dates' stalks.'
	So may your breasts be like clusters of the vine; may the fragrance of your breath be *as sweet* as apples. May your mouth be like the best wine.
Woman to King	*The wine is* going smoothly to my beloved; it flows gently over the lips of those who fall asleep together. I am my beloved's and his desire is for me.

The Woman's Invitation[213]

The Shulammite had now become well-known around the palace and in the city. Her deep love for the king may also have made her an object of scorn. As a consequence, she suggested to the king that they take a rural retreat.

Woman to King	Come, my beloved, let us go to the fields; let us spend a night in the villages. Let us get up early and go to the vineyards; let us see if the vines have budded; if its blossoms have opened. *Let us see if* the pomegranates are in bloom. I will give my love to you there.
	The mandrakes will give forth their fragrance *to stimulate our desire*. All choice fruits will be at our doors. *All things*, new and old, my beloved, I have treasured up for you.
	If only you were my brother, who nursed at my mother's breast. Then if I found you in the street, I could kiss you and no one would treat me with contempt. I could then lead you; I could bring you to the house of my mother, who taught me *about intimacy, and* I could give you a drink of spiced wine, from the nectar of my *own* pomegranate *wine*.
Woman to Friends	His left *hand* is under my head and his right hand embraces me. *But*, Daughters of Jerusalem, *do not be envious*. Swear that you will not arouse or awaken love *for yourselves* prematurely.

---

[213] The Song of Solomon 7:11-8:4

Establishing the Kingdom

The Woman's Love Song[214]

The Shulammite's love for the king was absolute. So she expressed the desire to be owned totally by her king.

Narrator	Who is this coming up from the wilderness, leaning on her beloved?
Woman to King	Under the apple tree I awakened you. There your mother was in labour with you; she was in labour *and* bore you there. *Own me*! Set me like a seal over your heart, like a seal on your arm. For love is as strong as death; jealousy as unyielding as Sheol. Its flames are flames of fire. *It is like* the flames of God. Much water cannot extinguish love; rivers can not wash it away. *But it will be tested. Because* if a man were to give all the wealth of his house for love, he would be held in utter contempt.

Brotherly Love[215]

As she had grown up, the Shulammite had been cared for by her brothers. It had been their responsibility to make sure she had remained pure, ready to be betrothed. So as her brothers reflected on this, the Shulammite was able to reassure them, that even when she had become sexually mature, she had kept herself pure for her beloved.

Brothers to Woman	Our sister is young, and her breasts are not *yet formed*. What shall we do for our sister, for the day that she will be spoken for? *We need to protect her from sexual misconduct. So,* if she *puts up a barrier like* a wall, we will *honour her; we will* build a battlement of silver on her. But if she is *promiscuous, as open as a* door, we will *stop her; we will* enclose her in boards of cedar.
Woman to Brothers	I am a wall, and my breasts are like towers. So I brought contentment to his eyes.

---

[214] The Song of Solomon 8:5-7
[215] The Song of Solomon 8:8-10

Establishing the Kingdom

Solomon's Vineyards[216]

As far as the Shulammite was concerned, everything she had, including her own body, belonged to the king. Despite that, she did not forgot the contribution her brothers had made to her well-being.

Narrator	Solomon had a vineyard in Baal Hamon. He put the vineyard *in the hands of* caretakers. Each would pay a thousand *shekels* of silver (*11.4 kilogrammes*) for its fruit.
Woman to King	My own vineyard is here before me. The thousand *shekels* are for you Solomon. But *there are* two hundred (*2.28 kilogrammes*) for the keepers, *my brothers*, who guarded its fruit.

Jealous Love[217]

The lovers were besotted by each other. So much so, that the king found it difficult to be apart from the love of his life—particularly when she had the attention of others.

King to Woman	You who sit in the gardens, my companions are listening to your voice. *But* let me hear *it*.
Woman to King	Make haste, my beloved! Be like a gazelle or a young stag on the mountains of spices.

---

[216] The Song of Solomon 8:11-12
[217] The Song of Solomon 8:13-14

C23. SOLOMON/JEDIDIAH
(991-930 BC)

d). The Highs and Lows of Solomon *(940-933 BC)*

Solomon's Navy[218]

King Solomon went to the land of Edom, to Ezion Geber and Elath on the edge of the Sea of Reeds. There at Ezion Geber, near Elath, he built a fleet of ships. Hiram *also* sent him *some* ships by his servants, who were experienced sailors. So they joined the fleet, *to sail* with Solomon's men.

They sailed to Ophir, and returned to Solomon with four hundred and twenty talents (*14.4 metric tonnes*) of gold. Moreover, the servants of Solomon and Hiram *also* returned with a great quantity of almug *wood* and precious stones from Ophir, in the ships in which they brought the gold from Ophir.

Then, with the almug trees, the king made steps for the house of YHWH and for the palace of the king. He *also* made harps and lyres for making music. *At the time this story was recorded*, such great quantities of almug trees had never been seen in Judah

The Queen of Sheba[219]

Sheba was either in Africa or Southern Arabia, and the queen of Sheba heard about the fame of Solomon (*in respect* to the name of YHWH). So she came to test him with difficult questions. She came to Jerusalem with a very big company. *She brought* camels carryings spices, a large quantity of gold, and precious stones. She came to Solomon and asked him everything that was on her mind. Solomon answered all her questions; there was nothing hidden from him which he was unable to explain to her.

The queen of Sheba saw all the wisdom of Solomon. She saw the palace he had built, the food on his table, the seating of his servants, and the attendance and dress of his waiters and cupbearers. She saw the Burnt Offerings that he made in the house of YHWH. *As a consequence,* her breath was taken away.

She said to the king, 'The report that I heard in my land, about your deeds and wisdom, is true. But I didn't believe it, until I came and saw for myself. Now see, not even half was told to me. The greatness of your wisdom and wealth go well beyond the report that I had heard.

'How happy are your men; how blessed are your servants who continually stand in your presence, hearing your wisdom. Blessed be YHWH, your God,

---

[218] 1 Kings 9:26-28; 10:11-12; 2 Chronicles 8:17-18; 9:10-11
[219] 1 Kings 10:1-10, 13; 2 Chronicles 9:1-9, 12

who has delighted in you, by putting you on the throne of Israel, as king for YHWH, your God. YHWH your God's love for Israel, and *his desire* to uphold them, is forever. So he has made you king over them, *to rule with* justice and righteousness.'

She then gave the king one hundred and twenty talents (*4.1 metric tonnes*) of gold, a large quantity of spices, and *some* precious stones. Never again did spices come in such great quantities, as the queen of Sheba gave to King Solomon.

King Solomon gave the queen of Sheba everything she desired and requested. *Indeed,* more than she had brought to the king. *That was* in addition to what he had given her from his own royal hand. Then she left, and she and her servants returned to her land.

Solomon's Wealth[220]

Every year Solomon received six hundred and sixty-six talents (*22.8 metric tonnes*) of gold. In addition, *he received* revenue from merchants and traders, and gold and silver from all the Arabian kings and governors of the land.

King Solomon made shields and put them in the House of the Forest of Lebanon.

Shields for the House of the Forest of Lebanon	
200 shields of hammered gold	600 *bekahs* (*3.4 kilogrammes*) of gold for each shield
300 hundred small shields of hammered gold	3 minas *or* 300 bekahs (*1.7 kilogrammes*) of gold for each shield

Then the king made a throne, the like *of which* had not been made in any *other* kingdom.

(See table on next page)

All of King Solomon's drinking utensils were *made* of gold; all the utensils in the House of the Forest of Lebanon were *made* of pure gold. Nothing *was made* of silver, because in the days of Solomon *silver* was not considered valuable.

The king had a fleet of *large ocean-going* ships of Tarshish at sea, with the ships of Hiram. Every three years the ships of Tarshish would return carrying

---

[220] 1 Kings 10:14-25, 27; 2 Chronicles 1:15; 9:13-24, 27

gold, silver, ivory, apes, and peacocks. So the king made silver and gold in Jerusalem *as common* as stones; and cedars as plentiful as the sycamore trees in the foothills.

King Solomon became greater in wealth and wisdom than all the *other* kings of the earth. All the world came seeking an audience with Solomon, *so they could* hear the wisdom that God had put on his mind. Year in, year out, each brought his gift: articles of silver and gold, garments, weapons, spices, horses, and mules.

King Solomon's Throne

Size	Large
Materials	Ivory, inlaid with pure gold
Description	There were 6 steps to the throne
	There was a gold footstool attached to the throne
	It's back had a rounded top
	It had arms on either side of the seat
	There were 2 lions standing beside the arms (*one on each side*)
	There were 12 lions standing on the steps, one on each end of each step

---

Solomon's Military Might[221]

Solomon acquired chariots and horsemen, and stationed them with him in Jerusalem and in *the designated* chariot cities. *Indeed*, he had four thousand stalls for *his* horses and chariots.

Solomon's Chariots and Horsemen

Type	*Number*
Chariots	1,400
Horsemen	12,000

Solomon's *chariots and* horses were imported from Egypt, Kue (*that is, Cilicia*), and from all other countries. The king's merchants acquired them from Kue at the *going* rate.

---

[221] 1 Kings 10:26, 28-29; 2 Chronicles 1:14, 16-17; 9:25-26, 28

> **Prices of Chariots and Horses**
>
> Type   Price
>
> *Chariots from Egypt*   600 *shekels* (*6.8 kilogrammes*) of silver
> *Horses from Kue*   150 *shekels* (*1.7 kilogrammes*) *of silver*

They imported chariots and horses from Egypt, and using the same *method* they exported them to all the Hittite and Aramean kings.

Solomon ruled over all the kings from the River *Euphrates* to the land of the Philistines and to the border with Egypt.

Solomon's Wives[222]

Now King Solomon loved many foreign women. Besides Pharaoh's daughter, *he married* Moabites, Ammonites, Sidonians, and Hittites—all from the nations that YHWH had said to the Israelites, 'You are not to go into them, or they into you. They will surely turn your hearts after their gods.'

Solomon clung to them, *because he* loved *them*, but his wives turned his heart astray.

> **Solomon's Wives**
>
> Wives   700 princesses
> Concubines   300

By the time Solomon was in his old age, his wives had turned his heart after other gods. His heart was no longer totally devoted to YHWH his God, as *had been* the heart of his father, David. Solomon followed after Ashteroth, the goddess of the Sidonians, and Molech, the abomination of the Ammonites. So Solomon did what was evil in the eyes of YHWH; he did not completely follow YHWH, unlike his father, David.

Indeed on the hill, east of Jerusalem, Solomon built *two* high places: one for Chemosh, the abomination of Moab, and *the other* for Molech, the

---

[222] 1 Kings 11:1-13

abomination of the Ammonites. He did the same for all his foreign wives who burnt incense and slaughtered sacrifices to their gods.

Now YHWH, the God of Israel had appeared to Solomon twice *before*. But because Solomon's heart had turned away from him, YHWH became angry with him. YHWH had commanded him about not following other gods, but Solomon had not observed YHWH's command.

So YHWH said to Solomon, 'Since you are acting this way, and are not keeping my covenant and my decrees which I commanded you, I will surely tear the kingdom away from you and give it to your servant. Nevertheless, for the sake of your father, David, I will not do it in your days; I will tear it from the hand of your son. But I will not tear away the whole kingdom. For the sake of David, my servant, and for the sake of Jerusalem, which I chose, I will give one tribe to your son.'

Hadad, the Edomite[223]

Then YHWH raised up Hadad (*'thunderer'*) the Edomite, from the royal line of Edom, to be an adversary against Solomon.

Hadad *had only been* a small boy when David *had fought* against Edom. Joab, the commander of the *Israelite* army, had gone to bury the dead and had struck down all the men of Edom. Then for six months Joab and all Israel had stayed there, until they had cut off every male in Edom. But Hadad, and *some of the* Edomite men, his father's servants, had fled with him to Egypt.

They had set out from Midian and had gone to Paran. They had taken men from Paran with them and had gone to Egypt, to Pharaoh, the king of Egypt.

Pharaoh had given him a house, provided him food, and given him *some* land. Hadad had then found great favour in Pharaoh's eyes. Pharoah had given him a wife: his wife's sister, the sister of Tahpenes the queen. The sister of Tahpenes had borne him a son, Genubath (*'theft'*), and Tahpenes had brought up his son inside Pharaoh's palace. Indeed, Genubath had lived in Pharaoh's palace among Pharaoh's *own* children.

But while *still* in Egypt, Hadad had heard that David was resting with his fathers and that Joab, the commander of the army, was dead. So Hadad had said to Pharaoh, 'Send me away, so I can return to my *own* land.'

Pharaoh had then said to him, 'What do you lack with me, that you wish to return to your *own* land?'

Hadad had then said, 'Nothing. But let me go.'

So Hadad had returned to Edom, and caused Solomon much trouble.

---

[223] 1 Kings 11:14-22

Rezon, Son of Eliada[224]

God raised up *another* adversary against Solomon: Rezon, son of Eliada.

Now Rezon had been *the servant of* Hadadezer, king of Zobah. However, when David had slaughtered the *people of Zobah*, he had fled from his master. Rezon had then gathered men around him and he had become leader of a marauding band. The rebels had then gone to Damascus, settled there, and ruled over the city.

So Rezon loathed Israel, and was an adversary to Israel the rest of Solomon's days. He reigned over Aram and compounded the trouble caused by Hadad.

Jeroboam, the Ephraimite[225]

Jeroboam (*possibly 'the people contend'*), son of Nebat, was an Ephraimite from Zeredah. His mother was a widow named Zeruah (*'leper'*). He was *one of* Solomon's servants, a very capable man.

Solomon had been building a supporting terrace and had closed the breach in *the wall of* the city of David, his father. He had seen how well the young man worked, so Solomon put him in charge of the whole labour force of the house of Joseph. But Jeroboam rebelled against the king. This is the reason why:

Ahijah the prophet was from Shiloh, *the former home of the Ark and the Tabernacle. He had been instructed by YHWH to seek Jeroboam regarding the future of the kingdom.* So one day when *the terrace was being built and* Jeroboam was on the road out of Jerusalem, Ahijah found him. The two of them then spent *some* time alone in a field.

Now the Shilohnite was wearing a new cloak. But he took hold of it and tore it into twelve pieces. He then said to Jeroboam, 'Take ten pieces for yourself.

'This is what YHWH, God of Israel, says, "Behold, I am about to tear the kingdom out of the hand of Solomon. I will give you ten tribes. But one tribe will remain his, for the sake of my servant, David, and for the sake of Jerusalem, *because Jerusalem is* the city that I chose from all the tribes of Israel.

"'I am doing this, because Solomon has forsaken me. He has worshipped Ashteroth, the goddess of the Sidonians, Chemosh, the god of the Moabites, and Molech, the god of the Ammonites. He has not walked in my ways or done what is right in my eyes; *he has not kept* my statutes and my ordinances, unlike his father, David. *Despite that*, I will not take the whole kingdom out of his hand.

---

[224] 1 Kings 11:23-25
[225] 1 Kings 11:26-40

"'For the sake of David, my servant, whom I chose, who observed my commandments and my statutes, I made Solomon ruler all the days of his life. So I will take the kingdom from the hands of his sons and I will give ten tribes to you.

'I will give his son one tribe. That way my servant, David, may always have a lamp before me in Jerusalem, the city where I chose to place my name. But I will take you, and you will rule over all that your heart desires. You will be king over *the northern kingdom* of Israel.

"'If you listen to everything that I command you, and walk in my ways, I will be with you. So do what is right in my eyes; keep my statutes and my commandments, just as my servant, David, did. I will then build you an everlasting house, just as I built for David. I will give you Israel. I will afflict the descendants of David for this, but not forever.'"

So Solomon sought to kill Jeroboam. But Jeroboam arose and fled to Egypt, to Shishak, king of Egypt. He remained there until the death of Solomon.

C23. SOLOMON/JEDIDIAH
(991-930 BC)

e). Reflections on Life *(933-930 BC)*

Introduction[226]

There has been much debate about the book Ecclesiastes. Much of it relates to the identity of the 'teacher' (or in Hebrew 'qoheleth').

However, regardless of when the book was written and why, this book is about a king who ruled over Israel (not just Judah) in Jerusalem. It also claims to be the words of a son of David.

Now only Solomon meets both criteria. As a consequence, these reflections are placed here, at the end of Solomon's life, when everything was going terribly wrong.

The title of the book: The words of a teacher, a son of David, king in Jerusalem.

The Cyclical Nature of Life[227]

The book begins with an observation of the cyclical nature of life.

The teacher says, 'Totally futile! Totally futile! Everything is futile. What does a man gain for all his labour, as he toils under the sun?

'Generations come and generations go, but the land remains forever. The sun rises and the sun sets, then it returns to its place *so it can* rise *again*. The wind blows to the south, then turns to the north; it goes around and around, returning on its course. All rivers flow into the sea but the sea is never full; *the water returns* to the place from which rivers flow, only to return again.

'Everything is so tiresome; *it is* more than one can say.

'The eye is never satisfied with *the things that it* sees, nor is the ear content *with the things that it* hears. What has happened will happen *again*; what has been done will be done *again*. There is nothing new under the sun.

'Is there anything of which can be said, "Look! This is new!"? *No*! It was already in existence; it was from long ago, before us. *Among the current generation* there is no memory of former things. Neither will anyone yet to come remember.'

---

[226] Ecclesiastes 1:1
[227] Ecclesiastes 1:2-11

The Search for Wisdom[228]
Despite his pessimism, the teacher had devoted his life to the search for meaning and purpose in life.

'I, a teacher, have been king over Israel in Jerusalem. I have put my mind to seeking and studying, through wisdom, all that is done under the heavens. It is an evil task that God has given the sons of man to occupy them. I have seen every *type of* deed that is done under the sun. But, look, it is all futile; *it is like* chasing the wind. "What is crooked cannot become straight; *what is* missing cannot be counted."

'I spoke to myself. I said, "Look, I have grown. I have increased in wisdom beyond anyone who ruled over Jerusalem before me. My mind has experienced great wisdom and knowledge." I then set my heart on understanding wisdom; to know madness and folly. But I learned that this too was *like* chasing the wind. "With much wisdom *comes* much sorrow; with much knowledge comes much pain."'

'I said to myself, "Come now, I will test you with pleasure; I will see what is good." But look, it too was futile. I said, "It is foolish to laugh", and "What does pleasure accomplish?"

'In my mind, I tried to cheer myself with wine. But my mind guided *me* with wisdom. *I tried* to embrace folly until I could see what was worthwhile for the sons of man; the things they could do, under the heavens, in the few days of their lives.

'I made my works bigger. I built houses for myself, I planted my vineyards. I made gardens and parks for myself; I planted fruit trees in them of every kind. I made pools of water to water a forest of sprouting trees. I bought male and female slaves, and others were born in my house. I also owned more cattle, herds, and flocks than anyone who came before me in Jerusalem. I accumulated for myself silver and gold, and the treasure of kings and provinces. I gathered around me male and female singers. *I tasted* the delights of the sons of man— many concubines.

'So I became great, and was greater than anyone who came before me in Jerusalem. Indeed, my wisdom stood by me. I did not hold back from anything that my eyes desired, nor did I hold my heart back from any pleasure. My heart was glad in all my work, and this was my reward for all my labour.

'I then reflected on everything that my hands had achieved, the work that I had done. But look, it was all futile; *it was like* chasing the wind. Nothing under the sun had been gained.'

---

[228] Ecclesiastes 1:12-2:23

'So I turned. I considered wisdom and madness and folly. For what can the successor do, *apart from* what the king had already done?

'I saw that there was more profit in wisdom than folly, just as there is greater advantage in light than darkness. *I saw that* the wise man *uses* the eyes in his head, while the fool walks in darkness. But even I knew that they would both meet the same fate.

'Then I said to myself, "I will encounter the same *fate* as the fate of the fool. What then is the advantage of being wise?" I said in my heart, "This is also futile." For neither the wise man nor the fool will be remembered forever; in the coming days both will be forgotten. Indeed, both the wise and the foolish will die.

'So I have hated life. The deeds that have been done under the sun are evil to me. All is futile and like chasing the wind.

'I *have come to* hate everything that I have toiled for under the sun, because I will have to leave it *all* to my successor. Who knows whether he will be a wise man or a fool? Yet he will be master of everything for which I have laboured and used my skill under the sun. This also is futile.

'So I turned. My heart despaired of everything for which I had laboured under the sun. For a man who uses wisdom, knowledge, and skill in his work must leave his property to a man who has not laboured for it. This too is futile and a great evil. For what does a man get for all his labour, and for which he strives under the sun? All his days his work is painful and grievous. His mind doesn't rest, even at night. This too is futile.'

The Search for God[229]

For the teacher, any search for the meaning of life, without God, was futile. Despite that, he recognised that God's world was contaminated by those who wanted nothing to do with him.

'*There is* nothing better for a man than to eat and drink and see himself satisfied in his work. This I have also seen from the hand of God. For who can eat or find enjoyment without him? For God gives wisdom, knowledge, and joy to the man who pleases him. But to the sinner he gives the task of gathering and storing, to hand it to someone who is pleasing to God. This too is futile, and chasing the wind.'

'*There is* a set time for everything; a time for every activity under the heavens. A time to give birth, and a time to die. A time to plant, and a time to pluck what was planted. A time to kill, and a time to heal. A time to break down, and a time to build. A time to weep, and a time to laugh. A time to lament, and

---

[229] Ecclesiastes 2:24-3:22

a time to dance. A time to fling stones, and a time to collect stones. A time to embrace, and a time to be distant. A time to search, and a time to declare "lost". A time to keep, and a time to throw away. A time to tear, and a time to sew together. A time to be still, and a time to speak. A time to love, and a time to hate. A time for battle, and a time for peace.

'What does the worker profit from his labour? I have seen the tasks that God has given the sons of man to occupy them. God made everything beautiful in its time; he set eternity in men's hearts. Yet no man is able to discover the deeds of God from beginning to end.

'I know that there is nothing better for men than to be happy and to do good in life. Yes, that every man should eat, drink, and find satisfaction in all his work. This is a gift of God.

'I know that everything God does endures forever. Nothing can be added to it, and nothing taken away. God does this, so that men will fear him. Whatever is, has already been; whatever will be, has already been. God seeks what has passed by.'

'Furthermore, under the sun, I have seen wickedness in the place of justice; wickedness in the place of righteousness. I said to myself, "God will judge the righteous and the wicked. A time *has been appointed to consider* every activity and deed there." I said in my heart, regarding the sons of man, "God will test them. Then they will see that they are just like animals."

'For the fate of the sons of man and the fate of animals are the same. As one dies, so does the other; the breath *of life* is the same for all. Man does not have an advantage over the animal. Everything is futile. All go to the one place. All come from dust, and all turn back to dust. Who knows, *then*, whether the spirit of the sons of man goes up *into the heavens*, and *whether the* spirit of animals goes down into the earth?

'I have seen, therefore, that there is nothing better than for a man to enjoy his deeds. Because that is his lot. For who can take him to see what will unfold after he *has gone?*'

The Hardships of Life[230]

Having outlined his basic principles, the teacher's attention then moved to the hardships of life —oppression, toil, and being alone. However, even he recognised that one of the causes of those hardships was one's own foolishness. So he detailed his own experiences of foolishness, and provided a warning about being foolish with God.

'Then I turned, and I saw all the oppression that was being done under the sun. I saw the tears of the oppressed, with no one to console *them*. Power was

---
[230] Ecclesiastes 4:1-5:7

on the side of their oppressors; they had no comforter. So I praised those who had already died more than the living who were still alive. But better than both of them *is the one* who has not yet been; who has not yet seen *such* evil deeds that are done under the sun.'

'Then I saw all the labour and skill produced through the envy of a man and his neighbour. This is also futile, *like* chasing the wind.
'"The fool folds *both of* his hands; *in his laziness* he ruins himself." However, "*It is* better to rest one hand than to have two hands toiling and chasing the wind."'

'I looked again, and I saw *more* futility under the sun.
'There was someone who was all alone. He had no son or brother, yet there was no end to all his toil. But his eyes were not satisfied with *his* wealth. *He said to himself*, "For whom am I toiling and depriving myself of pleasure?" This also is futile; an evil business.
'Two are better than one, because they can get a good return for their labour. For if one falls, the other one can pick his friend up. But woe to the one who falls if there is no one to help him. Furthermore, if two lie down together they can *keep each other* warm. But how can one keep warm *on their own*? If one can be overpowered, two can make a stand against *an attacker*. "A triple-*braided* cord is not easily broken."'

'"A poor but wise youth is better than an old but foolish king who no longer knows how to heed warnings." *A youth* can come from prison to become king, or *a king* can be born in poverty in his kingdom. I have seen all who live and walk under the sun, with the youth who will succeed the king. There is no end to the number of people who came before him, but those who come later will not be happy with him. This indeed is also futile, *like* chasing the wind.'

'Watch your step when you go to the house of God. Go to listen, rather than to offer the sacrifice of fools. For they do not know they are doing evil. Do not be quick with your mouth and your heart. Do not be rash with your mouth, or quick in your heart, to say anything in the presence of God. For God is in the heavens and you are on the earth. For this *reason*, let your words be few. "As fantasies come with much work, so the sound of a fool comes with many words."
'When you make a solemn vow to God, do not delay to fulfil it. *God does* not delight in fools. Fulfil your vow. It is better to not make a vow than to make one and not fulfil *it*. Don't let your mouth cause you to sin. Don't say to *God's* messenger that it was a mistake. Why should God be angry because of what you

said, and destroy the work of your hands? An abundance of dreams and words is futile, so fear God.'

The Search for Contentment[231]

The teacher was concerned about attitudes to wealth. There was a common belief that wealth would bring happiness. But there were traps associated with the love of money and being a hoarder. He also recognised that the poor remained poor because of the demands of others for 'their share' of the profits.

Despite that, he was able to conclude that God is in control. Indeed, the hand of God is often responsible for excessively wealthy people being unable to enjoy the fruits of their labour.

'If you see the poor being oppressed, and justice and rightness being denied in a district, do not be surprised at *such* a thing. For *there is one* official over *another* official, *and there are* higher *officials* over them. The profit from the land *is taken* by all; *even* the king profits from the land.'

'"Whoever loves money never has enough." "Whoever loves wealth never *has enough* income." This is also futile. "As prosperity improves, so do the needs of the consumer."

'So what is the benefit *of wealth* to its owner except to see it with his eyes. "The sleep of a worker is sweet, whether he eats little or much, but the rich will be denied sleep by his plenty."'

'There is a sickening evil *which* I have seen under the sun: wealth being hoarded to the detriment of its owner; riches that are lost through a bad situation. So *when* he fathers a son, there is nothing to hand on to him. "As *a man* comes naked from his mother's womb, so he will return." He will take nothing from his labour, *not even* what he can carry in his hand. This also is a sickening evil. "As all *men* come, so do they go." So what profit is there for a man who toils for the wind? Indeed, all his days he eats in the darkness. He is greatly troubled, sick, and angry.

'Look, even I have realised that *it is* good *and* fitting *for a man* to eat and drink and to see a reward for all his labour. *After all*, he toils under the sun during the few days of his life that God has given him for his lot. God gives wealth and possessions, and enables *a man* to enjoy them. So any man who *has received this* has accepted his lot. He is happy in his work and has *received* the gift of God. Indeed, he will not often reflect on the days of his life, because God keeps him occupied with the gladness of his heart.'

---

[231] Ecclesiastes 5:8-6:12

'There is *another* evil that I have seen under the sun. It is common among men. God gives a man wealth, possessions, and honour. So he has all his heart's desires, then God does not allow him to enjoy them. Indeed, a stranger enjoys them. This is meaningless; a sickening evil.

'A man may father a hundred children *and* live many years. Yet, however long he lives, he may be unable to be satisfied with *all* the good things, and won't *even* get a *decent* burial. Then I say, "A stillborn child is better than that man." A stillborn child is born in futility; it goes in darkness. Its name is covered in darkness. Although it never saw the sun, and never knew *anything*, it enjoyed more rest than that man. Even if a man could live a thousand years twice over, he may not enjoy the good things. *But* doesn't everyone go to the same place *anyway*?'

'"A man's labour is totally for his mouth, yet his desires are never satisfied." Indeed, what advantage does the wise *man have* over the fool? What does a poor man *benefit, in* knowing how to walk in front of others? "What the eyes see is better than a wandering appetite." This is also futile, like chasing the wind.

'Whatever is, has already been named; what man is, is already known. No man can contend with *the one* who is stronger than he. The more words *that he speaks*, the more futile *it all becomes. So* what advantage *is there* for a man? For who knows what is good for a man in *his* life? His futile life *lasts but a* few days; he spends his days like a shadow. Who can tell a man what will be under the sun, after he *has gone*?'

The Search for Wisdom[232]

The teacher had great concerns about the fragility of life. So, in what, at times, seems to be a random collection of proverbs, the teacher looked at the problems of suffering and sin. He even questioned whether it would be better to be dead than alive.

Entangled within his observations was his ongoing search for meaning in life, which even he admitted still alluded him.

'"A good name is better than fine oil." "The day of death is better that the day of birth." "It is better to go to a house of mourning than to go to the house of feasting." For every man is destined to die, and the living should take this to heart. "Sorrow is better than laughter", because "when a face is sad, a heart is glad." "The hearts of the wise are in a house of mourning, but the hearts of fools are in a house of pleasure." "It is better to hear the rebuke of a wise man than to listen to the song of fools." Indeed, "Like the crackling of thorns under the pot, so is the laughter of the fool." This is also futile.'

---

[232] Ecclesiastes 7:1-8:1

'"Extortion makes a wise man foolish," and "A bribe corrupts the heart."'

'"The end of the matter is better than its beginning." "A spirit of patience is better than a spirit of pride." "Don't let your spirit be stirred into anger, for anger resides in the bosom of fools."'

'Don't say, "Why were the former days better than these?" For you do not ask this from wisdom. Wisdom is good, it is like an inheritance. It benefits those who see the sun. For to be in the shadow of wisdom, *is like being* in the shadow of money. However, the advantage of knowledge *is that* wisdom lives in its owner.

'Consider the works of God. Who is able to straighten what God has made bent? In good times be happy. But in bad times consider that God made this as well as the other. Man is unable to discover anything *that will come* after he *has gone*.'

'In *all* my days of futility I have seen everything. *I have seen* a righteous *man* perishing in his righteousness, and a wicked *man* living *a* long *life* in his wickedness. *So* do not be too righteous or too wise. Why *should you* destroy yourself? Do not be too wicked or be a fool. Why *should you* die before your time? *Avoid the extremes; take the middle path.* It is good that you take hold of one, but do not let your *other* hand let go of the other. The one who fears God will follow them both.'

'"Wisdom gives a wise *man* more strength than ten masters who live in a city."'

'There is no righteous man on earth who *always* does right and never sins.'

'Do not pay heed to everything that is said, then you will not hear your servant cursing you. For your heart knows that you yourself have cursed others many times.'

'All of this I have tested by wisdom. I have said, "I will be wise." But it was beyond me. However far off it may be, it is exceedingly deep. Who can find it?

'I have devoted myself and my mind to know, explore, and seek *both* wisdom and the scheme of things. *I also wanted to* know *about* the folly of wickedness and the stupidity of madness. So I have found that a woman who is a snare, whose heart is a trap *and* whose hands *are* chains, is more bitter than death. One who pleases God will slip away from her, but one who sins will be seized by her.

'The teacher says, "Look, this is what I have found. One *thing* needs to be added to another to find the sum of things. *However, there are* still *things* I am searching for, but haven't *found*. I have found one *wise* man among a thousand, but I haven't found any *wise* women among them all. So this is all that I have found: that *even though* God made man upright, man has sought out many schemes."

'*So* who is like the wise man? Who knows how to interpret things? Wisdom brings light to a man's face; it softens the hardness of his appearance.'

The Search for Justice[233]

The teacher was concerned about justice in the world. Indeed, in a world where evil seemed to prevail, he found justice difficult to find, including sometimes within his own royal court. However, even when he was the cause of injustice, he recognised that justice could still be sought, but only if done in the right way.

So the teacher examined how the world treated the good and the bad, and pursued an understanding of the issue from God's perspective. His conclusion, however, was that much of life is beyond our understanding. But despite everything, God wants the righteous to enjoy the pleasures of life that he has given them.

'I *say*, "Keep the word of the king, because of *your* oath before God. Do not rush from his presence. Do not stand *with others* to malign *him*, for he will do whatever he pleases. Since the word of a king is supreme, who can say to him "What are you doing?"

'He who keeps *a king's* command will not face anything evil, for a wise heart will know the time and the way *to speak up*. For even though a man's misery lies heavy upon him, there is a *right* time and *a proper* procedure for every matter.

'As a man does not know what is coming, who can tell him when it has come? No man has mastery over the wind, to shut up the wind. So no one has mastery over the day of death. "As no one is discharged *in time of* war, so wickedness does not release its owners."

'I have seen this, *and* I have applied my mind to every deed that has been done under the sun. *This includes* when a man has dominated another to hurt him.'

'I have also seen the wicked—indeed, those who went in and out of the holy place—being buried *like anyone else*. But they are *now* forgotten in the city where they did this. This is also futile.'

'"If the sentence for an evil deed is not carried out quickly, the hearts of the sons of men will become filled with evil intent." A sinner may commit a

---

[233] Ecclesiastes 8:2-9:10

hundred evil *deeds*, but *if his execution is delayed, he will* live a long life. I know that those who fear God will go well before God, because they fear him, but it will not go well with the wicked. Their days will not be lengthened *even* like a shadow, because he does not fear God.'

'There is a futility about life on earth. There are righteous *men* who are touched by the deeds of the wicked, and there are wicked *men* who are touched by the deeds of the righteous. I say that this too is futile. As for myself, I commend pleasure. For there is nothing better for a man under the sun but to eat, drink, and be glad. This will then go with him in his toils, *all* the days of the life God has given him under the sun.'

'I devoted myself to know wisdom and to observe everything that is done on the earth. Even though it is impossible to see with your eyes closed, day or night, I saw everything that God has done. *But I concluded* that that no man is able to understand *everything* that is done under the sun. Despite a man's attempts to search *for meaning*, he cannot discover *it*; even a wise man who claims he knows, cannot comprehend it.'

'So I have taken all this to my heart. It is clear in all of this that the righteous and the wise, and their deeds, are in the hands of God. No man knows whether love or hate awaits *him*. All is before him. It is the same for everyone. There is one fate for the righteous and the wicked, for the good and *the bad*, for the clean and the unclean, for the one who sacrifices and the one who doesn't sacrifice, for the good *man* and the sinner, and for the one who swears an oath and the one who is fearful of swearing. This is an evil in everything that is done under the sun: there is one fate for all.

'In addition, the hearts of the sons of men are full of evil. There is madness in their hearts while they live. After that, they go to be with the dead. Indeed, there is hope for anyone who is joined with all the living. For "Even a dog that is alive is better than a dead lion." For *while* the living know they will die, the dead know nothing. Indeed, they will have no further reward, because even the memory of them will be forgotten. So their love, their hate, and their jealousy will have already perished. They will no longer have any part in anything that is done under the sun.

'*So* go, eat your bread with joy. Drink your wine with a merry heart. For God is pleased with your deeds. Wear white clothes at all times and never lack putting oil on your head. Enjoy life with a woman you love all the days of your futile life. For *God* has given you a life of futility under the sun. This is your lot—in life and in your toil—for which you are toiling under the sun. All that your hand finds to do, do it with *all* your might, because there is no work or thought or knowledge or wisdom in Sheol, where you are going.'

The Continuing Search for Wisdom[234]

The teacher's search then returned to wisdom. This time he contrasted it with folly. The teacher's use of proverbs to make his point is paramount. The sayings, at times, can seem disjointed, but the over-all effect is to emphasise the need for wisdom.

'Then I saw another thing under the sun—that the race is not for the fleet-footed, that the battle is not for the strong, that food is not for the wise, that wealth is not for the discerning, and that favour is not for the capable. Rather, time and chance affects them all. In addition, a man does not know *when* his time *will come*. "As fish are caught in a cruel net or birds are trapped in a trap, so the sons of man are lured by a time of evil, which suddenly falls upon them."

'I also saw this wisdom under the sun. It was great to me. *There was* a small town with *only a* few men in it. A great king came against it. He surrounded it, and built great siege works against it. But *in that town* a poor, but wise man was found, and using his wisdom the poor man saved the town. But no one remembered that man.

'So I say, "Wisdom is better than might." "The wisdom of a poor man is despised; his words are not heeded." "The quiet words of the wise are better heeded than the shout of a ruler of fools." "Wisdom is better than weapons of war," but "One sinner destroys much good." "As dead flies make a perfumer's oil give off a foul smell, so a little folly is *considered* more highly than wisdom and honour." "The heart of a wise *man leans* to his right, but the heart of a fool *leans* to his left." "Even as he walks along the road, a fool's senses are lacking; he says to everyone that he is a fool." "If a ruler's anger rises against you, do not leave your position, for composure can soothe major offenses."'

'There is an evil I have seen under the sun, an error which proceeds from a ruler. "Foolishness is elevated to high places, while the rich sit in low places." I have seen slaves on horses, while princes walk on the land like slaves.'

'"Whoever digs a pit may fall into it; whoever breaks through a wall may be bitten by a snake." "Whoever quarries stones may be hurt by them; whoever splits trees may be endangered by them." "If the axe is blunt, and the edge isn't sharpened, then more strength is required; but wisdom brings success." "If a snake bites before it is charmed, there is no profit for the owner of the tongue."'

'"Words from the mouth of a wise man are favourable, but a fool is engulfed by his *own* lips. *Indeed*, the words of a *fool* begin with folly and they end in wicked madness." Yet fools *speak* many words.'

---

[234] Ecclesiastes 9:11-10:20

'No man knows what is coming, and who can tell him what will happen after he *is gone?*'

'"Fools are so wearied by their labour, that they don't know *when they should go to town.*" Woe to the land whose king is a boy, and whose princes feast in the morning. Blessed is the land whose king is a nobleman and whose princes eat for strength, not to get drunk, at the proper time. "Through neglect the rafters sag; through slack hands the house leaks." "Food is prepared for laughter and wine makes life merry, but money is the answer to everything."'

'Do not make light of the king, even in your thoughts; do not make light of the rich, even in your bed chamber. Because a bird from the heavens may carry the sound; a winged creature may report *those* words.'

The Call for Action[235]

Despite the teacher's observation that everything was futile, he still called for action. He called people to a life of faith and a life of joy. In particular, he targetted the young to get into the habit of living life with their creator.

'Send out your bread on the surface of the waters, for you will find it *again* after many days. Give a portion *of what you own* to seven or even to eight *others*, for you do not know what evil may fall upon the land.

'When clouds are full, they pour rain upon the earth; when a tree falls, whether in the south or the north, it will lie where it has fallen. Those who watch the wind do not plant; those who look at the clouds do not reap. As you don't know the path of the wind, or how bones *are knit* in a mother's womb, so you don't know the works of God, the maker of all.

'*So* scatter your seed in the morning, and in the evening don't let your hand be idle. For you don't know which will succeed. It may be one or the other, or both may do equally well.'

'"Light is indeed sweet; it is good for the eyes to see the sun." "If a man lives many years, let him enjoy them all. But let him remember the dark days, for they will be many." All of what is to come is futile.

'Young man, be happy while you are young. Let your heart be glad in the days of your youth. Walk in the ways of your heart and follow what your eyes see. But know that God will call you to account for everything that you do. So turn aside *any* anger in your heart and turn away *any* pain in your body, for youth and vitality pass quickly away.

'Remember your creator in the days of your youth. Because days of trouble

---

[235] Ecclesiastes 11:1-12:8

will come, and years will draw near when you will say, "I take no pleasure in them."

'In those days, the sun, light, moon, and stars will grow dark. The clouds will return after the rain. The keepers of the house will tremble; strong men will stoop. Those who grind will stop *their work* because they are so few. Those who look through the windows will grow dim. The doors to the street will be closed. The sound of grinding will fade. A man will rise at the sound of a bird, but all the daughters of song will be faint. Men will be afraid of heights and the terrors of the road. The almond tree will be disgusting, the grasshopper will drag itself along, and the caperberry *bush* will be broken. For a man will go to his eternal home, while mourners go about in the street.

'*So remember your creator* before the silver cord is unbound, the golden bowl is smashed, the pitcher at the well is shattered, and the wheel at the cistern is crushed. Dust will return to the earth from which it came, and the spirit will return to God who gave it.

'The teacher says, "Futility of futilities! It is all futile."'

Epilogue[236]

The teacher's summary of the futility of life was now complete, so the compiler of his teachings added his own concluding comments.

'The teacher was not only a wise *man*, but he also taught the people knowledge. He tested, searched out, and arranged many proverbs. The teacher sought to find pleasing words, upright words of truth that were written down. For the words of the wise are like cattle prods; the owners of these collections are like firmly fixed nails. They are given by one who is a shepherd.

'But beware, my son, be warned: of making many books there is no end, and *too* much study tires the flesh.

'At the conclusion of the matter, when all has been heard, "Fear God, and keep his commandments." For this *is the duty* of every man. For God will judge every deed, including everything that is concealed, whether good or evil.'

The Death of Solomon[237]

Now the rest of Solomon's deeds, from beginning to end—all that he did and his wisdom—are they not written in the records?

(See table on next page)

---

[236] Ecclesiastes 12:9-14
[237] 1 Kings 11:41-43; 2 Chronicles 9:29-31

> **The Records of Solomon's Deeds**
>
> The Book of the Acts of Solomon
> The records of Nathan, the prophet
> The prophecy of Ahijah, the Shilohnite
> The visions of Iddo, the seer (concerning Jeroboam, son of Nebat)

Solomon reigned in Jerusalem, over all Israel, for forty years, then he lay down with his fathers, and was buried in his father's city, the City of David. Then Rehoboam, his son, became king in his place.

Section D

SONGS, SAYINGS, AND YHWH'S TEMPLE

D1. DAVID'S SONG BOOK

a). Introduction and Songs of Praise

1. INTRODUCTION TO THE SONGS OF DAVID

There are seventy-three psalms which are noted as being 'of David'. Some were probably written by David, others may have been written on his behalf, and some may simply have been part of his collection.

It has also been suggested that the psalms may relate to the Davidic line, rather than to David himself. Particularly as some of them refer to YHWH's Temple—which was not built in David's time—while others seem to describe later historical events.

However, references to YHWH's Temple, do not prove that a psalm was written at a later time. Indeed, many of the references to the Temple refer to God's heavenly Temple or to the Tabernacle in which the Ark of the Covenant was placed. Furthermore, as David made many arrangements for the building of the Temple, it is also possible that he provided psalms for future use.

Furthermore, in regard to the apparent links with future events, that doesn't mean they were written later either. Indeed, it is not impossible that the situations described reflect incidents in David's reign that have not survived in any other written form.

As a consequence, all the psalms 'of David' which have not been included in the Narrative section of this book are included here. They are presented in thematic order, in accordance with their major theme—Songs of Praise, The Life of Faith, Sin, or Enemies.

The 'psalms' themselves are a mixture of psalms, songs, and poems. Many borrow ideas and phrases from each other. Some include notes, the meaning of which is now uncertain or forgotten.

For example, the term 'Selah', is believed to be either a musical instruction indicating an interlude, or a change of musical accompaniment, or an instruction for the congregation to bow down in worship.

Underlying many of the psalms are the common problems of sin, suffering, and attacks by enemies. Indeed, the concept of sickness and suffering as God's punishment for sin is a common theme.

2. SONGS OF PRAISE

a). An Alphabetical Song of Praise[238]

This psalm celebrates the attributes of YHWH. In the original Hebrew, it is an

---

[238] Psalm 145:1-21

alphabetical acrostic psalm, with each couplet beginning with a different letter of the twenty-two-letter alphabet.

> *Notes:*
> A psalm of praise.
> Of David
>
> *David, to YHWH*
> א I will exalt you my God, the king;
>   I will bless your name forever and ever.
> ב I will bless you every day;
>   I will praise your name forever and ever.
>
> *David, to those around him*
> ג YHWH is great; he is to be praised most highly;
>   his greatness is beyond understanding.
>
> *David, to YHWH*
> ד *Each* generation will commend your works to the next;
>   they will declare your mighty deeds.
> ה *They will tell of* the glorious splendour of your majesty,
>   and I will meditate on the deeds of your wonderful works.
> ו They will speak of the power of your awesome deeds,
>   and I will recount your greatness.
> ז They will overflow with memories of your abundant goodness;
>   they will cry out about your righteousness.
>
> *David, to those around him*
> ח YHWH is gracious and compassionate,
>   slow to anger and generous in love.
> ט YHWH is good to all;
>   he has compassion on everything he has made.
>
> *David, to YHWH*
> י Everything you made will praise you, YHWH;
>   your holy people will bless you.
> כ They will talk of the glory of your kingdom;
>   they will tell of your might.
>
> *David, to those around him*
> ל *They will* make known to the sons of man his mighty acts,
>   and the glorious splendour of his kingdom.

Establishing the Kingdom

מ	*David, to YHWH* Your kingdom is a kingdom without end; your rule *will continue* through every generation.
	David, to those around him
נ	YHWH is the one who is faithful to all his promises; he is loving to all his creation.
ס	YHWH supports everyone who falls; he raises up all who are bowed low.
	David, to YHWH
ע	The eyes of all look to you; you give them their food at the appropriate time.
פ	You open your hand, and, with your favour, satisfy every living thing.
	David, to those around him
צ	YHWH is just in all his ways, and kind in all his works.
ק	YHWH is near to all who call on him; to all who call on him in truth.
ר	He fulfils the desires of those who fear him; he hears their cries and saves them.
ש	YHWH protects all those who love him, but he will exterminate all the wicked.

ת	My mouth will extol the praise of YHWH;
	    let every living thing bless his holy name
	        for ever and ever.

b). Contrasting God and Man[239]

This psalm contrasts the nature of YHWH as creator, saviour, and redeemer with that of the mortality of man.

The psalmist praises God for the forgiveness of sins, the healing of sicknesses, the rescue from Sheol, and for being a loving, caring God.

> *Note:*
> Of David.

---

[239] Psalm 103:1-22

David, to himself

Praise YHWH, my soul;
    all that is within me, *praise* his holy name.
Praise YHWH, my soul;
    do not forget all his dealings.

David, to those around him

He is the one who forgives all your sins.
    He is the one who heals all your diseases.
He is the one who redeems your life from the pit.
    He is the one who crowns you with love and compassion.
He is the one who satisfies you in life with good *things*.
    Indeed, like the well-known fable,
    your youth is renewed like the eagle's.

YHWH is the one who works righteous deeds
    and *delivers* justice for all those who are oppressed.
He made his ways known to Moses;
    his deeds to the sons of Israel.
YHWH is compassionate and gracious,
    slow to anger, and generous in love.
He will not always contend *against us*,
    nor will he maintain *his anger* forever.
Indeed, he has not dealt with us according to our sins;
    he has not repaid us as our iniquities *deserve*.
For as high as the heavens are above the earth,
    so is the greatness of his love toward those who fear him.
As far as the east is from the west,
    he has distanced our transgressions from us.
As a father has compassion on *his* children,
    so YHWH has compassion on those who fear him.
For he knows of what we are formed;
    he is reminded that we are *just* dust.
A man's days are like the grass,
    so he blossoms like a flower of the field.
But when the *hot dry* wind blows over it, *it withers* and dies;
    its place regards it no longer.
In contrast, the love of YHWH is eternal,
    and his love is with those who fear him.
His righteousness *extends* to their children's children;
    to those who keep his covenant;
    to those who remember to carry out his precepts.

> YHWH has established his throne in the heavens;
>> his kingdom rules over all.
>
>> *David, to the whole of creation*
> Praise YHWH, his angels;
>> you who are mighty in strength;
>> you who do his bidding, obeying the voice of his word.
> Praise YHWH, all his hosts;
>> you who serve him; you who do his will.
> Praise YHWH, all his works,
>> in all the places of his dominion.
>
>> *David, to himself*
> Praise YHWH, my soul.

c). Praise in the Face of Difficulty[240]

This psalm deals with the tension between maintaining a living relationship with YHWH and facing the difficulties of life. The psalmist may have been surrounded by his enemies, but he still wanted to praise his God.

As a consequence, the psalmist's emphasis is on the majesty and grace of YHWH, rather than on his own needs. However, he does offer thanks for the help he has received and for the strength he has been given. He also expresses the hope that God will come to his permanent rescue.

>> *Note:*
>> Of David.
>
>> *David, to YHWH*
> I will praise you with all my inner *being*;
>> I will sing your praises before the gods.
> I will bow down *to you*
>> facing your holy Temple.
> I will praise your name,
>> for *both* your goodness and your faithfulness.
> For you have made your word great;
>> *it has* exceeded *the expectations* of your name.
> On the day I called out *to you*, you answered me;
>> you made me bold, *you made* my heart strong.

---

[240] Psalm 138:1-8

> All the kings of the earth will praise you, YHWH,
>> because they have heard the words of your mouth.
> They will sing of YHWH's ways,
>> for great is YHWH's glory.
> *For* although YHWH is exalted, he still sees the lowly;
>> *and even* from a distance he knows the proud.
>
> *So even* though I *still* walk *around* surrounded by trouble,
>> you will restore my life.
> You will stretch out your hand against the wrath of my enemies;
>> you will deliver me with your right hand.
>> YHWH will fulfil *his purpose* for me.
> Your love is forever, YHWH;
>> do not desert the works of your hands.

3. THE NATURE OF GOD

a). *A Creator God*[241]

This psalm marvels at YHWH's creative works. In particular it emphasises the place of man in God's creation.

> *Notes:*
> For the *musical* director.
> According to the gittith (*probably a musical instrument or melody*).
> A psalm.
> Of David.
>
> *David, to YHWH*
>
> YHWH, our Lord,
>> how glorious is your name in all the earth.
>
> I will adore your majesty
>> *which is* above the heavens—
> *even though the best I can do is little more*
>> *than what comes out of* the mouths of children and babies.
>
> You have established *your* fortress *above*—
>> because of those who are hostile—
>> to silence the enemy and the avenger.

---

[241] Psalm 8:1-9

Establishing the Kingdom

> *However*, when I look up at the sky
> > *at* the works of your fingers—
> > the moon and stars you have created—
> what is man that you remember him?
> > *Who is* the son of man that you attend to him?
> You created him a little lower than the gods (*YHWH's heavenly court*);
> > yet you crowned him with glory and honour.
> You gave him dominion over the works of your hands;
> > you have put all things under his feet—
> flocks and herds (*domesticated animals*);
> > the beasts of the field (*wild animals*);
> birds of the air; fishes of the sea;
> > *and everything else that* swims in the sea.
>
> YHWH, our Lord,
> > how glorious is your name in all the earth.

b). A Covenant God[242]

This psalm expresses the magnificence of YHWH, in terms of his relationship with mankind. He is depicted as a covenant God: all seeing, all knowing, and ever present.

The final section of the psalm reflects the two-way nature of the covenant. It emphasises the need for God's people to take an active role in its upkeep, which includes the need to be jealous of God's honour.

> *Notes:*
> For the *musical* director.
> Of David. A Psalm.
>
> *David, to YHWH*
> YHWH, you have searched me,
> > and you know *everything*.
> You know when I sit down and when I stand up;
> > you discern my thoughts *even* from a distance.
> You distinguish *my movements*—when I go out, and when I lie down;
> > you are well aware of all my ways.
> Indeed, a word is not *even* on my tongue,
> > yet you, YHWH, know *what* all *my* words *will be*.
>
> You surround me—*you are* behind *me* and in front;
> > you have laid your hand on me.

---

[242] Psalm 139:1-24

Your knowledge is incomprehensible to me;
>   it is so high that it is out of my reach.
Where can I go from your Spirit?
>   Where can I escape from your presence?
If I ascend to the heavens *above*, you are there;
>   if I spread my bed out in Sheol *below, I will* see you *there*.
If I ride the wings of dawn *in the east*,
>   *and* take up residence on the farthest side of the sea *in the west*,
even there your hand will guide me;
>   your right hand will grasp me.
If I say, 'Surely, darkness will envelop me,
>   the light around me will be night,'
even *then* the darkness will not be dark to you;
>   the night will be as light as the day,
>   for darkness and light are the same *to you*.

Yes, you indeed created my kidneys *and my* inward parts;
>   you wove them together in my mother's womb.
I thank you, for I am awesomely and wonderfully *made*;
>   your works are extraordinary,
>   I know *that only too* well.
My bones were not hidden from you,
>   when I was made in seclusion.
I was made from the dust of the ground;
>   I was fashioned in great detail in the depths of the earth.
>   Your eyes *even* saw me as an embryo.
Furthermore, in all your books, the days ordained *for me* were written,
>   before any of it had come to be.

How precious are your thoughts to me, God;
>   how innumerable is their sheer number.
If I *tried to* count them,
>   they would exceed the *grains of* sand.
And *even* if I *could* finish *the count*,
>   I would still be with you.

God, if you would *only* slay the wicked;
>   *may* bloodthirsty men be taken away from me.
For they speak against you with wicked intent;
>   your adversaries take *your name, and* misuse *it*.
Look, YHWH, I hate those who hate you;
>   I loathe those who rise against you.

> I hate them with the utmost hatred;
>> they are my enemies *too*.
> Search me God. Know my heart.
>> Examine me. Know my uneasy thoughts,
> lest I follow in any ways which are offensive.
>> Guide me in the everlasting way.

c). *A Generous God*[243]

This psalm reflects God's generosity to his people. It acknowledges that God answers prayer, grants forgiveness, blesses his people, provides rain, and that he is both the creator and the saviour of mankind.

It is a psalm which may well have been sung at a harvest festival, where vows were taken, renewed, or fulfilled.

> *Notes:*
> For the *musical* director.
> A psalm.
> Of David.
> A Song.
>
> *David, to YHWH*
>
> We wait for you *in silence;*
>> *we* praise *you*, God, in Zion;
> to you *our* vow will be paid.
> All men will come to you,
>> *because you are* the one who hears prayers.
>
> *As for me*, sinful deeds *have* overwhelmed me;
>> *but you*, you atone for our transgressions.
> Blessed is the one you have chosen, and brought near
>> to live in your courts.
> We will be satisfied with the good things of your house;
>> the holiness of your Temple.
>
> You respond to us with wondrous *deeds* of righteousness,
>> God, our deliverer.
> *You are the* hope of all the ends of the earth
>> and of the most distant seas.
> *You are* the one who used his power to form the mountains;
>> the one who armed himself with might.

---

[243] Psalm 65:1-13

> *You are* the one who stills the roar of the seas,
>   the crashing of their waves,
>   and the murmur of the peoples.
> Those who live in distant places stand in awe of your wonders.
>   You call forth both dawn and sunset to bring cries of joy.
>
> You visit the earth and water it;
>   you make it rich *and fertile*.
> God's streams are full of water;
>   you provide *the people with* their grain,
>   for so you ordered it.
> *You* fill its furrows to settle its ridges;
>   you soften it with showers;
>   you bless its crop.
> You crown the year with your abundant *harvest*;
>   your carts overflow with the fat *of the land*.
> The grasslands of the wilderness have become lush *pastures*;
>   the hills have become clothed with joy.
> The meadows are covered with flocks;
>   valleys are enveloped with grain.
> They shout for joy;
>   they also sing.

d). *A Shepherd King*

This psalm reflects YHWH's provision for the spiritual and physical well-being of his covenant people. It acknowledges both the difficulties of life and the help that God provides the faithful.

It was written from the perspective of someone who had knowledge of what it meant to be both a shepherd and a king. In it, however, the writer visualised God as being far greater than any human shepherd or king could ever be.

> *Notes:*
> A psalm. Of David.
>
> *David, to those around him*
> YHWH is my shepherd;
>   I will lack nothing.
> He lets me rest in grassy meadows;
>   he refreshes me beside quiet waters;
>   he restores my soul.

---

[244] Psalm 23:1-6

> He leads me along paths of righteousness
> > for his name's sake.
> Even though I walk in the darkest valley,
> > I will not fear evil.
>
> *David, to YHWH*
>
> For you are *present* with me;
> > your club and your *shepherd's* staff bring me comfort.
>
> *But, YHWH, you are also my king.*
> > *You* have set a table before me.
> > and *I can feast* in the presence of my *captured* enemies.
> *As your special guest*, you have anointed my head with oil.
> > You are a generous host—
> > indeed, the cup *you have given* me is overflowing.
>
> *David, to those around him*
>
> Surely goodness and mercy will pursue me
> > all the days of my life.
> I will live in YHWH's house
> > for the rest *of my life*.

e). A God of Revelation[245]

This psalm acknowledges that YHWH is a God of revelation and can be found in both his creation and in his laws.

The psalmist recognises that knowledge of God's revelation has its consequences, admits his own weaknesses and failures, and seeks to be made right with God.

> *Notes:*
> For the *musical* director.
> A psalm.
> Of David.
>
> *David, to those around him*
>
> The heavens recount the glory of God;
> > the sky declares the work of his hands.
> Day after day their words pour out;
> > night after night they reveal *their* knowledge.
> *Yet* there is no speech, there are no languages,
> > *and* their voice cannot be heard.

---

[245] Psalm 19:1-14

Their message has gone out into all the earth;
> their words to the ends of the earth.

For the sun has pitched a tent in them,
> *where it spends the night.*

In the morning, it emerges from its canopy,
> like a bridegroom *at his wedding.*
>> It rejoices, like a strong man, to run *its* course.

The sun rises at *one* end of the heavens,
> and it traverses to the *other* end.
>> Nothing is concealed from its heat.

The law of YHWH is flawless;
> it restores the soul.

The covenant of YHWH is trustworthy;
> even *the simple* who enter into it *will become wise.*

The directions of YHWH are right;
> they give joy to the heart.

The commandments of YHWH shine *like the sun*;
> they give insight to the eyes.

The laws of YHWH are pure, *like refined silver*;
> they endure forever.

The judgements of YHWH are truth;
> they are all righteous.

Indeed, they are more desirable than gold;
> much more than pure gold.

They are sweeter than honey;
> even the honey *dripping* from the comb.

David, to YHWH

So your servant is warned by them;
> *there is* great reward in observing them.

But who can discern *his own* errors?
> Clean me of hidden, *inadvertent, faults.*

In addition, keep your servant from deliberate, *habitual*, sins,
> so they don't rule over me.

Then I will be blameless;
> I will be innocent of great rebellious acts.

YHWH, my Rock and my Redeemer,
> may the words of my mouth be pleasing *to you,*
>> *and* may the meditation of my heart *be acceptable* in your sight.

f). A Powerful God[246]

A psalm describing the majestic power of God, as illustrated in a violent thunderstorm.

> Notes:
> A psalm.
> Of David.
>
> *David, to heavenly beings*
> Give *honour* to YHWH, sons of the mighty one;
>   give *honour to* YHWH *for his* glory and might.
> Give to YHWH the glory due to his name;
>   bow down to YHWH in his holy splendour.
>
> The sound of YHWH is strong;
>   the sound of YHWH is full of majesty.
> *At sea*, the sound of YHWH is *heard* above the waters;
>   the God of glory thunders,
>   YHWH *thunders* over mighty waters.
> *On land*, the sound of YHWH breaks the cedars into pieces;
>   YHWH shatters the *strong* cedars of Lebanon.
> *In the north*, he makes *the mountains of* Lebanon skip like a calf;
>   and Sirion (*Mount Hermon*) like a young wild ox.
> *In the south*, the sound of YHWH makes the wilderness tremble;
>   YHWH stirs up the wilderness of Kadesh.
> The sound of YHWH divides
>   with flashes of lightning.
> The sound of YHWH makes the deer give birth *prematurely*.
>   He strips the forests bare.
> *But all the* while in his *heavenly* Temple,
>   all *in* it cry 'Glory'.
>
> YHWH sat *in judgement with* the flood;
>   YHWH sits enthroned as king forever.
> YHWH will give his people strength;
>   YHWH will bless his people with peace.

---

[246] Psalm 29:1-11

D1. DAVID'S SONG BOOK

b). The Life of Faith

1. LIVING A HOLY LIFE

a). Basic Characteristics of the Righteous Life[247]

This psalm recognises that if YHWH is holy, then his followers need to be holy too. As a consequence, the psalm identifies some of the basic characteristics expected of every genuine believer.

> *Notes:*
> A Psalm.
> Of David.
>
> *David, to YHWH*
> YHWH, who may enter your Tabernacle?
> Who may dwell on your holy mountain?
>
> Someone whose walk is blameless;
>   someone who is righteous.
> Someone who speaks truth from the heart
>   and does not slander with his tongue.
> Someone who does not wrong his neighbour
>   or take up *a report* discrediting his fellow man.
>
> In the eyes *of a godly man* a vile man is despised;
>   he honours those who fear YHWH.
> *When* he *is rash in* swearing an oath,
>   *even though* it *may* hurt, he doesn't change *it.*
> He does not lend his money at interest,
>   nor does he accept a bribe against the innocent.
>
> The *faith of someone* who abides by these *principles,*
>   will never be shaken.

---

[247] Psalm 15:1-5

b). A Profession of Loyalty[248]

This psalm provides a very personal expression of faith and loyalty to YHWH. Indeed, the psalmist knows well the goodness of God, both personally and through others. He also knows the inherent dangers of mixing with those who have chosen a different path.

So the psalmist acknowledges the many blessing that faith provides. But he also indicates a need for jealousy in regard to God's name.

Notes:
A miktam *(perhaps a contemplative prayer).*
Of David.

David, to YHWH

Watch *over* me, God,
    for I seek refuge in you.
I have said to *you*, YHWH, 'You are my Lord.
    Without you I would have nothing good.'
Regarding the godly who are in the land,
    even the glorious,
    all my delight is in them.
However, for those who have chosen other *gods*,
    their sorrows will increase.
I will not pour out their drink offerings of blood;
    nor will I take their names upon my lips.
YHWH, *you are* my allotted inheritance and my cup;
    you make my lot secure.
The borders allotted to me *are* in pleasant places;
    indeed, the inheritance is delightful to me.

David, to those around him

I will praise YHWH, who advises me;
    at night, my heart disciplines me.
I have put YHWH unceasingly before me;
    indeed, *he is* at my right hand.
    I will not be shaken.
So my heart is glad, and my spirit rejoices;
    my body will rest securely too.

David, to YHWH

For you will not abandon me to Sheol;
    you will not allow your holy one to see the pit.

---

[248] Psalm 16:1-11

> *Rather*, you will make the path of life known to me:
> the fullness of joy in your presence,
> *and the* pleasures at your right hand, for *the rest of my* life.

c). A Childlike Spirit[249]

This psalm emphasises the right way to approach a relationship with God. Indeed, it expresses the need to put away all ambitions and schemes, and to come to YHWH with a simple, uncomplicated, child-like faith.

> *Notes:*
> A song of ascents *(possibly a devotion for those on a pilgrimage to Jerusalem).*
> Of David.
>
> *David, to YHWH*
> YHWH, my heart is not proud;
> nor are my eyes arrogant;
> I do not occupy myself with lofty matters,
> or with things that are beyond me.
> Instead, I have kept my soul composed and still.
> Like a weaned child with its mother,
> *no longer crying for its mother's milk,*
> my soul is like a weaned child within me.
>
> *David, to Israel*
> Put your hope in YHWH, Israel,
> from now and for evermore.

d). A Life of Integrity[250]

This psalm points to the need to live a life fitting for YHWH.

Located in the house of God, the writer distinguishes his life—a life of integrity—with that of worthless men. He knows the importance of sincerity and the need for true allegiance. As a consequence, he appeals to God to be counted among the righteous and not to be included with those who are sinners.

> *Note:*
> Of David.

---

[249] Psalm 131:1-3
[250] Psalm 26:1-12

David, to YHWH
Judge me, YHWH, for I have walked *a life of* integrity.
    I have trusted in YHWH.
    I have not wavered.
Examine me, YHWH. Put me on trial.
    Refine my heart and my mind *in the furnace*.
For your love is *continually* before my eyes;
    I *constantly* walk in your faithfulness.

I do not sit with worthless men;
    I do not go *along with* those who pretend.
I abhor the assembly of those who do evil;
    I do not sit with the wicked.
I bathe my hands in innocence
    so I can go about your altar, YHWH.
Then, I can proclaim *your praise*;
    with a voice of thanksgiving,
    I can recount all your wonderful deeds.
YHWH, I love your house, the place where you live;
    the place where your glory dwells.

So do not gather my soul with *those of the* sinners;
    nor my life with *the lives of* men *who have* shed blood,
those whose hands plan wickedness,
    or those whose right hands are full of bribes.
As for me, I will walk *a life of* integrity.
    So redeem me, and be gracious to me.
My feet stand on level ground,
    and I will bless YHWH in the great assembly.

e). Dependence on God[251]
The psalmist was facing difficulties beyond his means to resolve. As a consequence, he appeals to God to be his rock and refuge.
The psalm particularly asks for security for both the king and his successors.

Notes:
For the *musical* director.
With stringed instruments (*perhaps intending to exclude other instruments*).
Of David.

---

[251] Psalm 61:1-8

> *David, to God*
> God, hear my cry;
> > incline *your ear* to my prayer.
> I call to you from the end of the earth,
> > because my heart grows faint.
> Guide me to a rock that is out of my reach,
> > for you are my refuge,
> > a tower of strength against those who are hostile.
> Let me dwell in your tent for the rest of my life;
> > let me seek refuge in the shadow of your wings.
> > > > > Selah
>
> For you, God, have heard my vows;
> > you have granted the inheritance
> > of those who fear your name.
> You add days to the days of a king;
> > his years *and his house will extend* to all generations.
> May *his line* remain in the presence of God forever;
> > may you designate kindness and faithfulness
> > to watch *over* him.
> Then, as I fulfil my vows day by day,
> > I will forever sing praises to your name.

f). Seeking Deliverance from Evil and Temptation[252]

The psalmist was aware of how easy it was to stray from God's ways, so he prays for deliverance from evil and temptation. In doing so, he was aware of the opposition he would face for taking such a godly stance.

> *Notes:*
> A psalm.
> Of David.
>
> *David, to YHWH*
> YHWH, I call to you. Come hastily to me;
> > listen to my voice when I call to you.
> May my prayer come before you, *like* incense;
> > may my hands be lifted up, *like the* evening sacrifice.
>
> Put a guard over my mouth, YHWH;
> > keep watch over the door of my lips.

---

[252] Psalm 141:1-10

> Prevent my heart from leaning towards evil things
> > *and* from participating in wicked deeds.
> Do not let me eat the delicacies
> > of men who act wickedly.
>
> *If I go astray*, let a righteous *man* strike me—*it will be* a kindness;
> > let him judge me—*it will be* oil upon *my* head.
> My head will not refuse *being chastised*,
> > for I pray continuously against their evil deeds.
> Their leaders will be thrown down the sides of a rock;
> > they will learn my words, for they are sweet.
> In the same way that someone ploughs and breaks up the earth,
> > *so* their bones will be scattered at the entrance to Sheol.
>
> But my eyes are on you, YHWH;
> > in you I seek refuge—do not take away my life.
> Keep me from the grasp of the trap they have baited for me,
> > and from the snares of those who act wickedly.
> Let all the wicked fall into his nets;
> > while I myself pass by.

2. WAITING ON GOD

a). Waiting on God (1)[253]

In this psalm, the psalmist illustrates the difficulties of life and faith, and admits to being in need of God's rescue. However, he also recognises that any rescue may not be immediate. Indeed, he has to learn the lesson: the need to wait on YHWH. That was his experience in the past, and now he needs to wait on YHWH again.

> *Notes:*
> For the *musical* director.
> Of David.
> A psalm.
>
> *David, to those around him*
> I waited and waited for YHWH.
> > He then reached out to me and heard my cry for help.
> He pulled me out of the pit of despair
> > from the miry mud *of Sheol*.

---

[253] Psalm 40:1-17

He set my feet upon a rock;
>> he made my footsteps firm.
He put a new song in my mouth;
>> a hymn of praise to our God.
Many *people* will see, be filled with awe,
>> and will trust in YHWH.
Blessed is the man who puts his trust in YHWH;
>> who does not turn to pagan idols
>> or deviate after false *gods*.

David, to YHWH

YHWH, my God, you have done many wonders;
>> no one can list *all* the plans you have for us.
If I could speak of you,
>> I would say that there are too many to count.

You opened my ears for me.
>> *You told me that* you do not delight in sacrifices or offerings.
>> You do not require Burnt Offerings and Sin Offerings.
But I replied, 'Behold, I am here.
>> It is written for me to do so in the scroll of the book.
I delight to do your will, my God;
>> your law is within my heart.'
I have borne tidings of righteousness in the great assembly.
>> Indeed, I do not restrain my lips, YHWH,
>> as you well know.
I have not concealed your righteousness within my heart;
>> I speak of your faithfulness and salvation.
I have not hidden your kindness and faithfulness
>> from the great assembly.

As for you, YHWH, do not hold back your compassion from me;
>> may your love and truth always protect me.
For I am surrounded;
>> evils without number encircle me.
>> my sins have overtaken me.
They are so many that I cannot see;
>> indeed more *numerous* than the hairs on my head.
>> My heart is failing me.
YHWH, be pleased to deliver me;
>> hasten to my help, YHWH.

> May those who seek to snatch away my life
> > be altogether shamed and humiliated.
> May those who delight in my distress
> > be turned back and humbled.
> May those who taunt me, *saying*, 'Aha, aha,'
> > be horrified at their *own* shame.
>
> *But* may all those who seek you, rejoice and be glad in you;
> > may those who love your salvation always say,
> > 'YHWH is great.'
> As for me, may the Lord consider me,
> > *for* I am afflicted and *in great* need.
> My God, you are my help and the one who delivers me.
> > Do not delay.

b). *Waiting on God (2)*[254]

The psalmist was facing attack from his enemies. But knowing that God would respond in his own time, he was willing to wait on God, and place his life in his hands.

The psalm expresses great faith in the Rock to deal with the difficulties that he faced. It also recognises that trusting in God is the only real hope.

> *Notes:*
> For the *musical* director.
> To Jeduthun (*A chief musician appointed by David*).
> A psalm.
> Of David.
>
> *David, to those around him*
> My soul waits quietly for God alone,
> > *for* from him comes my salvation.
> He alone is my rock and my salvation;
> > *he is* my fortress, so I will not be totally shaken.
>
> *David, to his enemies*
> How long will you shout at a man?
> > Will you all push him over,
> > > like a leaning wall, or a tottering fence?

---

[254] Psalm 62:1-12

David, to those around him
They have unanimously agreed
    to remove him from his exalted position;
    they delight in *telling* lies.
They bless with their mouths;
    but inwardly they curse.

                                                        Selah

David, to those around him
My soul waits quietly in God alone;
    for from him comes my hope.
He alone is my rock and my salvation;
    he is my fortress,
    so I will not be shaken.
I depend upon God for my salvation and my honour;
    he is my mighty rock, my shelter is in God.
Trust in him at all times, people;
    pour out your heart in his presence,
    for God is our refuge.

                                                        Selah

Men of lowly birth are but a breath;
    men who are highborn are a lie.
If they were weighed on scales the balance would rise;
    combined *they would weigh* only a breath.
Do not put *your* confidence in extortion;
    do not put *your* pride in anything stolen.
Although *your* riches may increase,
    do not set *your* heart *on them*.

Once God spoke,
    and two things I heard:
That power belongs to God,

David, to YHWH
and that you, Lord, are *a* loving *God*.
You will surely reward every man
    according to his deeds.

c). Future Hope[255]

The psalmist had been suffering, at the very least, from attacks from his enemies. The situation was grave and, although he had prayed, he had not received a response from YHWH.

But there was a day approaching when matters would come to a head. So the psalmist appealed to God to hear him, to teach him his ways, and to resolve matters in his favour.

Notes:
A prayer. Of David.

David, to YHWH

Incline your ear, YHWH.
    Answer me, for I am afflicted and in want.
Keep watch of my life, for I am godly;
    save your servant, who trusts in you, my God.
Be gracious to me, Lord,
    for I cry out to you all day *long*.
Gladden the soul of your servant,
    for I lift up my soul to you, Lord.
Because, Lord, you are kind and forgiving;
    and rich in love to those who call on you.

Listen, YHWH, to my prayer;
    take heed to the sound of my humble petition.
On my troubled day, I will call to you,
    for *I know* you will answer me.

There is no one like you among the gods, Lord;
    there are no deeds like yours.
Every nation you created will come
    and worship in your presence, Lord.
    They will glorify your name.
For you are great, you do extraordinary things;
    you alone are God.

YHWH, teach me your ways;
    then I will walk in your truth.
Make me single-hearted,
    so I can fear your name.
Lord, my God, I will thank you with all my heart;
    I will glorify your name forever.

---

[255] Psalm 86:1-17

> Because your goodness towards me is great;
>> you have snatched my soul from the depths of Sheol.
>
> God, *a group of* arrogant men *have taken a* stand against me;
>> a band of merciless men are seeking my life.
>> They have put themselves before you.
> But you, Lord, are a God *who is* compassionate and merciful;
>> *you are* slow to anger, and rich in goodness and faithfulness.
> Turn to me. Show me your favour.
>> Give your servant your strength.
>> Save your maidservant's son.
> Give me a sign of your favour,
>> so that those who hate me can see *it* and be humiliated;
>> for you YHWH have aided and consoled me.

3. HONOURING GOD

a). *A Pilgrimage to Jerusalem*[256]

This psalm is about the holy city of Jerusalem, where YHWH's Temple was located and where justice could be sought. The psalm was probably written to be used at one of the annual pilgrimage festivals, as the pilgrims entered or were leaving Jerusalem.

This psalm assumes a time when the Temple was in existence in Jerusalem. In its current form, it would not have been used during King David's lifetime. However, it may have been used during the time of King Solomon.

> *Notes:*
> A song of ascents (*possibly a devotion for those on a pilgrimage to Jerusalem*).
> Of David.
>
> *A pilgrim, to Jerusalem*
> I rejoiced with the company *of pilgrims* who invited me,
>> 'Let us go to the house of YHWH.'
> *And now* our feet are standing
>> within your gates, Jerusalem.
>
> *A pilgrim, to his fellow pilgrims*
> Jerusalem, built as a *strong and mighty* city,
>> united together *in fellowship.*

---

[256] Psalm 122:1-9

Establishing the Kingdom

> The tribes go up there;
> > the tribes of YHWH.
> *It was* decreed *for* Israel *to go there*,
> > to praise the name of YHWH.
> For there stand the thrones *to mete out justice*;
> > the judgement thrones of the house of David.
> > Pray for the peace of Jerusalem.
>
> > *A pilgrim, to Jerusalem*
> May those who love you remain safe.
> > May there be peace within your walls;
> > > serenity within your towers.
> For the sake of my brothers and my companions,
> > I now say, 'Peace be within you.'
> For the sake of the house of YHWH, our God,
> > I will pray for your well-being.

b). Moving the Ark of the Covenant[257]

The people were returning to Jerusalem, accompanied by the Ark of the Covenant. It may have been when the Ark was being moved from Kiriath Jearim to Jerusalem, when the Ark was being returned to the city after a battle, or on some other ceremonial occassion.

The movement of the Ark required some ceremony at the gates to the city. However, whether it involved the elders and those conducting business at the gates, or a group of singers waiting for the Ark's arrival, is not known.

> > *Notes:*
> > A psalm.
> > Of David.
>
> > *David, to those around him*
> The earth and everything in it belongs to YHWH—
> > the world and all who live in it.
> For he created it upon the *cosmic* seas;
> > he made it firm upon the rivers.
>
> Who may climb up *the holy* mountain of YHWH?
> > Who may stand in his holy place?
> *The one who has* clean hands and *are* pure of heart;
> > the one who doesn't worship idols;
> > *and* the one who doesn't swear deceitfully.

---

[257] Psalm 24:1-10

He will receive a blessing from YHWH;
> a vindication from the God of his salvation.

David, to YHWH
Such is *in store for us*, the generation of those who seek him;
> *for we are* those who seek your face, *God of* Jacob.
>> Selah

David, to those at the gates of Jerusalem
Lift up your heads, *you at the* gates;
> may the *height of the* ancient doors be raised,
> so that the glorious king may enter *the city*.
Who is this glorious king?
> *It is* the strong and mighty YHWH;
> *the* YHWH *who is* mighty in battle.
Lift up your heads, *you at the* gates;
> raise *the height of the* ancient doors,
> so that the king of glory may enter *the city*.
Who is this king of glory?
> Almighty YHWH, he is the king of glory.
>> Selah

D1. DAVID'S SONG BOOK

c). Sin

1. SIN

a). The Sin of Pride[258]

The psalmist had recovered from a near fatal illness—the direct result of his arrogance and pride. As a consequence, this psalm acknowledges the sin of pride, gives thanks to YHWH for his healing and forgiveness, and encourages his listeners to learn from his experience.

The note 'A Song for the Dedication of the House' most likely refers to either the Royal Palace or the House of God.

If the note relates to the dedication of the Temple, then it is not beyond possibility that the Temple was dedicated during David's lifetime, before it was built.

> *Notes:*
> A Psalm.
> A Song for the Dedication of the House.
> Of David.
>
> *David, to YHWH*
> I will exalt you, YHWH, for you have drawn me up *from the depths*;
>   you have not allowed my enemies to rejoice over me.
> YHWH, my God, I cried out to you *for help*
>   and you healed me.
> YHWH, you lifted me out of Sheol;
>   from those going down to the pit.
> You have let me live.
>
> *David, to those around him*
> Sing to YHWH, his godly people;
>   praise his holy name.
> For *while* his anger lasts *only* a moment;
>   his favour lasts a lifetime.
> The night may be passed with weeping;
>   but in the morning there will be rejoicing.

---

[258] Psalm 30:1-12

> *David, to YHWH*
> As for me, I said in my prosperity *and arrogance*,
>   'I will never be moved.'
> YHWH, by your favour, you made me stand firm *like a* mountain.
>   *But then* you hid your face *and* I was terrified.
> I called out to you, YHWH;
>   I cried for the Lord to be merciful.
> *I said*, 'What gain is there in my blood
>   if I descend into the pit?
> Will *my body* praise you *when it has turned to* dust?
>   Will it make known your faithfulness?
> Hear *me*, YHWH, and be favourable to me;
>   YHWH, be the one to help me.'
>
> For me, you changed my wailing into dancing;
>   you took off my sackcloth and surrounded me with joy.
> So, YHWH, my God, I will give you thanks forever;
>   my heart will sing to you and will never be silent.

b). The Importance of Confession[259]

The psalmist was well aware of the consequences of doing wrong, and he knew from personal experience the importance of admitting his mistakes to YHWH.

As a consequence, this psalm speaks of the need for godly people to confess their sins to YHWH. Furthermore, even though the psalmist's sin is not actually identified, he also expresses the great joy and relief of being forgiven.

> *Notes:*
> Of David.
> A maskil (*possibly a contemplative poem*).
>
> *David, to YHWH*
> Blessed is the one whose transgression is forgiven;
>   the one whose sin is covered *over*.
> Blessed is the man whose guilt has not been counted against him by YHWH,
>   and in whose spirit there is no denial.
>
> When I kept silent *about my sin*, I groaned all day long,
>   and my bones wasted away.

---

[259] Psalm 32:1-11

> For your hand was heavy upon me day and night;
>> and my energy dried up, like a drought in summer.
>>> Selah
>
> Then I made my sin known to you;
>> I uncovered my guilt.
> I said, 'I will reveal my transgression to YHWH.'
>> Then you took away the guilt of my sin.
>>> Selah
>
> Therefore, let every godly person pray to you
>> at *this* time *when you may* be found.
> *So* as surely as the mighty waters *of troubles* rise,
>> they will not strike him.
> You are the place in which I hide;
>> you keep me from trouble;
>> you surround me with cries of deliverance.
>>> Selah
>
> *YHWH, to David*
> I will instruct you, and teach you to walk in the *right* ways;
>> I will advise you. My eye will be upon you.
> You are not to be like a horse—like a mule without understanding—
>> who is controlled with the bit and bridle of his harness,
>> *otherwise* he would not come to you.
>
> *David, to those around him*
> The torments of the wicked are many;
>> but the one who trusts in YHWH
>> is surrounded by his goodness.
> Those who are righteous, rejoice and be glad in YHWH;
>> sing, all those who are upright in heart.

c). A Prayer for Forgiveness[260]

This psalm asks YHWH for forgiveness of sins, guidance in his ways, and preservation from his enemies.

In the original Hebrew, this is an alphabetical acrostic psalm. However it has suffered through its transmission over time or at the hand of an editor. Indeed, the letters ו *(waw) and* ק *(qop) are missing, and the letters* פ *(pe) and* ר *(res) have been included twice.*

---

[260] Psalm 25:1-22

Note:
Of David.

David, to YHWH

א   I lift my soul to you,
       YHWH, my God.
ב   I trust in you,
       do not let me be put to shame,
       do not let those who are hostile to me rejoice over me.
ג   Indeed, do not let any of those who wait on you be shamed;
       but let those who deal treacherously,
       for no *valid* reason, be shamed.

ד   Make your ways known to me, YHWH;
       teach me your paths.
ה   Lead me in your faithfulness.
       Teach me, for you are the God who saves me.
       I wait on you all day long.
ז   Remember your compassion and your goodness, YHWH,
       for they *have endured* from of old.
ח   Do not remember the sins of my early years,
       or my acts of rebellion.
       Remember me, in accordance with your covenant love,
       for the sake of your goodness, YHWH.

David, to those around him

ט   YHWH is good and upright;
       for this reason, he directs sinners in *his* ways.
י   He guides those who are afflicted in *his* justice;
       he teaches the poor his ways.
כ   For those who keep his covenant and his decrees,
       all YHWH's ways are good and faithful.

David, to YHWH

ל   *So* forgive my wickedness, great though it is,
       for the sake of your name, YHWH.

David, to those around him (about himself)

מ   Who, *then*, is this man who fears YHWH?
       YHWH will instruct him in the way he chooses.
נ   The days of his life will be spent in prosperity;
       his descendants will inherit land.

Establishing the Kingdom

ס	YHWH's counsel *will be* with those who fear him;
	he will make his covenant known to them.
ע	My eyes are on YHWH continuously,
	for he will disentangle my feet from the *hunter's* net.
	David, to YHWH
פ	Turn to me. Show me *your* favour,
	for I am alone and afflicted.
צ	The troubles of my heart have increased;
	release me from my distress.
ר	See my affliction and my trouble;
	take away all my sins.
ר	See those who are hostile to me, how many they have become;
	they hate me with a fierce hatred.
ש	Keep watch *over* my life. Deliver me.
	Do not let me be shamed, for I take refuge in you.
ת	May integrity and uprightness guard my *life*,
	because I wait on you.
פ	God, redeem Israel
	from all their troubles.

d). God's Punishment for Sin (1)[261]

The psalmist believed that he was being chastised by YHWH because of his sins. He was also being persecuted by his enemies. But whether his enemies were responsible for his predicament, or were simply being opportunists is not clear.

As a consequence, the psalmist appeals to God to ease his punishment, while requesting that his enemies be put in their place.

> *Notes:*
> For the *musical* director.
> With stringed instruments (*perhaps intending to exclude other instruments*).
> According to the sheminith (*possibly an eight-stringed instrument*).
> A psalm.
> Of David.
>
> *David, to YHWH*
> Do not condemn me in your anger, YHWH;
>   do not chastise me in your wrath.
> Show me *your* favour, YHWH, for I am weak;
>   heal me, YHWH, for my bones are racked *with pain*.

---

[261] Psalm 6:1-10

> My soul is greatly disturbed.
>> But you, YHWH, how long *will it be before you come to my aid?*
>
> Turn back, YHWH, deliver my soul;
>> save me, in accordance with your covenant love.
> For there is no remembrance of you in death;
>> who praises you in Sheol?
>
> I am weary with my groaning;
>> all night *long* I flood my bed with my tears,
>> I soak my couch.
> My eyes have grown dim with sorrow;
>>> they are failing, because of all those who are hostile to me.
>
>> *David, to his enemies*
> Go away from me, all *you* who act wickedly,
>> for YHWH has heard the sound of my weeping.
> YHWH has heard my humble petition;
>> YHWH has *also* accepted my prayer.
>
>> *David, to YHWH*
> Let all my enemies be disgraced and greatly troubled;
>> let them turn back,
>> let them suddenly be ashamed.

e). God's Punishment for Sin (2)[262]

The psalmist was suffering from an illness—the direct result of being chastisd by God for his sins. So he appeals to God using four basic themes: his illness, his guilt, his abandonment by his friends, and the opportunism of his enemies. Having confessed his sins, he then waits on God's mercy and restoration.

This psalm may have been written, or been adopted, for the sacrificial system—hence the title 'For the Memorial Offering'.

> *Notes:*
> A psalm. Of David.
> For the Memorial *Offering*.
>
>> *David, to YHWH*
> Do not reprimand me in your fierce anger, YHWH;
>> do not admonish me in your rage.

---

[262] Psalm 38:1-22

For your arrows have penetrated my *body*;
    your hand weighs heavily upon me.
Because of your strong displeasure, my flesh is unhealthy;
    my bones are unsound because of my sin.
Indeed, my guilt, *as if a flood*, is flowing over my head;
    like a heavy burden, it is too heavy for me.

My wounds stink and fester
    because of my foolishness.
I am twisted and bowed down *in mourning*;
    I go about all day in gloom.
Indeed, my loins are completely inflamed;
    my flesh is unsound.
I am numb; I am badly crushed;
    I yell out, because of the groaning of my heart.

Lord, every part of my desire is *open* before you;
    even my sighing is not concealed from you.
My heart pounds; my strength has abandoned me;
    and the light of my eyes—even that has failed me.
My friends and companions stay away *from me* and my wounds;
    my kinsman keeps right away.
Those who seek my life set their traps;
    those who would cause me injury, threaten destruction;
    they mutter treachery all day long.

As for me, I am like a deaf *man*. I cannot hear;
    I am like someone who is dumb, whose mouth won't open.
Indeed, I am like a man who cannot hear
    and whose mouth will not respond.
So, YHWH, I will wait for you;
    and Lord, my God, you will answer.
For I said, 'Do not let them rejoice over me;
    when my foot slips, do let them raise themselves over me.'

Yet I am about to stumble;
    my pain is constantly with me.
I have admitted my guilt
    and I am fearful because of my sin.
But those who are hostile to me are alive and mighty;
    those who wrongfully hate me are many.

> When I chase after that which is good,
>> those who repay evil for good are hostile to me.
>
> Do not abandon me, YHWH, my God;
>> do not keep your distance from me.
> Lord, my deliverer,
>> hurry to my aid.

f). God's Punishment for Sin (3)[263]

The psalmist was aware that he was being punished by God because of his sin. He also wanted to hold his tongue, particularly to those who were hostile to YHWH. Yet, despite his good intentions, the severity of his punishment was too great and he could no longer remain silent.

As a consequence, this psalm reflects his prayer to YHWH for deliverance, and to ask for an opportunity to enjoy God's favour one last time.

> *Notes:*
> For the *musical* director.
> *According* to Jeduthun (*one of David's chief musicians*).
> A psalm. Of David.
>
> *David, to YHWH*
> I said, 'I will keep watch over my ways,
>> so that I don't sin with my tongue.
> I will restrain my mouth with a muzzle,
>> while the wicked are in my presence.'
> *So* I remained mute and silent;
>> I didn't even say anything good.
> Yet my suffering increased
>> and my heart grew warmer inside me;
> In my thinking, a fire began to burn.
>> *Only then did* I speak with my tongue.
>
> Let me know *when* my *life will* end, YHWH;
>> *tell me* the length of my days;
>> remind me how fleeting my *life is.*
> Look, you have made my days *as short* as the span of a hand;
>> my duration is as nothing in your sight.
>> Indeed, even men of standing are just a breath.
>>>> Selah

---

[263] Psalm 39:1-13

> Surely, man walks around like a shadow;
> > he rushes around in vain.
> He accumulates wealth,
> > but has no idea who will get it.
>
> But now, Lord, what am I waiting for?
> > My hope is in you.
> Deliver me from all my transgressions.
> > Do not let fools treat me with contempt.
> I remained mute; I did not open my mouth
> > because you had brought *this suffering on me*.
> Turn aside your punishment from me;
> > the hostility of your hand has exhausted me.
> You discipline a man with reprimands for *his* sin;
> > like a moth, you consume the things he treasures.
> > Indeed, every man is just a breath.
> >   Selah
>
> Hear my prayer, YHWH, listen to my cry;
> > do not *turn a* deaf *ear* to my weeping.
> For I am a *resident* alien with you;
> > a sojourner, like all my fathers.
> Look away from me, so that I might smile *once more*
> > before I pass away, and am no more.

2. THE UNGODLY

a). A Godless World[264]

The psalmist was very aware of the godless world in which he lived. Indeed, the psalm describes the foolishness and the depth of depravity of those who continue to live as though God does not exist.

The psalm exists in two forms, much of which is common to both. However, in addition to expressing the foolishness of the ungodly, the second form also celebrates a miraculous deliverance from an attacking enemy.

> *Notes:*
> For the *musical* director.
> Of David.

---

[264] Psalms 14:1-7; 53:1-6

David, to those around him
A fool thinks in his heart,
    'God does not exist.'
Such people are debased, they commit abhorrent things.
    Indeed, those who do good are no *more*.

YHWH looks down from the heavens
    on the sons of man.
He *looks to* see if there is anyone who understands,
    anyone who is seeking God.
But all have turned aside;
    together they have become corrupt.
Of those who do good, none *remain*;
    not a single person.

Will all those who do evil ever gain knowledge?
    They devour my people, like they eat bread,
    but they do not call upon YHWH.
Despite that, they live in great fear,
    for God is with the righteous generation.
The assembly of the afflicted will put them to shame,
    for YHWH is their refuge.

Who will bring the salvation of Israel from Zion?
    When YHWH brings back the prosperity of his people,
    Jacob will rejoice, Israel will be glad.

Notes:
For the *musical* director.
According to mahalath (*possibly the name of a tune or a musical instrument*).
A maskil (*possibly a contemplative poem*).
Of David.

David, to those around him
A fool thinks in his heart,
    'God does not exist.'
Such people are debased, they commit abhorrent injustices.
    Indeed, those who do good are no *more*.

> God looks down from the heavens
>> on the sons of man.
> He *looks to* see if there is anyone who understands,
>> anyone who is seeking God.
> *But* all have gone astray;
>> together they have become corrupt.
> Of those who do good, none *remain*;
>> not a single person.
>
> Will those who do evil ever gain knowledge?
>> They devour my people like they eat bread,
>> but they do not call upon God there.
> *Despite that*, they live in great fear,
>> where no fear had been.
> But God scatters the bones of the one who encamps against you.
>> You will put *them* to shame, for God has rejected them.
>
> Who will bring the salvation of Israel from Zion?
>> When God brings back the prosperity of his people,
>> Jacob will rejoice, Israel will be glad.

b). The Reality of the Ungodly[265]

The psalmist was very aware of the ungodly people around him, who behaved very differently to himself. The wicked plotted and schemed, yet he was determined to be faithful to God.

Neverttheless, he was confident that God would prevail—he had done so in the past, and would do so again.

> *Notes:*
> For the *musical* director.
> Of David, a servant of YHWH.
>
> *David, to those around him*
> *I have received* an oracle concerning the sinfulness of the wicked *man*;
>> *it* is within my heart.
> There is no fear of God
>> in his eyes.
> For in his *own* eyes he prides himself
>> that his sin *will not be* detected,
>> or *that he will not be* hated *for it*.

---

[265] Psalm 36:1-12

> From his mouth come words which are wicked and perverse;
>> he has ceased to act wisely or do good.
> He plots *his* evil *schemes, even* on his bed;
>> he commits himself to a course *that is* not good;
>> he does not reject evil.
>
> *David, to YHWH*
> YHWH, your covenant love extends to the heavens;
>> your faithfulness *stretches out* to the clouds.
> Your righteousness is *as insurmountable* as the mountains of God;
>> your justice is *as immeasurable as the* deepest sea.
> YHWH, you deliver *both* man and beast.
>> God, how priceless is your covenant love.
> The sons of man seek refuge
>> in the shadow of your wings.
> They feast from the fatness of your house;
>> you quench their thirst from the river of your delights.
> For in you *alone* is the fountain of life;
>> *only* in your light *can* we see light.
>
> Maintain your covenant love with those who know you,
>> and your righteousness to the upright of heart.
> Protect me from the foot of the arrogant;
>> do not let the hand of the wicked drive me away.
>
> *David, to those around him*
> Look, those who have done evil have fallen;
>> they have been thrown down and are unable to rise.

c). *The Prosperity and Power of the Wicked*[266]

This psalm comments on the apparent prosperity and power of the wicked, and their contribution to the suffering of the righteous. Despite that, the psalmist is confident that God's righteousness will prevail, and that the righteous will receive their reward.

In the original Hebrew, it is an alphabetical acrostic psalm, with a different letter of the alphabet beginning every other verse.

> *Note:*
> Of David.

---

[266] Psalm 37:1-40

Establishing the Kingdom

David, to those around him

א Do not burn with anger over *the prosperity of* those who do evil;
    do not be jealous of *the success* of those who do wrong.
For they will quickly wither *away* like grass;
    like a green plant they will fade away.

ב Trust in YHWH. Do good.
    Live in the land and feed on faithfulness.
Delight in YHWH
    and he will give you your heart's desires.

ג Commit your way to YHWH;
    trust in him, and he will act:
He will bring forth your righteousness like the dawn;
    and the justice *of your cause* like the noonday *sun*.

ד Be still in YHWH's presence;
    wait patiently for him.
Do not burn with anger over someone who prospers in his way;
    over a man who carries out evil plans.

ה Cease from anger; turn from wrath.
    Do not burn with anger, *as it* only leads to evil.
For those who are evil will be cut off;
    but those who wait for YHWH will inherit the land.

ו *In* a little while, the wicked will be no more;
    although you look for his place, he will not be *there*.
But those who are humble will inherit the land;
    they will delight in abundant peace.

ז The wicked man plots against the righteous man;
    he gnashes his teeth at him.
But the Lord laughs at the wicked man,
    for he sees that his day is coming.

ח Wicked *men* draw their swords and bend their bows
    to bring down the poor and needy,
    to slaughter those whose ways are righteous.
But their swords will enter their *own* hearts,
    and their bows will be shattered.

ט The little that the righteous *have* is better
    than the abundance of many wicked.
For the strength of the wicked will be shattered,
    while YHWH cares for the righteous.

י YHWH knows the days of the righteous;
    their inheritance will last forever.

Establishing the Kingdom

	They will not be put to shame in times of disaster;
	in days of famine they will be satisfied.
כ	But the wicked will perish.
	YHWH's enemies are like the splendour of the pastures.
	They will vanish;
	they will disappear like smoke.
ל	The wicked borrow and never repay;
	but the righteous are gracious and *keep* giving.
	Indeed, those blessed by YHWH will inherit the land;
	but those cursed by him will be cut off.
מ	The steps of a man are established by YHWH,
	and he delights in his way.
	Although he stumbles he will not fall headlong,
	for YHWH holds onto his hand.
נ	I was young. Now I am old.
	However I have never seen a righteous *man* forsaken *by God*,
	or his child begging for bread.
	A righteous man is generous and lends *freely* all day *long*;
	his child will be a blessing.
ס	Turn from evil. Do good.
	then you will live forever.
	For YHWH is the one who loves justice;
	he will not forsake those who are faithful to him.
ע	They will be kept *safe* forever;
	but the offspring of the wicked will be cut off.
	The righteous will inherit the land;
	they will live in it forever.
פ	The mouth of the righteous utters wisdom;
	his tongue speaks justice.
	The law of his God is in his heart;
	his feet never slip.
צ	The wicked *man* keeps watch on the righteous;
	seeking *an opportunity* to kill him.
	But YHWH will not abandon him into his hand;
	he will not condemn him *even* if he is on trial.
ק	Wait for YHWH;
	keep his ways.
	Then he will exalt you to possess the land.
	You will see *it* when the wicked are cut off.
ר	I have seen a wicked and overbearing man
	spreading *himself* like a native green tree.

> But he passed away. Look, he is no more.
> > Even though I sought him, he could not be found.
> ש Watch the blameless. Observe the upright.
> > For a man of peace will have a future.
> But those who sin will be totally destroyed;
> > the future of the wicked will be cut off.
> ת The salvation of the righteous is from YHWH;
> > *he is* their refuge in time of trouble.
> YHWH helps them; he rescues them.
> > He delivers them from the wicked;
> > he saves them because they take refuge in him.

d). *The Oppression of the Poor and Afflicted*[267]

The psalmist was conscious of deceit and dishonesty all around him. Indeed, he felt surrounded by people who oppressed the poor and the afflicted. In one sense he felt alone, yet his prayer was that YHWH would provide safety and security for the faithful, and that he would deal with those who lie and practice double standards.

> *Notes:*
> For the *musical* director,
> According to the sheminith *(possibly an eight-stringed instrument)*.
> A psalm.
> Of David.
>
> *David, to YHWH*
> Help, YHWH, for no *one who is* pious remains;
> > those who were faithful
> > have disappeared from the sons of men.
> *Instead*, they all speak lies, *even to* their friends;
> > they speak with smooth lips and a double heart.
> May YHWH cut off all *who have* flattering lips;
> > *all who* utter boasts *with their* tongues.
> *Indeed, all* that say, 'With our tongue we will do great things.
> > Our lips belong to us, *so* who *can be* lord over us?'
>
> *David, to those around him*
> YHWH says, 'Because of the violence against those who are afflicted,
> > because of the crying of those in need,

---

[267] Psalm 12:1-8

> I will now make a stand,
> > I will place *the afflicted* in the security
> > for which they have longed.'
> YHWH's words are unadulterated words;
> > *like* silver *that has been* refined in a ground furnace,
> > purified seven times.
>
> > *David, to YHWH*
> You, YHWH, will keep watch over them;
> > you will forever protect us from this generation.
> *Even if* those who are wicked walk about *everywhere*;
> > and all that is vile is praised among the sons of men.

e). The Injustice in the World[268]

The need for justice was paramount in the psalmist's mind. Indeed, as he looked around him, he lamented over the injustices that he saw. He even brought charges against those who were responsible for such corruption and perversion.

But the psalmist was also convinced that justice would prevail. That in the end, YHWH would come to the rescue of his people, and not let the ungodly go unpunished.

> > *Notes:*
> > For the *musical* director.
> > *To the tune* 'Do Not Destroy'.
> > Of David.
> > A miktam *(perhaps a contemplative prayer)*.
>
> > *David, to those around him*
> You who are silent, do you truly speak justly?
> > Are you upright in your justice of the sons of man?
> No, in your heart you contrive injustice;
> > with your hands you measure out violence on the earth.
> The wicked have strayed *ever since* leaving the womb;
> > those who speak lies have erred since birth.
> Their venom is like the venom of a serpent;
> > *such a one is obstinate,* he has blocked his ears.
> *He is* like the cobra that is deaf;
> > who does not heed the tune of the charmer,
> > nor the skilful spells of the enchanter.

---

[268] Psalm 58:1-11

Establishing the Kingdom

> *David, to YHWH*
> God, break the teeth in the mouths *of the unjust;*
>   YHWH, pull out the teeth of *these* young lions.
> Let them wash away like water that runs away;
>   let his arrows be headless when he draws his bow.
> Let him be like a slug, *whose slime trails give the appearance*
>   *of* melting away as he moves along;
> May he be like the stillborn child of a woman
>   who has never seen the sun.
>
> *David, to those around him*
> *God* will sweep the ungodly away *in a whirlwind,*
>   before the thorns (whether green or dry)
>   *that you have collected in* your pots *to start a fire, can be lit.*
> The righteous will rejoice when he sees *such* vengeance;
>   he will bathe his feet in the blood of the wicked.
> Then a man will say, 'Surely there is a reward for the righteous;
>   surely there is a God who judges over the earth.'

f). A King's Struggle with Injustice[269]

    This is a psalm which reflects the reality of a king's life—that he is surrounded by many who are motivated by their own self-interest.

    As a consequence, the psalm emphasises the need for a king to distance himself from the ungodly around him, to live a blameless life, and to administer justice to his people.

> *Notes:*
> Of David.
> A psalm.
>
> *David, to YHWH*
> I will sing of your loyalty and justice;
>   I will make music to you, YHWH.
> I will observe a life that is blameless—
>   *so* when will you come to me?
>
> I will walk with integrity of heart within my house.
>   I will not place any worthless thing before my eyes.
>
> I hate the deeds of those who have fallen away;
>   they shall not remain close to me.

---

[269] Psalm 101:1-8

> I have turned away from the wicked heart;
> > I will not engage in evil.
> I will put an end to anyone
> > who slanders his neighbour in secret.
> I will not tolerate anyone
> > with an arrogant look or a proud heart.
>
> My eyes *will be* on the faithful of the land,
> > that they may remain with me.
> Only those who observe a life that is blameless
> > will serve me.
>
> No one who practices deceit
> > will be allowed to live in my house.
> No one who speaks lies
> > will *be permitted to* stand in my presence.
>
> *In my judgements* in the mornings, I will put an end
> > to all who are wicked in the land.
> I will cut off all who do evil
> > from the city of YHWH.

g). A Prayer for Protection Against the Ungodly[270]

The psalmist was surrounded by people consumed with worldly ways. As a consequence, he looked forward to the day when he would come face-to-face with his God.

This psalm is a prayer for the paslmist to be declared innocent. It also appeals for protection from ungodly men in general and, perhaps, from one man in particular (identity unknown).

> *Notes:*
> A prayer.
> Of David.
>
> *David, to YHWH*
> Hear *my* righteous *plea*, YHWH;
> > incline your ear to my cry.
> Listen to my prayer,
> > *which* does not *come* from lying lips.
> Let me be vindicated in your presence;
> > let your eyes see the upright.

---

[270] Psalm 17:1-15

Examine my heart, visit *me* at night,
> test me *in the flames*.
You will find nothing,
> *for* I have determined that my mouth will not sin.
Contrary to the deeds of men,
> *I have lived* by the word of your lips;
> I have guarded myself from the ways of the violent.
My steps have stayed firmly on your paths;
> my feet have not faltered.

I personally call on you, God,
> for you will respond to me.
Incline your ear to me;
> hear what I have to say.
Demonstrate your distinct covenant love.
> Deliver, with your right hand,
> those who take refuge *in you* from their foes.
Maintain my *reflection* in the pupil of your eye;
> conceal me in the shadow of your wings.

Protect me from the wicked who attack me
> *and from* my deadly foes who encircle me.
In their fatness they have become closed *to others*;
> with their mouths they speak such pride.
Now *they are* surrounding us in our tracks;
> their eyes are set to cast *us* to the ground.

He is like a hungry lion, *eager* to tear its prey;
> like a young lion, *waiting* in hiding, ready *to pounce*.
Stand up *and* face him, YHWH; bring him down;
> deliver me from *this* wicked *man with* your sword.

With your hand, *rescue me* from *such* men, YHWH;
> *save me* from *these* men of the world,
> whose *only* reward *is* in *this* life.
May you fill their bellies with what you have in store *for them*—
> *the things of this life*.
May they be satisfied with *their* sons;
> may they accumulate wealth for their children.
However I, in *my* righteousness, will see your face;
> *Indeed*, I will *only* be satisfied when I awake to *see* your image.

h). A Prayer to Overthrow the Wicked[271]

The psalmist was concerned that he would be numbered with the evil-doers around him. So he appeals to YHWH to deliver him from such men.

Then, with his expectation that his prayer would be answered, the psalmist continues by giving thanks to God for being the strength and shield of both himself and his people.

Note:
Of David.

David, to YHWH

YHWH, my rock, I call to you;
    do not be deaf towards me.
For if you are silent to me,
    I will be like those who go down to the pit.
Hear the sound of my humble prayer
    as I cry out to you for help,
and as I raise my hands
    in the direction of your Most Holy Place.

Do not take me away with those who are wicked;
    with those who do evil.
They speak peace with their neighbours,
    but have evil in their hearts.
Repay them according to their deeds;
    according to their evil practices.
Repay them according to the works of their hands;
    pay them what they deserve.

David, to those around him

For they do not show any regard for the works of YHWH
    or for the deeds of his hands.
So he will throw them down
    and he will never rebuild them.

Let YHWH be praised,
    for he has heard the sound of my humble prayer.
YHWH is my strength and my shield;
    my heart trusts in him, so I am helped.
My heart rejoices,
    and I will thank him with my song.

---

[271] Psalm 28:1-9

> YHWH is the strength of the people;
> > a saving refuge *for* his anointed *one*.
> Save your people, and bless your inheritance;
> > shepherd them, and carry them forever.

D1. DAVID'S SONG BOOK

d). Enemies

1. FALSE ACCUSATIONS

a). Falsely Accused[272]

The psalmist was under attack from those who sought his demise—and from one person in particular. Even though he believed he had done nothing wrong, and had given no grounds for complaint, he was facing a number of charges.

> *Note:*
> Of David.
>
> *David, to YHWH*
> Fight against my adversaries, YHWH;
>   do battle against those who fight against me.
> Take up *your* shield and armour;
>   stand up and come to my aid.
> Get ready the spear,
>   and block *the way* of those who are pursuing me.
> Tell my soul,
>   'I am your salvation.'
>
> Let those who seek my life
>   be shamed and humiliated;
> Let those who plot my ruin
>   be turned away and mortified.
> Let them be like chaff before the wind,
>   with the angel of YHWH blowing *them* away.
> Let their way be dark and slippery,
>   with the angel of YHWH in their pursuit.
>
> For they dug *a pit* for me, for no *valid* reason;
>   for no reason they concealed their pit *with* a net.
> Let destruction come upon him, without warning;
>   let his hidden net ensnare him;
>   let him fall into it, into *his own* ruin.

---

[272] Psalm 35:1-28

Then my soul will rejoice in YHWH;
> I will take great pleasure in his salvation.

Every one of my bones will say,
> 'Who is like you, YHWH?

You are the one who rescues the weak *man*
> from a stronger *man*.

You even help a poor and needy *man*
> from *the man who* robs him.'

Malicious witnesses stand up;
> they ask me about things I do not know.

They repay me evil for good.
> I am bereft.

But I, when they were sick, *I wore* sackcloth for my clothing;
> I humbled myself with fasting;
> I prayed with *my head* bowed to my breast.

I went about like a friend or brother;
> I bowed down grieving like a weeping mother.

But when I faced disaster they were glad; they gathered *together*;
> *even* those I didn't know gathered to attack me
> and they slandered *me* continuously.

Like a circle of ungodly mockers
> they gnashed their teeth against me.

Lord, how long will you look on?
> Rescue my life from their devastation;
> my solitary *life* from the lions.

Then I will thank you in the great assembly;
> I will praise you in the mighty crowd.

Do not let those who are hostile to me, without cause,
> rejoice over me.

Do not let those who hate me, without cause,
> wink the eye.

For they do not talk of peace;
> but they conceive words *intended to* deceive
> those who *live* quietly in the land.

They open wide their mouths at me;
> they say, with a triumphant cry,
> 'Our eyes have witnessed *what he has done*.'

YHWH you have seen *this*, so do not be silent;
> Lord, do not be distant from me.

Establishing the Kingdom

> Rouse yourself.
>> Stir yourself to my defence;
>>> fight for me, *my* Lord and my God.
> In your righteous *judgements*,
>> clear me YHWH, my God, *of their accusations*;
>>> do not let them rejoice over me.
> Do not let them say in their hearts,
>> 'Aha! *We have achieved* our heart's desire.'
> Do not let them say,
>> 'We have swallowed him up.'
>
> Let all those who take pleasure in my misery
>> be shamed and humiliated.
> Let those who elevated themselves over me
>> be clothed in shame and reproach.
> *But* let those who take pleasure in my vindication
>> be glad and sing out with joy.
> Let them say for evermore, 'YHWH is great,
>> he delights in his servant's well-being.'
> Then my tongue will mutter of your righteousness,
>> and I will praise you all day long.

b). *A Lament at Bedtime*[273]

The psalmist had been accused of something he hadn't done and, at night, events could easily be taken out of proportion. But he was not defeated. Indeed, he expresses trust that God would come to his rescue and would enable him to sleep in peace.

> *Notes:*
> For the *musical* director.
> With stringed instruments.
> A psalm.
> Of David.
>
> *David, to YHWH*
>
> My righteous God,
>> answer me when I call.
> You have relieved me from distress *before*;
>> *so* show me favour and hear my prayer.

---

[273] Psalm 4:1-8

> *David, to his accusers*
> Sons of men,
> > how long *will you* insult my honour?
> *How long* will you love vain *words*?
> > *How long* will you pursue lies?
> > > > > > > > Selah
>
> Know that YHWH has set apart the pious for himself,
> > for YHWH will hear when I call to him.
> Be perturbed, but do not sin.
> > Think about it *as you lie* on your beds—and be still.
> > > > > > > > Selah
>
> Offer the right sacrifices,
> > and *put your* trust in YHWH.
>
> *David, to YHWH*
> There are many who say, 'Who can show us *anything* good?'
> > Let the light of your face, YHWH, shine upon us.
> You have put more joy in my heart,
> > than *my accusers enjoy* when their grain and new wine abound.
> In peace, I will lie down and I will sleep,
> > for you alone, YHWH, cause me to dwell securely.

c). A Lament in the Morning[274]

The psalmist had been accused of wrongdoing by fellow Israelites. But he didn't trust his accusers because they were both flatterers and slanderers. Indeed, he believed that his accusers were blood-thirsty and willing to go to any lengths to fulfil their plans.

This psalm assumes that the Temple has already been built in Jerusalem, and may have been adapted from its original use.

> *Notes:*
> For the *musical* director
> For the flutes.
> A psalm.
> Of David.
>
> *David, to YHWH*
> Listen to my words, YHWH;
> > Give heed to my groaning.

---

[274] Psalm 5:1-12

> Incline your ears to the sound of my cry.
> > For I pray to you, my God and my king.
> *Every* morning you hear my voice;
> > *every* morning I set *my petitions* before you.
> > Then I wait.
>
> For *you are* not a God who delights in evil;
> > wickedness cannot stay, even temporarily, with you.
> Those who are arrogant are unable to stand in your presence;
> > you hate all who do evil.
> You eliminate those who speak falsely, YHWH;
> > *you* abhor men of blood and deceit.
>
> As for me, by the greatness of your covenant love,
> > I will enter your house.
> I will bow down in reverence to you,
> > in the direction of your holy Temple.
> Guide me in your righteousness, YHWH.
> > There are some who are watching me with evil intent—
> > so make your way straight before me.
>
> For nothing from their mouth can be trusted;
> > their hearts *bring nothing but* destruction.
> Their throats are *like* open graves *desiring more victims*;
> > they flatter with their tongues.
> Pronounce them guilty, God;
> > let their plans *be the grounds for* their *own* overthrow.
> Cast them out *of your presence* for their many sins,
> > for they *continue to* rebel against you.
>
> But let all who seek refuge in you rejoice;
> > let them sing for joy forever.
> Put your *protective* cover over them;
> > surround them with favour, like a shield.
> Let those who love your name rejoice in you.
> > For it is you, YHWH, who blesses the righteous.

d). Being Slandered and Hunted Down[275]

The psalmist was not only being slandered, but was being hunted down. What he was accused of is not known, but the accusations were serious. Indeed, they were likened to poison.

---

[275] Psalm 140:1-13

Establishing the Kingdom

Notes:
For the *musical* director.
A psalm.
Of David.

David, to YHWH
Deliver me, YHWH, from an evil man;
    guard me against a man of violence.
Because they plot evil in *their* hearts;
    they stir up wars all *the time*.
They make their tongues sharp, like *that of* a serpent;
    a viper's venom is on their lips.
                                    Selah

Keep me, YHWH, from the hands of the wicked;
    guard me against a man of violence.
    They plan to trip up my feet.
The proud have concealed a trap for me;
    with *their cords* they have spread out a net;
    they have set traps for me at the side of the road.
                                    Selah

I say to *you*, YHWH, 'You are my God.
    YHWH, listen to the cry of my humble prayer.
YHWH, *you are my* Lord, my strong deliverer;
    you cover my head in the day of battle.
YHWH, do not grant the wicked what he desires;
    do not let his schemes succeed.
    Otherwise they will become proud.'
                                    Selah

Let the trouble of their lips
    be upon the heads of those who surround me.
Let burning coals fall upon them;
    let them be thrown into muddy pits,
    from which they *will* never rise.
Let evil quickly hunt a man of violence down.
    Do not let a slanderer become settled in the land.

I know that YHWH will secure justice for the afflicted;
    he will maintain the cause of the needy.

> Surely those who are righteous will give thanks to your name;
> those who are upright will dwell in your presence.

e). On Trial[276]

The psalmist had been cursed and accused of a serious offence by his enemies. Indeed, the accusation had been so serious that he was put on trial. Furthermore, his enemies had tried to manipulate the court to obtain a conviction.

Despite that, the psalmist was confident of his innocence and that YHWH was on his side. As a consequence, he prays that the situation will rebound on his accusers, and that he will be acquitted of any wrong doing.

> *Notes:*
> For the *musical* director.
> Of David.
> A psalm.
>
> *David, to YHWH*
>
> God, whom I praise,
>   do not be silent.
> For wicked and treacherous *men*
>   have opened their mouths against me;
>   they speak against me with deceptive tongues.
> They encircle me with words of hatred;
>   they do battle with me, without cause.
> In response to my love, they act as my adversaries,
>   even *while I am in* prayer.
> *With my* good, they have repaid evil;
>   *with my* friendship, *they have returned* hatred.
>
> *They said,* 'Appoint a wicked *judge* against him;
>   let an adversary take their stand at his right hand.
> When he is tried, let him be found guilty;
>   may his *mocking* prayer be *recognised as* a sin.
> May his days be few;
>   may another take his position.
> May his son be fatherless,
>   and his wife a widow.
> May his children be forever wandering and begging;
>   may they be driven from the ruins they inhabit.

---

[276] Psalm 109:1-31

May the creditor seize all that he owns;
>> may strangers plunder *the produce of* his labour.
May no one extend kindness to him,
>> or show favour to his fatherless children.
May his future be cut off;
>> may the next generation's name be erased.
May YHWH recall the wickedness of his fathers;
>> may his mother's sin never be wiped out.
May their *sins* be continually before YHWH,
>> so that he can erase *all* memory of them from the earth.'

They continued, 'For he never remembered to do *acts of* kindness;
>> but *instead* pursued *the* poor, *the* needy,
>> and *the* broken-hearted to death.
He loved to curse;
>> so let *a curse* come on him;
He took no delight in blessing,
>> so let *a blessing* be far from him.
Instead, he put on cursing
>> as *though it were* a garment.
He drank it, and it entered his body like water;
>> *he rubbed it in,* like oil into his bones.
So let *the curses be* like a garment he wraps around himself;
>> like a belt he continually ties.'

David, to those around him
May this be YHWH's reward for those who accuse me,
>> and those who say evil *things* against me.

David, to YHWH
But you, YHWH, *my* Lord,
>> for your name's sake, deal *graciously* with me;
>> in your good *and* loving kindness deliver me.

For I am afflicted and in need;
>> my heart is pierced within me.
I am fading like a lengthening shadow;
>> I have been brushed off like a locust.
My knees are giving way from fasting;
>> my flesh is lean from *lack of* fat.
I myself am *an object of* scorn to them;
>> they shake their heads when they see me.

> Help me YHWH, my God;
> > in your goodness, deliver me.
> Let them know that this *is the work of* your hand,
> > *and* that you, YHWH, did it.
> Let they themselves curse *me*,
> > while you yourself bless.
> Let them stand up, but *only* to be shamed.
> > Then your servant will rejoice.
> Let my adversaries be clothed in disgrace;
> > let them be wrapped, like a cloak, in their shame.
>
> > *David, to those around him*
> I will express, with my mouth, great thanks to YHWH;
> > in the midst of the multitude I will praise him.
> For he takes a stand at the right hand of the one in need,
> > to deliver *him* from those who judge his life *falsely*.

2. BETRAYAL

a). Facing Betrayal[277]

Wickedness had pervaded the whole city, and the psalmist was facing attack from a former close friend. The psalmist had been tempted to flee the city, but instead chose to remain and put his faith in YHWH, his deliverer.

> *Notes:*
> For the *musical* director.
> With stringed instruments.
> A maskil (*possibly a contemplative poem*).
> Of David.
>
> > *David, to YHWH*
> Give ear to my prayer, God;
> > do not turn a deaf ear to my humble prayer.
> Minister to me; answer me;
> > for my complaint has made me restless,
> > and I am deeply troubled.
> *I am* threatened by those who are hostile to me;
> > *I am* oppressed by the wicked.

---

[277] Psalm 55:1-23

For they create trouble for me;
> in *their* anger they display animosity towards me.

My heart is in a whirl within me;
> the terrors of death have descended upon me.

I am overcome with fear and trembling;
> I shudder with the horror that hangs over me.

I have said, 'If only I had wings like a dove,
> I would fly *away* and live *in peace*.'

Look, I would flutter far *away*;
> I would pass the night in the wilderness.

Selah

I would speed to my place of shelter,
> *away* from the violent wind and storm.

Swallow *them* up, Lord; confuse their tongues;
> for I have seen violence and strife in the city.

Day and night the *evil-doers* patrol its walls;
> wickedness and trouble lie within it.

Destruction is in its midst;
> oppression and deceit are never absent from its marketplace.

David, to the former friend

Now if someone *else* was hostile to me,
> and found fault with me, I could take it.

If someone who hated me raised *himself* up against me,
> then I could hide from him.

But you *are* a man like me,
> *you were* my companion, the one I knew.

We enjoyed a close fellowship together,
> as we walked among the multitude in the house of God.

David, to those around him

Let death creep up on *evil-doers unawares*;
> let them descend to Sheol alive.

For evil is in the places that they live;
> *it is* in their very heart.

But I myself call to God;
> YHWH will deliver me.

> *Every* evening, morning, and noon I will complain;
> > *as* I moan he will hear my voice.
> He will deliver my soul,
> > unharmed from the battle against me;
> > *even* though many *strive* against me.
> God, who from of old remains on his throne, will hear;
> > he will answer them.
>
> > > > > > Selah
>
> They are men who never change;
> > they have no fear in God.
> He has attacked those with whom he was at peace;
> > he has violated his solemn promise.
> His mouth was smooth like butter;
> > but war was on his heart.
> His words were softer than oil;
> > yet they were drawn swords.
> Cast your burdens on YHWH, for he will sustain you;
> > he will never allow the righteous to fall.
>
> > > *David, to YHWH*
> But you, God, will hurl them down
> > into the pit of destruction.
> Bloodthirsty and treacherous men
> > will have their days cut short.
> As for me,
> > I will trust in you.

3. PERSONAL ENEMIES

a). Facing Little Support[278]

The psalmist's life was being threatened and he was receiving very little support from those around him. Logic suggested that he should flee for his life. But the psalmist preferred to stand firm and place his trust in YHWH.

> *Note:*
> For the *musical* director.
> Of David.

---

[278] Psalm 11:1-7

Establishing the Kingdom

> *David, to those around him*
> I have taken refuge in YHWH.
> > *So* how can you tell me,
> > 'Fly like a bird to the mountains.
> Look, those who are wicked are bending their bow,
> > they are placing their arrow on the string,
> > *and they will* shoot the upright of heart from the shadows.
> When the foundations *of society* are broken down,
> > what can a righteous *man* do?'?
>
> YHWH is in his holy Temple;
> > YHWH's throne is in the heavens.
> *With* his eyes he sees *everything;*
> > *indeed,* he closely examines the sons of man.
> YHWH tests the righteous;
> > but he himself hates the wicked *man*
> > and the one who loves violence.
> Let him rain down fire—coals and sulphur—on the wicked;
> > let a scorching wind be their lot.
> For YHWH, who loves righteousness, is just,
> > *and* the upright *man* will see his face.

b). The Ongoing Nature of Enemies[279]

The psalmist had been facing up to his personal enemies. Some had been dealt with, but others remained. In the meantime, he was confident that he had nothing to fear, and that his salvation and future hope remained firmly in the hands of YHWH.

> *Note:*
> Of David.
>
> *David, to those around him*
> YHWH is my light and my deliverer;
> > who *then* should I fear?
> YHWH is my security in life;
> > of whom should I be afraid?
> Evil men approached me
> > *seeking* to devour my flesh.
> My enemies, those who hate me, *came,*
> > *but* they *all* stumbled and fell.

---

[279] Psalm 27:1-14

So even if an army encamp against me
    my heart will not be fearful.
Even if armed men rise up against me,
    I will *remain* confident.

I have asked *only* one *thing* of YHWH,
    and this is what I seek:
to live in the house of YHWH
    as long as I live;
to behold the benevolence of YHWH,
    and to inquire *of him* in his Temple.
For in the day of trouble
    he will hide me in his lair.
He will conceal me in the secret place of his Tabernacle;
    he will set me high, *out of reach*, upon a rock.
Then my head will be lifted up
    above any who are hostile to me *and* surround me.
I will offer a sacrifice at his Tabernacle:
    a sacrifice of shouts of joy.
I will sing;
    I will make music to YHWH.

David, to YHWH

YHWH, listen to my voice when I call;
    show me favour and answer me.
My heart responds to *your command*, 'Seek my face.'
    I seek your face, YHWH.
Do not conceal your face from me;
    do not, in your anger, deny your servant,
    for you are my help
Do not leave me or abandon me,
    for you are the God of my salvation.
Even if my father and mother forsake me,
    gather me up, YHWH, *like a little child.*
Instruct me in your way, YHWH;
    guide me along a level path
    lest those who watch me *have reason for complaint.*
Do not give me away to the desires of my adversaries;
    for false witnesses, puffing out violence,
    have stood up against me.

> *David, to those around him*
> Despite that, I am sure
> > that I will see the goodness of YHWH
> > in the land of the living.
> *So* wait on YHWH. Be strong.
> > Be courageous in your heart, and wait on YHWH.

c). A Persecuted Man[280]

The psalmist had accumulated many enemies. Despite giving no cause, he faced many accusations, was treated scornfully, and was being persecuted because of his religious beliefs. He knew he wasn't perfect, and he believed he was being afflicted by YHWH as punishment for sin. But his enemies were compounding his suffering. As a consequence, this psalm is an appeal to God for restoration and for protection against his enemies.

Historically, this psalm may well reflect a later time—possibly during the reign of Hezekiah (when the Assyrians attacked the towns of Judah, and Jerusalem was under siege), or after the Babylonian exile. Despite that, it is not impossible that these verses are a record of events that occurred during the time of King David, which are otherwise not recorded. For this reason, this psalm is placed here with the other psalms 'of David'.

> *Notes:*
> For the *musical* director.
> To *the tune* 'Lilies'.
> Of David.
>
> *David, to YHWH*
> Deliver me God;
> > for I am up to my neck in water.
> I have sunk into a deep mire;
> > *I have* no firm footing.
> I have entered deep waters
> > and the flood is washing over me.
> I have grown tired from calling out;
> > my throat is sore.
> My eyes are failing,
> > while I wait for my God.
> Those who hate me, without cause,
> > are more numerous than the hairs on my head.
> Those who are hostile to me, without cause (and there are many),
> > wish to destroy me.

---

[280] Psalm 69:1-35

> *Indeed*, I am *forced to* pay back
> > what I haven't stolen.
>
> You God, you know my foolishness;
> > none of the things I have done wrong are hidden from you.
>
> May those who wait on you
> > not be ashamed because of my *predicament*,
> > Lord, Almighty YHWH.
> May those who seek you
> > not be humiliated because of my *plight*,
> > God of Israel.
> For I take the blame for your sake;
> > dishonour covers my face.
> I have become a stranger to my brothers;
> > an alien to my mother's sons.
> I am consumed with jealousy for your house;
> > the insults of those who find fault with you, fall on me.
> When I fasted, I wept;
> > then I was insulted.
> When I wore sackcloth for my clothing,
> > they made sport of me.
> Those who sit at the *town* gate talk about me;
> > drunkards *make up* songs.
>
> But as for me, my prayer *is* to you, YHWH;
> > *so look* favourably *on* me now, God.
> In your abundant goodness,
> > respond to me with your saving faithfulness.
> Deliver me from the mire;
> > do not let me sink *any further*.
> May I be delivered from those who hate me
> > and from the deep waters.
> Do not let the flood waters *continue to* wash over me;
> > do not let the deep *waters* swallow me up;
> > and do not let the pit close its mouth over me.
>
> Respond to me, YHWH, for your covenant loyalty is good;
> > in your abundant compassion, turn to me.
> Do not conceal your face from your servant;
> > be quick; answer me, for I am in trouble.

Draw near to me; redeem me; ransom me;
> otherwise my enemies *will question your honour*.

You know the blame, shame, and dishonour that I *have endured*;
> all who show hostility towards me are before you.
The scorn has shattered my heart;
> I am so sick.
I looked for pity, but found none;
> I didn't find anyone to console *me*.
They put poison in my food
> and gave me vinegar to drink for my thirst.

Let their table, set before them, become a snare;
> *let their* peace *offerings* be a trap.
Let their eyes grow dim, so they *are unable* to see;
> let their loins (*the source of their strength and vigour*)
> continually shake.
Pour out your righteous anger on them;
> let your burning anger seize them.
Let their dwellings become abandoned;
> let no one live in their tents.
For they pursue him, whom you yourself have afflicted;
> they recount the pain of those you have pierced.
So add *your* punishment to their injustices;
> do not let them enter into your salvation.
May they be wiped from the book of the living;
> may they not be recorded with those who are righteous.

I am afflicted and in pain;
> may your salvation, God, put me out of reach *of my enemies*.

David, to those around him

I will praise God's name in song;
> I will magnify him with *hymns of* thanksgiving.
For this will please YHWH more *than the sacrifice of* an ox,
> *or* a bull with its horns and hoofs.
Others who are afflicted will see *and* rejoice.
> May the hearts of those who seek God be restored.
For YHWH is the one who hears the needy;
> he does not despise his *people* who are in bonds.

> Let the heavens and the earth praise him—
>   the seas and everything that moves in them.
> For God will deliver Zion and rebuild the cities of Judah;
>   they will live there and take possession of it.
> The offspring of his servants will take possession of it,
>   and those who love his name will settle in it.

d). *Surrounded by Enemies*[281]

The psalmist was surrounded by enemies and felt abandoned by YHWH. Nevertheless, he was confident to call on God to uphold his covenant, come to his rescue, and deal with his enemies.

> *Notes:*
> For the *musical* director.
> A psalm.
> Of David.
>
> *David, to YHWH*
> How long, YHWH? Will you forget me forever?
>   How long will you conceal your face from me?
> How long must my soul wrestle with thoughts,
>   *feeling* sorrow in my heart all day *long*?
>   How long will my enemy be exalted over me?
>
> Look! Answer me, YHWH, my God;
>   brighten my eyes, or I will sleep the *sleep of* death.
> Then my enemy will boast, 'I defeated him.'
>   My foes will rejoice at my misfortune.
>
> But I trust in your covenant love;
>   my heart will rejoice in your salvation.
> I will sing to YHWH,
>   for he has treated me generously.

e). *A Troubled Man*[282]

The psalmist was at a very low ebb and facing death. But rather than face the final judgement by YHWH, he wanted God to restore him to full life. He also wanted God to judge his enemies.

This is a prayer intended to be spoken in the evening, expecting God's response at dawn.

---

[281] Psalm 13:1-6
[282] Psalm 143:1-12

Establishing the Kingdom

Notes:
A psalm.
Of David.

David, to YHWH

Hear my prayer, YHWH;
    listen to my humble petition.
Answer me in your firmness of purpose
    and in your righteousness.
But do not put your servant on trial,
    for no one alive can be justified in your presence.

The enemy pursues me;
    he squeezes my life *from me* on the ground.
He has made me sit in the dark,
    like those long dead.
My spirit within me is weak;
    my heart inside me is desolate.

I recall former days;
    I think about all your deeds;
    I reflect on the works of your hands.
I stretch out my hands to you;
    like *a throat* in a parched land, *so* my soul *thirsts* for you.
                                       Selah

Be quick. Answer me, YHWH;
    my spirit is failing.
Do not hide your face from me,
    or I will resemble those who go down to the pit.
Tomorrow morning, let me hear of your goodness;
    for I put my trust in you.
Let me know the direction I should be going;
    for I lift my soul to you.
Deliver me from my enemies YHWH;
    my protection is in your *hands*.
Teach me to do your will,
    for you are my God.
Guide me in *an* upright *manner*,
    with your good Spirit.

> Restore my life for the sake of your name;
>> in your righteousness, rescue me from *my* distress.
> Silence my enemies, with your loving kindness;
>> destroy all my enemies,
>>> for I am your servant.

f). Facing Mental Anguish[283]

The psalmist was in deep mental anguish. The causes were various, but they included being hunted, being alienated, and being subjected to false accusations. As a consequence, his life was fading away.

The depth of his anguish, however, is reflected in his repeated shifting backwards and forwards—from describing his state of mind, to that of his assurance in YHWH.

> *Notes:*
> For the *musical* director.
> A psalm.
> Of David.
>
> *David, to YHWH*
> I have sought refuge in you, YHWH,
>> *so* let me never be ashamed *of you*;
>> in your righteousness, deliver me.
> Lean down and listen to me;
>> in haste, come to my rescue.
> Be a rock of refuge for me;
>> *be* a strong fortress to save me.
>
> You are my rock and my fortress;
>> you will lead and guide me for your name's sake.
> You are my security;
>> you will free me from the concealed net they set.
> You have paid a ransom for me, YHWH, God of truth;
>> I entrust my spirit into your hands.
>
> I hate those who follow false gods;
>> but as for me, I trust in YHWH.
> I will rejoice and be glad in your faithful love,
>> for you have seen my affliction,
>> you are aware of my troubled soul.

---

[283] Psalm 31:1-24

You have not given me into the hand of the enemy;
> *Instead*, you have placed my feet in a *safe* roomy place.

Show favour to me, YHWH, for I am in distress;
> my eye is growing dim with grief,
> *and* my soul and my body *are fading too*.

For my life has become exhausted with anguish;
> *and* my years with groaning.

My strength is failing because of my guilt;
> my bones are growing weak.

I have become an object of scorn, particularly to my neighbours,
> because of all who are hostile to me.

I am an object of dread to those who know me;
> those who see me on the street flee from me.

I have been forgotten as *though I was* dead;
> *I have been erased* from the memories *of family and friends*.
> I have become *as useless as* a broken pot.

For I hear many *people* whispering;
> *there is* terror all around.

Together they conspire against me;
> they plot to take my life.

But I, I trust in you, YHWH;
> I say, 'You are my God.'

Every event of my life is in your hands.
> *So* deliver me from the hands of those who are hostile to me,
> and from those who pursue me.

Let your face shine upon your servant;
> in your faithful love, deliver me.

Do not let me be shamed, YHWH,
> for I have called to you *for help*.

Instead, let the wicked be shamed *for the sins they commit*;
> let them be silenced in *the depths of* Sheol.

Let their deceiving lips be bound,
> *because* they speak arrogantly against the righteous,
> with pride and contempt.

How many *more* good things have you in store
> for those who fear you?

You have done *so many things* for those who take refuge in you,
> in *plain* sight of the sons of men.

> You have *even* hidden them in a secret hiding place, in your presence,
>> *away* from the schemes of man.
> You have kept them hidden in your dwelling,
>> *away* from the accusations of tongues.
>
> *David, to those around him*
> Kneel down to YHWH,
>> for he has surpassed his loyal love—
>> *he helped* me in a city under siege.
>
> *David, to YHWH*
> I myself said when I was extremely fearful,
>> 'I have been cut off from your sight.'
> Yet when I cry out to you for help,
>> you hear the sound of my humble prayer.
>
> *David, to those around him*
> Love YHWH, all *you* who are pious.
>> YHWH is the one who watches over the faithful;
>> but he repays in full those who act with pride.
> Be strong and take courage,
>> all those who wait on YHWH.

g). A Prayer at a Time of Persecution[284]

Being persecuted and facing false accusations are common themes in the psalms. As a consequence, this psalm, which is almost identical to the last verses of Psalm 40, reflects a simple prayer to YHWH for help.

The psalm may also have been designed, or come to be adopted, for the sacrificial system—hence the title 'For the Memorial Offering'.

> *Notes:*
> For the *musical* director.
> Of David.
> For the Memorial *Offering*.
>
> *David, to YHWH*
> God, *be quick to* deliver me;
>> hasten to my help, YHWH.
> May those who seek my life
>> be shamed and mortified.

---

[284] Psalm 70:1-5

> May those who delight in my distress
>   be turned back and humbled.
> May those who *taunt me*, saying, 'Aha! Aha!'
>   be turned back because of their shame.
> *But* may all those who seek you
>   rejoice and be glad in you.
> May those who love your salvation continually say,
>   'YHWH is great.'
>
> As for me, I am afflicted and in *great* need;
>   hasten to me, God.
> You are my help and my deliverer, YHWH;
>   do not delay.

h). Malicious Enemies[285]

The psalmist was on his sickbed—the consequences of a sinful act—and his enemies were taking full advantage of his weakened state.

> *Notes:*
> To the *musical* director.
> A psalm of David.
>
> *David, to those around him*
> Blessed is the one who considers the weak;
>   YHWH will deliver him in troubled times.
> YHWH will watch over him, and preserve his life;
>   he will bless him in the land;
>   he will not give him over to the desires of his enemies.
> YHWH will provide him aid on his sickbed;
>
> *David, to YHWH*
> you will completely restore his bed from his illness.
>
> *In my illness*, I have said, 'YHWH, show me your favour;
>   heal me, for I have sinned against you.'
> My enemies speak maliciously of me,
>   'When will he die, and his name perish?'
> When one comes to see *me*,
>   he speaks falsely in his heart.

---

[285] Psalm 41:1-12

> He gathers trouble for his own use;
>> he *then* goes outside and speaks *mischief*.
> All those who hate me whisper together against me;
>> they consider the worst for me,
> 'A deadly disease has been poured out upon him;
>> he will not get up again from where he lies.'
> Even my best friend whom I trusted—
>> the one who ate my bread—has lifted *his* heel against me.
>
> But you, YHWH, show me favour;
>> raise me up, so that I can repay them.
> Then, because my enemy will no *longer* rejoice over me,
>> I will know that you are pleased with me.
> As for me, you have upheld me in my integrity;
>> you have stood me forever in your presence.

i). Enemies, Suffering, and Unanswered Prayer[286]

The psalmist was surrounded by enemies, was facing intense suffering, was close to death, and was feeling abandoned by YHWH. Despite that, this psalm recalls times when God had come to his rescue and the rescue of his people.

> *Notes:*
> For the *musical* director.
> To *the tune* 'The Hind of the Dawn'.
> A psalm.
> Of David.
>
> *David, to YHWH*
> My God, my God, why have you abandoned me?
>> *Why are you so* far from rescuing me?
>> I roar out my words *like a lion, but you do not hear.*
> My God, I call out during the day, but you give no answer;
>> *I cry out* at night, but I find no peace.
>
> But you are holy;
>> you are enthroned in the praises of Israel.
> Our fathers trusted in you;
>> they trusted and you delivered them.
> They cried out to you and they were saved;
>> they trusted in you and were not put to shame.

---

[286] Psalm 22:1-31

Establishing the Kingdom

But I am a worm; I am not a man.
> *I am* the scorn of men, despised by the people.

All those who see me deride me;
> they make mouths at me; they shake *their* heads.

They say, 'Let him trust in YHWH to rescue him.
> He delights in him, so let him deliver him.'

But you pushed me out of the womb,
> *and* you taught me to trust *in you* at my mother's breasts.

I was thrown upon you from birth;
> *and since* my mother's womb, you have been my God.

Do not remain distant from me,
> for trouble is near *and* there is no one to help.

Many bulls (*powerful and cruel*) surround me;
> *the* mighty ones of Bashan (*prime cattle land*) encircle me.

Like a lion roaring and tearing *its prey*,
> they open wide their mouths against me.

Like water, I am drained *of energy*;
> all my bones are dislocated.

My heart is like wax;
> it is melting away within me.

My strength has withered like an old dry pot;
> my tongue clings to my mouth.
> You have set me down on the dust of death.

Indeed, I am surrounded by *scavenging* dogs;
> a band of evil-doers have hemmed me in.
> They have pierced my hands and my feet.

I can count all my bones.
> *Meanwhile*, they stare at me *and* mock.

They share my garments among themselves;
> they draw lots for my clothing.

So you, YHWH, do not be *so* far away;
> My help, come quickly to my assistance.

Snatch my life from the sword;
> my one and only *life* from the hand of the dog.

Deliver me from the lion's mouth;
> and from the horns of the wild oxen.

Establishing the Kingdom

> You have answered me.
> I will make your name known to my brothers;
> > I will praise you in the midst of the congregation.
>
> *David, to those around him*
> Those who fear YHWH, praise him;
> > all Jacob's offspring, honour him;
> > > every descendant of Israel, stand in awe before him.
> For he has not *treated* the suffering of the afflicted
> > with *either* contempt or abhorrence.
> He has not hidden his face from him,
> > but has heard his cry for help.
>
> *David, to YHWH*
> You are the source of my praise in the great assembly;
> > I will fulfil my vows in the presence of those who fear you.
>
> *David, to those around him*
> The afflicted will eat and be satisfied;
> > those who seek YHWH will praise him.
> > May your hearts live for ever.
> The entire world will remember and turn back to YHWH;
> > the clans of every nation will worship before him.
> For sovereign authority belongs to YHWH;
> > he rules over the nations.
> All who have grown fat off the land will feast and worship;
> > all who go down to the dust will bow down before him.
> *Even* he who cannot keep himself alive will be served by *his* offspring;
> > the *next* generation will be told about the Lord.
> *So* a people yet to be born will come;
> > they will proclaim his righteousness, for what he has done.

4. OTHER ENEMIES

a). Attack on the Innocent[287]

The psalmist was not alone in facing attack from enemies. But he had been plotted against and threatened—and the images of swords, arrows, and traps indicate the kind of opposition that he faced. Despite that, he was sure that YHWH would take those weapons and turn them against their enemies.

---

[287] Psalm 64:1-10

> *Notes:*
> For the *musical* director.
> A psalm.
> Of David.
>
> *David, to YHWH*
> Hear my voice, God, as I complain *about my enemies*;
> > guard my life from the menace of those who are hostile.
> Conceal me from the designs of those who are evil;
> > from the multitude of trouble-makers.
>
> They sharpen their tongue like a sword;
> > they aim their bitter word *like* an arrow.
> They shoot at the innocent from their hiding places;
> > they shoot without warning and without fear.
> They harden themselves with *their* evil words;
> > they talk of setting hidden traps;
> > *indeed*, they say, 'Who will see them?'
> They plot unrighteous *acts*;
> > *they convince themselves*, 'Our plan is well-devised.'
>
> *David, to those around him*
> The heart and mind of a man is deep;
> > but God will shoot them *with an* arrow;
> > they will be struck down without warning.
> They will be made to stumble;
> > their *own* tongues will be against them.
> > All who see them will shake their heads.
> Then every man will fear *God*;
> > they will speak out about God's deeds;
> > they will meditate on what he has done.
>
> Let the righteous *man* rejoice in YHWH;
> > let him seek refuge in him;
> > let all the upright of heart boast *of him*.

b). Foreign Enemies, and Locally Grown Oppressors[288]
The psalmist had been facing oppression by his enemies and was thankful that YHWH had come to his aid. He knew others would rise up against him, but he was confident that

---

[288] Psalms 9:1-20; 10:1-18

Establishing the Kingdom

God would hear him and help him again. Indeed, God would come to the rescue of other righteous people too.

This is a Hebrew alphabetical acrostic psalm, which traditionally has been divided into two distinct psalms: Part One, because it appears to be dealing with a specific military victory; and Part Two, because it seems to be addressing a more local problem.

The psalm has suffered through transmission over time or at the hands of an editor. In the original psalm, every other verse would have begun with a different letter of the twenty-two letter alphabet. However, the letter ד *(dalet) is missing from Part One, and the letters* מ *(mem),* נ *(nun),* ס *(samek), and* ע *('ayin) are absent from Part Two.*

PART ONE

Notes:
For the *musical* director,
To *the tune* 'The Death of a Son'.
A psalm.
Of David.

David, to YHWH

א   I will give thanks *to you*, YHWH, with all my heart.
      I will declare all your wonderful deeds.
   I will rejoice. I will rejoice exceedingly in you.
      I will make music *in praise* of your name, Most High.

ב   When those who were hostile to me retreated *in defeat*,
      they stumbled and perished in your presence.
   For you maintained my just cause;
      you sat on *your* throne, judging righteously.

ג   You rebuked the nations; you slayed the wicked;
      you blotted out their name for ever and ever.
   The enemy was overtaken, *they faced* everlasting ruin,
      you uprooted *their* towns, *and* memory of them perished.

David, to those around him

ה   But YHWH sits *on his throne* forever.
      he has set up his throne for judgement.
   He alone will judge the world in righteousness;
      he will judge the people with equity.

ו   So let YHWH be a shelter for the oppressed;
      a fortress in troubled times.

Establishing the Kingdom

David, to YHWH

Those who know your name will put their trust in you;
    for you, YHWH, do not abandon those who seek you.

David, to those around him

ז   Sing praises to YHWH, who sits *enthroned* in Zion.
    declare his deeds among the peoples.
For the avenger of blood is mindful of those *who shed blood*;
    he does not neglect the cry of the afflicted.

David, to YHWH

ח   Have mercy on me, YHWH.
    See *how* I am afflicted by those who hate me.
    Lift me up from the gates of death.
Then I will *sing* all your songs of praise
    in the gates of the daughter of Zion;
    I will rejoice in your salvation.

David, to those around him

ט   The nations have sunk into the pit *of destruction* they made;
    their feet are entangled in their *own* concealed net.
YHWH has made himself known in his execution of justice;
    the wicked are trapped by the work of their *own* hands.

Higgagion *(perhaps an instruction for some meditative music).*
                                                                 Selah

י   The wicked will go down to Sheol,
    including every nation that forgets God.
כ   For the needy will not always be forgotten;
    the hope of the afflicted will not always perish.

David, to YHWH

Rise up, YHWH.
    Stop a *mortal* man from *claiming* to be strong;
    let the nations be judged in your presence.
Put fear into them, YHWH;
    let the nations know they are *but* men.
                                                                     Selah

PART TWO

David, to YHWH

ל YHWH, why do you stand so far away?
    Why do you hide in troubled times?

In his arrogance the wicked *man* pursues the afflicted;
    let the wicked be trapped by the schemes they have devised.
For the wicked *man* boasts of the desires of his heart;
    he blesses others who are greedy,
        and he treats you, YHWH, with contempt.
With his superior attitude, the wicked *man* does not seek *God*;
    none of his thoughts are of God.
His ways prosper all the time.
        Your judgements, from above, are beyond him.
        He treats those who are hostile to him with contempt.
He says to himself, 'Nothing can trip me up.'
    He swears, 'I will always be happy;
    I will never face adversity.'

פ His mouth is full of deceit and harm;
    wickedness and trouble are under his tongue.
He sits in ambush near the villages;
    he slays the innocent in *his* secret places.

צ   His eyes eagerly watch for an unfortunate *victim*.
He lies in wait in his hiding place, like a lion in a thicket;
    He lies in wait to seize the afflicted.
    He catches the afflicted *and* drags him off in his net.
In this way, his victims are crushed;
    the hapless *victim* falls under his might.
The victim says to himself, 'God has forgotten.
    He has covered his face. He will never witness it.'

ק Stand up, YHWH. Raise up your hand, God.
    Do not forget the afflicted.
For why does the wicked *man* treat God with contempt?
    Why does he say to himself,
    'You will not call me to account'?

ר But you have seen; you *have noted* the trouble and distress;
    and you consider what actions your hand will take.
The unfortunate *victim* commits *his cause* to you—
    the one who helps the fatherless.

> ש   Shatter the arm of the wicked;
>   call the evil man to account for his wickedness,
>   until no *evil* remains.
>
> *David, to those around him*
> YHWH is king forever and ever;
>   nations have perished from his land.
>
> *David, to YHWH*
> ת   YHWH, you hear the desires of the afflicted;
>   you incline your ear *and* strengthen their hearts.
>   Bring justice to the fatherless and the oppressed,
>   so that a mortal man may no longer terrify *others*.

c). *Deliverance from Foreign Enemies*[289]

Although his local enemies were being subdued by YHWH, the psalmist still faced attack from his foreign enemies. But then his foreign enemies were liars and even their most solemn vows could not be trusted.

> *Notes:*
> Of David.
>
> *David, to those around him*
> Blessed be YHWH, my rock;
>   the one who instructs my hands for war
>   *and* my fingers for battle.
> He is my steadfast love and my fortress;
>   *he is* my stronghold and the one who delivers me.
> *He is* my shield and I take refuge in him;
>   he is the one who subdues my *rebellious* people under me.
>
> *David, to YHWH*
> YHWH, what is man that you take notice of him?
>   *What is the* son of man that you consider him?
> Man is *as transitory* as a breath,
>   his days pass like shadows.
>
> Extend your heavens *to earth*, YHWH. Come down.
>   Touch the mountains so they smoke.

---

[289] Psalm 144:1-15

> Send a flash of lightning. Scatter *your enemies*.
>> Release your arrows, and throw them into confusion.
> Stretch out your hand from on high
>> and rescue me.
> Deliver me from deep waters
>> and from the hands of foreign men.
> *When swearing oaths*, they utter lies with their mouths;
>> they *raise* their right hands *to God* deceitfully.
>
> God, I will sing a new song to you;
>> I will play music to you on a ten-*stringed* harp.
> *You are* the one who gives victory to kings;
>> *you are* the one who delivered David, your servant.
>
> Deliver me from the wicked sword;
>> rescue me from the hands of foreign men.
> *Because* their mouths speak lies
>> and they *use their* right hands deceitfully.
>
>> *David, to those around him*
> May our sons *grow up* like plants,
>> *that have been* well-nurtured in their youth.
> *May* our daughters *become* like carved pillars,
>> *fitting* to adorn a palace.
> *May* our barns be filled
>> with every kind of produce.
> *May* our sheep increase by thousands;
>> *may* there be tens of thousands in our fields.
>> *May* our oxen draw heavy loads.
> *Let there be* no breach *in the walls of the city*,
>> no going away, and no cries of distress in our streets.
>
> Blessed are those people of whom this is true;
>> blessed are the people whose God is YHWH.

d). *YHWH's Promise of Dominion over Enemies*[290]

This psalm was used to address to the king. It either celebrated a military victory, or was used in remembrance of YHWH's promise to provide dominion over his enemies.

It was intended to be sung to the king—the mighty sceptre of the nation.

---

[290] Psalm 110:1-7

> *Notes:*
> Of David.
> A psalm.
>
> *A leader, to David*
> The words of YHWH to my lord, *the king*,
>   'Remain at my right hand,
> until I have made your enemies
>   a footstall for your feet.'
> YHWH will stretch out your mighty sceptre from Zion,
>   *telling you*, 'Rule in the midst of your enemies.
> Your people will offer themselves freely
>   on your day of battle.
> In holy splendour, from the womb of dawn,
>   your youth *will be* your dew.'
>
> YHWH has sworn *a solemn vow*;
>   he would not change his mind,
> 'You are a priest *living* forever,
>   like Melchizedek.'
>
> The Lord is at your right hand.
>   On the day of his wrath he will shatter kings.
> He will judge the nations;
>   he will fill them *with their* corpses;
>   he will shatter the rulers of all the earth.
> *But my lord the king* will drink from the brook beside the road.
>   Therefore *YHWH* will lift up *your* head.

5. WAR

a). *At a Time of War*[291]

This psalm shares much of its content with two other psalms. The first (Psalm 57:7-11) has David hiding in a cave from Saul; the second (Psalm 60:5-12) has David battling hostile neighbours.

As a distinctly separate psalm, however, it has a very different feel. The two parts linked together look forward to a time when YHWH's lordship would be established among the nations. In particular, it envisaged a time when the surrounding nations of Moab, Edom, and Philistia would be subdued.

---

[291] Psalm 108:1-13

Establishing the Kingdom

Notes:
A song.
A psalm.
Of David.

David, to YHWH
God, my heart is unwavering.
　With all my soul I will sing, I will make music.

David, to the harp and lyre
Rouse yourself, harp and lyre;
　I will wake up the dawn.

David, to YHWH
In the midst of the people, I will thank you, YHWH;
　I will sing of you before the nations.
For your goodness is great, it is higher than the heavens;
　your faithfulness *reaches* the clouds.
God, you are elevated above the heavens,
　yet your glory is over all the earth.

So save with your right hand. Answer me,
　so that those you love can be delivered.

David, to those around him
God spoke in his holiness, 'I will be triumphant.
　I will divide up Shechem (*west of the Jordan River*);
　I will measure out the valley of Succoth (*in the east*).
Gilead (*in the east*) is mine; so too is Manasseh (*in both east and west*);
　Ephraim (*in the centre*) is the *safety* helmet for my head;
　Judah (*in the south*) is my *kingly* sceptre.
Moab is my *lowly* wash basin;
　I will fling my sandal in Edom;
　I will shout in triumph over Philistia.'

David, to YHWH
So who will take me to the fortified city?
　Who will lead me to Edom?
Have you not rejected us, God?
　God, you do not go out with our armies.

Establishing the Kingdom

> Give us assistance against our adversaries,
>   for a man's help is worthless.
>
> *David, to those around him*
> We will *only* be strong with God's *help*;
>   he will trample over our foes.

b). A Prayer Before Going to War

The king had prayed, made the appropriate sacrifices, prepared his war plans, and arranged his men ready for battle. But before the fight could begin, the community needed to pray for their king and for success.

> *Notes:*
> For the *musical* director.
> A psalm.
> Of David.
>
> *A leader, to David*
> May YHWH answer you on the day of battle;
>   may the name of the God of Jacob be on high.
> May he send you help from the sanctuary;
>   may he sustain you from Zion.
> May he remember all your *sacrificial* offerings;
>   may he have grown fat on your Burnt Offerings.
>   Selah
>
> May he grant you your heart's *desire*;
>   may he fulfil all your plans.
>
> Our cries will ring out over your victory;
>   we will parade our standards in the name of our God.
>   May YHWH fulfil all your humble requests.
>
> Now I know that YHWH will deliver his anointed;
>   he will respond to him from his holy heavens,
>   with a mighty victory by his right hand.
> Some *sit* in a chariot, others *ride on* horses,
>   but we will remember the name of YHWH our God.
> *Our enemies* will be bowed down; they will fall *to the ground*.
>   But we will rise up and stand upright.

---

[292] Psalm 20:1-9

> YHWH has given victory *to* the king;
>   may he answer us on the day we call.

c). Taking the Ark into Battle[293]

It was common practice to take the Ark of God into battle. As a consequence, this psalm begins with the formula, 'Let God arise'. Then, as the march proceeded, the psalm also served as a reminder of God's might. God had helped them in the past, and he would help them again. Of all the places God had chosen to live, it was among his people on Mount Zion. They could therefore be assured of victory, and that others would come to them to pay tribute.

> *Notes:*
> For the *musical* director.
> Of David. A psalm.
>
> *David, to those around him*
> Let God arise, let his enemies be scattered;
>   let those who hate him flee before him.
> As smoke is driven away,
>   drive *them* away.
> As wax melts before a fire,
>   so let the wicked perish from the presence of God.
> But let the righteous rejoice,
>   let them be glad before God;
>   let them rejoice with joy.
>
> Sing to God; make music to his name;
>   lift up *your voices* to the one who rides through the deserts.
> YHWH is his name;
>   rejoice before him.
> *He is* father to the fatherless, a protector of widows;
>   God is in his holy dwelling.
> God provides a house for the lonely,
>   and leads captives into prosperity;
>   while those who rebel live in a sun-scorched land.
>
> *David, to YHWH*
> God, you led your people out;
>   you marched through the wilderness.
>   Selah

---

[293] Psalm 68:1-35

When *you did*, the earth shook, and the heavens poured rain
> before the God of Sinai;
> before God, the God of Israel.
God, you sprinkled your inheritance with abundant rain;
> you restored those who were weary.
Your creatures settled in *the land*,
> *and* out of your goodness, God, you provided for the poor.

> *David, to those around him*

The Lord gave the word,
> *and* those who proclaimed it were a great company.
The kings of armies fled for their lives,
> while those who remained divided the plunder.
When you laid down by the camp fires, *you were like* a dove,
> but with its wings covered in silver
> and its feathers with greenish gold.
When the Almighty scattered the kings there,
> it snowed on *Mount* Zalmon.

The mountains of Bashan, which have many peaks,
> were the mountains of God,
> But why look in envy, *many* peaked mountains?
God has taken pleasure to live *on Mount Zion;*
> Indeed, YHWH will live *there* forever.
The chariots of God are twice ten thousand,
> thousands *of thousands*;
> the Lord *came* in them *from* Sinai, into *his* holy *place*.

> *David, to YHWH*

You have ascended to the heights,
> you have taken *our* captives, *our enemies*, captive.
You have received gifts from men,
> even from the rebellious,
> *so that you*, YHWH God, may dwell *there*.

> *David, to those around him*

Blessed be YHWH.
> Day by day he carries our load;
> he is the God of our salvation.

Selah

Our God is a God of salvation;
>through the Lord YHWH comes escape from death.
Surely God will strike the heads of those who are hostile to him;
>the hairy crown of the one who continues his offense.
The Lord says, 'I will bring *them* back from Bashan;
>I will bring *them* back from the depths of the sea.
So that your foot can strike the enemies *with* blood,
>*and* your dogs' tongues *can have* their share.'

David, to YHWH

They have seen your processions, God;
>the processions of my God and king to the holy *place*.
The singers were in front,
>with those playing stringed instruments behind;
>between them were maidens sounding tambourines.

David, to those around him

Bless God in the assembly;
>*Bless* YHWH, fountain of *our patriarch*, Israel.
There is insignificant Benjamin, leading them;
>the leaders of Judah are in the crowd.
>*So too are the* leaders of Zebulun and Naphtali.
Your God has commanded *that* you *be* strong.

David, to YHWH

>Show *your* strength, God, as you *have* done for us *before*.

Because your Temple is in Jerusalem,
>kings will bear you gifts.
So rebuke the beast of the reeds;
>the herd of bulls among the calves of the peoples.
Trample on those *who lust* for pieces of silver;
>scatter the peoples who delight in wars.

David, to those around him

Let bronze be brought from Egypt;
>let Cush stretch out its hands to God.

David, to the nations

Sing to God, kingdoms of the earth;
>make music to the Lord.

>>>>>>>>>>Selah

> *David, to those around him*
> The one who rides in the heavens—the heavens of old—
> > behold, he speaks with his voice, a mighty sound.
> Ascribe strength to God,
> > his majesty over Israel,
> > and his might in the clouds.
>
> *David, to YHWH*
> You, God, are to be feared
> > in your holy place.
>
> *David, to those around him*
> He is the God of Israel,
> > he gives strength and might to the people.
>
> Blessed be God.

d). *A Prayer at the Conclusion of a Battle*[294]

When they had won a battle, the king and people expressed their thanks to YHWH, their true deliverer. But they were also aware of other battles to be fought. Indeed, they knew there would be other plots against them. Despite that, they were confident that with the help of God and their king, they would prevail.

> *Notes:*
> For the *musical* director.
> A psalm.
> Of David.
>
> *A leader, to YHWH*
> YHWH, the king delights in your might;
> > he rejoices greatly in your deliverance.
> You have granted him his heart's desire;
> > you have not denied the request of his lips.
> > > > > Selah
>
> Indeed, you came to him; you blessed *him* richly;
> > you placed a crown of fine gold on his head.
> He asked you *to preserve his* life, and you gave it to him;
> > a long life, *living* on in his descendants for ever and ever.

---

[294] Psalm 21:1-13

He *has received* great glory through your deliverance;
> you have favoured him with majesty and honour.

You have surely laid blessings upon him in perpetuity;
> you have made him rejoice
> with *the* joy *of being* in your presence.

For the king trusts in YHWH,
> and in the covenant love of the Most High,
> he will not be moved.

A leader, to David

Your hand will find all who are hostile to you;
> your right hand will find those who hate you.

When you face them,
> you will make them burn, like *in a portable* furnace.

In his anger, YHWH will swallow them up;
> fire will consume them.

You will eliminate the fruit *of* their *loins* from the earth;
> their seed from *among* the sons of men.

For they plot evil against you; they contrive schemes,
> *but* will not succeed.

For when you *set your arrows* on their strings,
> and aim *them* at their faces,
> you will see *their* backs *in retreat*.

A leader, to YHWH

Be exalted, YHWH, in your power;
> we will sing and make music to your might.

D2. SOLOMON'S SONG BOOK

1. INTRODUCTION

Like the psalms 'of David', the psalms 'of Solomon' were not necessarily written by Solomon. Indeed, the 'enthronement' psalm is more likely to have been written for Solomon, rather than by him.
Of all the psalms only two are noted as being 'of Solomon'; both relate to the life of faith.

2. THE LIFE OF FAITH

a). Putting YHWH First[295]

This psalm depicts two basic themes: the futility of life without God and the blessings that come from God through a life of faith.

The term 'house' in the first line has been understood in a variety of ways. If the psalm was later adopted as a song of accents, it would originally have meant the family unit. But as a song of ascents, it would be considered to be a reference to Solomon's Temple.

Notes:
A song of ascents (*possibly a devotion for those on a pilgrimage to Jerusalem*).
Of Solomon.

Solomon, to those around him
If YHWH does not build a house,
    those who build it labour in vain.
If YHWH does not keep watch over a city,
    the watchman stays awake in vain.
It is pointless to be an early riser, or to stay up late,
    or to eat the bread of painful toil,
    for he gives sleep to the one he loves.

Look, sons are an inheritance from YHWH;
    the fruit of the womb, *a man's* wages.
Like arrows in the hands of a warrior
    are the sons of *one's* youth.
Blessed is the man whose quiver is full of them;
    they will not be shamed with enemies by the gate.

---

[295] Psalm 127:1-5

b) A Prayer for the King[296]

This psalm, addressed to God, is a prayer for the king of Israel. The prayer is that the king would be faithful to God, that he would uphold God's laws, and that he would mete out God's justice.

The psalm would have been suitable for use at the enthronement of a king, or at the annual celebration of his kingship.

> *Notes:*
> Of Solomon.
>
> *Leader, to God*
> Give your ordinances to the king, God;
> > your righteousness to the son of a king.
> May he judge your people with righteousness;
> > your poor with justice.
> May the mountains bring prosperity to the people;
> > *may* the hills *bring* righteousness.
> May he defend the afflicted of the people,
> > give deliverance to the sons of the needy,
> > and crush those who oppress.
> *Then* the people will fear you while the sun *endures*
> > and in the presence of the moon,
> > generation after generation.
>
> May *his rule be* like rain coming down on mown grass,
> > like showers dropping *water* on the earth.
> *Then*, in his days, the righteous will flourish,
> > and peace will abound until the moon is no more.
>
> May he have dominion from sea to sea;
> > from the River *Euphrates* to the ends of the earth.
> May desert dwellers bow before him;
> > may his enemies lick the dust.
> May the kings of Tarshish and the coast return with tribute;
> > and the kings of Sheba and Seba approach with gifts.
> Let all the kings bow down to him;
> > let all the nations serve him.

---

[296] Psalm 72:1-19

For he will deliver a needy *man* crying out *for help*,
    and an afflicted *man*, who has no one to help him.
He will look upon the weak and the needy with compassion;
    he will save the lives of the needy.
He will rescue their lives from oppression and violence;
    for their blood is precious in his eyes.

Long may he live.
    May gold of Sheba be given to him.
May people always pray for him;
    may they bless him all day.
Let there be an abundance of grain throughout the land;
    let it sway on the hill tops.
Let its fruit flourish like the *trees of* Lebanon
    and thrive like the grass of the land.
May his name endure forever;
    may his fame increase before the sun.
May the people be blessed through him;
    may all the nations call him blessed.

Blessed be YHWH God, the God of Israel,
    he alone does extraordinary deeds.
Let his glorious name be blessed forever;
    may his glory fill all the earth. Amen. Amen.

D3. OTHER SONGS

1. INTRODUCTION

Many other psalms were written in addition to the psalms of David and Solomon. Where appropriate, they are included in parts 1, 3 and 4 of A Twenty-First-Century Bible. Only the psalms which appear to relate to the historical time-frame of this volume are recorded here.

2. SONGS OF PRAISE

a). Praise to the Creator and Lord[297]

This psalm calls the faithful to praise YHWH, and to wait on him, knowing that he is faithful and his word can be trusted.

The psalm, which may have been written after a military victory, describes God in terms of his faithfulness, his creation, his authority, his vigilance, and his readiness to save his people.

Psalmist, to those around him
Cry out *joyfully* to YHWH, righteous ones;
    it is fitting for the upright to praise.
Give thanks to YHWH with the lyre;
    make music to him on the ten-*stringed* harp.
Sing to him a new song;
    play *your* instruments well, with a shout *of joy*.

For the word of YHWH is upright,
    and all his deeds *are done* in faithfulness.
He loves righteousness and justice;
    the earth is full of the goodness of YHWH.

The heavens were made by the word of YHWH;
    all their host by the breath of his mouth.
He gathered the waters of the sea into a heap;
    he put the deeps into storehouses *to use as he sees fit*.
Let the whole earth fear YHWH;
    let all who live in the world hold him in awe.

---

[297] Psalm 33:1-22

> For he spoke and it came to pass;
> > he commanded and it took its stand.
>
> YHWH frustrates the plans of the nations;
> > he hinders the schemes of the peoples.
> The counsel of YHWH stands forever;
> > the thoughts of his heart from generation to generation.
> Blessed is the nation whose God is YHWH;
> > the people he chose for his inheritance.
>
> YHWH looks down from the heavens;
> > he sees all the sons of men.
> From his throne he gazes
> > on all who live on the earth.
> He who formed all their hearts
> > considers all their deeds.
>
> No king is saved by a mighty army;
> > no warrior is delivered by great power.
> *When it comes to* deliverance, the horse is a disappointment;
> > it cannot save, *even* with all its great strength
> *But* look, the eye of YHWH is on those who fear him;
> > on those who wait on his unfailing love.
> *He will* deliver their soul from death;
> > and sustain them in famine.
>
> Our soul waits for YHWH;
> > he is our help and our shield.
> For our hearts rejoice in him;
> > in his holy name we trust.
>
> > > *Psalmist, to YHWH*
> May your unfailing love, be upon us, YHWH,
> > even as we wait on you.

b). God the Creator and Sustainer[298]

This is a psalm of praise to the God of creation. It sings the praise of YHWH, the creator and sustainer of the heavens and the waters, and for the order and diversity of creation.

The psalmist is in awe of his God, and the least he can do is to call on his own being, his own soul, to praise YHWH.

---

[298] Psalm 104:1-35

Establishing the Kingdom

Psalmist, to himself
Praise YHWH, my soul.

Psalmist, to YHWH
YHWH my God, you are exceedingly great.
You are clothed with majesty and honour;
   you wrap yourself in light, like a garment.
You stretched out the heavens, like a curtain;
   you laid the beams of your upper chambers on the waters.
You made the dark clouds your chariot;
   you come on the wings of the wind.
You made the winds your messengers;
   flames of fire your ministers.

You set the earth on its foundations,
   so that it can never be shaken.
You covered it with the deep, as a garment;
   the waters took their stand above the mountains.
At the sound of your thunder the waters shook;
   at your rebuke they fled.
The mountains rose *and* the valleys sank,
   to the place you had appointed for them.
You set a boundary *for the waters* they cannot cross;
   they will never return to cover the earth.

You made springs to pour *water* into the valleys;
   to flow between the mountains.
They give water to all the beasts of the field;
   they quench the thirst of wild donkeys.
The birds of the air nest nearby;
   they sing among the foliage.
You water the mountains from your upper chambers;
   the earth is satisfied with the fruit of your works.
You make the grass spring up for the cattle,
   and vegetation for a man to till—
to bring forth food from the earth;
   to make wine which gladdens his heart;
to produce oil to make *his* face shine;
   and to make bread which sustains his heart.
The trees of YHWH are satisfied;
   the cedars of Lebanon which you planted.

It is the trees where birds make *their* nests;
> the pine trees *where the* stork *makes* its home.
The high mountains *are the homes of* the mountain goats;
> crags *are the* refuge for badgers.

You made the moon *to mark* the seasons;
> the sun knows when to set.
You set darkness *in its place*, and it became night;
> in it, all the beasts of the forest move around.
Young lions roar for prey;
> to seek their food from God.
When the sun rises they gather together;
> they lie stretched out in their dens.
Then a man goes out to his work
> and he labours until evening.

How various are your works, YHWH.
> You have made all of them with wisdom;
> the earth is full of your possessions.
There is the great and wide sea,
> in which things that move *live* without number;
> living things, both great and small.
Ships move about on it;
> *so does* the leviathan which you formed to laugh in it.

They all wait on you
> to give *them* their food at the appropriate time.
You give to them *and* they gather;
> you open your hand *and* they are satisfied *with* good *things*.
You hide your face *and* they are disturbed;
> you take away their breath and they perish,
> they return to their dust.
You send your spirit *and* they are created;
> you renew the face of the ground.

Psalmist, to himself

May the glory of YHWH last forever;
> may YHWH rejoice in his works.
He looks at the earth and it quakes;
> he touches the mountains and they smoke.
I will sing to YHWH while I live;
> I will make music to my God while I *have breath*.

> May my musings be pleasing to him,
>> *for* I rejoice in YHWH.
> Let sinners be consumed from the earth;
>> let the wicked be no more.
>
> Praise YHWH, my soul;
>> praise YHWH.

c). The Sovereignty of YHWH[299]

This psalm acknowledges the sovereignty of YHWH over the whole of creation. It compares God with created order, and the majesty of God with the power of the sea.

> *Psalmist, to those around him*
> YHWH reigns;
>> he is robed in majesty;
> YHWH is clothed;
>> he is girded with strength.
> Furthermore, the world is established;
>> it cannot be shaken.
>
> *Psalmist, to YHWH*
> Your throne was established long ago;
>> you are from everlasting.
> The rivers have lifted up, YHWH,
>> the rivers have raised up their voice;
>> the seas have lifted up their pounding *waves*.
>
> *Psalmist, to those around him*
> YHWH in the heights is majestic.
>> *He is* greater than the sound of many waters;
>> *more* majestic *than the* breakers of the sea.
>
> *Psalmist, to YHWH*
> Your decrees stand very firm, YHWH;
>> holiness befits your house forevermore.

d). The God of David and Zion[300]

This psalm remembers, and celebrates, the bringing of the Ark into Jerusalem. It includes part of the prayer that Solomon used at the dedication of the Temple.

---

[299] Psalm 93:1-5
[300] Psalm 132:1-18

Establishing the Kingdom

As a consequence, it served as a suitable psalm to be sung by pilgrims as they approached Jerusalem.

> *Note:*
> A song of the ascents (*possibly a devotion for those on a pilgrimage to Jerusalem*).
>
> *Psalmist, to YHWH*
> Remember David, YHWH,
>   and all his afflictions.
>
> *Remember* that he swore a solemn oath to YHWH;
>   he made a vow to the mighty one of Jacob.
> *He said,* 'I will not enter the *bed* chamber of my house,
>   I will not go up to the couch, which is my bed,
> I will not give sleep to my eyes
>   or slumber to my eyelids,
> until I find a place for YHWH,
>   a dwelling place for the mighty one of Jacob.'
>
> Look, we heard *about* it in Ephrathah;
>   we found *his words* in the fields of Jaar.
> *He said,* 'Let us go to his Tabernacle;
>   let us bow down at the footstool for his feet.'
> *We said,* 'Arise, YHWH, *go* to your resting place,
>   you and the ark of your might.
> May your priests be clothed in righteousness;
>   may your godly ones give out a ringing cry.
> For the sake of your servant, David,
>   do not turn away *from* the presence of your anointed.'
>
> *Psalmist, to those around him*
> YHWH swore a solemn oath to David,
>   he will truly not turn away from it.
> *He said,* 'I will put *your son* on your throne;
>   the fruit of your body.
> If your sons keep my covenant,
>   my decrees that I will teach them,
> then their sons will sit on your throne,
>   forever.'

> For YHWH chose Zion;
> > he desired it for his dwelling place.
> *He said,* 'This is my resting place forever;
> > I will dwell here, for this *is what* I desire.
> I will truly bless her food *supply*;
> > I will satisfy her poor with bread.
> I will clothe her priests with salvation;
> > her godly will truly cry out *with joy*.
> I will cause a horn to grow up for David there;
> > I will arrange a lamp for my anointed.
> I will clothe those who are hostile to him in shame;
> > but on him, his crown will sparkle.'

e). YHWH, Creator and Helper[301]

This psalm is a call to praise YHWH in his holy Temple in Jerusalem.

It is a reminder that God is the creator of all things, and that he has chosen Israel to be his people. It contrasts YHWH's might with the futility of making and worshipping idols.

> *Psalmist, to those around him*
> Praise YHWH.
>
> Praise the name of YHWH;
> > praise him, servants of YHWH,
> who take your stand in the house of YHWH;
> > in the courts of the house of our God.
>
> Praise YHWH, for he is good;
> > make music to his name, for *he is* delightful.
> For YHWH has chosen Jacob for himself;
> > Israel as his possession.
> As for me, I know that YHWH is great;
> > our Lord is greater than all *other* gods.
> YHWH does everything that he pleases
> > in the heavens and on the earth,
> > in the seas and in all depths.
> He makes clouds rise in the distant *parts* of the earth;
> > he makes lightning with rain;
> > he brings out wind from his storehouses.

---

[301] Psalm 135:1-21

He struck down the firstborn of Egypt,
    both man and beast.
He sent signs and wonders into your midst, Egypt,
    against Pharaoh and all his servants.
He struck down many nations
    and killed mighty kings—
including Sihon, king of the Amorites;
    Og, king of Bashan;
    and all the kings of Canaan.
He gave their land as a possession;
    an inheritance to his people, Israel.

Psalmist, to YHWH

Your name, YHWH, is forever;
    your fame, YHWH, *is remembered*
    generation after generation.
For YHWH judges his people;
    he has compassion on his servants.

The idols of the nations are *merely* silver and gold;
    they are the work of a man's hands.
They have mouths, but cannot speak;
    they have eyes, but cannot see.
They have ears, but cannot hear;
    nor is there breath in their mouths.
Their makers, and all who trust in them,
    will become *just* like them.

Psalmist, to Israel

So bless YHWH, house of Israel;
    bless YHWH, house of Aaron.
Bless YHWH, house of Levi;
    Bless YHWH, *all* who fear YHWH.

May YHWH, who dwells in Jerusalem,
    be blessed from Zion.

Praise YHWH.

3. THE LIFE OF FAITH

a). A Call to Worship[302]

This psalm is a call to gather to worship YHWH in his sanctuary. But whether at the Tabernacle or the Temple is not known.

The psalmist reminds the people that God is not only the creator but the shepherd of his people, and that he indeed is worthy of praise.

He also reminds the people of what will happen to those who ignore the call.

> *Psalmist, to those around him*
> Come let us cry out *with joy* to YHWH;
>   let us raise a shout to the rock of our salvation.
> Let us come into his presence with thanksgiving;
>   let us raise a shout to him with songs.
>
> For YHWH is a great God;
>   a great king above all gods.
> In his hand are the depths of the earth;
>   the peaks of the mountains are his *too*.
> The sea is his, for he made it;
>   his hands formed the dry land.
>
> Come let us bow down, let us worship;
>   let us kneel in front of YHWH, our maker.
> For he is our God
>   and we are the people of his pasture.
> *We are* the flock under his care.
>   So if *you would only* hear his voice today.
>
> *YHWH, to the Israelites*
> Do not harden your heart, as *you did* at Meribah,
>   as *you did* on the day at Massah in the wilderness.
> There your fathers tested me;
>   they tried me, *even* though they had seen my deeds.
> For forty years I felt a loathing with *that* generation;
>   I said, '*They are a* people whose heart strays,
>   they do not know my ways.'
> So in my anger I swore an oath,
>   'They will never enter my resting place.'

---

[302] Psalm 95:1-11

Establishing the Kingdom

b). A Call to Worship YHWH in Zion[303]

This psalm is a call for all the peoples of the world to come to Jerusalem, to worship YHWH in his sanctuary. It emphasises God's kingship and holiness, as well as his justice and righteousness.

> *Psalmist, to those around him*
>
> YHWH is king;
> > let the peoples tremble.
>
> He sits enthroned between the cherubim;
> > let the earth quake.
>
> YHWH is great in Zion;
> > he is on high, over all the peoples.
>
> *Psalmist, to YHWH*
>
> Let them praise your great
> > and fearful name.
>
> *Psalmist, to those around him*
>
> He is holy;
> > the mighty king loves justice.
>
> *Psalmist, to YHWH*
>
> You are the one who established equity;
> > you are the one who executed
> > justice and righteousness in Jacob.
>
> *Psalmist, to those around him*
>
> Rejoice in YHWH, our God;
> > bow down at his feet, at his footstool. He is holy.
>
> Moses and Aaron were among his priests;
> > Samuel was among those who called on his name.
>
> They called on YHWH and he answered them;
> > from a pillar of cloud he spoke to them.
>
> They kept his decrees and the laws
> > that he gave them.
>
> *Psalmist, to YHWH*
>
> YHWH, our God, you answered them;
> > you were a forgiving God to them,
> > but an avenger of their rebelliousness.

---

[303] Psalm 99:1-9

> *Psalmist, to those around him*
> *So* magnify YHWH, our God;
> > bow down on his holy mountain,
> > for YHWH, our God, is holy.

c). *A Call for the Whole World to Praise YHWH*[304]

This psalm is a call for the whole world to praise God. It calls the faithful to proclaim God to the nations, and for the nations to bring their sacrifices to YHWH.

YHWH is described as creator, king, and judge—and far superior to all other gods who are considered worthless.

> *Psalmist, to the whole world*
> Sing a new song to YHWH;
> > sing to YHWH all the earth.
> Sing to YHWH, bless his name;
> > bear the news of his salvation day after day.
> Recount his glory among the nations;
> > his extraordinary *deeds* among all the peoples.
>
> For YHWH is great and is *to be* overflowingly praised;
> > he is *to be* feared above all gods.
> None of the gods of the peoples have any worth;
> > but YHWH made the heavens.
> Splendour and majesty are before him;
> > might and glory are in his sanctuary.
>
> Clans of the peoples, give to YHWH;
> > give to YHWH glory and might.
> Give to YHWH the glory of his name;
> > take an offering and bring it into his courts.
> Bow down to YHWH in his sacred glory;
> > dance before him, all the earth.
>
> *Psalmist, to those around him*
> Say among the nations, 'YHWH reigns.
> > *He has* founded the world well,
> > it cannot be shaken;
> > he will judge the peoples with equity.'

---

[304] Psalm 96:1-13

> Let the heavens be glad, let the earth rejoice;
> > let the sea thunder, with all it contains;
> > let the field rejoice, with all that is in it.
> Then all the trees of the forest
> > will cry out *for joy* before YHWH.
> For he is coming, he is coming to judge the earth;
> > he will judge the world in righteousness
> > and the peoples in his steadfast *truth*.

d). Pilgrimage to Jerusalem[305]

This psalm is principally a call for the whole world to praise YHWH in Jerusalem. But it was almost certainly written with pilgrims in mind.

Indeed, the second part of the psalm locates the pilgrims at the gates to the city, where they sang this psalm before passing through to worship YHWH in his sanctuary.

> *Notes:*
> A psalm of thanksgiving.
>
> *Psalmist, to the whole world*
> Raise a shout to YHWH, all the earth;
> > serve YHWH with gladness.
> Come before him
> > and cry out *with joy*.
> Acknowledge that YHWH, alone, is God;
> > he made us, and to him *we belong*.
> We are his people;
> > the sheep that he pastures.
>
> *Psalmist, to those around him*
> Enter his gates with thanksgiving;
> > *come into* his courts with praise.
> Give thanks to him;
> > bless his name.
> For YHWH is good;
> > his steadfast love is forever.
> His faithfulness *will continue*
> > from generation to generation.

---

[305] Psalm 100:1-5

e). A Call to Trust in YHWH[306]

This psalm is a call to have faith in YHWH.

The psalmist recognised that life wasn't easy and that there were many dangers to face. However, he also knew that God had helped him in the past and that he would be ready to come to the aid of others too.

Psalmist, to those around him

He who sits in the shelter of the Almighty,
    lodges in the shadow of the Most High.
I say to YHWH, '*You are* my refuge and my stronghold;
    you are my God.'
I trust in him.

For he will deliver you from the fowler's trap;
    from deadly pestilence.
He will cover you with his feathers;
    you can seek refuge under his wings;
    his faithfulness will be your shield and buckler.
You will not fear the terror of the night;
    the arrow that flies by day;
or the pestilence that prowls in the darkness;
    the destruction that strikes at noon.
A thousand may fall at your side;
    ten thousand at your right hand.
    But it will not draw near to you.
You will only watch with your eyes;
    and see the reward of those who are wicked.

So make YHWH your shelter,
    the Most High your dwelling.
Then no evil will befall you;
    no plague will come near to your tent.
For he will charge his angels concerning you,
    to keep watch *over* you in all his ways.
They will lift you up with their hands,
    so you will not strike your foot against a stone.
You will tread upon a lion and a cobra;
    you will trample a young lion and a serpent.

---

[306] Psalm 91:1-16

> *YHWH, to others (about the psalmist)*
> Because he loves me, I will rescue him;
> > I will *set him inaccessibly* high, because he knows my name.
> He will call upon me, and I will respond to him;
> > I *will be* with him in trouble;
> > I will deliver him and bring him honour.
> I will satisfy him with a long life;
> > I will let him see my salvation.

4. ENEMIES

a). Threats to the Kingdom[307]

It was common for surrounding nations, and vassal states, to look for weaknesses in the defences of a nation. As a consequence, a change of king was seen as an opportunity to test a nation's strength.

Traditionally, this psalm was thought to have been used at the enthronement of a new king and the subsequent annual celebrations, but there is little to suggest that that was its original purpose.

> *Psalmist, to those around him*
> Why do the nations conspire
> > and the peoples plot in vain?
> The kings of the earth set themselves;
> > the rulers plot together
> > > against YHWH, and his anointed one.
> *They say,* 'Let us tear off their bonds,
> > let us cast off our cords.'
>
> The one who sits in the heavens laughs;
> > the Lord mocks them.
> At the *right* time he will speak to them in his anger;
> > he will terrify them in his burning anger.
> *He will say,* 'I have indeed set my king on Zion,
> > my holy mountain.'
>
> *Psalmist, to the surrounding nations*
> I will recount YHWH's decree.
> > He said to me, 'You are my son;
> > > today I have begotten you.

---

[307] Psalm 2:1-12

> Ask of me, and I will give the nations to you
> > as an inheritance;
> > the ends of the earth *as* your possession.
> You will break them with a rod of iron;
> > you will shatter them like a potter's pot.'
>
> So, kings, be prudent;
> > rulers of the earth be warned.
> Serve YHWH with fear;
> > rejoice with trembling.
> Kiss *God's royal* son, lest he be angry
> > and you perish *on the* road.
> For his anger will quickly burn.
> > *But* blessed are all who take refuge in him.

b). *An Old Man Facing Attack*[308]

This psalm, the words of an old man, is a prayer for help. In his lifetime he had seen much trouble, and in his latter years nothing had changed. But the psalmist remained confident in his faith. YHWH had come to his rescue before, and he was certain that he would do so again.

> *Psalmist, to YHWH*
> I have sought refuge in you, YHWH,
> > do not let me ever be ashamed.
> Deliver me in your righteousness, rescue me;
> > incline your ear to me and save me.
> Be a rock of refuge to me, to *which I can* always come;
> > give the command to save me,
> > for you are my rock and my stronghold.
>
> My God, deliver me from the hand of the wicked;
> > from the grasp of the evil-doer and the ruthless.
> For you are my hope, Lord YHWH;
> > I have trusted *in you* since my youth.
> I have leaned on you since birth;
> > you brought me from my mother's womb.
> > I have always praised you.
> I have become an omen to many,
> > *for* you are my strong refuge.

---

[308] Psalm 71:1-24

My mouth is filled with your praise
> *and* your splendour, all day *long.*

Do not cast me off at a time of old age;
> do not abandon me now my strength has gone.

For my enemies speak against me,
> those who watch my life consult together.

They say, 'God has abandoned him.
> Pursue him! Seize him!
> for there is no one to rescue *him.*'

God, do not be distant from me;
> make haste to help me, my God.

May my adversaries be shamed and consumed;
> may those seeking to hurt me
> be enveloped with blame and disgrace.

However I, I will always hope;
> I will add to all of your praise.

My mouth will recount your righteousness
> *and* your saving *deeds*, all day—
> although I cannot know *their* number.

I will enter into the mighty acts of Lord YHWH;
> I will remember your righteousness, *and* yours alone.

God, you taught me since my youth,
> and I still proclaim your extraordinary *deeds.*

Do not abandon me, God,
> even *though I am* in old age and have a grey head.

Let me declare your *mighty* arm to *another* generation;
> your strength to all who are to come.

Your righteousness, God, *reaches* to the heights;
> you have done great things, God.
> Who is like you?

Although you have made me see many troubles and evils,
> you will restore my life;
> you will lift me up from the depths of the earth.

You will add to my greatness
> and console me again.

Moreover I will praise you with a lute
> for your faithfulness, my God.

I will make music to you with a lyre,
> Holy One of Israel.

> My lips will cry *for joy* when I make music to you;
> > *so will* my soul, which you have redeemed.
> My tongue will also muse on your righteousness all day,
> > because those who are seeking to hurt me
> > will have been humiliated and put to shame.

c). *Victory over Israel's Enemies*[309]

This psalm celebrates a great victory over the enemies of Israel. At its heart is the acknowledgement that YHWH had given his people victory and, in doing so, had shown himself to the whole world.

As a consequence, the people, and indeed the whole of creation, are called on to sing YHWH's praises, and to look forward to a time when God will come to judge the world.

> *Note:*
> A psalm.
>
> *Psalmist, to those around him*
> Sing a new song to YHWH,
> > for he has done extraordinary *things*.
> His right hand and his holy arm
> > have brought him victory.
> YHWH has made his salvation known;
> > he has revealed his righteousness
> > to the eyes of the nations.
> He has remembered his steadfast love;
> > his faithfulness to the house of Israel.
> All the ends of the earth have seen
> > the salvation of our God.
>
> *Psalmist, to all creation*
> Raise a shout to YHWH, all the earth;
> > break out, cry out, and make music.
> Make music to YHWH with the lyre;
> > with the lyre and melodious sounds.
> Raise a shout in the presence of YHWH, the king,
> > with trumpets and the sound of the horn.
>
> Let the sea thunder, with all it contains;
> > *let* the world *join in*, with those who live in it.

---

[309] Psalm 98:1-9

> Let the rivers clap *their* hands;
>> let the mountains cry out,
>> united *with joy* before YHWH.
> For he is coming to judge the earth;
>> he will judge the world with righteousness
>> and the peoples with equity.

d). Being Treated as an Outcast[310]

The psalmist had spent some time living in foreign lands. In particular, he had lived in Meshech near the Black Sea, and Kedar in northern Arabia. He had now returned to his people, but he was being treated like an outcast. Indeed, some were saying things which were clearly untrue. As a consequence, the psalmist appeals to YHWH to come to his rescue.

Traditionally, this psalm has been considered to be one sung by pilgrims to Jerusalem. But if that is true, it may be an indication that not all pilgrims were welcomed as they should have been.

> *Note:*
> A song of the ascents (*possibly a devotion for those on a pilgrimage to Jerusalem*).
>
> *Psalmist, to those around him*
> In my distress I called to YHWH
>> and he answered me.
> *I said,* 'YHWH, deliver me from false speech,
>> and from treacherous tongues.'
>
> *Psalmist, to his slanderer*
> What will YHWH do to you?
>> What more will he do to you, treacherous tongue?
> *You will be pierced with* the sharp arrows of a warrior;
>> with *the burning* coals from a broom tree.
>
> *Psalmist, to those around him*
> Woe to me, for I have wandered in Meshech;
>> I *have* settled among the tents of Kedar.
> *For* many *years* I have lived
>> among those who hate peace.
> I am for peace, but when I speak
>> they are for war.

---

[310] Psalm 120:1-7

D4. THE SAYINGS OF SOLOMON

a). Introduction and Priority of Wisdom

A. INTRODUCTION TO THE SAYINGS OF SOLOMON

a). Introduction[311]

The book of Proverbs includes three collections of Solomon's sayings. The third of which was compiled during the reign of King Hezekiah, which began two hundred and fourteen years after the death of Solomon.

Collection	First
Title:	The proverbs of Solomon, son of David, king of Israel
Purpose:	To learn wisdom and correction; to discern words of insight.
	To receive instruction on how to be prudent; to be righteous, just, and upright.
	To give prudence to the open-minded; to give knowledge and purpose to the young. (A wise *man will* listen and add to his learning; a discerning *man* will receive direction).
	To understand proverbs and satire: the sayings and riddles of the wise.

Collection	Second
Title:	The proverbs of Solomon.

Collection	Third
Title:	Other proverbs of Solomon, collected *together* by the men of Hezekiah, king of Judah.

Each collection includes many sayings, and groups of sayings, which appear to have been included at random. In order to bring some order, they are presented here in thematic order—using the Ten Words (or Ten Commandments) as the basic framework.

The meaning of some of the proverbs may, today, seem to be ambiguous. But it is not unreasonable to suggest that at least some of them may have been deliberately written that way.

---

[311] Proverbs 1:1-6; 10:1a; 25:1

B. THE PRIORITY OF WISDOM

1. PRINCIPLE

The priority of wisdom, for Solomon, was a reflection of the covenant relationship with YHWH. If God had acted in love for his people, then the people needed to demonstrate that they were faithful to him.

This first group of sayings emphasises the priority of wisdom, and the need to remain faithful to all 'her' principles.

2. THE PRIORITY OF YHWH

a). The Creator[312]

> YHWH has made both the ear that hears and the eye that sees.

> *The point at which* a rich *man* and a poor *man* meet is that YHWH made them both.

b). The All-knowing God[313]

> YHWH's eyes are everywhere, watching the good and the bad.

> The breath of man is a lamp of YHWH; it searches all the chambers of *his* body.

c). Guidance[314]

> A man's mind considers his way, but YHWH directs his steps.

> A man's mind has many thoughts, but it is YHWH's counsel that will stand.

> A man's steps are from YHWH, so how can a man discern his way?

d). Blessings[315]

> YHWH's blessing brings riches; sorrow is not part of them.

> Commit your deeds to YHWH and your plans will succeed.

---

[312] Proverbs 20:12; 22:2
[313] Proverbs 15:3; 20:27
[314] Proverbs 16:9; 19:21; 20:24
[315] Proverbs 10:22; 16:3, 20

> A man who prudently follows the word will receive good *things*; *a man* who trusts in YHWH will be blessed.

e). Security[316]

> The name of YHWH is a mighty tower; a righteous *man* who runs to him will be safe.

f). Justice[317]

> The lot *may* be cast into the lap, but every judgement comes from YHWH.

> There is no wisdom, understanding, or counsel that *can stand* in opposition to YHWH.

3. THE NEED TO FEAR YHWH

a). The Need to Fear YHWH[318]

> A man who walks uprightly is one who fears YHWH, but *a man* who has turned aside in his ways is one who despises him.

> Whoever fears YHWH *will enjoy* confidence *in his* might; it will be a refuge for his sons. *For* the fear of YHWH is a wellspring of life, turning *a man* aside from the snares of death.

> It is better to fear YHWH, *and have* little, than to have much treasure with turmoil.

> *Whoever* fears YHWH has life; he passes the night satisfied, untouched by evil.

> The consequences of fearing YHWH and having humility are riches, honour and life.

---

[316] Proverbs 18:10
[317] Proverbs 16:33; 21:30
[318] Proverbs 14:2, 26-27; 15:16; 19:23; 22:4

4. THE PRIORITY OF RIGHTEOUSNESS

a). The Pursuit of Righteousness[319]

> Along the path of righteousness is life; along the path there is no death.

> Without a vision the people let go; but a man who observes the law is blessed.

5. THE PROMOTION OF WISDOM

a). Wisdom Is Better than Gold[320]

> It is so much better to acquire wisdom than gold, to get understanding than choose silver.

> Whoever pursues righteousness and goodness attains life, righteousness, and honour.

> A *good* name should be chosen *in preference to* great wealth; to be favoured is better than silver and gold.

> As water *reflects* a face, so a man's heart *reflects* the man.

b). The Blessings of Wisdom[321]

> A grey head is a crown of glory; it is attained through a life of righteousness.

> The glory of young men is their strength; the honour of old *men* is their grey head.

c). Family Wisdom[322]

> Listen, sons, to the discipline of a father; incline your ears *so that you may* gain understanding. I put before you sound teaching, so do not abandon my direction. For I was a son *of* tender *age* in my father's presence; I was the only child in my mother's eyes.
>
> My father taught me. He said to me, 'Let your heart grasp my words; keep my commands and live. Get wisdom! Get understanding! Do not forget, and

---

[319] Proverbs 12:28; 29:18
[320] Proverbs 16:16; 21:21; 22:1; 27:19
[321] Proverbs 16:31; 20:29
[322] Proverbs 4:1-9

> do not turn aside from the words of my mouth. Do not abandon wisdom, and she will guard you; love her, and she will keep watch over you. The acquisition of wisdom is the beginning of wisdom; and with all that you acquire, gets understanding. If you lift her up, she will raise you up; if you clasp her, she will honour you. She will place a garland of grace on your head; she will present you with a glorious crown.'

6. THE CHOICE OF WISDOM

a). Acknowledging One's Limitations[323]

> Who can say, 'I have cleansed my heart; I am clean; *I am free from* sin'?

b). Choosing the Right Path[324]

> My son, take my words; treasure my commands within you. Incline your ear to wisdom; turn your heart to understanding. Call out for insight; raise your voice for understanding. Seek wisdom, as *though she was* silver; search for her, as *you would for* hidden treasure. Then you will understand the fear of YHWH; you will find the knowledge of God.
>
> For YHWH gives wisdom; from his mouth *comes* knowledge and understanding. He stores up *the rewards of* wisdom for the upright; *he is* a shield for those who walk with integrity. He keeps watch over the path of justice; he preserves the way of the faithful. *Follow him and* you will discern righteousness, justice, and equity—every good way. For wisdom will come into your heart; knowledge will be delightful to your soul. Discretion will preserve you; understanding will keep watch over you.
>
> She will deliver you from the path of evil, from a man who speaks wickedly. *For* they abandon the straight paths to walk in the ways of darkness. They delight in doing evil; they rejoice in the wickedness of evil. For their paths are twisted, they have turned aside in their ways.
>
> *She will* deliver you from the woman who is a stranger; from the foreigner whose words are smooth. For the woman has left the partner of her youth and has forgotten the covenant of her God. Her house sinks down to death, her tracks *lead* to the spirits *of the dead*. None of those who go to her will ever come back; they will never reach the paths of life.

---

[323] Proverbs 20:9
[324] Proverbs 2:1-22

> For this reason, you should walk in the way of the good; you should keep to the paths of the righteous. For the upright will dwell in the land; the blameless will remain in it. But the wicked will be cut off from the land; those who act treacherously will be uprooted from it.

c). *Wisdom or Stupidity?*[325]

> Wisdom has built her house; she has fashioned out its seven pillars. She has slaughtered her animals; she has mixed her wine; she has set her table. She has sent out her maid*servants*; she calls from the highest places in the city. *She says to the* simple, 'Turn aside here.' She says to those who lack sense, 'Come, eat my food; drink the wine that I mixed. Leave *your* simple *ways* and live; walk straight *along* the path of understanding.'
>
> Whoever admonishes a scoffer takes on his own dishonour; whoever rebukes a wicked man *will receive* that man's abuse. *So* do not rebuke a scoffer or he will hate you; *but* rebuke a wise man and he will love you. Give *instruction* to a wise *man* and he will become wiser still; give knowledge to a righteous *man* and he will add *to his* learning. For the beginning of wisdom is the fear of YHWH; understanding *comes through* knowledge of the Holy One. Through wisdom your days will be many; years will be added to your life. If you are wise, you *will benefit* from that wisdom; if you are a scoffer, you will be on your own.
>
> A stupid woman is rough and coarse; she is simple and knows nothing. She sits at the entrance to her house, on a 'throne' at the heights of the city. *She* calls out to those passing along the road; those who are going straight on their way. *She says* to the simple, 'Turn aside here.' She says to those who lack sense, 'Water that has been stolen is sweet; food that has been hidden is delightful.' But the simple are unaware that the dead are there; *that* her guests are in the depths of Sheol.

d). *Abominations to YHWH*[326]

> Those whose hearts are twisted are an abomination to YHWH, but he delights in those whose way is blameless.

> The ways of a wicked *man* are an abomination to YHWH, but he loves a *man* who pursues righteousness.

---

[325] Proverbs 9:1-18
[326] Proverbs 11:20; 15:9

7. THE REJECTION OF WISDOM

a). The Wrong Way[327]

> There is a way *that seems* right to a man, but its end is the way of death.

> There is a way *which appears* straight to a man, but its end is the way of death.

b). Self-Sufficiency[328]

> A rich man's wealth is his mighty city; in his imagination it has an *inaccessibly* high wall.

c). Pride[329]

> Wisdom cries out in the street; she makes her voice known in public squares. She calls out at the top of noisy *corners*; she utters her speeches at the entrance to the gates of the city.
>
> *Wisdom, to fools*
> 'How long, simple ones, will you love being simple? *How long will* mockers take pleasure in their mocking? *How long* will fools hate knowledge?
>
> 'If you had taken heed of my criticism, I would have poured out my spirit on you; I would have made my words known to you. But I called and you refused *to listen*; I stretched out my hand and no one was inclined to hear. You ignored all my counsel; you refused to accept my rebuke. So I myself will laugh at your affliction; I will mock when you are struck with dread. Your dread will hit you like a devastating storm; your affliction will come upon you like a whirlwind; distress and anguish will come upon you.'
>
> *Wisdom, to the whole city*
> 'They will call to me, but I will not answer; they will look diligently for me, but not find me. Because they hated knowledge, and refused to choose the fear of YHWH, they were unwilling to accept my counsel and treated my rebuke with contempt. So they will eat of the fruit of their *own* ways; they will be glutted with their *own* plans.
>
> 'The simple will be killed through their rejection of faith, and fools will perish through their complacency. But whoever listens to me will live securely; he will *live in* peace from the dread of evil.'

---

[327] Proverbs 14:12; 16:25
[328] Proverbs 18:11
[329] Proverbs 1:20-33; 21:4

Haughty eyes and a proud heart are the lamp of the wicked; *they are* sinful.

D4. THE SAYINGS OF SOLOMON

b). The Nature of Wisdom

1. PRINCIPLE

If the pursuit of wisdom was imperative, so was the need to distinguish between what it is and what it isn't.
Wisdom needed to be nurtured, and all obstacles removed.

2. A DEFINITION OF WISDOM

a). The Fear of YHWH[330]

> The fear of YHWH is the beginning of knowledge, *but* fools treat wisdom and correction with contempt

3. BEING WISE

a). A Winner of Souls[331]

> The fruit of righteousness is a tree of life; a *man* who wins souls is wise.

b). A Wellspring of Life[332]

> The instruction of the wise is the wellspring of life, turning away from the lures of death.

> The path of life is upward for a wise *man*, in order to turn away from Sheol below.

> Whoever acquires wisdom loves his soul; whoever preserves understanding finds a good thing.

---

[330] Proverbs 1:7
[331] Proverbs 11:30
[332] Proverbs 13:14; 15:24; 19:8

c). A Discerning Man[333]

> *A man who is* wise in heart is called 'discerning'; the sweetness of lips adds to learning.

> A wise man's heart controls his mouth; with his lips he adds to learning.

> The mind of a discerning *man* acquires knowledge; the ears of the wise seek knowledge.

d). The Accomplishments of a Wise Man[334]

> A wise *man* goes up *against* a city of mighty *men*; he brings down the stronghold *in which they* trust.

4. BEING FOOLISH

a). No Desire to Learn[335]

> Why would a fool have money in his hand to buy wisdom, when he has no desire *to learn*?

b). Exposing One's True Self[336]

> A fool takes no delight in wisdom; only in exposing his *own* mind.

> *Like* the legs of a lame *man* that hang *uselessly*, so is a proverb in the mouth of fools.

> A thorn that enters the hand of a drunken *man is like* a proverb in the mouth of fools.

c). Repeating the Same Mistake[337]

> Like a dog which returns to its vomit, so is a fool who repeats his folly.

---

[333] Proverbs 16:21, 23; 18:15
[334] Proverbs 21:22
[335] Proverbs 17:16
[336] Proverbs 18:2; 26:7, 9
[337] Proverbs 26:11

d). The Place of the Fool[338]

> It is not seemly for a fool *to live in* luxury, or for a slave to have dominion over rulers.

e). Causing Strife[339]

> The mouth of a fool brings strife; with his mouth he calls out for beatings.

> The mouth of a fool is his destruction; his lips are the lure of his soul.

> A stone is heavy and sand is weighty, but the incitement of a fool is heavier than both of them.

f). Requiring Discipline[340]

> A whip is for a horse, a halter is for an ass, and a rod is for the backs of fools.

> *Even* if you *were to* pound a fool in a mortar with a pestle, mixed with crushed grain, he would not be separated from his folly.

g). Raging Against YHWH[341]

> A man's folly perverts his *own* way; his heart rages against YHWH.

h). Without Honour[342]

> *Like* snow in summer or rain at harvest time, so honour is not seemly for a fool.

> Like tying a stone to a sling, so is giving honour to a fool.

i). Considered Wise[343]

> Even a fool who remains silent is thought to be wise; if he seals his lips *he is considered to be* discerning.

---

[338] Proverbs 19:10
[339] Proverbs 18:6-7; 27:3
[340] Proverbs 26:3; 27:22
[341] Proverbs 19:3
[342] Proverbs 26:1, 8
[343] Proverbs 17:28

5. FACING A FOOL

a). Facing a Fool[344]

Leave the presence of a foolish man, for you will not find knowledge on *his* lips.

It is better to meet a bear robbed of a cub *than to face* a fool in his folly.

b). Responding to a Fool[345]

Don't respond to a fool according to his folly, or you yourself will become like him.

Respond to a fool according to his folly, otherwise he will see himself as being wise.

c). Employing a Fool[346]

Sending a message by the hand of a fool *is like* cutting off one's feet or drinking violence.

6. WISDOM VS. FOOLISHNESS

a). Wisdom for All[347]

Wisdom rests in the heart of a discerning *man*; she has made herself known even in the hearts of fools.

b). Wisdom vs. Foolishness[348]

A wise *man* fears and turns aside from evil, but a fool is arrogant and overconfident.

The simple have taken possession of folly, but the prudent are surrounded with knowledge.

The crown of the wise is their wealth; the folly of fools is their foolishness.

---

[344] Proverbs 14:7; 17:12
[345] Proverbs 26:4-5
[346] Proverbs 26:6
[347] Proverbs 14:33
[348] Proverbs 14:16, 18, 24; 17:24; 21:20; 28:26

> The face of a discerning *man reveals* wisdom; but the eyes of a fool are *focussed* on the ends of the earth.

> In the house of a wise *man* are desirable treasures and oil; a foolish man swallows it *all* up.

> *A man* who trusts in himself is a fool; *a man* who walks in wisdom will be delivered.

c). Wisdom vs. Wickedness[349]

> Planning wickedness is like laughter to a fool, but wisdom is *the pleasure* of a man of understanding.

d). Wisdom vs. Temper[350]

> A fool's anger is revealed within a day, but a prudent *man* conceals *his* dishonour.

> *Whoever is* slow to anger has great understanding, but *whoever is* short-tempered rises to foolishness.

> A fool expresses every *aspect of* his temper, but a wise *man* soothes it within.

e). Wisdom vs. Ruin[351]

> The wise store up knowledge, but the mouth of the fool brings ruin near.

> Whoever walks with wise men will become wise, but whoever associates with fools will *come to* harm.

f). Counsel vs. Self[352]

> The way of the fool is right in his *own* eyes, but a wise man listens to the counsel *of others*.

g). Knowledge vs. Folly[353]

> All prudent men act from knowledge, but the fool spreads folly.

---

[349] Proverbs 10:23
[350] Proverbs 12:16; 14:29, 29:11
[351] Proverbs 10:14; 13:20
[352] Proverbs 12:15
[353] Proverbs 13:16; 15:7, 14, 21; 16:22

> The lips of the wise scatter knowledge; not so the minds of fools.

> The mind of a discerning *man* seeks knowledge, but the mouth of fools grazes on folly.

> Folly brings joy to *a man* who lacks heart, but a man of understanding walks a straight *path*.

> Insight is a fountain of life to its owners; but folly is the discipline of fools.

h). Discernment vs. Deception[354]

> The wisdom of the shrewd is to discern his *own* way; but the folly of fools is deception.

> A simple *man* believes in anything, but a shrewd *man* discerns his steps.

i). Favour vs. Guilt[355]

> Fools mock at guilt, but the upright enjoy YHWH's favour.

j). Integrity vs. Being Twisted[356]

> It is better to be a poor *man* walking in integrity than to have twisted lips and be a fool.

k). Advice[357]

> Arrogance results in nothing but strife; but wisdom *can be found* in those who can take advice.

7. FOOLISHNESS VS. SELF-DECEPTION

a). Self-Deception[358]

> *There is* more hope for a fool than for a man who you can see is wise in his *own* eyes.

---

[354] Proverbs 14:8, 15
[355] Proverbs 14:9
[356] Proverbs 19:1
[357] Proverbs 13:10
[358] Proverbs 26:12

8. THE DISCIPLINE OF WISDOM

a). *Wisdom as the Rule of Life*[359]

Doesn't wisdom call out? *Doesn't* understanding raise her voice? On the heights beside the road, where the paths meet, she takes her stand. Beside the gates, at the entrance to the city, at the approach of the doorway, she cries out, 'I call out to you, men; my voice *calls out* to the sons of man. You who are simple discern prudence; you who are foolish discern understanding. Hear the noble things I have to say; I will open my lips *for what is* right. For my mouth will speak *the* truth, *because* wickedness is detestable to my lips. All the words of my mouth are righteous; *there is* nothing twisted or perverse in them. They are all straight to the discerning; they are all right to those who have found knowledge. *So* take my correction, not silver; *take* knowledge, rather than the choicest gold. For wisdom is better than rubies; no pleasures can compare with her.

'As for me, I, wisdom, live with prudence; I have attained knowledge *and* purpose. The fear of YHWH *is* to hate evil. So I hate pride, arrogance, evil ways, and perverted mouths. Counsel and success are mine; I have understanding and might. By me, kings reign; rulers decree what is just. By me, rulers and nobles govern—all those who rule in righteousness. As for me, I love those who love me; *so* those who look diligently for me will find me. With me, are riches and honour; *with me*, is wealth beyond measure and righteousness. My fruit is better than gold, even fine gold; my produce is better than the choicest silver. I walk in the way of righteousness, in the midst of the paths of justice. So I can endow with wealth those who love me; I can fill their storehouses.

'YHWH procreated me at the beginning of his way, before his *creative* works of old. From everlasting, I was installed; from the beginning, from the former times of the earth. I was born before the depths *were created*; before springs abounded with water. I was born before the mountains were settled and the hills *had come into being. Indeed*, even before he had made the land, the fields, or even the first dust of the world.

'I was there when he established the heavens *and* when he inscribed a horizon on the face of the deep. *I was there* when he made firm the skies above *and* when he secured the springs of the deep. *I was there* when he prescribed the laws for the sea, so the waters would not disobey *the word of* his mouth; *and again* when he inscribed the foundations of the earth. I was with him as a

---

[359] Proverbs 8:1-36

> master craftsman; I was a delight *to him*, day after day. I rejoiced in his presence at all times. I rejoiced in the world, in his earth; I delighted in the sons of man.
>
> 'So now, *my* sons, listen to me; blessed are those who keep my ways. Listen to correction and become wise; don't leave it alone. Blessed is the man who hears me; who watches day by day at my door; who keeps watch at my doorposts. For whoever finds me finds life; he is furnished with YHWH's favour. But whoever passes me by does violence to himself; all who hate me love death.'

9. CORRECTION

a). Accepting Correction[360]

> The ear that hears a life-giving rebuke will dwell among the wise.

> The correction that brings wisdom is the fear of YHWH; humility *comes* before honour.

> Listen to advice and accept correction, so that in the end you will be wise.

> Blows that bruise scour away evil; blows *reach every* chamber of the body.

> It is better *to be* open to rebuke than *to* conceal love.

> *Just as* iron is *used to* sharpen *the edge of* iron, so a man sharpens the face of his friend.

b). Rejecting Correction[361]

> Do not reject the chastening of YHWH, my son; do not abhor his reproof. For YHWH censures those he loves, as a father *does to the* son in whom he delights.
>
> Blessed is the man who finds wisdom; the man who attains understanding. For wisdom is more profitable than silver; her return is better than gold. She is more precious than rubies; nothing you desire can compare with her. In her right hand is a long life; in her left hand are riches and honour. Her ways

---

[360] Proverbs 15:31, 33; 19:20; 20:30; 27:5, 17
[361] Proverbs 3:11-20; 15:12; 19:27

are delightful ways; all her paths are sound. She is a tree of life to those who adopt her; those who grab hold of her are blessed.

YHWH fixed the earth in place through wisdom; with understanding he established the heavens. With his knowledge the deeps were divided, and the clouds drip down with dew.

A scoffer does not like *a man who* rebukes him; he will not go to the wise.

Cease listening to correction, my son, *and you will* stray from words of knowledge.

c). Accepting vs. Rejecting Correction[362]

Whoever heeds instruction *reveals* the path to life, but whoever ignores rebuke leads *others* astray.

Whoever loves correction loves knowledge, but whoever hates rebuke *remains* coarse.

Whoever ignores correction *will face* poverty and dishonour, but whoever heeds rebuke will be honoured.

Whoever ignores correction rejects himself; whoever hears rebuke gains understanding.

A rebuke descends further into a discerning *man* than one hundred lashes on a fool.

Strike a scoffer and the simple may become shrewd; rebuke a discerning *man and* he will gain knowledge.

The wounds a friend *inflicts* are faithful, but the kisses of an enemy are abundant.

---

[362] Proverbs 10:17; 12:1; 13:18; 15:32; 17:10; 19:25; 27:6

D4. THE SAYINGS OF SOLOMON

c). The Use and Abuse of Wisdom

1. PRINCIPLE

Wisdom needed to be honoured, and not manipulated to suit the user. The use of wisdom needed to reflect well on YHWH at all times.

2. WALKING WITH YHWH

a). A Child-like Faith[363]

> Do not forget my instruction, my son; let your heart observe my commands. For *they will add* to the length of *your* days, the years of *your* life, and they will bring you peace. Do not let goodness and truth ever leave you; bind them around your neck. Write them on the table of your heart, then you will find favour and *have* a good reputation in the eyes of God and man.
>
> Trust in YHWH with all your heart; do not depend on your *own* understanding. Acknowledge him in everything you do, and he will make your paths straight.
>
> Do not see yourself as wise, *but* fear YHWH and turn away from evil. It will be healing for your body; refreshment for your bones.
>
> Honour YHWH with your wealth, with the first fruits of all your produce. Then your storehouse will be filled with plenty; your vats will burst with new wine.

b). Walking with YHWH[364]

> Do not lose sight of *wisdom and understanding*, my son; guard sound judgement and discretion. They will be life for your soul and grace for your neck. Then you will be secure as you walk in your way; your foot will never stumble. When you lie down, you will not be afraid; when you lie down, your dreams will be sweet. Do not fear sudden dread or the ruin that comes to the wicked,

---

[363] Proverbs 3:1-10
[364] Proverbs 3:21-35

> for YHWH will be your confidence. He will keep your foot from being captured.
>
> Do not withhold good from those to whom it belongs, when it is in your power to do *good*. Do not say to your friend, 'Come, return tomorrow. I will give *it to you then*,' when you have it with you.
>
> Do not devise evil against your friend who is living in safety with you. Do not strive against *another* man without reason, and who has not caused you injury.
>
> Do not envy a violent man; do not choose any of his ways. For the one who turns away is an abomination to YHWH, who keeps counsel with the upright.
>
> YHWH's curse is on the house of the wicked; his blessing is on the home of the righteous. Indeed, he treats mockers with contempt, but he shows favour to the afflicted. Those who are wise inherit honour, but fools rise *only* to dishonour.

3. GUARDING AGAINST EVIL

a). Guarding Against Evil[365]

> Listen, my son, to the instruction of your father; do not abandon the teaching of your mother. For they are an elegant garland for your head, and are pendants about your neck.
>
> My son, if sinners entice you, do not be willing *to join them*. Some may say, 'Come with us. Let us lie in wait to *shed someone's* blood; let us ambush the innocent for no reason. Let us swallow them alive, like Sheol; *let us swallow them* whole, like those going down to the pit. *Then* we can take all *their* precious wealth; we will fill our houses with spoil. Throw your lot in with us, *and* we will all share the one purse.'
>
> My son, do not walk in *that* manner with them; withhold your foot from their path. For *with* their feet they rush into evil; they are quick to shed blood. Surely it is useless spreading out a net while a bird is watching. But they lie in wait for their *own* blood; they ambush themselves. So is the way of all who pursue unjust gain; it takes away the life of *all* who possess it.

---

[365] Proverbs 1:8-19; 4:10-19; 16:17; 19:2; 22:5

Listen, my son, take my words, and the years of your life will be many. I will instruct you in the way of wisdom; I will lead you along straight paths. Your steps will not be obstructed when you walk; you will not stumble when you run. *So* take a firm grip of instruction; do not let go. Guard wisdom, for she is your life. Do not enter the path of the wicked; do not advance in the way of evil *men*. Leave it alone! Do not pass through it! Turn aside from it and move on. For unless they do evil, they cannot sleep; until they cause *someone* to stumble, they are robbed of sleep. For they eat the bread of wickedness and they drink the wine of violence.

The path of the righteous is like the bright light *of the dawn*, which gets brighter until the full of day. *But* the way of the wicked is like darkness; they don't know what they are stumbling over.

The highway of the upright is to turn aside from evil; *a man* who guards his way preserves his soul.

Passion without knowledge is not good; one who is hasty misses his step.

A twisted *man's* path is *littered with* thorns and traps; whoever guards his life will distance *himself* from them.

b). Keeping on Track[366]

My son, pay attention to my words; incline your ear to my words. Do not let them slip away from your sight; guard them within your heart. To those who find them, they are life; they are health to the whole body. With all watchfulness, guard your heart, for from it *flows the* spring of life. Turn aside from having a crooked mouth; put lying lips far from you. Let your eyes look to the front; let your gaze be directed in front of you. Make level a path for your feet; let all your ways be firm. Do not bend to the right or left; turn your foot aside from evil.

When pride comes, it is followed by dishonour, but with modesty comes wisdom.

---

[366] Proverbs 4:20-27; 11:2

4. SEEKING WISDOM

a). Seeking Wisdom[367]

> A scoffer who seeks wisdom will never *find her*, but to a discerning *man* knowledge comes easily.

6. VOWS

a). Vows[368]

> *A* snare for a man is to declare wildly, 'It is set apart,' only later to examine his vows.

---

[367] Proverbs 14:6
[368] Proverbs 20:25

D4. THE SAYINGS OF SOLOMON

d). The Celebration of Wisdom

1. PRINCIPLE

Setting aside time for rest, and times to celebrate their relationship with YHWH—as a community—was an important aspect of Hebrew life. But so too was the need to acknowledge their sins and to depend upon YHWH for his forgiveness.

However, they needed to demonstrate that they were truly genuine.

2. YHWH'S COVENANT

a). *Atonement for Sins*[369]

> Sin is atoned for through covenant love and faithfulness; through fear of YHWH *a man can* turn aside from evil.

b). *Covenant of Peace*[370]

> When a man's ways are accepted favourably by YHWH, he makes a covenant of peace even with his enemies.

3. SACRIFICES

a). *Sacrifices*[371]

> The sacrifices of the wicked are an abomination to YHWH, but the prayers of the upright find his favour.

> A righteous and just deed is more preferable to YHWH than *to offer a* sacrifice.

> *If* the sacrifices of the wicked are an abomination, how much more, then, when a man brings a sacrifice with wicked intentions.

---

[369] Proverbs 16:6
[370] Proverbs 16:7
[371] Proverbs 15:8; 21:3, 27

D4. THE SAYINGS OF SOLOMON

e). Family Responsibilities

1. PRINCIPLE

The structure of society was an important part of Hebrew life, for it was within the family unit that intimate relationships were nurtured and built. As a consequence, the family unit was at the very core of the covenant community, and for a community to work well it was vital that the concept of belonging to one's 'father's house' was maintained.

2. THE FAMILY

a). Inheritance[372]

A *man* who stirs up his *own* house will inherit wind; the foolish will be the servant of the wise of heart.

b). Crowning Glory[373]

The crowns of the elderly are their sons' sons; the glory of sons are their fathers.

c). A Troublesome Wife[374]

It is better to have a meal of vegetables *served* with love, than to have a fatted ox with hatred.

It is better to live *alone* on the corner of a roof, than to share a house with an antagonistic wife.

It is better to live in a land of wilderness, than with an antagonistic and angry wife.

It is better to live on the corner of a roof, than share a house with a wife who quarrels.

---

[372] Proverbs 11:29
[373] Proverbs 17:6
[374] Proverbs 15:17; 21:9, 19; 25:24; 27:15-16

> Like the continual dripping of rain on a *rainy* day, so is a quarrelsome wife. Whoever hides her, hides a *storm* wind; his right hand grasps oil *which slips through his fingers*.

d). A House Full of Strife[375]

> It is better to have a dry fragment *of food* with quiet than a house full of sacrificial *meat* with strife.

> A foolish son is his father's destruction; the arguments of his wife are *like* constant dripping.

3. FATHERS

a). Fathering a Fool[376]

> Whoever fathers a fool *brings* grief upon himself; the father of a fool does not rejoice.

b). Training a Son[377]

> Train a boy in the manner *he should live*, so that when he is old he will not turn away from it.

c). Disciplining a Son[378]

> Whoever withholds his rod hates his son, but whoever loves his son disciplines him early.

> Chastise your son while there is hope; do not set your heart on his death.

> A boy's heart is bound up with folly; a chastening rod will distance it from him.

> A rod and rebuke bring wisdom, but a boy who is undisciplined brings shame to his mother.

> Discipline your son and he will give you rest; he will bring delight to your soul.

---

[375] Proverbs 17:1; 19:13
[376] Proverbs 17:21
[377] Proverbs 22:6
[378] Proverbs 13:24; 19:18; 22:15; 29:15, 17

4. WIVES

a). A Noble Wife[379]

> A noble wife is the crowning *glory* of her husband, but a shameful *wife* is like decay in his bones.

> *A man* who finds a wife finds a good *thing*; he will be furnished with favour from YHWH.

> A house and wealth are an inheritance from *a* father, but an understanding wife comes from YHWH.

b). A Foolish Woman[380]

> A beautiful woman who lacks judgement, *is like a* gold ring in a swine's snout.

> A wise woman builds her house, but a foolish *woman* tears it down with her *own* hands.

5. SONS

a). A Righteous Son[381]

> A righteous *man* walks his blameless life; *how* blessed are his sons who follow him.

> Even a child is regarded by his deeds, *by* whether his deeds are pure and upright.

b). A Disgraceful Son[382]

> A fool treats his father's discipline with contempt, but a shrewd *man* heeds correction.

> A wise servant will rule over a son who acts shamefully; he will share in the inheritance with the brothers.

---

[379] Proverbs 12:4; 18:22; 19:14
[380] Proverbs 11:22; 14:1
[381] Proverbs 20:7, 11
[382] Proverbs 15:5; 17:2, 25; 19:26; 20:20, 21: 28:24

A foolish son is grief to his father and bitterness to the one who bore him.

A man who deals violently with *his* father makes his mother flee; *he is* a son who brings shame and disgrace.

A man who slights his father or mother, *like* a lamp, will be extinguished *into* pitch black.

An inheritance obtained by greed from the start, will not be blessed at the end.

A man who robs his father or mother, and says, 'It is not a sin,' is an associate of a man who destroys.

c). *Wise vs. Shameful Sons*[383]

A wise son brings *his* father joy, but a foolish son *brings* grief to his mother.

A wise son is one who gathers the summer fruit, but a shameful son is one who sleeps during the harvest.

A wise son *accepts* the discipline of *his* father, but a scoffer does not hear the rebuke.

A wise son makes *his* father glad, but a foolish man is one who despises his mother.

Whoever observes a command preserves his soul; whoever despises his ways will die.

Be wise, my son. Make my heart rejoice. Then I can respond to *any*one who rebukes me.

A discerning son is one who keeps the law, but *a son* who associates with worthless *men* humiliates his father.

A man who loves wisdom brings his father joy; a man who associates with harlots squanders *his* wealth.

---

[383] Proverbs 10:1b, 5; 13:1; 15:20; 19:16; 27:11; 28:7; 29:3

6. BROTHERS

a). Comparison with a Friend[384]

A friend is loving at all times, but a brother is born for adversity.

7. SERVANTS

a). A Faithful Messenger[385]

Like the cool of snow in the heat of harvesting is a faithful messenger to those who send him. He refreshes his master's soul.

b). A Thankless Servant[386]

A man who indulges his servant from youth will later find him to be thankless.

c). Discipline[387]

A servant cannot be disciplined by words *alone*; although he may understand *them*, he will give no answer.

---

[384] Proverbs 17:17
[385] Proverbs 25:13
[386] Proverbs 29:21
[387] Proverbs 29:19

D4. THE SAYINGS OF SOLOMON

f). The Sanctity of Life

1. PRINCIPLE

The need to uphold the sanctity of life was an important principle in maintaining the covenant community. As a consequence, it involved not only the need to protect people from harm, but the responsibility to preserve life and promote well-being.

2. LIVING AS A COMMUNITY

a). Caring for Others[388]

A *man with a* generous soul will grow fat; a *man* who refreshes *others* will also be refreshed.

Whoever tends a fig tree will eat its fruit; whoever keeps watch over his master will be honoured.

Make certain you know the state of your flock; set your heart on *the state of your* herds. For riches do not *last* forever, nor does a crown *continue* generation after generation.

b). The Value of Friendship[389]

Oil and incense make the heart glad, but the sweetness of a friend is in his counsel of the soul.

Do not abandon your friend or your father's friend; do not go to your brother's house when you are in distress. A close neighbour is better than a distant brother.

c). Promoting Peace[390]

Kings delight in righteous lips; they love a man who speaks truthfully.

---

[388] Proverbs 11:25; 27:18, 23-24
[389] Proverbs 27:9-10
[390] Proverbs 16:13; 17:14; 20:3; 26:20

> The beginning of strife is *like* allowing water to escape; so abandon the dispute before it breaks out.

> It is honourable for a man to cease strife; any fool *can start a* quarrel.

> Without wood a fire goes out; without a whisperer strife quietens down.

d) Neighbourly Advice[391]

> Rarely set foot in your neighbour's house, otherwise he will become full of you and hate you.

> A blessing in a loud voice early in the morning will be considered a curse by his neighbour.

e). The Value of Advisors[392]

> The people fall through lack of direction, but *there is* deliverance in *having* many advisors.

3. RIGHTEOUSNESS

a). Being Genuine[393]

> Many men call themselves good men, but who can find a man who is *truly* faithful?

b). Slipping[394]

> *Like* a muddied spring, or a polluted fountain, is a righteous *man* who slips up in the presence of the wicked.

4. WICKEDNESS

a). Abominations to God[395]

> There are six things that YHWH hates; seven *that are* abominations to him:

---

[391] Proverbs 25:17; 27:14
[392] Proverbs 11:14
[393] Proverbs 20:6
[394] Proverbs 25:26
[395] Proverbs 6:16-19; 16:12; 28:9

Establishing the Kingdom

> proud eyes; a deceitful tongue; hands that shed the blood of the innocent; a heart that devises wicked schemes; feet that are quick to run to evil; a false witness who breaths lies; and someone who stirs strife between brothers.

> It is an abomination for kings to act wickedly, for a throne is established by righteousness.

> When a man turns aside from listening to the law, even his prayer is an abomination.

b). Pride[396]

> An insolent *and* proud *man*— 'Scoffer' is his name—acts with arrogant pride.

c). Selfishness[397]

> Whoever separates himself *from others* seeks *his own* desires; he shows contempt for all sound wisdom.

d). Greed[398]

> The wealth of a rich *man* is his fortified city; the ruin of the poor is their poverty.

> Eating too much honey is not good, neither is seeking honour honourable.

> *Like* Sheol and Abaddon, the eyes of a man are never satisfied.

e). Lack of Self Control[399]

> *Like* a city that has been breached, with no wall *to protect it*, is a man who is unable to restrain his spirit.

f). Plotting Evil[400]

> The man who winks his eye plans wicked things; the man who puckers his lips accomplishes evil.

> A twisted mind cannot attain good; a perverted tongue falls into evil.

---

[396] Proverbs 21:24
[397] Proverbs 18:1
[398] Proverbs 10:15; 25:27; 27:20
[399] Proverbs 25:28
[400] Proverbs 16:30; 17:20; 26:10, 23

Like an archer who wounds all, is *a man* who hires a fool or someone passing through.

Like an earthenware *pot* overlaid with the dross from silver, are burning lips and an evil heart.

g). Being Treacherous[401]

Like a mad *man* who shoots flaming and deadly arrows, is a man who deals treacherously with his neighbour and *then* says, 'I was only having a laugh.'

Men who shed blood hate the blameless; they seek the lives of the upright.

h). Bribery[402]

A bribe is an amulet in the eye of its owner; wherever he turns he succeeds.

A wicked *man* takes a bribe *hidden* in the bosom, to pervert the way of justice.

A man's gift opens wide *his way*; it leads him into the presence of great *men*.

A gift *given* in secret subdues anger; a bribe *hidden* in the bosom *eases* a mighty rage.

i). Lacking Compassion[403]

A wicked soul desires evil; his eyes show his neighbour no favours.

Whoever takes a garment off on a cold day, *or* pours vinegar on soda, *is like a man* who sings songs *to a man* with a heavy heart.

A poor man who oppresses the lowly, *is like* driving rain which destroys the crops.

j). Leading Others Astray[404]

A violent man entices his neighbour; he leads him on a way that is not good.

---

[401] Proverbs 26:18-19; 29:10
[402] Proverbs 17:8, 23; 18:16; 21:14
[403] Proverbs 21:10; 25:20; 28:3
[404] Proverbs 16:29

k). Sin and Destruction[405]

Whoever loves strife loves sin; whoever makes his doorway high seeks destruction.

l). A Wicked Ruler[406]

A king's wrath is like a lion's roar; whoever makes him angry risks his *own* life.

Like a lion that roars, and a bear that charges, is a wicked ruler over poor people.

m). An Offended Brother[407]

An offended brother is stronger than a mighty city; *such* strife is like the barred *gates* of a citadel.

n). A Ransom for the Upright[408]

A wicked *man* is the ransom for the righteous; an unfaithful man is *the ransom for the upright*.

5. RIGHTEOUSNESS VS. WICKEDNESS

a). Righteousness vs. Wickedness[409]

A godless *man* destroys his neighbour with *his* mouth, but through knowledge the righteous will escape.

A man is praised for his words of discernment, but a man is despised for his twisted mind.

A short-tempered *man* acts foolishly; a schemer is hated.

A glad heart is good for healing; a troubled spirit withers the bone.

A wicked man puts on a bold face; an upright *man* makes his way firm.

---

[405] Proverbs 17:19
[406] Proverbs 20:2; 28:15
[407] Proverbs 18:19
[408] Proverbs 21:18
[409] Proverbs 11:9; 12:8; 14:17; 17:22; 21:29; 28:28

> When the wicked rise up, men hide; when they perish, the righteous become great.

b). Accepting Commands[410]

> The wise of heart accepts commands, but the fool will be thrust away by his *own* talk.

c). Firm Foundations[411]

> A man cannot *establish* firm *foundations* through wickedness, but the root of the righteous will never be moved.

d). Having Sense[412]

> A man who lacks sense treats his neighbour with contempt, but a man of understanding remains silent.

> Good judgement wins favour, but the way of the treacherous is unchanging.

e). Plotting and Planning[413]

> The plans of the righteous are *for* justice; the counsels of the wicked are *for* deceit.

> Deceit is in the heart of those who plot evil, but those who counsel peace have joy.

> Don't those who devise evil go astray? But those who devise good find goodness and truth.

> The plans of an evil *man* are an abomination to YHWH, but pleasing words *come from* the pure.

f). Life vs. Sin[414]

> The mouth of the righteous is a wellspring of life, but the mouth of the wicked conceals violence.

> The wage of a righteous *man* is life; the income of a wicked *man* is sin.

---

[410] Proverbs 10:8
[411] Proverbs 12:3
[412] Proverbs 11:12; 13:15
[413] Proverbs 12:5, 20; 14:22; 15:26
[414] Proverbs 10:11, 16; 13:6; 14:34; 28:1

> Righteousness watches over *those whose* way is blameless, but wickedness perverts the sinner.

> Righteousness lifts up a nation, but sin is the shame of the people.

> A wicked *man* flees although no one is chasing *him*, but the righteous have the confidence of a lion.

g). Good vs. Evil[415]

> The desire of the righteous is surely *for the* good *of others*, but the hope of the wicked is *to inflict their* wrath *on others*.

> The heart of a righteous *man* considers how to answer, but the mouth of the wicked bubbles over with evil *things*.

> Crooked are the ways of a guilty man; upright are the deeds of the pure.

> Those who abandon the law praise the wicked; those who observe the law strive against them.

> When the righteous rejoice, *there is* great glory, but when the wicked rise up, men go into hiding.

> When the righteous become great, the people rejoice; when a wicked *man* has dominion, the people groan.

> An unrighteous man is an abomination to the righteous; a man whose way is righteous is an abomination to a wicked *man*.

h). Rich vs. Poor[416]

> There are some who pretend to be rich but have nothing, *while others* pretend to be poor but have great wealth.

> The ransom for a man's life is his riches, but the poor receive no threat.

> A poor *man* is hated even by his neighbour, but those who love the rich are many.

---

[415] Proverbs 11:23; 15:28; 21:8; 28:4, 12; 29:2, 27
[416] Proverbs 13:7-8; 14:20-21, 31; 16:8, 19; 19:4; 28:6

> Whoever despises his neighbour is a sinner; whoever shows favour to the poor is blessed.

> Whoever oppresses a poor *man*, finds fault with his maker, but whoever shows the needy favour, honours him.

> It is better to be righteous and have little than to have much income *and remain* unjust.

> It is better to be lowly in spirit with the poor than to share in the spoils with the proud.

> A wealthy *man* attracts many friends; a poor *man* is abandoned by his friend.

> *It is* better to be a poor *man* who walks with integrity than a *man* whose ways are twisted, *even* though he is rich.

i). *Unity vs. Disunity*[417]

> A rebellious land has many rulers, but with a discerning and knowledgeable man *order is* prolonged.

j). *Goodwill vs. Violence*[418]

> Blessings are on the head of the righteous, but the mouth of the wicked conceals violence.

> A gracious woman receives honour; but men who strike terror receive riches.

k). *Goodwill vs. Greed*[419]

> The people will curse *a man* who withholds grain, but they will bless the head of the *man* who is selling.

l). *Compassion*[420]

> Hatred stirs up discord, but love covers every transgression.

---

[417] Proverbs 28:2
[418] Proverbs 10:6; 11:16
[419] Proverbs 11:26
[420] Proverbs 10:12; 12:10, 26

> A righteous *man* knows the needs of his cattle, but the *only* compassion *that* the wicked *have* is for cruelty.

> A righteous *man* seeks out his neighbour, but the way of the wicked leads them astray.

m). Circle of Friends[421]

> A wicked *man* takes pleasure in the net of evil *men*, but the root of the righteous bears *fruit*.

> A man with *many* friends will be broken, but there is a friend who clings closer than a brother.

n). Honour vs. Dishonour[422]

> It is better to be dishonoured but with a servant, than to honour yourself and lack food.

o). The Heart[423]

> A desire fulfilled is pleasing to the soul, but to turn away from evil is detestable to fools.

> The heart knows its bitterness of spirit, and does not share its joys with a stranger.

> A heart may be in pain even in laughter, but grief follows joy.

6. ANGER AND JEALOUSY

a). Slow to Anger[424]

> A man's prudence makes him slow to anger; *it is to* his glory to pass over an offense.

b). Hot-Tempered[425]

> An angry man stirs up strife; a hot-tempered man sins abundantly.

---

[421] Proverbs 12:12; 18:24
[422] Proverbs 12:9
[423] Proverbs 13:19; 14:10, 13
[424] Proverbs 19:11
[425] Proverbs 29:22

c). Hot-Tempered vs Slow-to-Anger[426]

> A man who is hot-tempered stirs up strife, but a *man who is* slow to anger calms a dispute.

> It is better to be *a man* who is slow to anger than a mighty *man*; a man who rules his temper than *a man* who captures a city.

d). A King's Wrath[427]

> A king's rage is a messenger of death, but a wise man will pacify it.

> When a king's face is bright, *there is* life; his favour is like a cloud *which brings the* spring rain.

> A king's wrath is like a lion's roar, but his favour is like dew on the grass.

e). Jealousy[428]

> Rage *may* be fierce and anger *may flow like* a flood, but who can stand in the presence of jealousy?

7. RESPONSE TO ONE'S ENEMIES

a). The Hungry and Thirsty[429]

> If *a man* who hates you is hungry give him food to eat; if *he is* thirsty give him water to drink. For *by doing so* you will be piling up coals on his head, and YHWH will reward you.

b). A Murderer[430]

> A man burdened with the guilt of *spilling* human blood—*let him* flee to the pit, let no one offer him support.

---

[426] Proverbs 15:18; 16:32
[427] Proverbs 16:14-15; 19:12
[428] Proverbs 27:4
[429] Proverbs 25:21-22
[430] Proverbs 28:17

8. INDEBTEDNESS

a). Loans[431]

A rich *man* has dominion over the poor; *a man* who borrows *is* a servant to the man who lends.

b). Pledges for a Loan[432]

My son, if you have given a pledge for your neighbour—*if* you have shaken your hand with a stranger—*then* you have been lured *and* caught by the words of your *own* mouth. So do this, my son: deliver yourself, because you have come into your neighbour's power. *Do whatever is necessary to get out of the contract.* Go, stamp, and act boisterously to your neighbour. Do not let your eyes sleep or your eyelids slumber. Deliver yourself, like a gazelle from the hand *of the hunter*; like a bird from a trapper's hand.

If a *man* guarantees a pledge for another, he will surely suffer; he who hates clasping *hands, as a guarantor*, will be safe.

A man who lacks judgement clasps a hand *as guarantor*; he gives his pledge in the presence of his neighbour.

When a *man* gives a pledge for a stranger, take his garment; hold the pledge given for a foreigner.

When *a man* takes on a pledge for a stranger, take his garment; hold it in pledge for a foreign *woman*.

c). Interest[433]

Whoever increases his wealth by *charging* high interest *will* accumulate it for *a man* who shows favour to the poor.

9. POVERTY AND RICHES

a). Poverty and Riches[434]

Many entreat the favour of a generous *man*; all are friends to a man *who* gives.

---

[431] Proverbs 22:7
[432] Proverbs 6:1-5; 11:15; 17:18; 20:16; 27:13
[433] Proverbs 28:8
[434] Proverbs 19:6-7; 22:9; 27:7

Establishing the Kingdom

> *If* a poor man is hated by all his brothers, then how much more *do* his friends become distant to him. *Although* he pursues them *with* words, they are no longer *there*.

> Blessed is the man with a generous eye, for he gives from his food to the poor.

> A satisfied soul tramples down honey; but to a hungry soul everything bitter is sweet.

10. WAR

a). Planning[435]

> Plans are established through consultation; war is waged *after seeking* advice.

b) Promoting Peace[436]

> Casting a lot can cease strife, and divide *and* separate mighty *men*.

> Men who mock, breathe *incitement into* a city, but wise men turn away anger.

c). YHWH, the Redeemer[437]

> A horse is made ready for the day of battle, but deliverance belongs to YHWH.

11. RUNNING FROM CONFLICT

a) Taking Flight[438]

> Like a bird that takes flight from its nest, is a man who flees his home.

---

[435] Proverbs 20:18
[436] Proverbs 18:18; 29:8
[437] Proverbs 21:31
[438] Proverbs 27:8

D4. THE SAYINGS OF SOLOMON

g). The Sanctity of Marriage

1. PRINCIPLE

Marriage involved a binding commitment of one partner to the other. As a consequence, unfaithfulness in marriage closely mirrored unfaithfulness to God.

2. ADULTERY

a). The Destructive Power of Adultery[439]

> My son, take heed of my wisdom; lend your ear to my understanding. Then you may maintain discretion and your lips may guard knowledge. For the lips of an adulteress drip honey; her mouth is smoother than oil. But afterwards she is as bitter as wormwood; *as* sharp as a two-edged sword. Her feet go down to death; her steps grasp hold of Sheol. She doesn't consider the path of life; she doesn't know her paths are unstable.
>
> So now, *my* sons, listen to me; don't turn away from the words of my mouth. Keep your path far away from her; don't approach the door of her house. Otherwise, you will give your majesty to others, and your years to *those who are* cruel. Otherwise, strangers will take their fill of your wealth and *the rewards of* your labours *will go* to the house of another. At the end *of your life*, when your flesh and body are spent, you will groan. You will say, 'How I have hated correction; *how* my heart has treated reproof with contempt. I refused to listen to the voice of my teachers; I refused to turn my ear to my instructors. I am near total ruin, in the midst of the congregation and assembly.'
>
> Drink water from your *own* well; *drink* water flowing from your *own* well. Why scatter your springs outside? *Why spread* your streams of water in open places? Let them be for you, alone; not for strangers with you. May your fountain be blessed; be glad with the wife of your youth. *She is* a loving hind and a graceful doe. *So* may her breasts satisfy you at all times; may you continually be captivated with her love. Why then, my son, would you go astray with a stranger? *Why would* you embrace the bosom of a foreigner? For the ways of

---

[439] Proverbs 5:1-23

> a man are before YHWH's eyes; YHWH weighs up all his paths. A wicked man will be entrapped by his *own* wickedness; he will be held fast by the cords of his *own* sin. He will die for refusing correction; he will be led astray by the greatness of his folly.

b). *A Neighbour's Wife*[440]

> My son, guard your father's command; do not abandon your mother's instruction. Bind them continually on your heart; tie them around your neck. They will guide you as you walk; they will watch over you when you lie down; they will talk to you when you awake. For the commands are a lamp and the teaching is a light; the reproofs of correction are a way of life. *They will* keep you from an evil woman; from the smooth tongue of a stranger.
>
> Do not *let* your heart lust after her beauty; do not let her eyelashes captivate you. For a prostitute's fee *may only be the equivalent* of a loaf of bread, but *another* man's wife hunts for precious life. Can a man carry embers in his bosom without his clothes being burned? Can a man walk on coals without his feet being scorched? So is the one who goes into his neighbour's wife; no one who touches her will remain unpunished.
>
> A thief is not despised if he steals to satisfy his hunger. *But* if he is caught he must pay back seven times; he must give all the wealth of his house. A man who commits adultery with a woman lacks common sense; a man who does so ruins himself. He will be beaten and disgraced; his infamy will never be wiped away. For a husband's fury *will be fuelled by* jealousy; he will show no pity on the day of vengeance. He will not take any compensation; he will refuse *to accept* a bribe, no matter how large.

3. PROSTITUTION

a). *The Dangers*[441]

> The mouth of a *female* stranger is a deep pit; *a man* who has provoked YHWH to wrath will fall into it.

b). *The Art of Seduction*[442]

> My son, guard my words; treasure my commands within you. Observe my commands and live; *make* my instruction like the apple of your eye. Bind

---

[440] Proverbs 6:20-35
[441] Proverbs 22:14
[442] Proverbs 7:1-27

them on your fingers; write them on the tablet of your heart. Say to wisdom, 'You are my sister.' Call to understanding, 'You are my kinsman.' They will keep you from a wife who is unfaithful; from a foreigner whose words are smooth.

For I have looked out of the window of my house through the lattice. I have watched the open-minded, and I have noticed among the young men, a youth lacking common sense. He went down the street, *to* near the corner *where an immoral woman lived*; he went the way to her house. It was twilight, early in the evening, as night approached and darkness *gathered*. When behold, a woman *came out* to meet him; she was wearing the clothes of a prostitute and she was sly of heart.

She was loud and rebellious; her feet never stayed *still* at home. *She was* now in the street, now in the square; *she* lay in wait at every corner. So she grabbed him and kissed him, and without blushing she said to him, '*I have* Fellowship Offerings *at home* with me; I fulfilled my vows today. I came out to meet you for this reason; I have looked diligently for you and found you. I have covered my couch with a coverlet, with colourful linens from Egypt. I have perfumed my couch with myrrh, aloes, and cinnamon. Come, let us drink our fill of love until morning; let us enjoy ourselves with love. For my husband is not in his home; he has gone on a distant journey. He has taken a pouch of silver in his hand; he will return to his home at *the next* full moon.' So she seduced him with her multitude of reasons; she compelled him with her smooth lips.

Then immediately he followed after her; he went like an ox to the slaughter, as in chains *used* to discipline a fool. He did not know that this *would cost* him his life, *like* an arrow piercing his liver *or* a bird flying into a trap.

So now, *my* sons, listen to me; lend your ears to the words of my mouth. Don't let your heart be deviated to her ways; do not err in her paths. For she has wounded men *and* laid *them* low; numerous are all she has slain. Her house is the highway to Sheol; it descends to the chambers of death.

D4. THE SAYINGS OF SOLOMON

h). Respect for Other People's Property

1. PRINCIPLE

In a society where the ownership of property was both limited and necessary for survival, there was a need to respect other people's property. People had a right to possess the means of their livelihood. What was produced could then be used for the common good.

2. THEFT

a). A Poor Man's Field[443]

The untilled *field* of a poor man *produces* an abundance of food, but it is snatched away by injustice.

b). Honest and Dishonest Scales[444]

Dishonest scales are an abomination to YHWH, but correct weights are his delight.

Honest scales and balances are from YHWH; all the stones in the bag are his concern.

Replacing measures—one stone for another, or one ephah for another—is indeed an abomination to YHWH.

Replacing one weighing stone for *another* is an abomination to YHWH; dishonest scales are not good.

c). Dishonesty[445]

Wealth gained by dishonesty dwindles away, but whoever gathers by *their own* hand makes it grow.

'*It is* bad. *It is* bad,' says the buyer, but when he leaves he boasts *of the quality*.

---

[443] Proverbs 13:23
[444] Proverbs 11:1; 16:11; 20:10, 23
[445] Proverbs 13:11; 20:14, 17; 21:6

> Bread obtained by deceit *may be* sweet to a man, but after *he has eaten*, his mouth will be full of gravel.

> Acquiring treasures with a lying tongue is *like* driving steam and seeking death.

d). False Promises[446]

> *Like* clouds and wind with no rain is a man who boasts deceptively of a gift.

---

[446] Proverbs 25:14

D4. THE SAYINGS OF SOLOMON

i). Justice

1. PRINCIPLE

For a community to remain healthy, its members needed to exude integrity, honesty, and fairness. As a consequence, laws needed to be made, any breaches investigated, and the processes of law upheld.

2. JUSTICE FOR ALL

a). *Justice for All*[447]

A man who shows favour to the poor lends to YHWH; he will repay him for his deed.

It is not good to regard *one person over another*, for a man will do wrong *even* for a morsel of bread.

b). *Being Found Out*[448]

Whoever walks in integrity walks securely, but whoever *walks* a twisted path will be found out.

c). *Removing the Dross*[449]

Remove the dross from silver, and the silversmith can produce a utensil.

3. YHWH AND JUSTICE

a). *YHWH Brings Light*[450]

YHWH brings light to the eyes of both a poor *man* and an oppressor.

---

[447] Proverbs 19:17; 28:21
[448] Proverbs 10:9
[449] Proverbs 25:4
[450] Proverbs 29:13

b). Nothing Hidden from YHWH[451]

> *If* Sheol and Abaddon *lie open* before YHWH, how much more the hearts of the sons of man.

> YHWH has made everything to answer *for itself*, even the wicked for the day of trouble.

c). The Testing of Hearts[452]

> All a man's ways are pure in his *own* eyes, but YHWH is the one who measures motives.

> A crucible is for silver and a furnace is for gold, but the testing of hearts is for YHWH.

> Every way of a man is right in his *own* eyes; but YHWH weighs hearts.

d). Justice Belongs to YHWH[453]

> Do not say, 'I will repay evil.' Wait on YHWH, and he will deliver you.

> Many seek the presence of a ruler, but it is from YHWH that a man *receives* justice.

e). The Fear of YHWH[454]

> Blessed is a man who continually fears YHWH, but evil falls on *a man* who hardens his heart.

f). The Judgements of YHWH[455]

> YHWH will not let the righteous go hungry, but he will frustrate the desires of the wicked.

> When a storm wind passes through, the wicked will be no more, but the righteous *will remain standing on* the everlasting foundation.

> The way of YHWH is a stronghold for the upright, but destruction for those who do evil.

---

[451] Proverbs 15:11; 16:4
[452] Proverbs 16:2; 17:3; 21:2
[453] Proverbs 20:22; 29:26
[454] Proverbs 28:14
[455] Proverbs 10:3, 25, 29; 15:25, 29; 21:12; 22:12

> YHWH tears down the houses of proud men, but he takes his stand on the boundary of a widow.

> YHWH *remains* distant from the wicked, but he hears the prayer of the righteous.

> The Righteous One is prudent towards the house of the wicked, but turns the wicked to *their* ruin.

> YHWH's eyes guard the knowledgeable, but frustrate the words of the unfaithful.

4. THE RIGHTEOUS

a). Beware of Wicked Men[456]

> A very angry *man* will incur a fine; if you deliver *him* you will surely have to do it again.

> *Like* a broken tooth or a slipping foot, is confidence in a treacherous *man* on a day of trouble.

b). The Fear of Wicked Men[457]

> A trap is set through the fear of *another* man, but *a man* who trusts in YHWH will be raised on high.

c). Driving Out the Wicked[458]

> Overthrow the wicked and they are no more, but the house of the righteous will remain standing.

> Drive out a scoffer and strife will go *too*; quarrelling and dishonour will cease.

> Remove a wicked *man* from the king's presence, and his throne will be established in righteousness.

---

[456] Proverbs 19:19; 25:19
[457] Proverbs 29:25
[458] Proverbs 12:7; 22:10; 25:5

d). Joy for the Righteous[459]

> A city rejoices when it goes well with the righteous; there are joyful cries when the wicked perish.

e). The Righteous Acknowledged[460]

> Evil *men* will bow in the presence of the good; wicked *men will bow down* at the gates of the righteous.

5. THE WICKED

a). Worthless Men[461]

> A worthless man *is* a wicked man; he goes about speaking wicked *things*. He winks his eyes; he shuffles his feet; he points with his fingers. In his wicked heart he plots evil; he continually stirs up strife. For this reason, a calamity will suddenly come upon him; he will be shattered, unable to be restored.

> An evil man seeks only rebellion, so a cruel messenger will be sent against him.

> A man who strays from the path of prudence rests in the assembly of the dead.

b). Proud Men[462]

> All who are proud of heart are an abomination to YHWH; be sure they will not get clean *away*.

> A proud man's heart will be crushed; before honour *comes* humility.

c). Stiff-necked Men[463]

> A man often rebuked is stiff-necked; he will be shattered suddenly, beyond cure.

---

[459] Proverbs 11:10
[460] Proverbs 14:19
[461] Proverbs 6:12-15; 17:11; 21:16
[462] Proverbs 16:5; 18:12
[463] Proverbs 29:1

d). Payment for Evil[464]

> When a wicked man dies, *his* hope perishes; the hope of power dies.

> Whoever mocks the poor rebukes his maker; whoever rejoices at calamity will not go unpunished.

> Evil will not leave the house of anyone who repays evil for good.

> When a wicked man comes, contempt comes too; with dishonour comes disgrace.

> The wicked will be dragged away by their *own* violence, for they refuse to do *what is* just.

> *A man* who oppresses the poor to make more for himself—or *a man* who gives to the rich—will surely *come* to poverty.

> An evil-eyed man terrifies *others* to gain wealth, but does not know that poverty will come upon him.

> A man who *is* slippery with his neighbour spreads out a net for his *own* feet.

6. THE RIGHTEOUS VS. THE WICKED

a). Righteousness vs. Wickedness[465]

> The righteousness of the upright will keep their way straight, but the wicked will fall by their *own* wickedness.

> Evil pursues sinners, but the righteous will be rewarded with good *things*.

> Whoever walks in blamelessness will be delivered; whoever *walks along* a twisted path will suddenly fall.

> An evil man is baited by his *own* sin, but a righteous *man* gives a ringing cry and rejoices.

---

[464] Proverbs 11:7; 17:5, 13; 18:3; 21:7; 22:16; 28:22; 29:5
[465] Proverbs 11:5; 13:21; 28:18; 29:6-7

A righteous *man* knows about justice for the poor, *but* a wicked *man* does not discern *such* knowledge.

b). Good vs. Evil[466]

A *man* who delights in seeking good will find goodwill, but if a *man* seeks evil, evil will come to him.

A prudent man sees evil and hides himself; the simple continue on and pay the penalty.

A shrewd *man* sees evil *and* hides himself; those who are simple continue on and pay the penalty.

Evil men cannot discern justice; but those who seek YHWH can discern all *things*.

c). Integrity vs. Crookedness[467]

The upright are guided by their integrity, but the treacherous are ruined by their crookedness.

d). Light and Hope[468]

The hope of the righteous is joy, but the hope of the wicked perishes.

The light of the righteous rejoices, but the lamp of the wicked goes out.

e). Fears and Desires[469]

What a wicked man fears will come upon him; what the righteous desire will be given *them*.

The upright will be delivered by their righteousness, but the treacherous will be captured by their *own* desires.

A righteous *man* eats to satisfy his appetite, while the belly of the wicked remains empty.

---

[466] Proverbs 11:27; 22:3; 27:12; 28:5
[467] Proverbs 11:3
[468] Proverbs 10:28; 13:9
[469] Proverbs 10:24; 11:6; 13:25; 14:14

> Whoever turns his heart away will get his fill of his *own* ways, but a good man *will be rewarded* for his *deeds*.

f). Wealth[470]

> *Being* wealthy will have no benefit on the day of wrath, but *being* righteous will deliver from death.

g). Righteousness vs. Greed[471]

> A *man* who trusts in his riches will fall, but like a leaf *in spring* the righteous will flourish.

> A man of faith *will receive* many blessings, but *a man* who is in a hurry to get rich will not go unpunished.

> A greedy man stirs up strife, but *a man* who trusts in YHWH will grow fat.

h). Generosity and Poverty[472]

> The *man* who scatters will gain *even* more, but the *man* who holds back what is due will surely *end* in poverty.

> *A man* who gives to the poor will lack nothing; *a man* who shuts his eyes will be cursed many *times*.

i). Scheming[473]

> Whoever winks his eye causes trouble, but the fool will be thrust away by his *own* talk.

> A good *man* promotes favour from YHWH, but a man who schemes he will condemn.

> The words of the wicked are to lie in wait for blood, but the mouth of the upright will deliver their *intended victims*.

---

[470] Proverbs 11:4
[471] Proverbs 11:28; 28:20, 25
[472] Proverbs 11:24; 28:27
[473] Proverbs 10:10; 12:2, 6

j). Correction and Advice[474]

Whoever despises advice will be bound by it; whoever fears the command will be rewarded.

Severe punishment awaits *a man* who leaves the path; *a man* who hates rebuke will die.

k). Inheritance[475]

A good *man* leaves an inheritance for his sons' sons, but the wealth of a sinner is stored up for the righteous.

l). Leading Others Astray[476]

Whoever leads the upright astray along an evil path will fall into his own pit, but the blameless will inherit good *things*.

m). Hiding One's Sins[477]

A man who covers up his sins will not prosper, but *a man* who confesses and abandons *them* will be given mercy.

n). Pride[478]

A man's pride will bring him low, but *a man* who is lowly in spirit will obtain honour.

7. THE REWARDS OF THE RIGHTEOUS AND THE WICKED

a). A Man's Reward[479]

A kind man does himself good, but a cruel *man* stirs up trouble for himself.

A wicked *man* receives a wage *which is* deceptive, but those who sow rightness will receive a true wage.

You can be sure that an evil *man* will not get clean *away*, but the offspring of the righteous will slip away.

---

[474] Proverbs 13:13; 15:10
[475] Proverbs 13:22
[476] Proverbs 28:10
[477] Proverbs 28:13
[478] Proverbs 29:23
[479] Proverbs 11:17-18, 21, 31

> If a righteous *man* is rewarded on earth, how much more the wicked and the sinner.

b). Trouble[480]

> A righteous *man* will never be moved, but the wicked will not dwell in the land.

> A righteous *man* is drawn away from trouble; it comes upon a wicked *man* instead.

> The righteous will not be faced with sorrow, but the wicked will be filled with misery.

> *There is* much wealth in the house of a righteous *man*, but trouble is the income of a wicked *man*.

> A *man* who gains through violence troubles his *own* house, but a man who hates bribes will live.

c). Length of Days[481]

> The fear of YHWH adds days *to life*, but the years of the wicked will be short.

> A ruler who practices extortion lacks understanding; *a man* who hates profit gained through violence will lengthen *his* days.

d). Life and Death[482]

> Treasures gained by wickedness are of no *eternal* benefit, but being righteous will snatch you away from death.

> Whoever is truly righteous *will gain* life, but whoever pursues evil *will go* to his *own* death.

> The house of the wicked will be destroyed, but the tent of the upright will flourish.

---

[480] Proverbs 10:30; 11:8; 12:21; 15:6, 27
[481] Proverbs 10:27; 28:16
[482] Proverbs 10:2; 11:19; 14:11, 32

> A wicked *man* is brought down by his *own* evil doing, but a righteous *man* seeks refuge *even* at his *own* death.

e). The Overthrow of the Wicked[483]

> When the number of wicked *men* increases, *so* sin increases, but the righteous will watch their overthrow.

f). Being Remembered vs. Being Forgotten[484]

> The remembrance of the righteous *will be* a blessing, but the name of the wicked will rot.

8. THE MOUTH

a). Lying Lips[485]

> The mouth of a righteous *man* bears the fruit of wisdom, but a wicked tongue will be cut out.

b). False Witnesses[486]

> Whoever breathes truthfulness declares what is right, but a false witness *utters* deceit.

> A truthful witness does not lie, but a false witness breathes lies.

> A truthful witness is one who saves lives, but a false *witness* breaths deceit.

> A false witness will not get clean *away*; whoever breathes lies will not slip away *unpunished*.

> A false witness will not get clean away; a man who breathes lies will perish.

> A false witness will perish, but a man who listens will speak forever.

> *Like* a club, a sword, and a sharp *arrow* is a man who responds *as a* false witness against his neighbour.

---

[483] Proverbs 29:16
[484] Proverbs 10:7
[485] Proverbs 10:31
[486] Proverbs 12:17; 14:5, 25; 19:5, 9; 21:28; 25:18

c). Loose Talk[487]

> Whoever watches his mouth, preserves his life; whoever opens wide his lips, *goes to* his ruin.

d). YHWH's Response to the Tongue[488]

> The plans of the mind belong to man, but the response to the tongue belongs to YHWH.

9. THE COURT

a). Resolving Disputes outside Court[489]

> Argue your dispute with your neighbour; do not expose another *man's* secret. Or whoever hears may rebuke you, and the whispering about you will never go away.

b). Court Cases[490]

> The first *man* to state his case *will seem* right, until his neighbour comes and examines him.

> A poor *man* presents his humble petition, but a rich *man* responds harshly.

> Don't be in a rush to bring to court what your eyes have seen, for what will you do in the end when your neighbour shames you?

c). Witnesses[491]

> A worthless witness mocks justice; the mouths of the wicked swallow wickedness.

> A hateful *man* disguises himself with his lips, but he harbours a treacherous heart. Although he may sound gracious, do not believe him, for he has seven abominations in his heart. His hatred may be covered by guile, *but* his wickedness will be uncovered in the assembly.

> Whoever takes a share with a thief hates his *own* life; *when made to testify*, he hears the oath but says nothing.

---

[487] Proverbs 13:3
[488] Proverbs 16:1
[489] Proverbs 25:9-10
[490] Proverbs 18:17, 23; 25:7b-8
[491] Proverbs 19:28; 26:24-26; 29:24

10. JUSTICE

a). Just Verdicts[492]

> A divine verdict is on the king's lips; his mouth should not judge unfairly.

> A *man* who shuts his ear to the outcry of the poor, will surely also cry out—but he will not be answered.

> To do justice is joy to the righteous but ruin to trouble makers.

> *Unlike* a sparrow that flutters or a swallow which dives, a curse without reason comes *to nought*.

b). Perverted Verdicts[493]

> It is not good to fine a just man, or to strike a noble *man* for being upright.

> It is not good to elevate the head of a wicked *man*; to bend justice on the righteous.

c). Abominations to YHWH[494]

> Someone who justifies a wicked man, and someone who condemns an innocent man, are both alike—an abomination to YHWH.

d). Punishments[495]

> Punishments have been prepared for mockers; blows *await* the backs of fools.

> When a mocker is fined, a simple *man can* become wise; when a wise man is prudent, he gains knowledge.

> A man who sows injustice will reap trouble; the rod *he uses in his* arrogance will be spent.

> Whoever digs a pit will fall into it; whoever rolls away a stone will *have the stone* rolled back on him.

---

[492] Proverbs 16:10; 21:13, 15; 26:2
[493] Proverbs 17:26; 18:5
[494] Proverbs 17:15
[495] Proverbs 19:29; 21:11; 22:8; 26:27

e). A King's Verdict[496]

A king who sits on his judgement seat scatters all evil with his eyes.

A wise king scatters the wicked; he rolls the threshing wheel over them.

Goodness and truth guard a king; he sustains his throne through goodness.

A king who judges the poor faithfully—his throne will be established forever.

f). Responses to Verdicts[497]

Like golden apples in silver settings is a word spoken at *the right* time. *Like* a gold ring, or a gold ornament, is a wise *man's* judgement to a listening ear.

Whoever judges a man who repents, will find more favour than a man with a smooth tongue.

When a wise man *seeks* justice from a foolish man, *the fool will* rant and laugh, but there will be no resolution.

g). Bribery[498]

Through the justice *of* a king a land can take its stand, but a man who takes 'contributions' tears it down.

---

[496] Proverbs 20:8, 26, 28; 29:14
[497] Proverbs 25:11-12; 28:23; 29:9
[498] Proverbs 29:4

D4. THE SAYINGS OF SOLOMON

j). Right Thinking

1. PRINCIPLE

For the covenant community to work, they needed to focus their lives on two aspects: their relationship with YHWH and their relationship with each other. As a consequewnce, their neighbour was to be loved as a fellow member of the family of God.

In addition to all of the other topics, 'right thinking' was to be applied to every aspect of their lives.

2. HARD WORK

a). The Labourer's Appetite[499]

A labourer's appetite urges him; indeed his mouth presses him on.

When the hay has been harvested, new growth appears and mountain grass is gathered in. Lambs *will provide wool* for your clothing; male goats *will bring* the price of a field. There will be enough goat's milk for food for you, your house, and to sustain your housemaids.

b). False Economy[500]

Without oxen the feeding trough is empty, but much produce *comes* with the strength of an ox.

3. LAZINESS

a). The Sluggard[501]

Go to an ant, sluggard. See its ways and become wise. It has no chief, official, or ruler. *Yet* it organises its food in the summer; it gathers its food at the harvest. How long will you *remain* lying down, sluggard? When will you rise from your sleep? 'A little sleep, a little slumber, a little folding of hands before

---

[499] Proverbs 16:26; 27:25-27
[500] Proverbs 14:4
[501] Proverbs 6:6-11; 26:16

> lying down.' Destitution will come upon you, as it does a vagrant; what you have *will be taken*, as if *by* an armed robber.

> A sluggard is wiser in his *own* eyes than seven *men* who can respond judiciously.

b). Work[502]

> As vinegar is to the teeth and smoke to the eyes, so is the sluggard to those who send him.

> *A man* who is slack in his work, is a brother to *a man who* loves to destroy.

> A sluggard does not plough after the harvest, so the *next* harvest *time* he looks *for the crop*, but *finds* nothing.

c). Meal Times[503]

> The sluggard conceals his hand in the dish; he doesn't even return it to his mouth.

> A sluggard conceals his hand in the dish; he is too weary to return it to his mouth.

d). Sleep[504]

> Laziness *makes a man* fall into a deep sleep; a slack man suffers hunger.

> As a door swings on its hinge, so a sluggard *turns* on his bed.

e). Security[505]

> The sluggard says, '*There's* a lion outside. I will be slain in the middle of the street.'

> A sluggard says, '*There's* a lion on the road; *there's* a lion in the streets.'

---

[502] Proverbs 10:26; 18:9; 20:4
[503] Proverbs 19:24; 26:15
[504] Proverbs 19:15; 26:14
[505] Proverbs 22:13; 26:13

4. HARD WORK VS. LAZINESS

a). Poverty[506]

Slack hands make a *man* poor, but diligent hands make *a man* rich.

There is profit in every *kind of* labour, but words from the lips only *lead to* poverty.

If you love sleep you will inherit poverty; open your eyes and you will have an abundance of food.

The thoughts of the diligent are surely *focussed* on abundance, but all who are hasty surely *come* to poverty.

b). Hunger[507]

Whoever works his land will have plenty of food, but whoever chases worthless pursuits lacks sense.

A lax *man* cannot roast *even* wild game; but a diligent man *will roast an animal from* his *own* precious possessions.

The appetite of a sluggard craves and *gets* nothing, but the appetite of the diligent is to grow fat.

c). Chasing Empty Pursuits[508]

A man who works his land will have *his* fill of food; *a man* who chases empty *pursuits* will have *his* fill of poverty.

d). Forced Labour[509]

Diligent hands will have dominion, but slack *hands* will result in forced labour.

e). Obstacles[510]

The way of a sluggard is like *moving through* a hedge of briars, but the path of the upright is *like* a raised *highway*.

---

[506] Proverbs 10:4; 14:23; 20:13; 21:5
[507] Proverbs 12:11, 27; 13:4
[508] Proverbs 28:19
[509] Proverbs 12:24
[510] Proverbs 15:19

f). Desires[511]

> The desires of the sluggard will be his death, because his hands refuse to do *anything*. All day long he craves and craves, while a righteous *man* gives and does not hold back.

5. THE POSITIVE USE OF THE TONGUE

a). The Fruit of the Mouth[512]

> By the fruit of his lips a man is satisfied with good *things*; a man is rewarded by the work of his *own* hands.

> A man finds joy in an appropriate response; a timely word is agreeable.

> Words from a man's mouth *are like* deep waters; the wellspring of wisdom *is like* a bubbling brook.

> A man's stomach will be satisfied with the fruit of a mouth; he will be satisfied with the produce of his lips.

> Life and death are in the tongue's power; those who love it will eat its fruit.

> Advice in a man's mind is *like* deep water; *only* a man of understanding can draw it out.

> There is gold and an abundance of rubies, but knowledgeable lips are a *far more* precious thing.

> A *man* who loves a pure heart, *and whose* speeches are gracious, will have a king for a friend.

b). Persuading a Ruler[513]

> Through *exercising* patience a ruler can be persuaded; *even* a gentle tongue can break a bone.

---

[511] Proverbs 21:25-26
[512] Proverbs 12:14; 15:23; 18:4, 20-21; 20:5, 15: 22:11
[513] Proverbs 25:15

c). Praise[514]

A crucible is for silver and a furnace is for gold, but a man *is known* by the praise he is granted.

d). Bringing Hope[515]

A man is bowed down by an anxious heart, but a good word brings it joy.

Pleasant words are *like* a honeycomb—sweet to the soul and healing to the bones.

Like cool water to a weary soul is good news from a distant land.

e). Restraint[516]

Whoever withholds his words is a knowledgeable *man*; whoever is cool of spirit is a *man* of understanding.

Whoever guards his mouth and tongue preserves his life from trouble.

6. THE NEGATIVE USE OF THE TONGUE

a). Listening to Lies[517]

If a ruler inclines his ears to lies, all of his ministers will become wicked.

b). Indignant Faces[518]

The north wind brings rain; a sly tongue *brings* indignant faces.

c). Digging Up Evil[519]

A worthless man digs up evil; it is like a burning fire on his lips.

A perverse man projects strife; a whisperer divides close friends.

The words of a whisperer are like choice morsels; they go down into the chambers of the body.

---

[514] Proverbs 27:21
[515] Proverbs 12:25; 16:24; 25:25
[516] Proverbs 17:27; 21:23
[517] Proverbs 29:12
[518] Proverbs 25:23
[519] Proverbs 16:27-28; 18:8; 26:17, 22

> Like *a man* who takes a passing dog by its ears, is *a man* who meddles in a dispute *that is* not his own.

> The words of a whisperer are swallowed greedily as they descend to the chambers of the body.

d). Lying Lips[520]

> Whoever has lying lips conceals hatred; whoever comes out with an evil report is a fool.

e). Responses to Sin[521]

> A man who covers over *another's* sin seeks love; a man who repeats a matter divides close friends.

f). Quick to Speak[522]

> *When* you see a man who is hasty to speak, there is more hope for a fool than for him.

7. POSITIVE VS. NEGATIVE USE OF THE TONGUE

a). General Principles[523]

> Wisdom is found on the lips of the discerning, but is a rod for the back for those who lack understanding.

> A shrewd man conceals *his* knowledge, but the hearts of fools proclaim *their* folly.

> A man eats good *things* because of the fruit of his mouth, but the appetite of the unfaithful is for violence.

> A wicked messenger brings calamity, but a faithful envoy *brings* healing.

> The tongue of the wise makes knowledge pleasing, but the mouth of fools bubbles up with foolishness.

---

[520] Proverbs 10:18
[521] Proverbs 17:9
[522] Proverbs 29:20
[523] Proverbs 10:13; 12:23; 13:2, 17; 15:2, 4; 18:13

A healing tongue is a tree of life, but a crooked tongue crushes the spirit.

A man who answers before he hears, is both foolish and shameful.

b). Hostility[524]

In the mouth of a fool is a rod of pride, but the lips of the wise will protect them.

A delicate response turns back wrath, but a hurtful word raises anger.

c). Loose Tongues[525]

When there are many words, sin is not lacking; he who refrains from speaking is wise.

The tongue of a righteous *man is like* choice silver; the heart of the wicked *is worth* little.

The lips of the righteous are a pasture to many, but fools die for lack of understanding.

A city is exalted by the blessing of the upright, but is torn down by the mouth of the wicked.

An evil *man* is lured by the sinfulness of his *own* lips, but a righteous *man* escapes such trouble.

Whoever speaks thoughtlessly stabs like a sword, but the tongues of the wise *bring* healing.

d). Lying Lips[526]

The lips of a righteous *man* know what is good, but the mouth of the wicked *only speaks what* is perverse.

Truthful lips endure forever, but a lying tongue lasts only a moment.

---

[524] Proverbs 14:3; 15:1
[525] Proverbs 10:19-21; 11:11; 12:13, 18
[526] Proverbs 10:32; 12:19, 22; 13:5; 17:4, 7; 19:22; 26:28

Lying lips are an abomination to YHWH, but he looks with favour on those who do right.

A righteous *man* hates deceptive words, but a wicked *man* stinks and acts shamefully.

An evil *man* inclines his ears to wicked lips; a liar gives ear to a destructive tongue.

An eloquent speech is not fitting for a fool, any more than lying lips for a noble*man*.

What is desired of a man is his goodness; it is better to be poor than a man who lies.

A lying tongue hates those it oppresses; a smooth mouth causes stumbling.

e). Slander[527]

A slanderer reveals confidences, but someone who is trustworthy keeps matters hidden.

A man who goes about as a slanderer uncovers *secret* counsel, so have nothing to do with a chatterer.

f). Being Argumentative[528]

As charcoal is to embers, and wood is to fire, so is an argumentative man to the kindling of disputes.

8. OTHER MATTERS

a). Joy[529]

Bright eyes bring joy to the heart; a good report puts fat on the bones.

---

[527] Proverbs 11:13; 20:19
[528] Proverbs 26:21
[529] Proverbs 15:30

b). Seeking Pleasure[530]

> Whoever loves pleasure is a poor man; whoever loves wine and oil will never be rich.

c). Strong Drink[531]

> Wine is a mocker, strong drink a brawler; everyone who is led astray by them is unwise.

d). Jealousy[532]

> A healthy heart is life to the body, but jealousy is decay to the bones.

e). Pride[533]

> Pride *comes* before a crash; a spirit of arrogance before a stumble.

f). Greed[534]

> *If* you find honey, eat *only* what you need; do not eat your fill or you will vomit it up.

g). Desires[535]

> Drawn-out hope makes the heart sick, but a desire fulfilled is the tree of life.

> *When* the heart is full of joy, the face is glad; but when the heart aches, the spirit is crushed.

> Every day is bad for the afflicted, but a cheerful heart *leads to a* continual feast.

h). A Troubled Spirit[536]

> A man's spirit can endure his sickness, but who can bear a troubled spirit?

i). Planning[537]

> Plans are frustrated for lack of counsel, but *plans* succeed with many advisors.

---

[530] Proverbs 21:17
[531] Proverbs 20:1
[532] Proverbs 14:30
[533] Proverbs 16:18
[534] Proverbs 25:16
[535] Proverbs 13:12; 15:13, 15
[536] Proverbs 18:14
[537] Proverbs 15:22

j). Boasting[538]

Do not boast about tomorrow, for you do not know what the day will bring.

Let another *man* praise you, not your *own* mouth; a stranger, not your *own* lips.

A rich man is wise in his *own* eyes, but a poor discerning *man* sees through him.

9. A KING

a). A King's Glory[539]

A king's glory is in an abundant people; declining numbers are a prince's ruin.

Like a watercourse, a king's heart is in YHWH's hand; he bends it where he delights.

b). A King's Favour[540]

A king favours a wise servant, but his wrath falls on whoever acts shamefully.

Do not honour yourself in the presence of a king; do not take your stand where great *men* stand. For it is better *for him* to say to you, 'Come up here,' than for you to be made low in the presence of a noble *man*.

c). The Mind of a King[541]

It is God's honour to conceal a matter; *it is* a king's honour to search a matter out.

From the highest heavens to the depths of the earth, so the minds of kings are unsearchable.

---

[538] Proverbs 27:1-2; 28:11
[539] Proverbs 14:28; 21:1
[540] Proverbs 14:35; 25:6-7a
[541] Proverbs 25:2-3

D5. OTHER SAYINGS OF THE WISE

1. THE THIRTY SAYINGS

a). Advice for a Messenger[542]

Unlike the three collections of Solomon, no author is attributed to the following sayings. However, their style, with the use of the 'thirty sayings' motif, is not dissimilar to that used in Egypt around the time of Solomon.

The context of the sayings suggests that they constitute advice given by a father to a son, who was to act as a messenger or ambassador on behalf of the leaders of a nation. As a consequence, they may be sayings of Solomon to one of his sons, or they could simply be advice from a 'wise' man, whose identity is unknown.

	I make *my words* known to you, even you, today, *so let* your confidence be in YHWH. I am writing you thirty *sayings*, counsels of knowledge, *so that* you may know the truth. *They are* words *you can* rely *on as a messenger*, to return faithfully to those who send you.
	The Pursuit of Wisdom
1	Incline your ear; hear the words of the wise; set your mind on my knowledge. For it will be delightful if you keep them within your belly, if they are already on your lips.
	Robbing the Poor
2	Do not rob a poor *man* because he is poor; do not crush the afflicted at the gate. For YHWH will fight for their cause; he will rob those who rob them of life.
	Mixing with the Hot-tempered
3	Do not associate with an angry man; do not go along with a hot-tempered man. Otherwise you will learn his ways, and set a trap for your soul.
	Guarantor for a Loan
4	Do not be a man who clasps hands to pledge *a security for a* loan. Should you be unable to pay, why should he take your couch (*bed*) from under you?
	Theft of Property
5	Do not move an ancient boundary *stone* that your fathers set.
	Skilled Labourers
6	Do you see a man who is skilled in his work? He will take his stand in

---

[542] Proverbs 22:17-24:22

	the presence of kings; he will not take his stand before men of low *ranking*.
7	*Behaving in the Presence of a Ruler* When you sit down to eat with a ruler, carefully observe what is *set* before you. If you are a man with *a large* appetite, put a knife to your throat. Do not be inclined *to eat* his delicacies, for they are deceptive food.
8	*The Pursuit of Wealth* Do not weary yourself out *in order* to become rich; use your understanding to stop *working*. Flit your eyes on riches and they are gone. For, indeed, wealth makes itself wings; it flies off into the heavens like an eagle.
9	*An Unwilling Host* Do not eat the food of an evil-eyed *man*; do not desire his delicacies. For *it is* as if he calculates *the cost* within himself; he says to you, 'Eat! Drink,' but his heart is not with you. You will spew out the morsel you have eaten; your good words will be wasted.
10	*Talking to Fools* Do not speak in the ears of a fool, for he will despise your words of wisdom.
11	*Theft of Property* Do not move an ancient boundary *stone*; do not go in the fields of the fatherless. For their redeemer is mighty; he will fight their cause against you.
12	*The Pursuit of Knowledge* Apply your mind to instruction; your ear to words of knowledge.
13	*Discipline in the Home* Do not hold back from disciplining a youth; if you strike him with a rod, he will not die. *If* you personally strike him with a rod, you will snatch his soul away from Sheol.
14	*The Pursuit of Wisdom* My son, if you are wise of heart, my own heart will rejoice too: my innermost parts will be lifted up when your lips speak with equity.
15	*Fearing YHWH* Do not let your heart be jealous of sinners, rather fear YHWH at all times. For there is a future *for you*, and your hope will not be cut down.
16	*Drunkards and Gluttons* Listen, my son. Be wise and direct your heart along the straight path. Do not mix with those who drink large quantities of wine, or who make light of *eating* meat. For the big drinkers and the gluttons will take possession of poverty; drowsiness will clothe *them* in rags.

17	*Family Values*	
	Listen to your father who gave you life; do not despise your mother when she is old. Acquire truth; do not sell *it. Acquire* wisdom, discipline, and understanding. A righteous *man's* father will rejoice exceedingly; *a man* who gives life to a wise *man* will be glad in him. May your father and mother be glad; may she who gave birth to you rejoice.	
18	*Prostitutes*	
	My son, give me your heart; let your eyes be pleased with my ways. For a harlot is a deep pit; a foreign woman is a narrow well. Like a robber she lies in wait; she adds to the unfaithful among men.	
19	*Avoiding Strong Drink*	
	Who laments? Who groans? Who *faces* strife? Who has complaints? Who has been wounded without provocation? Whose eyes are dull? Those who remain behind *drinking* wine; those who go in search of mixed wine. Do not look at wine when it is red, when it is put in the cup, and when it goes down smoothly. *When* it is finished it bites like a serpent; it injects *venom* like a viper. *Then* your eyes will see strange *things*; your inner man will speak wicked *things*. You will be like *a man* who goes to sleep in the heart of the sea, *like a man who lives in a different world*; like *a man* who sleeps at the top of the mast. *You will say*, 'They struck me, but I am not weak; they struck me down, but I didn't know. When I wake up I will do it again; I will find another drink.'	
20	*Mixing with Evil Men*	
	Do not be jealous of evil men; do not be inclined to be with them. For their minds ponder violence; their lips speak trouble.	
21	*Family Values*	
	A house is built through wisdom; it is made firm through understanding. Through knowledge the rooms are filled with all precious and delightful treasures.	
22	*The Value of Counsellors*	
	A wise man *grows* in strength; a knowledgeable man grows in power. For with *wise* counsel you can wage war; with many counsellors there is victory.	
23	*Wisdom and the Fool*	
	Wisdom is too lofty for a fool; he cannot open his mouth at the *city* gate.	
24	*'Schemers'*	
	A man who plans evil *deeds* will be called 'a schemer' by men. The planning of folly is sinful; a scoffer is an abomination to man.	
25	*Rescuing Others*	
	If you sink *under pressure* on the day of distress, your strength will be *seen to be* weak. *So* snatch away those who are being lead to *their* deaths; hold	

	back those who are staggering to *their* slaughter. If you *are taken by surprise, and* say, 'Look, we knew nothing *about* this,' then won't the one who weighs hearts discern *it*? Won't the one who guards your life know *it*, and repay a man according to his deed?
26	*The Sweetness of Wisdom* Eat honey, my son, for it is good; the honey from the comb is sweet to your palate. So know that wisdom is sweet to your soul. If you attain *wisdom, you will* have a future; your hope will not be cut down.
27	*Lying in Wait for a Righteous Man* Do not lie in wait, *like* a wicked *man*, by the house of a righteous *man*; do not destroy the place where he sleeps. For a righteous *man* may fall seven *times*, and *each time* rise again, but the wicked will stumble at calamity.
28	*When an Enemy Falls* Don't be glad when a man, who is hostile to you, falls; don't let your heart rejoice when he stumbles. Otherwise, YHWH will see, it will be evil in his eyes, and he will turn back his anger from him.
29	*Attitude towards Evil Men* Don't burn with anger regarding evil *men*; don't be jealous of the wicked. For an evil *man* has no future; the lamp of the wicked will be extinguished.
30	*Fear YHWH and the King* Fear YHWH and the king, my son; do not exchange pledges with those who change *allegiances*. For disaster will suddenly rise against them, and who knows *what* disaster *will be sent by* the two of them.

2. MISCELLANEOUS SAYINGS

a). Other Sayings of the Wise[543]

This is small group of sayings, gathered together from different sources. King Solomon may have been the collector, or they may simply have been placed in the book of Proverbs, because they pick up similar themes.

These are also sayings of wise *men*:
Justice for All It is not good to show partiality in judgements. People will curse a man who says to a wicked *man*, 'You are righteous'; nations will show their indignation against him. But it will go well with those who prove him *guilty*; good blessings will come upon them.

---

[543] Proverbs 24:23-34

The Consideration of Equals
A man who kisses lips is *a man* who speaks honestly.
Getting Your Priorities Right
Complete your work outside, get everything ready in your field, then build your house.
Revenge and False Witness
Do not witness against your neighbour without reason; do not deceive with your lips. Do not say, 'I will do to him as he has done to me; I will pay the man back for what he has done.'
Laziness and Poverty
I passed by the field of a man—a sluggard; by the vineyard of a man lacking heart. I saw *that* his whole *field had* come up in thistles; its surface was covered in weeds and its stone wall had fallen down. When I saw *it*, I put my mind *to the problem*; I looked *again and* I took instruction: 'A little sleep, a little slumber, a little folding of the arms to lie down and poverty will come upon you *like* a robber. Your need *will come upon you like* an armed man.'

3. THE WORDS OF AGUR

a). The Words of Agur[544]

The following proverbs are clearly marked as the words of Agur, son of Jakeh. Who Agur was is unknown, but as Agur means 'gatherer', Agur may have been a court official who had a special interest in the collection of proverbs.

The words of Agur, son of Jakeh. An oracle the man declared to Ithiel; to Ithiel and Ucal.
To Ithiel
I do not have the understanding of a man, because I am more brutish than *any other* man. I have not learned wisdom, nor do I know the knowledge of the Holy *One*.
Who has ascended into the heavens? *Who has* descended? Who has gathered the wind in his hands? Who has bound up the waters in a cloak? Who has established all the ends of the earth? What is his name? What is his son's name? You must know. Every word of God has been tested *in the fire*; he is a shield to those who seek refuge in him. Do not add to his words, or he will decide *against* you; you will be found to be a liar.

---

[544] Proverbs 30:1-33

To God
Two *things* I ask of you; do not hold back from me before I die: keep empty words and deceit far from me, *and* do not give me *either* poverty or riches. *Rather*, rend me *only* my portion of food. Otherwise I will become *too* satisfied, and deny you, saying, 'Who is YHWH?' Or I will be *so* poor *that* I will steal and profane the name of my God.

Slandering a Servant
Do not slander a servant to his master, or he will curse you and you will be found guilty.
An Arrogant Generation
There is a generation *which* curses their father and refuses to bless their mother. *There is* a generation *which is* pure in their *own* eyes, but are not cleansed from their *own* filth. *There is* a generation whose eyes are proud; whose pupils are lifted up. *There is* a generation whose teeth are *like* swords; whose teeth are *like* knives. They devour the poor from the earth; the needy from among men.
Greed
The leech has two daughters: 'Give' *and* 'Give'.
Never Enough
There are three *things* which are never satisfied; four things that never say, 'Enough': Sheol, a barren womb, land that never has enough water, and fire that never says, 'Enough'.
Respect for Parents
An eye which mocks a father, and despises obedience to a mother, will be pecked out by the ravens of the valley, and eaten by young eagles.
Things Beyond Understanding
There are three *things* that are too wonderful to me; four that are beyond my knowledge: The way of the eagle in the heavens, the way of a serpent on a rock; the way of a ship in the heart of the sea, and the way of a man with a young woman.
An Adulterous Woman
This is the way of a woman who commits adultery: She eats, wipes her mouth, and then says, 'I have done nothing wrong.'
An Upside-Down World
There are three *things* which make the earth quake; four it is unable to bear: A servant who becomes king, a fool who is satisfied with food, a hated woman who gets married, and a maidservant who dispossesses her mistress.
Challenging a Superior Attitude
There are four *things* on earth that are small, but they are very wise: Ants are not *as* strong *as* people, yet they store up their food in summer; coneys are not *as* mighty *as* people, yet they locate their houses in the rocks; the locust

> has no king, yet they all swarm in their divisions; *and* a lizard *which* you can catch with *your* hands, but can be found in the palaces of a king.
>
> *Stately Things*
> There are three *things* that are pleasing by *the way* they stride; four *things* by *the way* they walk: A lion, mighty among beasts, who does not turn back from anything; a rooster which struts; a male goat; and a king surrounded by his army.
>
> *Playing the Fool*
> If you have been foolish, by exalting yourself or devising an *evil* plan, *put your* hand over *your* mouth. For as the pressing of milk produces curds, and the pressing of the nose produces blood, so the pressing of anger produces strife.

4. THE WORDS OF KING LEMUEL

a). *A Distracted King*[545]

It has been suggested that Lemuel ('devoted to God') was a pet name for Solomon. If that is true, then this oracle records an incident in which Bathsheba needed to discipline her son for neglecting his duties. But whoever Lemuel is, he is clearly distracted by women and drink, and needs to be reminded of his kingly duty of dispensing justice to his people.

> The words of King Lemuel.
> An oracle with which his mother disciplined him.
>
> O my son, O son of my womb, O the son of my vows. Do not give your strength to women; your ways wipe out kings. *It is* not for kings, Lemuel. It is not for kings to drink strong wine; *it is not* for rulers to desire strong drink. Otherwise he would drink and forget what has been decreed; he would change the judgements of all the oppressed.
>
> Give strong drink to whoever is perishing; *give* wine to those whose life is bitter. Let him drink, let him forget his poverty; let him remember his trouble no more.
>
> Open your mouth for those who are unable to speak for justice, for all who are perishing. Open your mouth, govern rightly; bring justice to the poor and afflicted.

---

[545] Proverbs 31:1-9

Establishing the Kingdom

5. THE NOBLE WIFE

a). The Noble Wife[546]

This is an alphabetical acrostic poem, by an author unknown. It has been suggested that the poem describes Ruth, or even Bathsheba—Solomon's mother. But more likely it was intended to be an archetypal role model to which all Hebrew daughters were intended to aspire.

	The Value of a Noble Wife
א	Who can find a noble wife?
	Her value is far greater than rubies.
ב	Her husband's whole being trusts in her;
	he doesn't lack *any of her* spoils.
ג	She does good things for him, not bad,
	every day of her life.
	The Activities of a Noble Wife
ד	She seeks out wool and flax;
	she works with willing hands.
ה	She is like a merchant's ships;
	she gathers her food from distant places.
ו	She gets up while it is still night;
	she sets food before her family,
	and portions for her *servant* girls.
ז	She inspects a field and buys it;
	she plants a vineyard with the fruit of her hands.
ח	She girds her loins with strength;
	she strengthens her arms.
ט	She sees that her trading is good;
	her lamp is not extinguished at night.
י	She puts her hands to the distaff (*a tool for spinning*);
	her palms grasp the spindle.
כ	She spreads out her hands to the poor;
	She stretches out her hands to those in need.
ל	She has no fear for her house when it snows,
	for her whole house is clothed in *wool, dyed* scarlet.
מ	She makes her own bed*spreads*;
	her clothing is *made of* fine linen and purple.
נ	Her husband is known at the gates *of the city*;
	he sits with the elders of the land.

---

[546] Proverbs 31:10-31

ס	She makes linen garments and sells *them*;
	she supplies *women's* sashes to the tradesmen.
ע	Her clothing is strength and honour;
	she can laugh at the coming day.
פ	Her mouth speaks with wisdom;
	good teaching is on her tongue.
צ	She keeps watch on the ways of her house;
	she doesn't eat the bread of tardiness.

The Praise of a Noble Wife

ק	Her sons stand up *in her presence*, and call her 'blessed.'
	Her husband boasts about her, *saying*,
ר	'Many daughters have acted nobly,
	but you have exceeded them all.'
ש	Grace is deceptive, and beauty passes away;
	but a woman who fears YHWH is to be praised.
ת	Give her the fruit of her hands;
	let her deeds praise her at the *city* gates.

D6. YHWH'S TEMPLE

1. INTRODUCTION

a). Introduction[547]

The house that King Solomon built for YHWH *was constructed* in Jerusalem, at the place David had provided. *It was built* on the threshing floor of *Araunah* (*or* Ornan) the Jebusite, on Mount Moriah, where *YHWH* had appeared to Solomon's father, David.

Only stone finished at the quarry was used when the Temple was being built. During its construction no hammer, axe, or iron tools of any kind were heard at the Temple *site*.

All measurements were according to the cubits of the old standard.

2. THE MAIN STRUCTURES

a). The Main Hall[548]

Item	The Main Hall
Foundations	Length: Sixty cubits (*27.4 metres*) Width: Twenty cubits (*9.1 metres*) Height: Thirty cubits (*13.7 metres*)
Outside walls	Stone
Roof	Wooden rafters and planks of cedar
Windows	Framed lattice
Offsets	These were put around the outside *wall*, to prevent things being inserted into the walls of the Temple
Entrances	The *ground* floor: on south side The middle floor: up the stairs from *the ground floor* The third floor: up the stairs from *the middle floor*

b). The Porch[549]

Item	The Porch
Position	At the front of the main hall of the house

---

[547] 1 Kings 6:2a, 7; 2 Chronicles 3:1b, 3b
[548] 1 Kings 6:2b, 4, 6b, 8, 9b; 2 Chronicles 3:3a
[549] 1 Kings 6:3; 2 Chronicles 3:4a

Establishing the Kingdom

Foundations	Width: Twenty cubits *(9.1 metres)*—the width of the house Depth: Ten cubits *(4.6 metres)* from front of main hall Height: Twenty cubits *(9.1 metres)*

c). The Inner Courtyard[550]

Item	The Inner Courtyard
Materials	Three layers of dressed stone One layer of cedar beams

d). Other Courtyards[551]

Item	The Priests' Courtyard The Outer Courtyard
Doors	Overlaid in bronze

3. OTHER EXTERIOR STRUCTURES

a). Pillars[552]

Item	Pillars
Number	Two
Material	Cast bronze
Location	At the front of the Temple, by the Porch—one on the right *(or south)* and one on the left *(or north)*. The right one Solomon named Jakin *(possibly 'he establishes')* and the one on the left he named Boaz *(possibly, 'in strength')*.
Height	Eighteen cubits *(8.2 metres)* each. A total of *about* thirty five cubits *(16 metres)* for both pillars
Circumference	Twelve cubits *(5.5 metres)*

Item	*Bowl-shaped* capitals—to be placed on the top of the pillars
Number	Two
Material	Cast bronze
Height	Five cubits *(2.3 metres)*
Design	Lilies, four cubits *(1.8 metres)* high

Item	Chains—for the capitals on the tops of the pillars
Number	Seven for each capital

---

[550] 1 Kings 6:36b
[551] 2 Chronicles 4:9b
[552] 1 Kings 7:15b, 16b-17, 18b-20, 21b-22a, 42b; 2 Chronicles 3:15b-16; 17b; 4:13b

Design	A latticework and interwoven threads

Item	Pomegranates—attached to the chains
Purpose	To decorate the capitals on the top of the pillars
Number	One hundred *for each row*. Two hundred in total *for each pillar*
Location	On the capitals, above the rounded projection
	In two rows encircling the latticework on each pillar

4. THE INTERIOR

a). Basic Interior Lining[553]

Item	Interior of Temple
Interior walls	Cedar and cypress boards of panelled wood—from floor to ceiling rafters
Floor	Cypress boards

b). Partition[554]

The Inner Sanctuary	Twenty cubits *(9.1 metres)—at the rear of the Temple*
The Main Hall	Forty cubits *(18.3 metres)*—in front of the Inner Sanctuary
Partition	Cedar boards *(from floor to ceiling rafters)*

c). Main Hall[555]

Item	The Main Hall or Holy Place
Lining	Cedar *panelling*, completely covering the stone walls
Decoration	The cedar carved with gourds, and open flowers

d). Inner Sanctuary[556]

Item	The Most Holy Place
Purpose	*To house the Ark of the Covenant of YHWH*
Dimensions	Length: Twenty cubits *(9.1 metres)*—the width of the house
	Width: Twenty cubits *(9.1 metres)*
	Height: Twenty cubits *(9.1 metres)*
Decoration	Overlaid in six hundred talents *(20.5 metric tonnes)* of pure gold

---

[553] 1 Kings 6:15b; 2 Chronicles 3:5
[554] 1 Kings 6:16b-17
[555] 1 Kings 6:18
[556] 1 Kings 6:20a; 2 Chronicles 3:8b-9

| Gold nails | Weighed fifty gold shekels (*570 grams*). |

e). Side Rooms[557]

Item	Side Rooms
Location	Built against the walls of the building around the Main Hall and the Inner Sanctuary
Floors	*Three—each floor being* five cubits (*2.3. metres*) high
Dimensions	The ground floor: Five cubits wide (*2.3 metres*)
	The middle floor: Six cubits wide (*2.7 metres*)
	The third floor: Seven cubits wide (*3.2 metres*)
Construction	Joined to the house with cedar beams

f). Main Hall and Side Rooms[558]

Item	*Main Hall and Side Rooms*
Panelling	Cypress wood panelling, overlaid with pure gold
Carving	Panelling decorated with cherubim, palm trees, open flowers, and chains
Pure Gold[1]	Overlaid in the inside of the Temple—beams, door frames, walls, and doors—including in the upper rooms
	Overlaid on the floors of the inner and outer rooms
Other	Precious stones
Note: [1]All the gold was from Parvaim (*location unknown*)	

g). Porch[559]

Item	Porch
Pure Gold	Overlaid on the inside

5. FURNISHINGS

5a). The Most Holy Place

a). Two Cherubim[560]

Item	Cherubim
Where made	In the Most Holy Place
Number	Two—each identical in shape and size

---

[557] 1 Kings 6:5-6a, 10
[558] 1 Kings 6:21a, 29b-30; 2 Chronicles 3:6-7
[559] 2 Chronicles 3:4b
[560] 1 Kings 6:23b-28; 2 Chronicles 3:10b-13

Material	Sculptured olive-wood, overlaid with gold
Height	Ten cubits (*4.6 metres*)
Wings	Each wing five cubits long (*2.3 metres*)
Wingspan	Ten cubits (*4.6 metres*) from tip to tip
Location	They were set up with their feet standing on the floor, and their faces towards the Main Hall. Their wings were spread out, so that they touched each other in the centre and their outer wings touched the side walls

b). Doors for the Inner Sanctuary[561]

Item	Doors for the Inner Sanctuary
Number	Two
Materials	Olive wood
Lintel and Doorposts	Five-sided
Design	The doors were carved with cherubim, palm trees, and open flowers—the cherubim and palm trees were overlaid with beaten gold

5b). The Main Hall

a). Curtain[562]

Item	Curtain
Materials	Blue, purple, and crimson linen
Design	Embroidered cherubim

b). Chains[563]

Item	Chains
Location	In front of the Inner Sanctuary
Decoration	Overlaid in pure gold

c). Doors for the Main Hall[564]

Item	Doors for the Main Hall
Doors	Two
Materials	Cypress wood

---

[561] 1 Kings 6:31b-32; 2 Chronicles 4:22b
[562] 2 Chronicles 3:14
[563] 1 Kings 6:21b
[564] 1 Kings 6:33-35; 2 Chronicles 4:22c

Design	Each door with two folding leaves, carved with cherubim, palm trees, and open flowers. Gold overlaid evenly over the carvings
Doorposts	Four-sided, made from olive wood

d). The Lampstands[565]

Item	Lampstands
Material	Pure gold
Number	Ten
Purpose	To burn in front of the Inner Sanctuary in the prescribed manner—five on the right (*south*) and five on the left (*north*)
Design	Gold floral work Solid gold lamps and snuffers

e). Tables[566]

Item	Tables
Number	Ten
Location	In the Temple, five on the right (*south*), and five on the left (*north*)

f). Altar of Incense[567]

Item	Altar *of Incense*
Materials	Cedar, overlaid in pure gold

g). Utensils for Burning Incense[568]

Item	Basins, snuffers, bowls, spoons, censers
Material	Pure gold
Purpose	For *burning incense*

h). The Table of the Presence[569]

Item	The Table *of the Presence*
Purpose	For the Bread of the Presence
Materials	*Overlaid in* Gold

---

[565] 1 Kings 7:49; 2 Chronicles 4:7b, 20-21
[566] 2 Chronicles 4:8b
[567] 1 Kings 6:20b; 7:48b
[568] 1 Kings 7:50a; 2 Chronicles 4:22a
[569] 1 Kings 7:48c; 2 Chronicles 4:19b

5c). Other Interior Furnishings

a). Gold Sockets[570]

Item	Sockets
Material	Gold
Purpose	*Hinges* for the doors of the Inner Sanctuary, the Most Holy Place
	Hinges for the doors of the Main Hall of the Temple

5d). The Inner Courtyard

a) The Sea[571]

Item	Sea (*or settling-tank*)
Purpose	For the priests to wash in
Location	On the right (*south*), at the south-east corner of the Temple
Materials	Cast *bronze*
Dimensions	Ten cubits (*4.6 metres*) from rim to rim
	Height: Five cubits (*2.3 metres*)
	Circumference: 30 cubits (*13.7 metres*)
	Thickness: a hand width (*i.e., 4 fingers*)
Capacity	Two thousand (*or three thousand*) baths (*44 or 66 kilolitres*)
Shape	Circular
Design	A rim: like the lip of a cup—as a lily blossom
	Under the rim, encircling the Sea: two rows of gourds (*or bulls*), ten to the cubit (*0.46 metres*), cast in one piece with the Sea

Item	Bases
Purpose	For the Sea to stand on
Number	Twelve
Design	Oxen
Location	Three facing *each direction of the compass*—north, south, west, and east—with their hindquarters facing the centre

---

[570] 1 Kings 7:50b
[571] 1 Kings 7:23b-26, 39c; 2 Chronicles 4:2b-5, 6c, 10

b) *Water Basin Stands*[572]

Item	Wheeled *Water Basin* stands
Purpose	To rinse the Burnt Offerings in
Number	Ten (all using the same moulds—and of identical size and form)
Location	Five on the left (*north*) and five on the right (*south*) of the Temple
Dimensions (each)	Length: Four cubits (*1.8 metres*) Width: Four cubits (*1.8 metres*) Height: Three cubits (*1.4 meters*)
Material	Bronze
Design	Panels attached to crossbars, all decorated with lions, bulls and cherubim Above and below the lions and the bulls were wreaths—hammered work The frames were square—not round Engraved opening on the crown (*top*)—a circular frame into the inside of the stand—one cubit (*45.7 centimetres*) deep. With its base work it measured one and a half cubits (*68.6 centimetres*) Four handles projecting from each stand—one on each of the four corners A circular band around the top of the stand—a half a cubit (*22.9 centiietres*) high Supports and panels attached to the top of the stand Engravings of cherubim, lions and palm trees on every surface, support and panel, surrounded by wreaths
Wheels, etc.	Four bronze wheels, like chariot wheels, under the panels, for each stand Dimensions: One and a half cubits (*68.6 centimetres*) in diameter Bronze axles, attached to the stand Four feet, as supports beneath the basin—each cast on the side with wreaths Axles, rims, spokes and hubs all of cast *bronze*

Item	Basins
Number	Ten
Material	Bronze
Capacity	Forty baths (*880 litres*)

---

[572] 1 Kings 7:27b-37, 38b, 39b; 2 Chronicles 4:6b

| Dimensions | Four cubits (*1.83 metres*) in diameter |
| Location | One basin for each of the ten stands |

c). Pots, Shovels and Bowls[573]

| Item | Pots, shovels, and bowls |
| Material | Burnished bronze |

d). The Altar of Burnt Offering[574]

Item	Altar
Purpose	*Where sacrifices are made*
Material	Bronze
Dimensions	Length: Twenty cubits (*9.1 metres*) Width: Twenty cubits (*9.1 metres*) Height: Ten cubits (*4.6 metres*)

e). Bowls[575]

Item	Bowls
Purpose	*Possibly for the draining of blood*
Number	One hundred
Material	Gold

---

[573] 1 Kings 7:40b, 45b; 2 Chronicles 4:11b, 16b
[574] 2 Chronicles 4:1b
[575] 2 Chronicles 4:8c

SELECT BIBLIOGRAPHY

Hebrew

The text of Aaron ben Moses ben Asher, 10th century AD, as printed in Snaith, Norman Henry (ed.), Torah, Nevi'im and Ketuvim *(a.k.a. Hebrew Old Testament)*, London, The British and Foreign Bible Society, 1958.

The text of the Leningrad Codex, 11th century AD, as printed in Elliger, K & Rudolph, Wilhelm (eds.), Biblia Hebraica Stuttgartensia, Stuttgart, Deutsche Bibelstiftung, 1977, and as reproduced as part of Kohlenberger III, John R. (ed.), The Interlinear NIV Hebrew-English Old Testament, Grand Rapids, Michigan, The Zondervan Corporation, 1979, 1980, 1982, 1985, 1987.

Brown, Francis (ed.), The New Brown-Driver-Briggs Gesenius Hebrew-English Lexicon, USA, Hendrickson Publishers, 1979.

Armstrong, Terry A., Bushby, Douglas, L., & Carr, Cyril F., A Reader's Hebrew-English Lexicon of the Old Testament, Volumes I and II – Genesis – 2 Kings, Grand Rapids, Michigan, Regency Reference Library, 1980, 1982.

Armstrong, Terry A., Bushby, Douglas, L., & Carr, Cyril F., A Reader's Hebrew-English Lexicon of the Old Testament, Volume IV – Psalms – 2 Chronicles, Grand Rapids, Michigan, Regency Reference Library, 1988.

Judges

Boling, Robert G., Judges, Garden City, New York, Doubleday & Company Inc., 1975. (The Anchor Bible)

Webb, Barry G., The Book of Judges, Grand Rapids, Michigan, Wm. B. Eerdmans Publishing Company, 2012. (The New International Commentary on the Old Testament)

Butler, Trent, Judges, Nashville, Tennessee, Thomas Nelson Inc., 2009. (Word Biblical Commentary)

Cundall, Arthur E., & Morris, Leon, Judges and Ruth, pp. 15-215, Leicester, England, Inter-Varsity Press, England and Downers Grove, Illinois, InterVarsity Press, USA, 1968. (Tyndale Old Testament Commentaries)

Ruth

Campbell, Edward F., Ruth, Garden City, New York, Doubleday & Company Inc., 1975. (The Anchor Bible)

Hubbard, Robert L., The Book of Ruth, Grand Rapids, Michigan, Wm. B. Eerdmans Publishing Company, 1988. (The New International Commentary on the Old Testament)

Hawk, L. Daniel, Ruth, Nottingham, England, Apollos & Downers Grove, Illinois, InterVarsity Press, 2015. (Apollos Old Testament Commentary)

Bush, Frederick W., Ruth, Esther, USA, Word Books, 1996. (Word Biblical Commentary)

Cundall, Arthur E., & Morris, Leon, Judges and Ruth, pp. 217-318, Leicester, England, Inter-Varsity Press, England and Downers Grove, Illinois, Inter-Varsity Press, USA, 1968. (Tyndale Old Testament Commentaries)

Fuerst, Wesley J., The Books of Ruth, Esther, Ecclesiastes, The Song of Songs, Lamentations, pp. 5-31, Cambridge, England, Cambridge University Press, 1975. (The Cambridge Bible Commentary)

1 and 2 Samuel

Tsumura, David Toshio, The First Book of Samuel, Grand Rapids, Michigan, Wm. B. Eerdmans Publishing Company, 2007. (The New International Commentary on the Old Testament)

McCarter, Jr., P. Kyle, I Samuel, Garden City, New York, Doubleday & Company Inc., 1980. (The Anchor Bible)

McCarter, Jr., P. Kyle, II Samuel, Garden City, New York, Doubleday & Company Inc., 1984. (The Anchor Bible)

Anderson, A.A., 2 Samuel, Dallas Texas, Word Books, 1989. (Word Biblical Commentary)

Firth, David G., 1 & 2 Samuel, Nottingham, England, Apollos & Downers Grove, Illinois, InterVarsity Press, 2009. (Apollos Old Testament Commentary)

Baldwin, Joyce, 1 and 2 Samuel, Leicester, England, Inter-Varsity Press, 1988. (Tyndale Old Testament Commentaries)

Hertzberg, H. W., I & II Samuel (Second Revised Edition), London, SCM Press Ltd, 1964 (Old Testament Library)

1 Kings 1:1-11:43

DeVries, Simon J., 1 Kings, pp. 1-151, Waco, Texas, Word Books, 1985. (Word Biblical Commentary)

Gray, John, I & II Kings (Third, Fully Revised, Edition), pp. 1-298, London, SCM Press Ltd, 1977. (Old Testament Library)

Wray Beal, Lissa M. 1 & 2 Kings, pp. 1-176, Nottingham, England, Apollos & Downers Grove, Illinois, InterVarsity Press, 2014. (Apollos Old Testament Commentary)

Wiseman, Donald J., 1 and 2 Kings, pp. 1-140, Leicester, England, Inter-Varsity Press, 1993. (Tyndale Old Testament Commentaries)

1 Chronicles 10:1 to 2 Chronicles 9:31

Myers, Jacob M., I Chronicles, USA, pp. 75-200, Doubleday & Company Inc., 1965. (The Anchor Bible)

Selman, Martin J., 1 Chronicles, pp. 131-263, Leicester, England, Inter-Varsity Press, 1994. (Tyndale Old Testament Commentaries)

Braun, Roddy, 1 Chronicles, Dallas Texas, Word Books, 1986. (Word Biblical Commentary)

Myers, Jacob M., II Chronicles, pp. 1- 60, Garden City, New York, Doubleday & Company Inc., 1965. (The Anchor Bible)

Selman, Martin J., 2 Chronicles, pp. 276-358, Leicester, England, Inter-Varsity Press, 1994. (Tyndale Old Testament Commentaries)

Dillard, Raymond B., 2 Chronicles, Dallas, Texas, Word Books, 1987. (Word Biblical Commentary)

Coggins, R. J., The First and Second Books of Chronicles, pp 62-180,

Cambridge, England, Cambridge University Press, 1976. (The Cambridge Bible Commentary)

Psalms (selections from)

deClaisse-Walford, Nancy, Jacobson, Rolf, A., & Tanner, Beth LaNeal, The Book of Psalms, Grand Rapids, Michigan, Wm. B. Eerdmans Publishing Company, 2014. (The New International Commentary on the Old Testament)

Longman III, Tremper, Psalms, Downers Grove, Illinois, InterVarsity Press USA & Leicester, England, Inter-Varsity Press, 2014. (Tyndale Old Testament Commentaries)

Broyles, Craig C., Psalms, Peabody, Massachusetts, Hendrickson Publishers & Paternoster Press, Milton Keynes, England, 1999. (New International Biblical Commentary – Old Testament Series)

Ross, Allen P., A Commentary on the Psalms, Volume 1 (1-41), Grand Rapids, Michigan, Kregel Publications, 2011. (Kregel Exegetical Library)

Ross, Allen P., A Commentary on the Psalms, Volume 2 (42-89), Grand Rapids, Michigan, Kregel Publications, 2013. (Kregel Exegetical Library)

Dahood, Mitchell, Psalms I (1-50), Garden City, New York, Doubleday & Company Inc., 1965. (The Anchor Bible)

Dahood, Mitchell, Psalms II (51-100) (Third Edition), Garden City, New York, Doubleday & Company Inc., 1968. (The Anchor Bible)

Dahood, Mitchell, Psalms III (101-150), Garden City, New York, Doubleday & Company Inc., 1970. (The Anchor Bible)

Anderson, A. A., Psalms (1-72), Grand Rapids, Michigan, Wm. B. Eerdmans Publishing Company & London, Marshall, Morgan & Scott, 1972. (The New Century Bible Commentary)

Anderson, A. A., Psalms (73-150), Grand Rapids, Michigan, Wm. B. Eerdmans Publishing Company & London, Marshall, Morgan & Scott, 1972. (The New Century Bible Commentary)

Kidner, Derek, Psalms 1-72, Leicester, England, Inter-Varsity Press, 1973. (Tyndale Old Testament Commentaries)

Kidner, Derek, Psalms 73-150, Leicester, England, Inter-Varsity Press, 1975. (Tyndale Old Testament Commentaries)

Craigie, Peter C., Psalms 1-50, Dallas, Texas, Word Books, 1983. (Word Biblical Commentary)

Tate, Marvin E., Psalms 51-100, Dallas, Texas, Word Books, 1989. (Word Biblical Commentary)

Allen, Leslie C., Psalms 101-150 (Revised Edition), Dallas, Texas, Word Books, 2002. (Word Biblical Commentary)

Proverbs

Waltke, Bruce K., The Book of Proverbs: Chapters 1-15, Grand Rapids, Michigan, Wm. B. Eerdmans Publishing Company, 2004. (The New International Commentary on the Old Testament)

Waltke, Bruce K., The Book of Proverbs: Chapters 15-31, Grand Rapids, Michigan, Wm. B. Eerdmans Publishing Company, 2005. (The New International Commentary on the Old Testament)

Kidner, Derek, Proverbs, Leicester, England, Inter-Varsity Press, 1964. (Tyndale Old Testament Commentaries)

Murphy, Roland E., Proverbs, Nashville, Tennessee, Thomas Nelson Inc., 1998. (Word Biblical Commentary)

Ecclesiastes

Longman III, Tremper, The Book of Ecclesiastes, Grand Rapids, Michigan, Wm. B. Eerdmans Publishing Company, 1998. (The New International Commentary on the Old Testament)

Eaton, Michael A., Ecclesiastes, Leicester, England, Inter-Varsity Press, 1983. (Tyndale Old Testament Commentaries)

Murphy, Roland E., Ecclesiastes, Nashville, Tennessee, Thomas Nelson Inc., 1992. (Word Biblical Commentary)

Fredericks, Daniel C., & Estes, Daniel J., Ecclesiastes & The Song of Songs, pp.

19-263, Nottingham, England, Apollos & Downers Grove, Illinois, InterVarsity Press, 2010. (Apollos Old Testament Commentary)

Fuerst, Wesley J., The Books of Ruth, Esther, Ecclesiastes, The Song of Songs, Lamentations, pp. 91-158, Cambridge, England, Cambridge University Press, 1975. (The Cambridge Bible Commentary)

Song of Songs

Longman III, Tremper, Song of Songs, Grand Rapids, Michigan, Wm. B. Eerdmans Publishing Company, 2001. (The New International Commentary on the Old Testament)

Carr, G. Lloyd, The Song of Solomon, Leicester, England, Inter-Varsity Press, 1984. (Tyndale Old Testament Commentaries)

Duguid, Iain M., The Song of Songs, Downers Grove, Illinois, InterVarsity Press USA & Leicester, England, Inter-Varsity Press, England 2015. (Tyndale Old Testament Commentaries)

Pope, Marvin H., Song of Songs, Garden City, New York, Doubleday & Company Inc., 1977. (The Anchor Bible)

Garrett, Duane & House, Paul, R, Song of Songs, Lamentations, Nashville, Tennessee, Thomas Nelson Inc., 2004. (Word Biblical Commentary)

Fredericks, Daniel C., & Estes, Daniel J., Ecclesiastes & The Song of Songs, pp. 265-444, Nottingham, England, Apollos & Downers Grove, Illinois, InterVarsity Press, 2010. (Apollos Old Testament Commentary)

Fuerst, Wesley J., The Books of Ruth, Esther, Ecclesiastes, The Song of Songs, Lamentations, pp. 159-200, Cambridge, England, Cambridge University Press, 1975. (The Cambridge Bible Commentary)

INDEX TO ESTABLISHING THE KINGDOM

All references are to the footnote numbers.

Judges	
1:1-4a	2
1:4b-5a	3
1:5b	2
1:6-11	3
1:12-15	Part 1
1:16-20	3
1:21	2
1:22-36	4
2:1-5	5
2:6-9	1
2:10-3:6	6
3:7-11	14
3:12-30	15
3:31	16
4:1-24	17
5:1-31	18
6:1-10	19
6:11-24	20
6:25-32	21
6:33-40	22
7:1-8a	23
7:8b-25	24
8:1-21	25
8:22-29	26
8:30-35	27
9:1-6	33

Judges	
9:7-21	34
9:22-41	35
9:42-49	36
9:50-57	37
10:1-2	38
10:3-5	39
10:6-16	40
10:17-11:11	41
11:12-28	42
11:29-40	43
12:1-7	44
12:8-10	45
12:11-12	46
12:13-15	47
13:1-25	48
14:1-20	49
15:1-8	50
15:9-19	51
15:20	54
16:1-3	52
16:4-21	53
16:22-31	54
17:1-6	11
17:7-13	12
18:1-31	13
19:1-10	7

Judges	
19:11-30	8
20:1-48	9
21:1-25	10

Ruth	
1:1-22	28
2:1-23	29
3:1-18	30
4:1-12	31
4:13-17a	32
4:17b-22	84

1 Samuel	
1:1-3a	55
1:3b	56
1:4-8	55
1:9-19a	56
1:19b-28	57
2:1-11	58
2:12-26	59
2:27-36	60
3:1-4:1a	61
4:1b-11	62
4:12-22	63

Establishing the Kingdom

1 Samuel	
5:1-12	64
6:1-12	65
6:13-16	66
6:17-18a	65
6:18b-7:4	66
7:5-17	67
8:1-22	68
9:1-10:8	69
10:9-16	76
10:17-27	71
11:1-11	72
11:12-15	73
12:1-25	74
13:1	75
13:2-15	76
13:16-14:1	77
14:2-14	78
14:15-23	79
14:24-48	80
14:49-51	81
14:52	80
15:1-35	82
16:1-13	83
16:14-23	86
17:1-18:4	85
18:5-16	87
18:17-30	88
19:1-8	89
19:9-17	90
19:18-24	91
20:1-42	92
21:1-10a	93
21:10b-22:1a	94

1 Samuel	
22:1b-5	96
22:6-23	97
23:1-5	98
23:6-29	99
24:1-22	100
25:1-42	101
25:43-44	102
26:1-25	104
27:1-28:2	105
28:3-25	106
29:1-11	107
30:1-31	108
31:1-13	109

2 Samuel	
1:1-16	110
1:17-27	111
2:1-11	113
2:12-3:5	114
3:6-21	115
3:22-39	116
4:1-12	118
5:1-4a	119
5:4b-5	180
5:6-10	121
5:11-12	122
5:13-16	143
5:17-21	120
5:22-25	129
6:1-11	123
6:12-15	124
6:16	127

2 Samuel	
6:17-19a	124
6:19b	125
6:20-23	127
7:1-17	133
7:18-29	134
8:1-14	130
8:15-18	135
9:1-13	136
10:1-19	137
11:1-27a	139
11:27b	141
11:27c-12:15a	140
12:15b-24a	141
12:24b-25	142
12:26-31	139
13:1-22	145
13:23-39	146
14:1-33	147
15:1-12	148
15:13-37	149
16:1-4	150
16:5-14	151
16:15-17:29	152
18:1-18	153
18:19-33	154
19:1-8a	155
19:8b-43	156
20:1-26	157
21:1-14	128
21:15-22	138
22:1-51	132
23:1-7	178
23:8-12	144

Establishing the Kingdom

2 Samuel	
23:13-17	120
23:18-39	144
24:1-17	158
24:18-25	159

1 Kings	
1:1-4	161
1:5-27	162
1:28-53	163
2:1-9	179
2:10-12	180
2:13-37	181
2:38-46	182
3:1	183
3:2-15	184
3:16-28	187
4:1-19	188
4:20-28	189
4:29-34	190
5:1-18	185
6:1	191
6:2a	547
6:2b	548
6:3	549
6:4	548
6:5-6a	557
6:6b	548
6:7	547
6:8	548
6:9a	191
6:9b	548
6:10	557

1 Kings	
6:11-15a	191
6:15b	553
6:16a	191
6:16b-17	554
6:18	555
6:19	191
6:20a	556
6:20b	567
6:21a	558
6:21b	563
6:22-23a	191
6:23b-28	560
6:29a	191
6:29b-30	558
6:31a	191
6:31b-32	561
6:33-35	564
6:36a	191
6:36b	550
6:37-38	191
7:1-12	196
7:13-15a	192
7:15b	552
7:16a	192
7:16b-17	552
7:18a	192
7:18b-20	552
7:21a	192
7:21b-22a	552
7:22b-23a	192
7:23b-26	571
7:27a	192
7:27b-37	572

1 Kings	
7:38a	192
7:38b	572
7:39a	192
7:39b	572
7:39c	571
7:40a	192
7:40b	573
7:40c-42a	192
7:42b	552
7:43-45a	192
7:45b	573
7:46-48a	192
7:48b	567
7:48c	569
7:49	565
7:50a	568
7:50b	570
7:51	192
8:1-21	193
8:22-61	194
8:62-66	195
9:1-9	197
9:10-14	198
9:15-24	199
9:25	200
9:26-28	218
10:1-10	219
10:11-12	218
10:13	219
10:14-25	220
10:26	221
10:27	220
10:28-29	221

Establishing the Kingdom

1 Kings	
11:1-13	222
11:14-22	223
11:23-25	224
11:26-40	225
11:41-43	237

1 Chronicles	
10:1-14	109
11:1-3	119
11:4-9	121
11:10-14	144
11:15-19	120
11:20-47	144
12:1-22	112
12:23-40	117
13:1-14	123
14:1-2	122
14:3-7	143
14:8-12	120
14:13-17	129
15:1-28	124
15:29	127
16:1-6	124
16:7-43	125
17:1-15	133
17:16-27	134
18:1-13	130
18:14-17	135
19:1-19	137
20:1-3	139
20:4-8	138
21:1-17	158

1 Chronicles	
21:18-27	159
21:28-22:19	160
23:1-32	164
24:1-19	165
24:20-31	166
25:1-31	167
26:1-19	168
26:20-28	169
26:29-32	170
27:1-15	171
27:16-22	172
27:23-24	158
27:25-34	173
28:1-21	174
29:1-9	175
29:10-20	176
29:21-23a	177
29:23b-25	186
29:26-30	180

2 Chronicles	
1:1	186
1:2-13a	184
1:13b	186
1:14	221
1:15	220
1:16-17	221
2:1-18	185
3:1a	191
3:1b	547
3:2	191
3:3a	548

2 Chronicles	
3:3b	547
3:4a	549
3:4b	559
3:5	553
3:6-7	558
3:8a	191
3:8b-9	556
3:10a	191
3:10b-13	560
3:14	562
3:15a	192
3:15b-16	552
3:17a	192
3:17b	552
4:1a	192
4:1b	574
4:2a	192
4:2b-5	571
4:6a	192
4:6b	572
4:6c	571
4:7a	192
4:7b	565
4:8a	192
4:8b	566
4:8c	575
4:9a	191
4:9b	551
4:10	571
4:11a	192
4:11b	573
4:11c-13a	192
4:13b	552

Establishing the Kingdom

2 Chronicles	
4:14-16a	192
4:16b	573
4:17-19a	192
4:19b	569
4:20-21	565
4:22a	568
4:22b	561
4:22c	564
5:1	192
5:2-6:11	193
6:12-7:1	194
7:2	193
7:3	194
7:4-10	195
7:11-22	197
8:1-3	198
8:4-10	199
8:11	197
8:12-15	200
8:16	192
8:17-18	218
9:1-9	219
9:10-11	218
9:12	219
9:13-24	220
9:25-26	221
9:27	220
9:28	221
9:29-31	237

Psalms	
2:1-12	307
3:1-8	149
4:1-8	273
5:1-12	274
6:1-10	261
7:1-17	103
8:1-9	241
9:1-10:18	288
11:1-7	278
12:1-8	267
13:1-6	281
14:1-7	264
15:1-5	247
16:1-11	248
17:1-15	270
18:1-50	132
19:1-14	245
20:1-9	292
21:1-13	294
22:1-31	286
23:1-6	244
24:1-10	257
25:1-22	260
26:1-12	250
27:1-14	279
28:1-9	271
29:1-11	246
30:1-12	258
31:1-24	283
32:1-11	259
33:1-22	297
34:1-22	94
35:1-28	272
36:1-12	265

Psalms	
37:1-40	266
38:1-22	262
39:1-13	263
40:1-17	253
41:1-12	285
51:1-19	140
52:1-9	97
53:1-6	264
54:1-7	99
55:1-23	277
56:1-13	94
57:1-11	95
58:1-11	268
59:1-17	90
60:1-12	131
61:1-8	251
62:1-12	254
63:1-11	151
64:1-10	287
65:1-13	243
68:1-35	293
69:1-35	280
70:1-5	284
71:1-24	308
72:1-19	296
86:1-17	255
91:1-16	306
93:1-5	299
95:1-11	302
96:1-13	304
98:1-9	309
99:1-9	303
100:1-5	305

Establishing the Kingdom

Psalms	
101:1-8	269
103:1-22	239
104:1-35	298
108:1-13	291
109:1-31	276
110:1-7	290
120:1-7	310
122:1-9	256
124:1-8	120
127:1-5	295
131:1-3	249
132:1-18	300
133:1-3	126
135:1-21	301
138:1-8	240
139:1-24	242
140:1-13	275
141:1-10	252
142:1-7	95
143:1-12	282
144:1-15	289
145:1-21	238

Proverbs	
1:1-6	311
1:7	330
1:8-19	365
1:20-33	329
2:1-22	324
3:1-10	363
3:11-20	361
3:21-35	364

Proverbs	
4:1-9	322
4:10-19	365
4:20-27	366
5:1-23	439
6:1-5	432
6:6-11	501
6:12-15	461
6:16-19	395
6:20-35	440
7:1-27	442
8:1-36	359
9:1-18	325
10:1a	311
10:1b	383
10:2	482
10:3	455
10:4	506
10:5	383
10:6	418
10:7	484
10:8	410
10:9	448
10:10	473
10:11	414
10:12	420
10:13	523
10:14	351
10:15	398
10:16	414
10:17	362
10:18	520
10:19-21	525
10:22	315

Proverbs	
10:23	349
10:24	469
10:25	455
10:26	502
10:27	481
10:28	468
10:29	455
10:30	480
10:31	485
10:32	526
11:1	444
11:2	366
11:3	467
11:4	470
11:5	465
11:6	469
11:7	464
11:8	480
11:9	409
11:10	459
11:11	525
11:12	412
11:13	527
11:14	392
11:15	432
11:16	418
11:17-18	479
11:19	482
11:20	326
11:21	479
11:22	380
11:23	415
11:24	472

Establishing the Kingdom

Proverbs	
11:25	388
11:26	419
11:27	466
11:28	471
11:29	372
11:30	331
11:31	479
12:1	362
12:2	473
12:3	411
12:4	379
12:5	413
12.6	473
12:7	458
12:8	409
12:9	422
12:10	420
12:11	507
12:12	421
12:13	525
12:14	512
12:15	352
12:16	350
12:17	486
12:18	525
12:19	526
12:20	413
12:21	480
12:22	526
12:23	523
12:24	509
12:25	515
12:26	420

Proverbs	
12:27	507
12:28	319
13:1	383
13:2	523
13:3	487
13:4	507
13:5	526
13:6	414
13:7-8	416
13:9	468
13:10	357
13:11	445
13:12	535
13:13	474
13:14	332
13:15	412
13:16	353
13:17	523
13:18	362
13:19	423
13:20	351
13:21	465
13:22	475
13:23	443
13:24	378
13:25	469
14:1	380
14:2	318
14:3	524
14:4	500
14:5	486
14:6	367
14:7	344

Proverbs	
14:8	354
14:9	355
14:10	423
14:11	482
14:12	327
14:13	423
14:14	469
14:15	354
14:16	348
14:17	409
14:18	348
14:19	460
14:20-21	416
14:22	413
14:23	506
14:24	348
14:25	486
14:26-27	318
14:28	539
14:29	350
14:30	532
14:31	416
14:32	482
14:33	347
14:34	414
14:35	540
15:1	524
15:2	523
15:3	313
15:4	523
15:5	382
15:6	480
15:7	353

Establishing the Kingdom

Proverbs		Proverbs		Proverbs	
15:8	371	16:8	416	17:10	362
15:9	326	16:9	314	17:11	461
15:10	474	16:10	492	17:12	344
15:11	451	16:11	444	17:13	464
15:12	361	16:12	395	17:14	390
15:13	535	16:13	390	17:15	494
15:14	353	16:14-15	427	17:16	335
15:15	535	16:16	320	17:17	384
15:16	318	16:17	365	17:18	432
15:17	374	16:18	533	17:19	405
15:18	426	16:19	416	17:20	400
15:19	510	16:20	315	17:21	376
15:20	383	16:21	333	17:22	409
15:21	353	16:22	353	17:23	402
15:22	537	16:23	333	17:24	348
15:23	512	16:24	515	17:25	382
15:24	332	16:25	327	17:26	493
15:25	455	16:26	499	17:27	516
15:26	413	16:27-28	519	17:28	343
15:27	480	16:29	404	18:1	397
15:28	415	16:30	400	18:2	336
15:29	455	16:31	321	18:3	464
15:30	529	16:32	426	18:4	512
15:31	360	16:33	317	18:5	493
15:32	362	17:1	375	18:6-7	339
15:33	360	17:2	382	18:8	519
16:1	488	17:3	452	18:9	502
16:2	452	17:4	526	18:10	316
16:3	315	17:5	464	18:11	328
16:4	451	17:6	373	18:12	462
16:5	462	17:7	526	18:13	523
16:6	369	17:8	402	18:14	536
16:7	370	17:9	521	18:15	333

Proverbs		Proverbs		Proverbs	
18:16	402	19:27	361	21:1	539
18:17	490	19:28	491	21:2	452
18:18	436	19:29	495	21:3	371
18:19	407	20:1	531	21:4	329
18:20-21	512	20:2	406	21:5	506
18:22	379	20:3	390	21:6	445
18:23	490	20:4	502	21:7	464
18:24	421	20:5	512	21:8	415
19:1	356	20:6	393	21:9	374
19:2	365	20:7	381	21:10	403
19:3	341	20:8	496	21:11	495
19:4	416	20:9	323	21:12	455
19:5	486	20:10	444	21:13	492
19:6-7	434	20:11	381	21:14	402
19:8	332	20:12	312	21:15	492
19:9	486	20:13	506	21:16	461
19:10	338	20:14	445	21:17	530
19:11	424	20:15	512	21:18	408
19:12	427	20:16	432	21:19	374
19:13	375	20:17	445	21:20	348
19:14	379	20:18	435	21:21	320
19:15	504	20:19	527	21:22	334
19:16	383	20:20	382	21:23	516
19:17	447	20:21	382	21:24	396
19:18	378	20:22	453	21:25-26	511
19:19	456	20:23	444	21:27	371
19:20	360	20:24	314	21:28	486
19:21	314	20:25	368	21:29	409
19:22	526	20:26	496	21:30	317
19:23	318	20:27	313	21:31	437
19:24	503	20:28	496	22:1	320
19:25	362	20:29	321	22:2	312
19:26	382	20:30	360	22:3	466

Establishing the Kingdom

Proverbs		Proverbs		Proverbs	
22:4	318	25:24	374	27:6	362
22:5	365	25:25	515	27:7	434
22:6	377	25:26	394	27:8	438
22:7	431	25:27	398	27:9-10	389
22:8	495	25:28	399	27:11	383
22:9	434	26:1	342	27:12	466
22:10	458	26:2	492	27:13	432
22:11	512	26:3	340	27:14	391
22:12	455	26:4-5	345	27:15-16	374
22:13	505	26:6	346	27:17	360
22:14	441	26:7	336	27:18	388
22:15	378	26:8	342	27:19	320
22:16	464	26:9	336	27:20	398
22:17-24:22	542	26:10	400	27:21	514
24:23-34	543	26:11	337	27:22	340
25:1	311	26:12	358	27:23-24	388
25:2-3	541	26:13	505	27:25-27	499
25:4	449	26:14	504	28:1	414
25:5	458	26:15	503	28:2	417
25:6-7a	540	26:16	501	28:3	403
25:7b-8	490	26:17	519	28:4	415
25:9-10	489	26:18-19	401	28:5	466
25:11-12	497	26:20	390	28:6	416
25:13	385	26:21	528	28:7	383
25:14	446	26:22	519	28:8	433
25:15	513	26:23	400	28:9	395
25:16	534	26:24-26	491	28:10	476
25:17	391	26:27	495	28:11	538
25:18	486	26:28	526	28:12	415
25:19	456	27:1-2	538	28:13	477
25:20	403	27:3	339	28:14	454
25:21-22	429	27:4	428	28:15	406
25:23	518	27:5	360	28:16	481

Establishing the Kingdom

Proverbs	
28:17	430
28:18	465
28:19	508
28:20	471
28:21	447
28:22	464
28:23	497
28:24	382
28:25	471
28:26	348
28:27	472
28:28	409
29:1	463
29:2	415
29:3	383
29:4	498
29:5	464
29:6-7	465
29:8	436
29:9	497
29:10	401
29:11	350
29:12	517
29:13	450
29:14	496
29:15	378
29:16	483
29:17	378
29:18	319
29:19	387
29:20	522
29:21	386
29:22	425

Proverbs	
29:23	478
29:24	491
29:25	457
29:26	453
29:27	415
30:1-33	544
31:1-9	545
31:10-31	546

Ecclesiastes	
1:1	226
1:2-11	227
1:12-2:23	228
2:24-3:22	229
4:1-5:7	230
5:8-6:12	231
7:1-8:1	232
8:2-9:10	233
9:11-10:20	234
11:1-12:8	235
12:9-14	236

Song of Solomon	
1:1	201
1:2-6	202
1:7-2:7	203
2:8-17	204
3:1-5	205
3:6-11	206
4:1-5:1	207

Song of Solomon	
5:2-6:3	208
6:4-7	209
6:8-10	210
6:11-13	211
7:1-10	212
7:11-8:4	213
8:5-7	214
8:8-10	215
8:11-12	216
8:13-14	217

www.ingramcontent.com/pod-product-compliance
Lightning Source LLC
Chambersburg PA
CBHW051415290426
44109CB00016B/1304